Mac OS® X Panther™ Timesaving Techniques

FOR DUMMIES®

by Larry Ullman and Marc Liyanage

WILEY

Wiley Publishing, Inc.

Mac OS® X Panther™ Timesaving Techniques For Dummies®

Published by
Wiley Publishing, Inc.
111 River Street
Hoboken, NJ 07030-5774

For general information on our other products and services or to obtain technical support, please contact our Customer Care Department within the U.S. at 800-762-2974, outside the U.S. at 317-572-3993, or fax 317-572-4002.

Wiley also publishes its books in a variety of electronic formats. Some content that appears in print may not be available in electronic books.

Library of Congress Control Number: 2004101049

ISBN: 0-7645-5812-9

Manufactured in the United States of America

10 9 8 7 6 5 4 3 2 1

1V/SS/QT/QU/IN

WILEY

About the Authors

Larry Ullman is the Director of Digital Media Technologies at DMC Insights, Inc., a firm specializing in information technology. He is the author of four other computer books. In addition to writing, Larry develops dynamic Web applications, conducts training seminars, and is an Extension Instructor for the University of California at Berkeley. He's been working with Apple computers for more than 20 years, starting with the Apple IIe back in the dark (or monochrome) ages.

When he's not tinkering on his Mac, he spends his time reading, working on his fixer-upper of a house, and, given the time, napping in front of the fireplace. Larry currently lives outside of Washington, D.C., with his wife of eight years, Jessica.

Marc Liyanage is a senior software engineer at futureLAB AG, a research and development company focusing on emerging Internet, telecommunications, and wireless technologies.

He's been using and programming Macintosh computers professionally for 15 years for desktop publishing, video and TV screen design, and software development. He's been a UNIX user and software engineer for the past eight years in the Internet/ISP industry, doing commercial Web application work and large-scale ISP systems design and implementation using open source software packages. He has also taught classes on XML and trained junior software engineers.

He's been a Mac OS X user and developer since the first beta versions, and he's very excited about the Panther OS because it brings together the elegance of the Macintosh with the power of UNIX. In his spare time, he runs the developer-oriented Mac OS X Web site `www.entropy.ch`, writes Cocoa software, and tinkers with his Mac.

His spare-time interests include graphic design, typography, and digital photography. He enjoys watching and reading science fiction movies and books. Marc lives in Zurich, Switzerland.

Dedication

We dedicate this book to the good people at Apple. Thanks for designing wicked hardware, putting out the best operating system we've ever used (that'd be Panther), giving away some top-notch software, and for demonstrating that there's nothing wrong with a computer that's cool, feature-rich, secure, and stable.

Marc would like to also dedicate this book to his mother, Martina.

Authors' Acknowledgments

Our thanks to Wiley and to Carole McClendon at Waterside.

As always, thanks to Jess for her support and willingness to listen to me complain.

A special shout-out to David S. just for being a swell guy.

Thanks to my excellent co-author, Marc, both for his much-needed assistance with this book as well as for the copious amount of work and support he has done for the Mac OS X platform over the years.

Last but not least, my sincerest gratitude goes out to you, the reader.

—Larry Ullman

First and foremost, big thanks to Larry Ullman for inviting me to join him on this book project and for being a great guy to work with. I enjoyed every minute and learned a lot on the way.

Thanks to my friends at futureLAB for making this the best work place in the world!

Finally, thanks to my brother Andy for being a great friend.

—Marc Liyanage

Publisher's Acknowledgments

We're proud of this book; please send us your comments through our online registration form located at www.dummies.com/register/.

Some of the people who helped bring this book to market include the following:

Acquisitions, Editorial, and Media Development

Project Editor: Linda Morris

Acquisitions Editor: Bob Woerner

Senior Copy Editor: Teresa Artman

Technical Editor: Ilene Hoffman

Editorial Manager: Leah Cameron

Media Development Supervisor: Richard Graves

Editorial Assistant: Amanda Foxworth

Cartoons: Rich Tennant (www.the5thwave.com)

Production

Project Coordinator: Courtney MacIntyre

Layout and Graphics: Beth Brooks, Joyce Haughey, Stephanie D. Jumper, Michael Kruzil, Kristin McMullan, Lynsey Osborn, Heather Ryan, Melanee Wolven

Proofreaders: Laura L. Bowman, Carl Pierce

Indexer: Tom Dinse

Publishing and Editorial for Technology Dummies

Richard Swadley, Vice President and Executive Group Publisher

Andy Cummings, Vice President and Publisher

Mary C. Corder, Editorial Director

Publishing for Consumer Dummies

Diane Graves Steele, Vice President and Publisher

Joyce Pepple, Acquisitions Director

Composition Services

Gerry Fahey, Vice President of Production Services

Debbie Stailey, Director of Composition Services

Contents at a Glance

Table of Contents

Introduction

We're fairly smart people, and presumably you're a really smart person (you are looking at the right book, after all), but it still seems like technology has eclipsed our ability to understand it. Even the magical Mac — the symbol of all things easy in computers — is overladen with features and gadgets and pretty lights. Make no mistake: We all like features and gadgets and pretty lights, but how are we supposed to make sense of it all and just do what we want to do, quickly and easily?

By reading this book, of course!

But if that isn't enough to convince you (and we can't imagine why not; after all, we've never lied to you before), take a moment or two to read through this Introduction. You'll see where we're coming from, what this book offers, and how it'll make you fall in love with your Mac all over again.

Saving Time with This Book

The *Timesaving Techniques For Dummies* books focus on high-payoff techniques that save you time, either on the spot or somewhere down the road. And these books get to the point in a hurry, with step-by-step instructions to pace you through the tasks you need to do, without any of the fluff you don't want. We've identified more than 60 Techniques that Mac OS X Panther users need to know to make the most of their time. In addition, each Technique includes lots of figures that make following along a breeze. Decide for yourself how to use this book: Read it cover to cover if you like, or skip right to the Technique that interests you the most.

In *Mac OS X Panther Timesaving Techniques For Dummies*, you can find out how to

✔ **Tame time-consuming tasks:** Because we demystify the inner workings of Mac OS X Panther for you, letting you in on more than 60 tips and tricks along the way, you can spend more time on creating great results and less time on fiddling with a feature so that it works correctly.

✔ **Take your skills up a notch:** You're already familiar with the basics of using Mac OS X. Now this book takes you to the next level, helping you become an even savvier Mac user.

✔ **Customize Mac OS X to meet your needs:** Spending some upfront time customizing Mac OS X so that it works faster, more reliably, and more like how you work on a daily basis can save you time (and aggravation) later.

Foolish Assumptions

Every book is written with certain assumptions about the reader, and this one is no exception. Don't be alarmed: We're not looking for an advanced degree in computer science or the ability to recall long lists of Mac trivia at parties. What we do expect of you are two things:

✔ **A Macintosh, running Panther (Mac OS X v.3):** Well, to be perfectly frank, if you aren't running Panther (but are running another version of Mac OS X), you'll still be able to get a lot of things out of this book; you just won't be able to do *everything* this book says you can do. This requirement is more of a highly advisable suggestion.

✔ **Basic familiarity with your computer:** In some ways, this is the same kind of *For Dummies* book you've come to know and love, but it's not the kind that shows you how to plug in a printer or save a document. (It will show you how easy it is to share a printer on a network and how you can save documents faster, though.) We promise that you won't be overwhelmed by anything in this book, but keep in mind that you won't be spoon-fed, either.

Having a fast Internet connection will help you get the most out of this book, and so will a little extra spending money (but just a little). But neither of these are required as long as you have a Mac and a willingness — or a need — to discover how to use your computer better.

How This Book Is Organized

As devoted Mac users, we've amassed a gazillion pieces of useful knowledge. By sheer luck, it turned out that these little pieces could be organized into *Techniques,* which are chapter-like sections grouped by application or the general theory being discussed. These Techniques, it turns out, are sorted into larger parts, which we're calling (appropriately enough) *parts* (we're clever that way). We give you the highlights as to what the parts are all about here, but remember that you can approach this book how *you* want to. Read a part straight through, skip from Technique to Technique, or just pick out the little pieces most relevant to the way you work. This book has a structure, but you can be a free thinker. You own a Mac, after all!

Part I: Starting, Stopping, and Running Your Mac Faster

This first part of the book focuses exclusively on how to get the machine and operating system to load and run faster — in other words, how to speed up the process between pushing the power button and actually doing anything. While we're at it, we also discuss some faster aspects of the installation process and the easiest ways to shut down and log out. These might be the basics of using your computer, but even here, you find ways to do things more efficiently.

Part II: Optimizing Your Interface

This part of the book discusses specific topics such as files, applications, and so forth. This is the general guide to doing *anything* better. The heart of Part II is navigation techniques, both with the keyboard and the mouse. You also discover how to customize the Finder, windows, and the Dock. All in all, the absolutely most-universal and most-helpful time-saving techniques are here.

Part III: Handling Files (And Other Stuff) Quickly

Like a teenager's closet, your Mac is full of stuff. Who knows what it all is? Okay, we know, and we think you should, too. Although your hard drive might not yet be bursting, there's always going to be a lot of junk in there. This third part of the book demonstrates how to best organize, manage, and find your (and your computer's) stuff. You'll also see how to save disk space and remove clutter by trashing unnecessary files.

Part IV: Improving Application Performance

Included on your computer (see Part III) are *applications* — software that does stuff with other stuff (not to be too technical about it). You won't read about any one specific application here but rather pick up some useful knowledge for using any application more efficiently.

Part V: Cranking Up Your Internet Activities

As Homer Simpson says, "They have the Internet on computers now." Well, the man's never been more correct. Accessing e-mail and the World Wide Web are why many people have computers. Most folks spend a decent portion of their computing life in this realm. Part V covers Web browsers, performing searches, using e-mail, and other timesaving online techniques. Tips on managing spam and using Google effectively can save you minutes per day — minutes you could spend surfing the Internet.

Part VI: Optimizing Your Network

The networking section of the book is Part V's counterpart. Although not every user has advanced networking needs, most could benefit from using locations, working with an iDisk, and knowing how to easily connect to other computers when the time comes.

Part VII: Fast and Furious Multimedia

Apple markets itself as the multimedia machine, and with good reason: The free software that comes with the operating system is exceptional. In the multimedia section of the book, we take a few of these applications and demonstrate how to more efficiently use them.

Part VIII: Security and Maintenance

Okay, so your Mac pretty much takes care of itself. Still, a little TLC couldn't hurt. Part VIII (that's *eight* to you and me) offers you all the motherly advice you can use on viruses, creating backups, keeping your software up-to-date, and the like. Think of this as the *An ounce of prevention is worth a pound of cure* section of the book.

Part IX: The Scary Or Fun Stuff

Whether you know it or not, your Mac is a powerful machine capable of some really, really cool things. The final part of the book strongly emphasizes our friend, the Terminal, with a nod given to AppleScript. If you're looking for something more fun and less scary, check out the Technique on using your cellphone with your Mac as well as the one on screen savers.

Conventions Used in This Book

This book, as you'll soon see, has a lot of visual stuff in it to serve as your roadmap. You know . . . different fonts and icons, indentations, and a few funny characters. Here's a Rosetta stone as to what they all mean:

- ✔ **Keyboard shortcuts:** This book has a healthy amount of keyboard shortcuts in it. These use a conjoining plus sign to indicate that two (or more) keys should be pressed in harmony. So when you see something like ⌘+A (the Select All shortcut), you should press and hold ⌘, press A once, and then release both. Something like Control+click means that you hold down the Control key while clicking the mouse button once.

- ✓ **Menu bar:** The menu bar is the thing going across the entire top of your window. It has all the, you know, menus.

- ✓ **Menu sequences:** Sequences of menus are referenced with an arrow. For example, Go⇨Recent Folders means that you should click the Go menu (on the menu bar) and then choose the Recent Folders submenu from there.

- ✓ **Apple menu:** The Apple menu, represented by the ⍟ symbol, is that blue Apple symbol in the upper-left corner of your window.

- ✓ **Application menus:** When we refer to an *application* menu, we mean the menu that has the title of the application and appears between the Apple menu and the File menu. So in the Finder, it's called *Finder;* in Microsoft Word, it's called *Word;* in iTunes, it's called *iTunes*.

- ✓ `Monospace font`: Web sites (URLs) and e-mail addresses are in their own special monospace font, which looks like `www.apple.com`. Onscreen messages and text in the Terminal also `look like this`.

- ✓ **User entry:** Stuff you should type appears in bold, like this: Type **How now, brown cow?**.

Icons Used in This Book

This book is littered with lots of little tidbits and notes, set aside by different icons. In due time, you'll probably identify the pattern for what each icon represents, but here's a quick heads-up.

 Tips are just extra ideas that we think you'll appreciate. Although not life-altering, tips are our way of saying, "Hey, you know what else you could try?"

 These icons reemphasize the timesaving point being made in a certain section. If you don't feel like reading through all those pesky words and get tired of our trite jokes, look for these.

 This icon means that you've seen this idea before, you'll see this idea again, and you ought to keep it in mind. These are publishing's version of sticky notes.

 For crying out loud, don't do anything marked with this icon! If you don't believe anything else that we say, trust us on these warning icons. Think *curiosity* and *cat* here and how that went. You won't see many warnings in this book, but when you do, understand that you might be about to take an irrevocable step.

Comments and Questions

We'd like to think that this book was everything you wanted or needed, and that you have no more comments, problems, questions, and the like. But writing can be a cruel mistress (we don't know what that means, either, but it sounds bad), and no book is ever comprehensive. If you have something to say or ask, here are some places to turn:

- ✓ **Wiley** (`www.dummies.com`): You can contact Wiley, the publisher of this book, at its *For Dummies* Web site. Feel free to leave all sorts of feedback, including praise (Woo-hoo!), complaints (D'oh!), and requests (that's okay, too).

- ✓ **Mac OS X Panther Timesaving Techniques For Dummies, the Web site** (`www.dmcinsights.com/ mactst`): At Larry's Web site, we're maintaining a separate section that focuses solely on this book. Its contents will vary, but basically you'll find news, links to useful Web pages, and extras (as we create them). Plus, you'll also find our contact information and the link to the supporting forum.

✔ **Mac OS X Panther Timesaving Techniques For Dummies, the support forum** (`www.entropy.ch/mactst/`): Marc has established a forum at his Web site where you can ask questions about the book, about us, and about your Mac. Not only will we reply (probably faster than we'll get to an e-mail), but you'll also hear what other readers have to say.

✔ **E-mail the authors:** If you'd like to contact us directly, you can e-mail us at `mactst@dmcinsights.com`. Although we do respond to every e-mail we receive, there's no guaranteeing how quickly that'll happen. Don't get us wrong: We absolutely appreciate the feedback, but there are only so many hours in the day.

Keep in mind that normally the quickest way to answer a general Mac question is to search Google. Also, if you're having problems with a particular application, you'll have the best luck contacting the manufacturer of that application. But still, if you drop us a line via one of the above methods, trust that we'll do our best to help out.

Part I

Starting, Stopping, and Running Your Mac Faster

The 5th Wave   By Rich Tennant

"I'm not saying I believe in anything. All I know is since it's been there, Panther is running 50% faster."

Technique

Installing Panther without the Hassle

Save Time By

✔ Discovering the benefits of Panther

✔ Selecting the appropriate installation method

✔ Using Disk Utility

✔ Installing Panther

✔ Working with Setup Assistant

✔ Transferring your existing files to a new installation

Before you can discover the magic of Apple's latest, greatest operating system, you need a version of it running on your Mac. You might even wonder whether Mac OS X Panther is right for you. Because you're holding this book, the answer is presumably yes, but to explain why, we begin this Technique by discussing some of Panther's benefits and new technologies.

The installation process itself has a few variables, and comprehending the different choices can not only save you time during the installation process but also give you a more reliable operating system over the long haul. You should also be able to make knowledgeable decisions about formatting and partitioning your disk drive before you install the OS. Finally, we show you how to breeze through the *Setup Assistant* (Apple's program for easing you through the startup process) and then wrap up with a discussion of foolproof file transfers.

What Panther Can Do for You

The benefits of using Panther break down into two broad categories: operating system improvements and better versions of Apple's many wondrous applications. What you'll find in Panther itself is

- A new style of Finder windows with improved navigation, much better search capability, and built-in *actions* (which are kind of like contextual menus)

- The return of *Labels,* the much maligned — but still used — Mac OS 9 feature that dropped off the radar in previous versions of OS X

- Greatly improved Open and Save dialogs for applications

- *Exposé,* which is a fantastic tool for immediate access to open windows and documents

- Built-in fax software that allows you to send and receive faxes via your computer without third-party applications

- Better integration with your iDisk for .Mac users

✔ Surprisingly easy security provided by *FileVault*, which is an encryption tool for your folders and files

✔ The ability to more readily access different user accounts thanks to Fast User Switching

Because the other Apple applications are critical to the functionality of the operating system as a whole, most of the applications that Apple provides with Panther have also had a makeover and some new ones have even been created. Specific benefits of these include

✔ The introduction of *Font Book*, which is a font management application that can take the place of third-party tools for most users.

✔ Even more reasons to use *Mail*, which is Apple's aptly named e-mail client (see Technique 33).

✔ A speedier and more useful version of *Preview*, which is Mac OS X's default viewer for PDF documents and images. More importantly, Preview now supports many common PDF features like hyperlinks, bookmarks, and full-text searching.

✔ Modest changes to *Address Book* (personal information management software), giving it even more cause to be a regular resource for every Mac user.

✔ A new version of the popular iChat messenger service, *iChat AV*. You can now save oodles of time and money doing video or audio conferencing with your computer and a FireWire-enabled video camera. (This application is available to Jaguar users for $29.95.)

✔ The advent of *Xcode*, which is a tool for creating applications. Xcode is a sophisticated new version of Project Builder, which developers will love and the general public can safely ignore. (This application is available to Jaguar users at no cost.)

All these improvements, new applications, and features can be yours for the low, low cost of . . . okay, the not-so-low cost of $129. But that's a beauty of an operating system.

 The price of Panther ($129) is the same whether you're upgrading from Jaguar or buying a version of OS X for the first time.

To further convince you, consider that an overriding benefit of installing Panther is that you'll be using the most current version of Apple's operating system. This means that you can take advantage of all of Apple's future development of applications and patches, which will be designed with Panther in mind.

 If you own more than one Macintosh, consider the Family Pack version of Panther, which gives you license to install the OS on up to five machines for the bargain price of $199. If time truly is money, this tip alone could save you hours!

Minimum System Requirements

In order to use Panther, Apple recommends that you have one of the following computers:

✔ Power Mac G5

✔ Power Mac G4

✔ Power Mac G3 (Blue and White)

✔ PowerBook G4

✔ PowerBook G3 with built-in USB

✔ iMac

✔ eMac

✔ iBook

Apple also recommends that you have at least 128MB of RAM (we recommend 256MB or more, but you can get away with less if you never use Panther's Classic mode), a supported display, and at least 2GB of available disk space. (You need 3.5GB if you want to install the Developer Tools as well.) You're welcome to attempt to install Panther even if you don't meet the above requirements, but you do risk having a bum computer and wasting a whole heck of a lot of time in the process.

Choosing an Installation Method

If you just purchased a brand new Mac, making yourself the envy of the neighborhood, you should be sitting there with a fresh copy of Panther purring away. In that case, you can skip ahead a bit to the section "Working with Setup Assistant" to see how to whip through the Setup Assistant. If you don't have Panther installed yet but are the proud owner of some shiny new installation discs, it's time to put them to use.

Before you begin, take a minute to think about what type of installation you want. You have three options:

✔ **Upgrade a previous version of Mac OS X:** Upgrading is the easiest and least time-consuming option to use — in the short run, that is. One drawback, however, to upgrading an existing OS is that your hard disk will be become bloated with deadwood files. The resulting OS can be a little buggy, inheriting problems from its predecessor.

 If you want to install Panther and get on with your life with a minimum of fuss, choose the upgrade option.

✔ **Erase and Install:** This option is the most taxing and time-consuming (and drastic) of the three. On the bright side, you do end up with an untouched hard drive and a brand spankin' new OS. On the other hand, you wipe out all your files and applications in the process.

 Absolutely, positively do not use the Erase and Install option unless you've got multiple backups of all your files, drivers, and software. This option does exactly what it says: erases the contents of your entire hard drive.

✔ **Archive and Install:** This happy medium between your other two install choices creates a new system folder with new copies of all the OS stuff, but it also allows you to maintain all the user files and non-Apple applications. Although Apple doesn't promote this feature as the recommended type of installation, we're quite fond of it ourselves. It gives you the benefit of a clean system folder (without the deadwood created by an upgrade) without the serious drawback of having to reinstall all your applications and files.

 The Archive and Install option throws all the existing system files and Apple applications in a folder called Previous Systems. After you're convinced that no valuable information has been overwritten by the recent installation, delete this folder to clear up space on your hard drive.

Managing Your Disk Drives

Along with deciding what type of installation you want to perform, another topic worth your consideration before you install Panther is the formatting and partitioning of your hard drive (or drives). To clarify:

✔ **Formatting** a disk drive is the process of erasing its contents and telling the blank drive how to structure the files stored on it.

✔ **Partitioning** a disk drive is the process of breaking a single drive into multiple volumes. Your computer still has the same number of physical hard drives, but the operating system behaves as if there were more. (Each volume appears as a separate drive in Finder and other software.)

 Practically anything you do with the Disk Utility application requires erasing your entire hard drive. Although Disk Utility warns you before it does anything so drastic, we'd advise you not to use the application unless you've first backed up everything that you need.

Both of these tasks are accomplished by using the Disk Utility application (see Figure 1-1), which can be found in the Utilities folder and on the first Panther installation disc. If you have multiple drives or volumes, Disk Utility can format or partition any volume except for the one on which it resides (because it can't erase itself). If you want to format or partition the drive that contains Disk Utility, you need to use the installation discs.

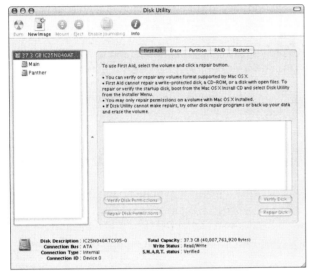

• **Figure 1-1: The Disk Utility application manages your hard drives.**

If you plan either an Upgrade or an Archive and Install installation, do not reformat or partition your hard drive because there will be nothing to upgrade or archive. If you're performing an Erase and Install, the installer can handle basic formatting (but not partitioning) for you.

1. **Start your computer with the first Panther installation disc.**

2. **At the first screen that appears (for language selection), select Open Disk Utility from the Installer menu (see Figure 1-2).**

3. **Follow the appropriate steps in one of the next two sections to either format or partition your drives and volumes.**

• **Figure 1-2: Click the Installer menu to access Disk Utility.**

Formatting a volume

To format a volume with Disk Utility:

1. **Click the volume icon in the left column. (A disk's volumes appear under the disk's icon.)**

2. **Click Erase.**

3. **Select a Volume Format.**

   The Volume Formats are

   ▶ **Mac OS Extended**

   This used to be the default format and is the safest choice.

   ▶ **Mac OS Extended (Journaled)**

   Journaling support has just recently been added by Apple. You don't really need to understand the details of what it does to appreciate that it allows you to more accurately recover your computer in the event of a disaster. Feel free to use this format because Apple now uses it as the default.

   ▶ **UFS (Unix File System)**

   If you choose to format with UFS, you render the hard drive unrecognizable by some operating systems (in particular, OS 9). For this reason, we'd advise you to stay away from it.

4. Enter the volume's name (see Figure 1-3) in the Name box.

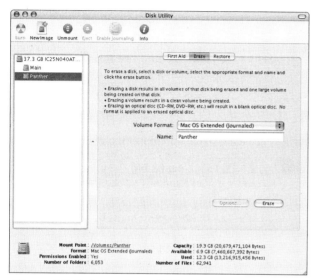

• **Figure 1-3:** Reformatting a disk's volume.

5. Click Erase to reformat the volume.

When reformatting a hard drive, you can choose to Zero All Data (available by clicking the Options button). Doing so will exponentially increase how long it takes to reformat the drive, but it's the best way to both clean the drive and ensure that it's working properly.

Partitioning a disk drive

To partition a disk drive into multiple volumes:

1. Click the drive's icon in the left column.

The drive will have a strange name consisting of the size and model of the device.

2. Click the Partition tab.

3. Select a scheme from the Volume Scheme drop-down menu (see Figure 1-4).

A volume's scheme refers to how many partitions you want to create. Hard drives 20GB or larger can be nicely divided into two partitions.

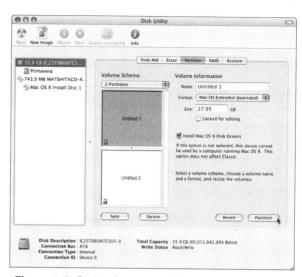

• **Figure 1-4:** Opting for two partitions as the volume's scheme.

4. One at a time, select every partition in the volume scheme window (named Untitled 1 and Untitled 2 in Figure 1-4). Type a name in the Name box and select a format type in the Format drop-down list for each.

Disk Utility automatically partitions a disk into equally sized volumes. You can override this by clicking and dragging the bar that separates the volumes in the scheme window.

5. Click the Partition button to enact the changes.

Using RAIDs

If your computer has multiple hard drives, you can establish a RAID (Redundant Array of *Inexpensive* Disks or Redundant Array of *Independent* Disks, depending upon whom you ask) on them with Disk Utility. A *RAID* treats multiple drives as one single device, offering either better performance or better reliability (or sometimes both), depending upon how it's defined.

Unless you're doing high-end video or image processing or are supremely concerned about a disk drive failure, a RAID is a waste of disk space. ***Remember:*** Creating a RAID on your disk drives erases all the current content.

Installing Panther

The installation process is fairly obvious, particularly after you understand the options, but we'll run through the steps and highlight a few important considerations nonetheless. To install Panther:

1. **Update your computer's firmware.**

Apple always recommends that you do this, pointing you to www.apple.com/support/downloads. Once there, click your computer model under Updates by Product in the right-hand column. This will take you to a results page where you probably *won't* find an update for your firmware. We're not suggesting that you skip this step, but don't be surprised if it's less than fruitful.

2. **Insert the first Panther disc into the disc drive (make sure that you have all three CDs), double-click the Install Mac OS X icon, click Restart (see Figure 1-5), and wait for your Mac to reboot.**

• **Figure 1-5: Restart your computer to begin installing Panther.**

 You can also begin installing Panther by holding down the C key while your computer starts up or selecting Mac OS X Install Disc 1 in the Startup Disk preferences panel (assuming the CD is in the CD drive).

3. **Select the language that you want to use and then click Continue.**

4. **Read through the introductory text on the first two pages, clicking Continue to go on.**

 The information presented on the second page is duplicated in the Read Before You Install PDF file found on the first installation disc. It mostly covers Panther's compatibility issues.

5. **Accept the license agreement by clicking Continue in the main window and then Agree on the sheet that appears from the top of the window.**

 You don't have to accept the license agreement — unless you want to install Panther, that is. If you click Disagree, you exit the installer and are returned to your normal operating system world. One could argue, therefore, that to save time, *you just skip reading the agreement* (because you have to agree with it regardless). We'd never be so irresponsible as to suggest that *you skip reading the agreement*, though. (Cough, cough.)

6. **On the Select a Destination page that appears, select the destination drive for the installation but don't click Continue just yet (see Figure 1-6).**

The installer will present a list of available volumes where you can place Panther. The installer will even mark the recommended destination with a green arrow and unusable destinations with a red X.

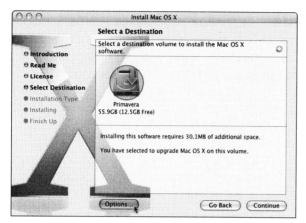

• **Figure 1-6: The destination determines where Panther will be installed.**

 If you have a decent-sized hard drive (20GB or more), hopefully you partitioned it into two or more separate volumes. If so, you can do a clean install of an OS onto the second volume, maintaining all your files and applications on the original volume, just in case. See "Managing Your Disk Drives" for more information on partitioning.

7. Before you leave the Select a Destination page, click Options at the bottom of the window.

8. In the Options dialog that appears (see Figure 1-7), select the appropriate installation method (see the earlier section "Choosing an Installation Method"). Click OK to close the Options dialog and then click Continue in the Select a Destination window.

Your choices are

▶ Upgrade

▶ Archive and Install

▶ Erase and Install

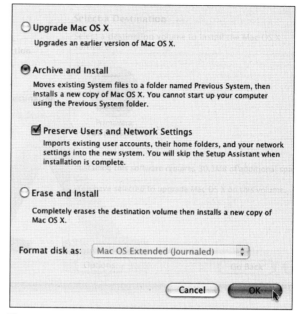

• **Figure 1-7: The Options dialog is where you select your installation type.**

 If you select the Archive and Install option, you absolutely, positively want to select the Preserve Users and Network Settings check box; otherwise, you'll need to recreate all your files from the archive, which is an unnecessary hassle.

If you select the Erase and Install option, you have the choice of formatting with either the Mac OS Extended (Journaled) or Unix File System (UFS) formats. You almost certainly want the former, but read the "Managing Your Disk Drives" section for more information.

 If you perform an Erase and Install of Panther, all your existing applications — along with your files — are wiped out. If you don't have all the application disks and serial numbers written down somewhere, you also lose some software in your transition.

9. On the Installation Type page that appears, click the Customize button at the bottom of the screen.

10. In the Customize dialog that appears, deselect all the features that you won't use (see Figure 1-8).

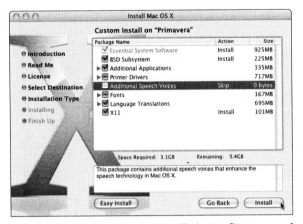

• **Figure 1-8:** Customize your installation to fit your needs.

The most important timesaving consideration when installing Panther is to avoid installing features that you'll never need. This will save you time now and disk space in perpetuity. The options that you can choose to forgo include

▶ **BSD Subsystem:** The BSD Subsystem takes up about 222MB of space but is well worth it, particularly if you're anything but the most basic Panther user. Don't skimp on this one!

▶ **Additional Applications:** The Additional Applications include Internet Explorer, StuffIt Expander, iTunes, iMovie, iPhoto, iCal, and iSync. You'll probably want all of these, but go ahead and drop those you won't use.

▶ **Printer Drivers:** If you don't have a printer, you won't need these at all, so deselect this option and save a whopping 922MB of disk space. If you do have a printer, choose to install the drivers that correspond to the make and model of your printer.

▶ **Additional Speech Voices:** The speech voices only require 29MB of space, but that's 29 more megabytes than necessary if you never use them. We don't. You probably won't either.

▶ **Fonts:** Although Apple's been kind enough to include the fonts, an informal poll of ours concluded that most Panther users don't read much text written in Inuktitut or Gujarati. If that accurately describes you, drop all the fonts, along with the standard Asian ones (Japanese, Chinese, and Korean). You'll save yourself 172MB of room (possibly for MP3s) in the process.

▶ **Language Translations:** If everyone using the computer primarily reads and writes English, deselect the 389MB of language translations that the OS will never use.

▶ **X11:** This option is admittedly close to our hearts and requires a meager 82MB of space. Installing it will open up your Mac to a whole world of free *(free!)* software and make these geeky authors proud. X11 provides a graphical user interface to UNIX applications, such as the GIMP image manipulation tool, games, various text-editing programs, and a wide array of scientific tools. Although these UNIX applications will not look or act as nice as native Mac OS X applications, the ability to run them is still very valuable, and the price is right.

 If you don't install the BSD Subsystem, be aware that you won't be able to use many of the more techie features of Panther, including a few that we list in this book. This includes command line utilities and some Internet and networking software.

11. After you select what you want installed, click OK to close. You can also click Easy Install to cancel the customization. Lastly, click Continue in the main installation window.

12. On the final installation page, click Install to begin the actual installation process.

You can quit the installer any time up until you click the Install button. After you do that, get out a good book because you'll have to wait out the installation (easily 15–30 minutes, depending upon your computer and the installation choices made).

13. **The first step that the installer takes is to check for problems on the destination volume. You have the option of skipping this step (click Skip in the lower-right corner), but you should let the installer do its thing.**

If the installer fails while checking the integrity of your disk, you need to use Disk Utility to perform repairs before attempting the installation again.

14. **When the installation finishes, your computer automatically restarts. (You can also click Restart at the prompt.)**

15. **If necessary, follow the onscreen instructions to insert discs 2 and 3.**

After your computer reboots — and is therefore running off the new OS on your hard disk — the installation process might continue if you've elected to install some of the optional components listed in Step 10. For example, if you're installing extra fonts and printer drivers, you'll be prompted for disc 2; if you elected to install X11, disc 3 will be required.

The installer CDs can also be used for three administrative purposes: changing the Startup Disk, resetting a password, and accessing a version of Disk Utility not running on the main hard drive (see "Managing Your Disk Drives"). Each of these is accessible through the Installer menu.

Working with Setup Assistant

If you perform an Erase and Install installation of Panther, or if you're using your computer for the very first time, you get the magic of the Setup

Assistant when your computer reboots. Like its Windows counterpart, Setup Assistant asks you a series of questions intended to make using the computer easier. Here are the highlights of the process so that you can whip through it more quickly:

1. **Select your language.**

2. **Select your keyboard layout.**

For both of the preceding steps, the defaults will most likely work. Apple's kind enough not to display all the options, but you can get them by clicking the box at the bottom of the window.

3. **Decide what you want to do for an Apple ID.**

You have three options:

▶ Enter your existing ID, if you have one.

▶ Create a new Apple ID.

▶ None of the above.

You already have an Apple ID if you've registered for any of the special areas at www.apple.com or if you have a .Mac account (which will be the same as your Apple ID).

If you don't already have an Apple ID or a .Mac account, we strongly recommend creating one, which will give you a 60-day trial .Mac account. If you like the trial, you can pay for a permanent account. We both have one and think it's well worth the $99 yearly price.

You can get a free trial .Mac membership when you go through Setup Assistant. Because we refer to some .Mac stuff throughout this book, you really ought to consider signing up, even temporarily.

4. **If you want, register.**

Unlike Windows XP, which requires activation of the operating system, you can forgo Panther registration entirely. If you don't feel like registering, press ⌘+Q to quit the registration application. You will then be given the option to skip registration entirely (and continue with Setup Assistant), shut down the computer, or cancel.

5. **Create your user account.**

To create your account, enter your full name, the short name (which the computer will treat as your username), and a password. Ideally, your short name should consist only of letters, numbers, and the underscore, and be eight characters in length or shorter.

 You can skip the password and verify prompts if you'd rather not have a password. This will expedite many tasks but will also make your computer far less secure.

6. **Select your Internet access type and then click Continue.**

There are four options:

▶ Two different ways of setting up an EarthLink account.

▶ Use your existing Internet service.

▶ I'm not ready to connect to the Internet.

7. **Follow the prompts to complete the Internet setup.**

As long as you didn't select I'm Not Ready to Connect to the Internet in Step 6, you're led through a connection setup wizard. If you're using an existing service, have your Internet information written down and ready for when you go through Setup Assistant. Getting the information correct here will save you the hassle of configuring your network later, although you always have that option.

You need to know some combination of the following:

▶ Connection type (telephone modem, cable modem, and so forth)

▶ User name

▶ Password

▶ Phone number (for telephone dialup)

▶ Subnet mask, router address, DNS hosts, and Domain Names (for DSL, cable modems, and other networks)

 Your Internet service provider should give you detailed connection information to use during the Internet setup process.

8. **Select your time zone, confirm the current date and time, and start using Panther!**

Transferring Files Flawlessly

In Technique 14, we discuss how to organize and maintain your files and folders. Panther comes with a good implicit organization scheme that you really ought to follow. If you do so, you can restore all your documents, bookmarks, e-mail, and so forth merely by copying the contents of your old Home directory to your new user directory. Even if you use the painless Archive and Install installation option, saving the contents of the Users folder to an external source before you begin installation (hard drive, CD-ROM, DVD) is a prudent move.

While we're at it, we recommend that you have at least one reliable backup of all your data at all times. If you're installing a new version of the operating system, you want two or more backups that use different media. (You can never be too careful.)

 The Backup application is provided free to .Mac users. Version 2 of the application can back up files to your iDisk, a CD or DVD, and even external hard drives.

Be sure that your backups aren't in a proprietary format (for example, the Retrospect Express cataloging system; www.dantz.com) because you won't be able to get to the data until your computer can read that format again.

 We highly recommend making a CD-ROM of installed applications that also contains a text document with all your serial numbers. This fairly simple step makes restoring the software on your computer a snap!

Starting Up with Speed

Technique 2

Save Time By

- Always keeping your computer on
- Selecting the proper operating system in a multiboot environment
- Managing the login process
- Loading applications automatically at startup

After you get Panther installed on your computer, it's time to get it humming. In this Technique, we discuss various ways to get your computer up and running as fast as possible. The timesaving ideas that we discuss here cover from the time you press the power button to using the actual applications.

We begin by pointing out the benefits of never shutting down your computer, which helps you start faster and is a reasonable option for many Panther users. Then we follow through steps that you can take to choose which Mac operating system (OS) to boot into if you have different ones installed on your machine. Finally, we show you how to best manage computers in a multiuser environment, concluding with how to bring up your must-have applications as soon as you log into Panther.

Faster Startups: Never Shut Down

Although obvious, many people never think of this: The fastest way to get your computer to start up is to never shut it down. Even on the fastest machines, the startup process takes several minutes — minutes that you don't need to spend sitting idly. The Unix operating system — which is at the heart of Mac OS X — was designed to run 24 hours a day, and your Mac is perfectly capable of this as well. Granted, keeping your computer on all the time will rack up the electrical bill a few cents per month, but that minimal extra cost can be easily offset by your increased productivity. Now, we're not arguing that you should *never* shut your computer down, but here are some different ways to limit shutdowns:

- Put the computer to sleep overnight, rather than shutting it down.
- Set the sleep mode (see Figure 2-1) by clicking the Show Details button from the Sleep tab of the Energy Saver panel.

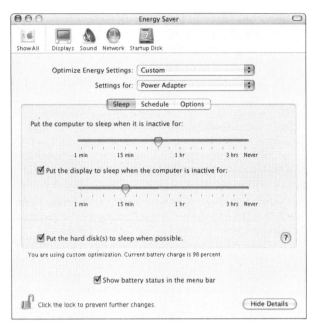

• **Figure 2-1:** You can adjust your computer's sleeping
habits in the Energy Saver panel.

You can access the Energy Saver panel by
choosing System Preferences from the Apple
menu and then clicking on Energy Saver
under Hardware. Figure 2-1 shows the Energy
Saver panel for a laptop, which has a few more
features than the same panel on a desktop
machine.

✔ Turn off the monitor (desktop users only).

✔ Close your laptop's monitor to engage the sleep
mode (laptop users only).

✔ Leave the computer active but engage the screen
saver.

If you're not going to use your computer for
days on end (like during a long holiday), shut
it down. Our main point is that you don't have
to shut down your computer on a nightly basis.

If you prefer to shut down your computer
nightly and bring it back up in the morning,
look into using the scheduling capability built
into the Energy Saver panel (see Figure 2-2).
You can have your computer automatically
start up at a certain time every morning.

• **Figure 2-2:** If you consistently use your computer on a
regular basis, use the scheduler to start up
automatically.

Laptop Power-Saving Suggestions

If you're running a laptop from its battery, be prudent
when choosing to shut down the computer versus putting
it to sleep. Sleep mode requires very little energy from your
computer. Conversely, starting up the machine (as well as
shutting it down) is a huge drain on its battery. In
Technique 3, we discuss some energy management suggestions in more detail.

Booting into a Different Mac OS

Many OS X users still use OS 9, thus creating a dual operating system computer. If you need to choose which operating system to boot into, here are some ways to make this process faster and easier:

✔ Use the Startup Disk (see Figure 2-3) preferences panel to set the most commonly used operating system. This OS should be your default, allowing you to change the game plan only when using another Mac OS. Click the lock icon to set this choice, thereafter requiring a password if someone wants to change Startup Disk preferences.

• **Figure 2-3: Use Startup Disk preferences to choose your primary OS.**

✔ Have your computer prompt you with a list of available operating systems by holding down the Option key while the computer starts up. Doing so generates a prompt (it will take a while) of the installed operating systems. Click the one that you want and then click the right arrow to boot into the selected operating system.

> If your computer is off and you need to start up in other than the default operating system, hold down the Option key after you've turned on the computer.

✔ Boot up from a system CD-ROM by holding down the C key while the disc is in the drive.

✔ If you happen to have both OS X and OS 9 installed on the same disk drive, automatically boot into OS X by holding down the X key at startup.

Booting from External Drives

The later versions of Jaguar (OS X 10.2) finally introduced the ability to boot from an OS stored on an external drive. This support is also included in Panther (OS X 10.3). Thanks to this, you now have the option of installing an entire OS on a FireWire drive and using that as the need arises.

Although this might seem like an unnecessary feature, it can be quite helpful. For example, if you want to experiment with a beta version of a new OS, install that on an external drive. If you think that you'll occasionally need to use OS 9 (or Classic), place it on that FireWire drive. Doing so will speed up the performance of your computer (it won't have to track multiple operating systems) and also save disk space on your primary drive.

Speeding Up Login

If your computer has multiple users, you have the same types of questions that you have with multiple operating systems:

✔ Should a user be automatically logged in?

✔ If a user should be automatically logged in, which user?

✔ How do you quickly switch to another user?

Panther includes many nice touches for using the computer in a multi-user environment. Simplify and speed up the login process like this:

✔ If you use the computer more often than other users, set the computer to automatically log in under your username by following these steps:

1. Open the Accounts panel under System Preferences.

2. Click Login Options at the bottom of the left-hand column.

3. Select the Automatically Log in As check box.

4. Select your username from the drop-down list (see Figure 2-4).

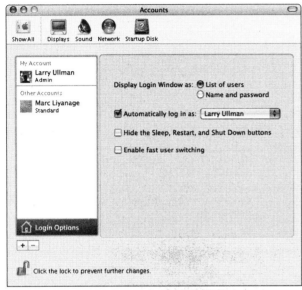

• **Figure 2-4: Use the Login Options in the Accounts panel to secure and speed up access to your computer.**

5. Click the lock in the bottom-left corner to make this setting permanent.

 Any locked System Preferences panel needs to be unlocked in order for changes to be made. Unlocking a panel requires an administrator's password. If you are the only administrator of your Mac, using the lock on any System Preferences page means that no one else can change that setting.

Keeping Peace with Multiple Users

Setting yourself as the default user might miff your co-users, but it'll save you time, and that's all we're really concerned with here, right?

Besides, Panther's new Fast User Switching feature (which we discuss in Technique 5) makes the automatic login much less of an inconvenience for the other users of the computer.

 Keep in mind that if you log on automatically, anyone who has physical access to your computer now has the power to use your computer without restraint. If your computer stays at home and you trust your dog, this might not be an issue; otherwise, be aware of this fact.

✔ If you must use the login prompt, select the List of Users radio button in the Login Options section of the Accounts panel. Doing so will allow you to skip typing in your username while still requiring a password.

✔ Again, if you must use the login prompt, at the prompt, type the first letter of your name and press Return. Assuming that letter isn't used by multiple users, this will quickly get you to the password prompt.

Security versus Convenience

As we say many times throughout this book, you might have to compromise security for greater convenience (or speed). In many of the examples of this book, you need to decide whether you want something to be easier or more secure. Mitigating factors in making this decision include

✔ Whether or not you share your Mac

✔ What type of information is stored on your Mac

✔ Who might have physical access to your computer

✔ What kind of potential exists for your computer being stolen

For example, the most secure login method is to require users to enter both a username and password to log into the computer, but this is really annoying if you are the only one who uses and has access to your Mac. In this case, automatically logging in as yourself, but password protecting sensitive files on your computer (such as a Quicken document) and keeping regular backups of everything makes sense.

In the course of this book, you find many techniques for making things convenient and many for making things secure. In the end, only you can decide where on that scale your total Mac usage should fall.

Starting Applications Automatically

After your computer is up and running and you've logged in, you're ready to start working with applications. In Part IV, we discuss applications in detail, but we can discuss at least one related technique here. From the Accounts panel, you can set applications to launch automatically when you start up your computer.

1. Open the Accounts System Preferences panel.

2. Select your username from the list on the left (assuming that you have multiple users).

3. (If necessary) Unlock the panel by clicking the lock icon in the lower left-hand corner and entering the administrative password.

4. Click the Startup Items tab (see Figure 2-5).

• **Figure 2-5: Larry's list of must-be-running applications are included in his Startup Items.**

At this stage, you have two options:

▶ Click the plus sign at the bottom of the Startup Items window, navigate to the application using the Open sheet that appears, select the application, and press Return.

▶ Open your Applications folder and drag-and-drop the application(s) into the Accounts panel. We find this method to be much, much faster.

5. After you're finished, click the lock icon to finalize the changes.

 Speed up the startup process by disabling automatic startup applications when you won't need them: Hold down the Shift key after logging in. This trick will work only if you've gone through the login panel (it won't work with automatic logins).

Startup Items: A Techie's Technique

Another (far more geeky) way to make things automatically happen when you turn on your computer is to use the Startup Items folder, located in /System/Library. Every item here gets its own folder, and the script within that folder is automatically called when the computer turns on. Unlike the login panel, these items are run for all users.

If you're comfortable with scripting, using the Startup Items folder is a great way to do some things, such as starting a database application each time that the computer runs. Marc has created a shell script for exactly that purpose (automatically starting the MySQL database server), which can be downloaded from www.entropy.ch/software/macosx/mysql. You can use this example (if you're feeling adventurous), or those already on your system, as templates for how to get really geeky with Panther.

The slightly less geeky (and, frankly, easier) solution is to use an AppleScript that runs your startup routine. An example is developed in Technique 60. This can then be added to your Startup Items in the Accounts panel.

While you're messing around with System Preferences is a good time to have the auto-loading applications do their things. For example:

✔ Set Mail to automatically check for new e-mail every so many minutes, using Mail's General preferences panel (see Figure 2-6).

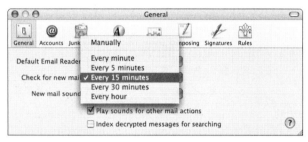

• **Figure 2-6:** Have Mail automatically fetch new messages if you have an always-on Internet connection.

✔ Set Safari to automatically open a specific URL when it's launched. Use Safari's General preferences panel to set a Home page and indicate that all new windows should open with that.

If it's applicable, you can even select a file to open at startup by adding it to the Startup Items list. Select the Hide check box next to a Startup Item (refer to Figure 2-5) to have it load without the visual fuss.

 Your computer must expend some time and a bit of power to start up applications. Therefore, you should only add those to your Startup Items list that you absolutely will use every time you start the computer.

Technique 3

Running Panther Faster

Save Time By

- ✔ Using System Optimizer X to pick up the pace
- ✔ Turning off unused options and features of the operating system
- ✔ Extending your laptop battery's life
- ✔ Spending your hard-earned money wisely on speed-enhancing improvements

Like many of the other techniques in the first part of the book, those in this Technique show you how to save time by adjusting system-wide settings. They're of the "do it once and forget about it" variety.

First, we cover a ridiculously cheap shareware application called System Optimizer X, which fine-tunes your computer for improved performance. We tested it ourselves, read the technical specifications, and were impressed by the reviews — now we think it should be part of your system, too. Much in the same vein, you then discover how to manually tune your computer by disabling some of Panther's unused features. Doing so will pare down a hefty OS (as much as possible, that is).

For those of you using a laptop, we give some attention to the related ideas of energy management and extending your battery's life. Finally, we cover the best ways to improve the performance of your computer through hardware.

Optimizing Your System with Shareware

One of the great things about the Mac OS X system is that where there's a need, there's shareware (and often freeware, too). One such application, System Optimizer X (available from www.mkd.cc/sox/ for the low, low price of only $12), fine-tunes several aspects of the operating system. The manufacturer's claim — and the evidence seems to support these claims — is that System Optimizer X will

- ✔ Improve the overall system speed and responsiveness
- ✔ Handle automated tasks that Panther has set to run overnight

 Mac OS X has several maintenance-type tasks set to run when you're not using the computer. Most of these are therefore scheduled to run during the middle of the night or early morning. For many users, these routines are never executed because their computers are off at those times. If you do regularly shut down your machine, System Optimizer X addresses these maintenance needs.

✔ Increase the stability of the operating system

✔ Perk up your Internet connection

✔ Give you feedback on what it's doing

If that hasn't convinced you to use this application, follow these steps to install and use System Optimizer X for a free trial. If you're pleased with the results, keep and pay for it; otherwise, you can easily uninstall it.

1. **Download the most current version of the application from** www.mkd.cc/sox/ **(see Figure 3-1).**

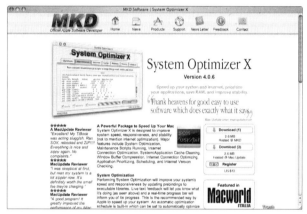

• **Figure 3-1: System Optimizer X helps speed up Mac OS X.**

2. **Double-click the downloaded file (which will be named something like** SystemOptimizerX406. dmg.gz**) to expand the file with StuffIt.**

3. **Double-click the resulting disk image file (again, named something like** SystemOptimizerX406.dmg, **depending upon your version) to automatically call the Disk Utility application to mount it as a drive.**

4. **Install System Optimizer X by dragging the folder on the disk image (see Figure 3-2) into your Applications or Utilities folder.**

• **Figure 3-2: Mounting the DMG file creates this disk image.**

5. **Launch System Optimizer X by double-clicking the installed application in the Finder.**

6. **Click Go Ahead at the prompt.**

This gives the application permission to install the files that it needs to run.

 We're not saying that it will happen, but just in case the application wreaks havoc on your machine, it's a very good idea to run a thorough backup before optimizing the system (see Technique 48). Again, we have not experienced any problems, but System Optimizer X works on your system files and removes some cached data, so you can never be too careful.

7. **After the installation is complete, you'll be presented with the main window.**

To optimize your system:

▶ 1. Click the lock in the lower-left corner.

▶ 2. Enter your system's administrative password.

▶ 3. Click the Optimize button.

8. **After the optimization process is complete (which could take a good half-hour or more), click the Restart button (see Figure 3-3).**

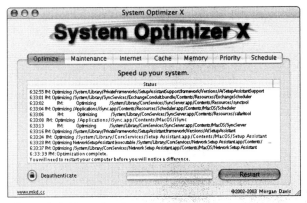

• **Figure 3-3: To notice the optimization effects, you must restart the computer.**

 Because it takes a while before the first time System Optimizer X does its thing, you might want to start it before you go to lunch (or maybe take a nap).

9. After your computer restarts, open System Optimizer X again to execute the remaining optimization techniques (click each tab — Maintenance, Internet, and so forth — for details).

10. If you appreciate the application and decide to keep it, be certain to register by going to www.mkd.cc/sox and clicking the Register link (it's only $12).

11. After you register, use the Schedule tab to set up routine maintenance.

 MDK Software recommends that you run the System (through the Optimize tab) and Cache optimizations monthly and the Maintenance routine weekly (or more often).

Disabling Unnecessary Features

Larry has a friend who was annoyed by how slowly her computer was performing. After taking a look, he quickly discovered one culprit: animated icons dancing around on her Desktop. Our point isn't to make you question Larry's choice of friends and their computer know-how, but this: There's frequently an inverse relationship between features and performance. The more features you have turned on and running, the more your computer has to do. The more your computer has to do, the slower it becomes. The trick is to find a balance between functionality and speed.

Common speed-enhancing techniques are

✔ **Removing CD-ROMs from your disc drive when you're not using them.**

Your Mac has to keep track of all mounted disks (and discs), be they CD-ROMS, DVDs, or external hard drives. Tracking discs does require some processor effort, which could be better used elsewhere.

✔ **Removing external disks when they're not being used.**

Keeping an eye on large FireWire drives takes a noticeable toll on your Mac. (Dismounting and unplugging an external drive might cut that electricity bill a bit, too.)

✔ **Turning off the iDisk synchronization.**

Panther has better built-in support for iDisk than its predecessors. Your iDisk can be always available for access and can also be in synchronization at all times. What this means, though, is that your computer is constantly checking on the status of your iDisk and updating it. This is a drag in terms of performance, network speed, and disk space. To disable automatic synchronization, do the following:

 Having an iDisk is one of the benefits of paying for a .Mac account (we discuss both in Technique 41). Simply put, the iDisk is 100MB of online storage. There's a little more to it than that — like a .Mac Web page, an easy way to download software, and a method for sharing documents online — but that's the gist of the idea.

▶ 1. Click on .Mac, found under the Internet & Network section of the System Preferences panel.

▶ 2. Click the iDisk tab and either deselect the Create a Local Copy of Your iDisk option (see Figure 3-4), or select the Manually radio button under Synchronize.

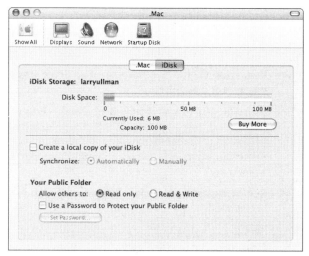

• **Figure 3-4: Turn off the iDisk synchronization option for better performance.**

✔ **Turning off the items in the Sharing panel if they're not going to be used regularly (see Figure 3-5).**

Panther supports several different kinds of services — Personal Web Sharing, Personal File Sharing, Printer Sharing — but using each of these requires an actively running process. Although most sit quietly in the background, waiting to be used, you don't need to have them turned on if you aren't regularly using them. Click Sharing under the Internet & Network section of System Preferences to access the panel and see Technique 39 for more information (including the related security issues).

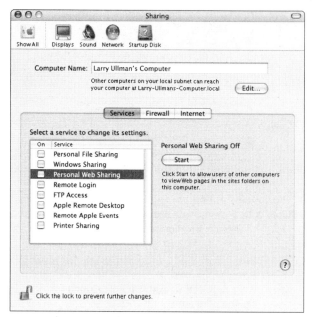

• **Figure 3-5: The Sharing panel provides easy access to different services.**

 The good people at Apple were smart enough to have all the Sharing items turned off by default. If you change these settings, try to remember that so you'll turn them back off again when the time is right. For example, if you're traveling (and therefore not on your normal network), you don't need to enable File or Print sharing.

✔ **Trying not to overburden your Internet connection.** Imagine simultaneously listening to online music through iTunes, running ESPN's GameCast Java applet to follow a Cubs game, instant messaging your friends, and transferring files via FTP. For some inexplicable reason, your computer is incredibly sluggish. By making better decisions (your friends can wait, so turn off iChat, and wouldn't you rather listen to a CD anyway?), Panther will start purring again.

Because of how Mac OS X manages CPU and memory usage, most open applications won't affect the overall performance when they're not being used. You can save yourself time without bringing the computer down by not continually closing and reopening applications.

✔ **Turn off your AirPort Card when you're not online.**

Using an AirPort Card requires some processing and battery power. If you're not currently online, turn off the AirPort Card. See Technique 37 for other wireless network-related ideas.

Longer Battery Life

If you're using a laptop, the life of your battery directly affects how fast you can get things done. If you don't believe us, try doing, well, anything on a dead battery with no outlets in sight. To minimize or altogether eradicate such occurrences, keep in mind the following principles:

✔ **Disable unnecessary features.** See the previous section of this Technique.

✔ **Keep running applications to a minimum.** It's not running applications that drain the battery as much as starting and stopping them does. Open only the applications you need and keep them open until you're finished.

✔ **Minimize how often the computer has to access the hard drive.** Writing to and reading from drives of any type is a big drain on a laptop's battery. In particular, most of the iLife applications suck the blood from your battery. Avoid listening to iTunes, editing videos in iMovie, or working with iPhoto unless you really have to or don't mind the shortened battery life.

✔ **Remove CDs and DVDs from the disc drive.**

✔ **Change your energy settings to Longest Battery Life.** Head over to the Energy Saver panel (see Figure 3-6) under System Preferences. One of the default configurations is Longest Battery Life (assuming you have a laptop). This option automatically configures your display, sleep, and other settings accordingly.

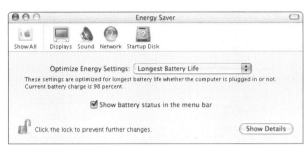

• **Figure 3-6:** Laptop users should stay on top of the Energy Saver panel.

 If you're using a laptop, get in the habit of enabling the battery status in the menu bar (see Figure 3-6) while you're not wired and disabling it otherwise. You'll want to monitor it when you're on battery, but it only clutters up your screen otherwise.

✔ **Keep the screen as dim as possible.** A fair portion of your battery's power will go into illuminating the monitor. To maximize your battery's life, dim the monitor as much as you can (use the screen brightness keys on the keyboard to do so). If you're working in a particularly dark place or at night, you can get away with almost entirely dimming the monitor while still being able to read it.

 If your laptop is running off the battery but you're not actively using it and you want to keep it awake (for example, if it's processing something or playing iTunes), dim the monitor to the point of blackness — you will save yourself lots of power for later use.

✔ **Don't play DVDs or CD-ROM-based games on your laptop.** Nothing drains a battery more quickly.

Faster Performance through Energy Management

Most computer users don't think about energy management, although it has a profound effect on both the computer's performance and a laptop's longevity. Apple set up energy management to work very well without help, but you might occasionally find reasons to make adjustments. Most users can and should keep the energy settings — found in the Energy Saver panel of System Preferences — on Automatic. The more curious user might want to consider switching among Highest Performance, DVD Playback, and Presentations, as the need arises. The latter two are particularly effective under their corresponding conditions: For example, each of them disables sleep mode.

Improving Performance through Hardware

You can do a fair amount of tweaking by using the built-in Panther software and running shareware, but if you really want to enhance your computer's performance, you'll have to part with some cash. Here are some hardware improvements that you can make from least to most expensive:

If you're looking through this book in a library or bookstore, we highly recommend that you purchase your own copy (or better yet, buy several, and you'll never need to read the same copy twice). The small price is well worth the timesaving techniques!

How to Upgrade Your Hardware

If you're not the type of person that likes to open up a computer and mess around with the insides, you have a couple of options for getting the job done:

- ✔ Have it performed at the store where you purchase the upgrades

- ✔ Go to an official Apple store

- ✔ Take your Mac to an authorized Apple dealer, such as CompUSA

Any of the above places will install the new hardware for a nominal cost (maybe $30, depending upon the item in question).

If you don't mind a little tinkering — and are willing to assume the risks involved — new RAM, hard drives, and video cards can often be installed using only basic tools. You'll most likely find installation instructions either with the purchased hardware or online. Search Google or the AppleCare Knowledge Base (http://kbase.info.apple.com) for specifics.

- ✔ **Add more RAM ($40–$200).** Adding RAM is far and away the most foolproof method for improving your computer's performance. RAM has become cheaper and cheaper and is ridiculously affordable these days. If you haven't maxed out your computer's RAM capabilities, consider doing so now.

We recommend that you have at least 384MB or more of RAM in your computer. You don't necessarily need to go up to 2GB, but 512MB is a nice, even number and befitting most Panther users.

- ✔ **Purchase a faster hard drive ($80–$300).** Sadly, Apple stopped using SCSI hard drives some time ago, opting to go with the cheaper but slower IDE drives instead. If you don't feel like upgrading to a SCSI drive (which isn't even an option for laptop users), consider buying a faster IDE drive. Most laptops use a 4,200 rpm drive by default, but 5,400 rpm drives can be acquired for a few dollars more. Desktop machines commonly use 7,200 rpm drives, but these can be replaced with 10,000 rpm drives without breaking the bank. We admit that the performance gap between SCSI and IDE drives has closed over the years, but there's still wiggle room for speed improvements in your machine.

- ✔ **Purchase an external FireWire drive ($150–$400).** If you need more storage space but do not want to replace your existing hard drive, add an external one. Such a device can be used only when you need it and can be shared among many computers.

✔ **Install a better video card ($150–$400).** People who aren't hard-core gamers often don't value a good video card and frequently fail to realize how a faster card improves the overall performance. Everything that happens on the screen has to go through this device, so the performance impact is real. Laptop users have little to no room for improvement in this area, but desktop users have many options. Consider buying a new card with as much RAM possible (64MB is fair) and use that Accelerated Graphics Port (AGP) slot if you have it.

 Ideally, any video card that you purchase should also support Panther's Quartz Extreme acceleration, which is a great benefactor to performance.

 Make sure that the video card manufacturer supports Panther by providing the appropriate drivers. If they don't, you either won't reap the performance benefits or the card might not work at all. Check a manufacturer's Web site for compatibility information before making the investment!

✔ **Replace the motherboard (desktop users only, $400–$900).** This is a pricey step and comes close to being impractical because motherboards are often almost as expensive as a new computer. But if you have a nice machine that you want to work with, you can upgrade to a newer, faster processor for a few hundred big ones.

✔ **Get that new Mac ($900–$3,000).** It used to be that as a Mac user, you knew that you would spend more for your computers, get less in return, and have fewer options than your Windows friends, but those days are long gone. Apple has had great success in developing separate computer lines (professional and home) with a decent range of prices and capabilities. You can now pick up an impressive eMac for under a grand and a low-end iBook for just over that amount.

✔ **Take out a second mortgage and get that new dual-processor G5, with all the RAM that you can, and a new 23-inch studio display ($5,000).** Buy us one while you're at it.

Technique 4

When Good Applications Go Bad

Save Time By

✔ Killing stalled-out applications

✔ Keeping an eye out for problems with the Activity Monitor

I'm sure we all agree that Panther is a most excellent operating system — perhaps the best that we've ever used. However, we still encounter the occasional problem or misguided application that mucks up the works. Fortunately, OS X brought us *protected memory,* meaning that a stalled-out application will no longer bring down the whole machine. But stalled applications do gum up the works and leave your computer hanging. In this Technique, we show you the best and fastest ways to monitor and shut down problematic software. In an ideal world, you'd never need to know these techniques, but in reality, following these steps can keep your system going.

Slaying Stalled Apps with the Dock

Panther has a few different ways to kill errant applications. The best-known method is to press ⌘+Option+Esc to bring up the Force Quit Applications window (see Figure 4-1).

• **Figure 4-1:** The Force Quit Applications window allows you to shut down applications.

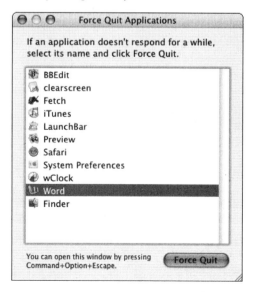

You can also bring up the Force Quit Applications menu by selecting Force Quit from the Apple menu.

An alternative method for killing an application is to use the Dock. Here's how:

1. Before you proceed, think back to make sure that you haven't assigned this application some monumental task (such as heavy image or video processing) that can explain its sluggishness.

2. If an application is not responding, click and hold its Dock icon to bring up a contextual menu (see Figure 4-2).

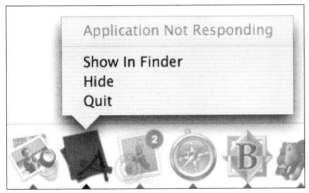

• **Figure 4-2:** Clicking and holding a **Dock** item brings up a contextual menu.

3. Press the Option key while still clicking the Dock icon to get the Force Quit option (see Figure 4-3).

4. If the contextual menu for the application (created in Steps 2 and 3) reads Application Not Responding and you can't think of a good reason why, select Force Quit.

5. Wait a couple of minutes to let the system stabilize; then reopen the application.

You should always attempt to quit an application in the usual way before performing a force-quit. Also get in the habit of giving your quits and force-quits a few moments to work before trying to nuke them.

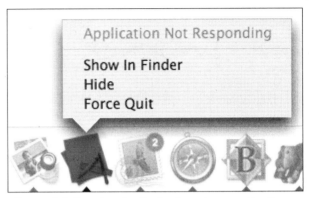

• **Figure 4-3:** Pressing the Option key gives you the Force Quit option.

Gaining Better Performance through Activity Monitoring

One of Panther's lesser-used applications is the Activity Monitor, found in the Utilities folder. This application does exactly what you'd think: It monitors the activity of the computer. The interface of the application is a bit techie, but it can be a very useful tool for catching problems and fine-tuning the performance of your computer. For example, you can set up a floating CPU window that allows you to continuously monitor your CPU's activity. You can use the CPU window to catch apps that might be slowing down your system performance. Follow these steps to set up the window:

1. Open the Activity Monitor, located in the Utilities folder.

2. Choose Monitor⇨Floating CPU Window and either Show Vertically or Show Horizontally (see Figure 4-4).

By default, the Activity Monitor does not display a floating CPU window. This step creates one that remains visible even after you hide the Activity Monitor application.

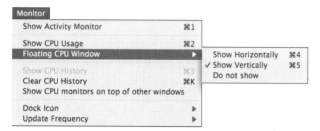

• **Figure 4-4:** Choose a type of floating CPU window to display: Horizontal or Vertical.

 Instead of using the menu bar, you can also create the floating CPU window by pressing ⌘+4 or ⌘+5.

3. While you have the Activity Monitor open, adjust the update frequency by choosing Monitor⇨Update Frequency⇨Less Often.

 Setting the Activity Monitor to update less frequently will minimize the performance effect that running the monitor has on your computer.

4. If the floating CPU window (see Figure 4-5) turns to solid green or solid green and red for more than a few seconds, some program is using up all the available processing power (thereby bringing down the performance of everything else).

5. Click the Activity Monitor icon in the Dock and press ⌘+1 to bring up the Activity Monitor screen (if it isn't already).

The Activity Monitor icon either looks like the monitor image next to the Finder in Figure 4-5 or it can be a graph itself (see Figure 4-6).

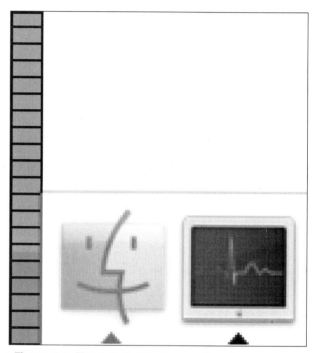

• **Figure 4-5:** The Activity Monitor creates a bar graph indicating CPU usage.

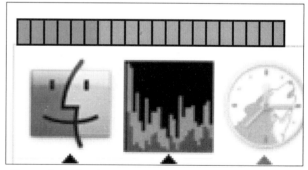

• **Figure 4-6:** The Activity Monitor can also be represented by a history graph of CPU usage.

 The Activity Monitor's Dock icon can be used to show CPU usage or history (Figure 4-6); disk or memory usage; or network activity.

6. Click the %CPU column so that CPU usage is displayed by process in descending order (see Figure 4-7).

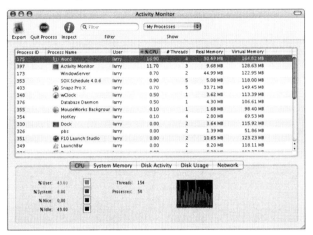

• **Figure 4-7:** Sort by the CPU usage to see what applications are hogging the machine.

In Figure 4-7, Microsoft Word is the guilty party.

7. If a process name appears in red, the application is no longer responding and needs to be shut down.

8. Determine whether it's reasonable to kill the application.

If the application in question is performing some intensive task (like iMovie compositing a video clip or iPhoto importing pictures), then the high CPU usage makes sense. However, if you haven't asked the application to do something taxing or it's a normally less intensive application (like Safari), you'll know there is a problem.

9. If the application should be stopped, try quitting it.

If so, highlight the application and click the stop sign icon in the toolbar (Quit Process), which will attempt to kill the application through normal means.

10. If the application still hasn't stopped, force it to quit by using one of the methods outlined in "Slaying Stalled Apps with the Dock," earlier in this chapter.

 If you have some time to kill or just really want to know what your computer is doing and why, the Activity Monitor is the perfect tool to spend some time with.

Understanding Processes

In the Unix world, a *process* refers to an *active* (that is, running) application, *daemon* (a special type of constantly running utility), or other service. (In fact, the Unix operating system blurs the lines between these ideas.) Panther uses the same notion of processes, of course, and therefore introduces an idea that may be foreign to many. The Activity Monitor displays not only your open applications but also behind-the-scenes system processes.

To learn more about any particular process, click the Process ID in the Activity Monitor and then press ⌘+I. This brings up another window with details for that particular application, as shown in the following figure. When you're done with your investigation, be sure to click Close to close the window — not Quit, which will attempt to shut down the process.

Another tool for monitoring your performance is *iPulse*, which is a shareware application created by the good people at the Iconfactory ($12.95 at iconfactory.com/ip_home.asp). iPulse tracks the CPU, memory, and hard drive usage and displays them graphically on the Desktop or Dock. It'll even monitor network activity.

If you want a free solution that only monitors CPU usage, check out Xload (http://s.sudre.free.fr/Software/Xload.html). If you are using a multiprocessor Mac, it will even report on each processor individually.

Logging Out and Shutting Down

Technique 5

Save Time By

✔ Logging out in different ways

✔ Switching between users quickly

✔ Shutting down fast

When it's time to call it a night, you want to get off your Mac as quickly as possible. In this final Technique of Part I, we show you a few inside tips for speeding up that process, covering the range of options: You can choose to log out of your computer, switch over to another user's account, or shut down the computer.

Logging Out

Before we discuss logging out techniques, it should be made clear that logging out of your computer is only necessary under two conditions:

✔ The Mac is being used by more than one person.

✔ You want to make sure no one messes with the computer while you're away from it.

If neither describes your situation or how your Macintosh is used, stick with your one login account and continue on your merry way.

If you share the computer and want to log out with ease, try any of the following:

1. Go to the Apple menu and select Log Out *User* (where *User* is your name; see Figure 5-1).

2. If you've enabled Fast User Switching (see the next section of this chapter to find out how), go to the user menu in the upper-right corner of the screen and select Login Window (see Figure 5-2).

Fast User Switching is a must-use feature of Panther for multi-user computers.

• **Figure 5-1: The Apple menu gives the option of logging out.**

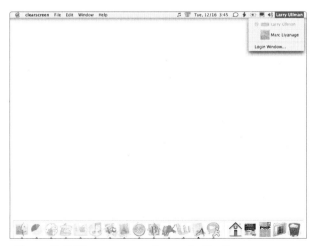

• **Figure 5-2: The user menu is new to Panther.**

3. **Press ⌘+Shift+Q to quit all applications and log out.**

You'll get a warning message like Figure 5-3.

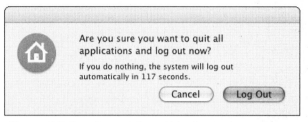

• **Figure 5-3: Logging out the standard way causes this annoying prompt.**

 To cut a step out of the log out process, hold down the Option key when selecting Log Out from the Apple menu or while pressing the keyboard shortcut. This eliminates Apple's warning.

4. **At the log out confirmation prompt (refer to Figure 5-3), press Return to log out or Esc to cancel.**

Unless you are using the Fast User Switching method of logging out, there are two considerations you should remember:

✔ Each logout method closes any open applications.

✔ If you have an unsaved document in any application, you cannot log out until you opt to Save or Don't Save that file.

Neither of these options applies to Fast User Switching, as the state of your account remains the same (all open applications remain open).

Every method of logging out — including Fast User Switching — does these two things, though:

✔ Automatically attempts to log you out after two minutes if you don't choose to either Log Out or Cancel (see Figure 5-3).

✔ Takes you to the main login screen after logging you out.

If you want to temporarily log out of your machine with the intention of returning to your work, enable Fast User Switching and log out from the user menu.

Adding User Icons

Each user on a Mac running Panther can have their own icon. This icon appears next to their name in the System Preferences⇨Accounts panel, in the main login screen, and in the Fast User Switching menu. Besides being a nice representation of you and your personality, user icons make finding your login name from among a list of names easy. You can change your icon using the Picture tab after selecting your account in the System Preferences⇨Accounts panel.

From there you have four options:

✔ Clicking one of the default Apple icons in the rightmost column.

✔ Click the Edit button and drag an image into the window.

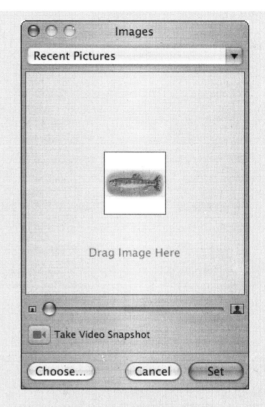

✔ Click the Edit button and take a picture of yourself using an attached camera.

If you have a FireWire video camera connected to your Mac, your image appears in the Edit window and you can click the Take Video Snapshot button to make a literal iconic representation of yourself.

✔ Click the Edit button, and then click the Choose button to find the image on your Mac.

If you click Choose in the Edit window, you get a dialog (like the Open/Save ones) so that you may navigate to and select an image on your hard drive.

The user icon you select also is updated in your Address Book and in iChat. If you like switching icons frequently, both iChat and the Edit window from the Accounts panel will remember your most frequently used images.

Securing Your System with a Screen Saver

On the other hand, if what you really want to accomplish by logging out is to protect your computer while you're away from your desk, here's an easier answer. You can instead use your screen saver and set it to require a password to deactivate.

1. Open System Preferences by selecting System Preferences from the Apple menu.

2. Click Desktop & Screen Saver under Personal.

3. If the panel appears in the Desktop mode, click the Screen Saver tab (see Figure 5-4).

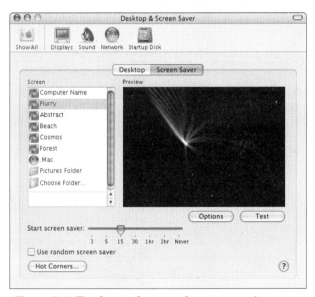

• **Figure 5-4: The Screen Saver preferences panel.**

4. Make sure that the screen saver is set to start after a certain length of time.

 For a higher level of security, set a *hot corner* that will start the screen saver. This way, you can immediately enact the screen saver before you leave your desk. Otherwise, you're trusting that no one gets to your machine between the time you leave and when it turns on.

Hot, Hot, Hot Corners

Your Mac has a feature called hot corners, wherein you can assign special meaning to the different corners of your screen. So, for example, moving the mouse into the upper-left corner may turn on your screen saver and moving the mouse into the lower-left corner may engage Exposé. Moving the mouse back out of a corner reverts the screen to its previous state (turns off the screen saver or Exposé, in these examples).

Hot corners are enabled and assigned using either the Hot Corners button in the Screen Savers panel (see Figure 5-4) or by using the Active Screen Corners section of the Exposé tab (see Technique 13).

5. Choose View⇨Security.

6. In the Security panel (see Figure 5-5), select the Require Password to Wake This Computer from Sleep or Screen Saver check box.

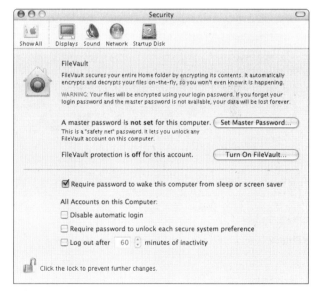

• **Figure 5-5: You can password-protect your computer through the Security panel.**

 While in the Security panel, you can also set your computer to log out after so many minutes of inactivity. You might find this option to be great (because it's more secure) or a pain (as you're consistently logging back in).

Fast User Switching

New to version 10.3 of the Mac OS X is the Fast User
Switching feature, and it's a wonderful addition for
those who share their computer. The main benefit of
Fast User Switching is that it allows a user to log out
without quitting every application. To enable Fast
User Switching, do the following:

1. **Open System Preferences.**

2. **Click Accounts under the System heading
(see Figure 5-6).**

The Accounts icon

• **Figure 5-6:** Configure Fast User Switching from the
Accounts panel.

3. **In the Accounts panel (see Figure 5-7), click
Login Options at the bottom of the left column.**

4. **In the panel that comes up next, check the
Enable Fast User Switching option (see
Figure 5-8).**

• **Figure 5-7:** The Accounts panel manages a computer's
users.

• **Figure 5-8:** Multi-user Macs should enable Fast User
Switching.

5. To switch to another account, select it from the Fast User Switching menu (refer to Figure 5-2).

6. Enter a password for the user selected in Step 5 and click Log In (see Figure 5-9).

Mac OS X
Larry Ullman's Computer

Marc Liyanage

Password : ••••••••

Cancel

Log In

• **Figure 5-9:** Enter the proper password to log in as another user.

7. To return to the previous account, or to log in under another account, repeat Steps 5 and 6.

 If multiple users are sharing a Mac, the Fast User Switching feature allows them to switch between accounts (and therefore preferences, Home folders, and more) without losing their place or re-establishing the work environment upon return.

Making the Quick Exit

After you finish for the night (or morning or afternoon) and it's time to close up for the day, you probably want to shut down your computer. Every Mac user knows how to do this, but not every Mac user knows how to do it as quickly as possible.

✔ **The old fashioned method is to select Shut Down from the Apple menu (refer to Figure 5-1).**

✔ **You can also shut down your computer by pressing the power button on your Mac or keyboard.** This brings up a prompt of options (see Figure 5-10). At this prompt, press Return to shut down your computer, Esc to cancel, S to sleep, and R to restart, or click the appropriate button with your mouse.

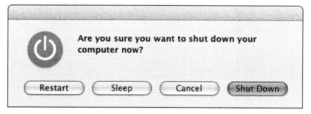

Are you sure you want to shut down your computer now?

Restart   Sleep   Cancel   **Shut Down**

• **Figure 5-10:** Use this prompt to specify what action your Mac should take.

 From the Energy Saver panel (in System Preferences), you can set your computer to automatically shut down at set times. This is great for lab environments or for those who tend to forget to shut down their computers at the end of the day.

✔ **Hold down the Option key while you select Shut Down from the Apple Menu.** Holding down the Option key causes your computer to shut down immediately without any other prompts.

 The Option key trick for suppressing the confirmation prompt also works for restarting the computer, putting it to sleep, or logging out.

Part II

Optimizing Your Interface

The 5th Wave   By Rich Tennant

"OKAY—ANTIDOTE, ANTIDOTE, WHAT WOULD AN ANTIDOTE ICON LOOK LIKE? YOU KNOW, I STILL HAVEN'T GOT THIS DESKTOP THE WAY I WANT IT."

Technique 6

Working with Displays

Save Time By

✔ Finding out how to change the screen resolution

✔ Figuring out color management

✔ Adjusting how the system handles fonts

✔ Conveniently using multiple monitors

The distant ancestor of today's Macs, the Apple IIe, had a small glass monitor that supported two colors: black and green. Today's modern computers come equipped with beautiful monitors, some of them liquid crystal display (LCD) or plasma flat-screen, capable of displaying millions of colors, and with a viewing area of nearly two feet. But there's more to your monitor than just the physical hardware: You also use many pieces of software to control what you see and how you see it.

In this Technique, for starters, you find out a thing or two about what screen resolution is, how to choose the proper setting, and how to easily manage these settings. Then you work with color management in Panther, using ColorSync. We discuss how Mac OS X handles fonts, why you might want to adjust that behavior, and how to do it. Finally, we cover how to configure your Mac to make the best use of multiple monitors. Determining and setting the optimal resolution for your monitor gives you more screen space to work with, a better interface, and more reliable results (for graphic designers). In short, the steps in this chapter make doing the things you need to do easier.

Managing Your Display Resolution

Most beginning computer users, whether they use a Mac or a PC, never concern themselves with the display resolution. So why should you? Because adjusting the display resolution directly affects everything you do with your computer. (Because it all goes through the monitor, right?)

Monitors create everything that you see onscreen by using *pixels,* which are small squares of colored light. Your screen resolution is set in terms of pixels, such as 800 x 600 pixels. Common measurements for standard monitors are

✔ 800 x 600

✔ 1024 x 768

✔ 1280 x 1024

✓ 1600 x 1200

✓ 1920 x 1440

Those of you who use laptops or a cinema display will also find these weird ratios:

✓ 896 x 600

✓ 1152 x 768

 The screen resolutions used on a display correspond to its aspect ratio. Like televisions, most traditional monitors use a 4:3 (width:height) ratio. Most Apple laptops and all Apple cinema displays use a 16:9 ratio (like a movie theater screen or a widescreen television).

These numbers refer to how many pixels comprise the width and height of the monitor; therefore, a higher resolution has more pixels. How does this affect you in practical terms?

If an icon — for example, for a folder — takes up 42 x 42 pixels, a higher resolution means that you can display more folder icons in the same monitor space (because the high resolution offers more pixels). However, each individual folder icon is smaller because 42 pixels takes up less monitor space. Compare the images on the left and right side of Figure 6-1. A higher resolution allows you to display more stuff, but everything is smaller.

1024 x 768   1280 x 1024

• **Figure 6-1: A folder icon at two different resolutions.**

 A higher screen resolution might increase your productivity (you'll spend less time toggling around), but also your need to see an ophthalmologist (you'll be looking at tiny, tiny things onscreen).

You set screen resolutions from the Displays dialog:

1. **Choose Apple Menu⇨System Preferences⇨Displays.**

2. **Making sure that the Display tab is selected (see Figure 6-2), select a higher resolution than the current (presumably default) one.**

The screen sizes available for use depend upon the display itself and the video card in the computer (in particular, the amount of VRAM — Video RAM — that it has).

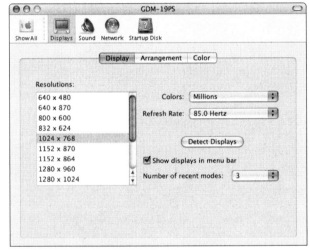

• **Figure 6-2: Control your screen resolution from the Displays dialog.**

3. **Select the Show Displays in Menu Bar check box.**

Marking this check box creates a monitor control in the menu bar (shown in Figure 6-3), saving you trips to the Display panel.

 You should click the Detect Displays button whenever you add or remove another monitor, including a projector. Doing so allows your Mac to recognize what monitors are currently in use. Alternatively, you can select Detect Displays from the pop-up menu that appears when you click the menu bar Display icon.

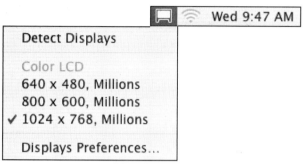

4. **Set the Number of Recent Modes drop-down box to 3, if you have that option.**

The Recent Modes drop-down menu dictates how many resolutions appear in the menu bar's Display menu. You probably have no reason to show more resolutions than three unless you've got some hog-wild resolution switching going on.

5. **Close the Displays panel.**

6. **Experiment with the new monitor setting.**

If it's too hard on the eyes, use the menu bar Display tool (refer to Figure 6-3) or the Display menu (see Figure 6-2) and switch to another resolution.

7. **Repeat Step 6 until you find the best resolution.**

 As a compromise for your vision, you can use a high resolution but also increase the default font sizes of the system (see "Handling Fonts" later in this chapter) and your applications.

 Many of the Display menu's features and more are duplicated in the shareware application SwitchResX (available from www.madrau.com for $15). It brings added support to some monitors and allows you to create bookmarks for display settings that can automatically be used when certain applications are started.

Virtual Desktops

Another method of getting more screen space for your buck is to use an application like CodeTek's VirtualDesktop (www.codetek.com, $30). This program creates *virtual desktops*. A virtual desktop is exactly like the Finder's Desktop except that you can have many of them instead of just the one.

After you create multiple desktops, each can have its own personality. By that, we mean that each individual Desktop can have its own background, Dock, set of preferences, open windows, and even open applications. For example: If you have multiple projects going on at once, a different Dock can be used for each environment. Or, you can have one Desktop in which you're playing games and using iTunes and another where you're actually working.

This idea, strange as it might seem to many, is familiar territory for users of the Linux operating system. Linux (and other variants of Unix) primarily uses the Gnome or KDE application as its version of the Finder. Each of these applications supports multiple desktops.

You might like the idea of virtual desktops — and you might not — but if you're whittling away time one afternoon, it's certainly worth your consideration. The free, demo version of CodeTek's VirtualDesktop allows you to use two different virtual desktops, which should be sufficient to get a taste for the idea.

Adjusting the Colors

Your monitor does not necessarily display colors in a manner that's consistent with other users' monitors: It's a foreign concept to many computer users and a hard lesson for the novice graphic designer to learn. In fact, historically, the colors of a Mac have been slightly brighter than those of a Windows PC. This is because coloring is a software issue. To help adjust for these variations, you can create different profiles with Apple's ColorSync application. For example, you can calibrate different color profiles for different purposes (graphic design, general use) and then switch among them from the Display panel. To create a custom ColorSync profile:

1. **Choose Apple Menu⇨System Preferences⇨ Displays to bring up the Display panel (refer to Figure 6-2).**

2. **Make sure that the Colors drop-down menu is set to Millions and that the Refresh Rate drop-down menu is set as high as possible.**

   The number of colors is just that: how many different colors the monitor will display. Although we can't name 256 colors (let alone a million), we can definitely tell the difference between the two settings on the monitor.

   The *refresh rate* determines how often everything on the screen is redrawn. (When you see computer monitors on television and in movies with lines scrolling down the page, a refresh is taking place.) The higher the number that you select in the Display panel, the faster the refresh. Even though you'll probably never be aware of it, except on the lowest settings, higher refresh rates are easier on the eyes.

3. **Click the Color tab (as shown in Figure 6-4).**

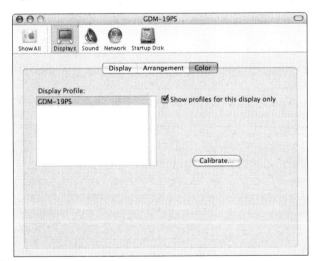

• **Figure 6-4: The Color panel of the Displays dialog.**

4. **Click the Calibrate button to begin the automated calibration process.**

   The Display Calibrator Assistant appears (see Figure 6-5).

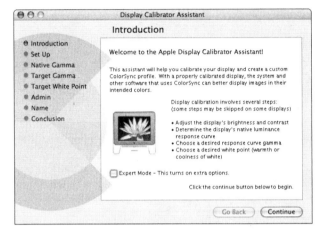

• **Figure 6-5: Use the Display Calibrator Assistant to create your monitor's color profile.**

5. **Follow the onscreen instructions to create your profile.**

   The assistant is easy to use and has clear instructions to help you through the process. The Display Calibrator Assistant even offers an expert mode, although if your needs are advanced enough to require that, you probably don't need our help.

   If you have a laptop, you can also adjust the brightness of your monitor from the Display panel, although doing so will throw off your colors.

6. **To change from one profile to another, select from the available options in the Color section of the Display panel (Figure 6-6).**

   Your Mac probably comes with a couple of profiles and every profile you add also is listed here. Select the new profile to make the switch.

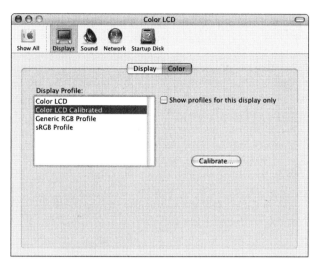

• **Figure 6-6: All of the available profiles appear under the Color panel of the Displays System Preferences panel.**

 Graphic designers can create a Mac profile for everyday use and a Windows profile for seeing how their work will look on that other operating system. After you create the two profiles, switching between the two is a snap!

Handling Fonts

Along with the color scheme and screen resolution, another parameter that you can adjust that affects your overall Panther experience is how the system treats fonts. On your Mac, you can adjust how the operating system handles anti-aliasing. As any graphic designer will tell you, *anti-aliasing* minimizes the jagged edges of characters to produce a smoother appearance. Like the refresh rate issue, this is something that you might not consciously appreciate, but it could have a subtle effect. You can adjust anti-aliasing by using the Appearance dialog:

1. **Open System Preferences, and under the Personal heading, click Appearance.**

2. **At the bottom of the Appearance dialog that appears (see Figure 6-7), select the appropriate font smoothing style.**

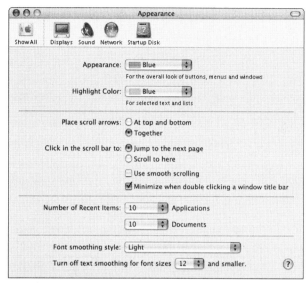

• **Figure 6-7: The Appearance dialog adjusts many cosmetic and user interface settings.**

▶ If you're using a traditional monitor, choose Standard.

▶ If you're using a flat-screen display (such as a plasma cinema display or a laptop), select Medium.

▶ If for some reason you want the least amount of font adjustment possible (like us, when writing this book), use Light.

▶ If none of these options apply to you and you're overwhelmed by the roughness of the fonts, opt for Strong.

3. **Just below the Font Smoothing Style menu, determine to what point sizes font smoothing should be applied.**

From this menu, you can choose 4, 6, 8, 9, 10, or 12. Any font of the size that you choose or smaller will be anti-aliased. Those larger won't be.

4. **Close the Appearance dialog.**

 The higher the font number set for smoothing in the Appearance dialog, the greater the toll that it'll take on your computer's performance.

Shareware Options

Unsanity Software (www.unsanity.com) is the maker of Silk, a *haxie* (a little computer hack) for manipulating fonts. The $10 application enables the text-rendering capabilities that Panther has thanks to its Quartz foundation. The result will be anti-aliased (smoother) fonts in all Carbon-ized applications such as the Netscape and Mozilla browser. Silk also allows you to more finely adjust the system fonts. If you really like a cleaner look, it's worth considering.

TinkerTool, a must-have freeware application provided by Marcel Bresink (www.bresink.de/en), adds many different customization options to Panther. It's been so popular in its many incarnations that its features frequently end up in later versions of OS X. One adjustment that TinkerTool can make is what fonts to use as the default system fonts, as shown in the following figure.

By adjusting these fonts, you can have a more personalized interface, correct for a screen resolution's settings, and more accurately control when font smoothing takes place.

Using Multiple Displays

Many Mac users already benefit from the Mac's ease of using multiple monitors. Graphic designers and video editors frequently use multiple monitors in order to improve workspace efficiency. High-end applications such as Apple's Final Cut Pro, Adobe Photoshop, and even Macromedia Dreamweaver have so many windows open at once that you almost need to have one monitor for open windows and another for the work in progress itself. Laptop users can dock their machine to another monitor, using both it and the laptop's built-in display simultaneously. (The same principle applies if you hook a Mac up to a projector for a presentation.) In all of these cases, the user needs to be able to manage the various displays, which is pleasantly simple with Panther.

To configure your Macintosh to work with two monitors (or a monitor and a projector), follow these steps:

 In order to use multiple monitors with your Mac, you need an extra video-out port. Laptop users have an extra by default; desktop users need a second video card or a video card with two ports.

1. **Connect both displays to your Mac.**

When connecting any new display, turn the display (monitor, television, or projector) off, make the connection, and then turn the display on. You do not have to turn your Mac off when connecting a display.

2. **Open the Displays dialog in System Preferences.**

3. **Click the Detect Displays button.**

This button brings the new monitor to the Mac's attention.

 You do not need to restart your Mac to connect or disconnect another monitor.

4. **Click the Arrangement tab in the main display window.**

When using the Displays dialog with multiple monitors, you will see two separate windows. The main display window (see Figure 6-8) appears on the display that also has the Dock and the menu bars. The second display (see Figure 6-9) appears on the subordinate monitor.

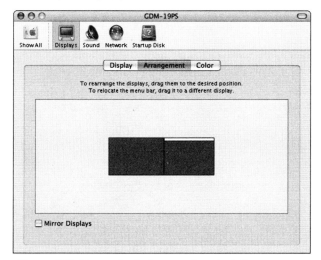

• **Figure 6-8:** The main display panel controls the arrangement of multiple monitors.

5. **In the main display, move the monitor icons around so that they correspond with their literal relation to each other.**

The two connected displays are represented by the two blue squares in the box below the Arrangement tab (refer to Figure 6-8). The main display is indicated by the white bar going across the top of the one icon, which represents the menu bar. When you understand which icon represents which monitor, you can click and drag the icons to arrange them the same way your displays are physically arranged. If you are using a monitor and a projector, then how they are arranged in the Displays panel doesn't matter (as the screens are not next to each other), but you still need to visualize how the two screens meet up.

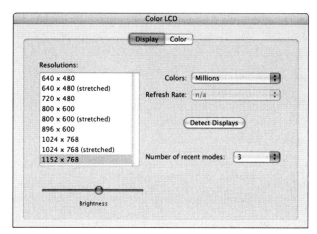

• **Figure 6-9:** A secondary display panel controls only the resolution and color settings for the second monitor.

 If you are using two monitors in a non-mirroring format, you have essentially one large workspace created by virtually combining the two display areas. Consequently, the cursor scrolls off the edge of one monitor and onto the other. For those to work best, the monitors should be arranged in the Displays dialog as they are physically arranged in your work area or you need to comprehend how the cursor gets from a monitor to the projector's screen (by scrolling off of one side or the other).

6. **Move the menu bar icon to dictate which monitor is the primary. (The primary monitor will have the menu bar and the Dock.)**

As we said in Step 5, the white bar on the top of the one display icon represents the menu bar. You can click and drag this from one monitor icon to the other in order to set the primary computer. Your primary computer will show the menu bar at the top, the Dock, and any mounted volumes on your Desktop (if it's set to do so).

If you possess two monitors, you can either use them to display two different things simultaneously, or to have them mirror each other. *Mirroring* means that both monitors display the same thing at the same time — which is useful when giving presentations because you can work on your computer while still controlling the overhead projection. The cursor moves in sync on both displays. To use mirroring:

1. If you haven't already, enable the Display menu bar icon (see "Managing Your Display Resolution," earlier in this chapter).

The Display menu bar tool provides you with quicker access to your monitor settings, including mirroring, resolution, and detecting new displays.

2. Click the Display menu bar icon and select Turn On Mirroring from the menu that appears (see Figure 6-10).

3. Still using the Display menu bar menu (refer to Figure 6-10), set the appropriate screen resolution for both monitors.

In earlier versions of OS X, both monitors had to use the same resolution for mirroring to work; fortunately, this is no longer the case.

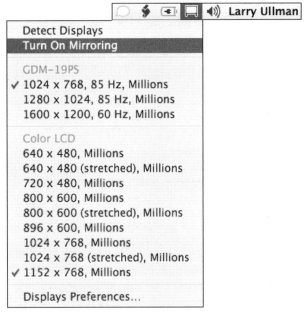

• Figure 6-10: Control mirroring and the resolution of both monitors by clicking the Display menu bar icon.

4. Use the menu bar Display icon to turn mirroring on and off as necessary.

When giving a presentation, you can use your Mac's ability to easily turn monitoring on and off to your advantage. If you want both monitors to present the same information, turn mirroring on. If you'd like to do something without everyone in the room seeing it, temporarily turn off mirroring and then use the nonprojected display.

Quartz Extreme

Panther now supports a feature called Quartz Extreme. Quartz is the underlying technology that handles 2-D graphics, which is most everything that you see on a daily basis. A system that uses Quartz Extreme performs significantly faster than one that isn't.

Unfortunately, running a second monitor might disable the Quartz Extreme feature because it requires AGP 2x (Advanced Graphics Port) with 16MB VRAM. Running Quartz Extreme on two monitors requires a video card that can provide these minimum requirements for each. In order to see whether your system is Quartz Extreme-accelerated (as shown in the following figure), check out the free Quartz Extreme Check tool on Marc's Web site (www.entropy.ch/software/macosx/).

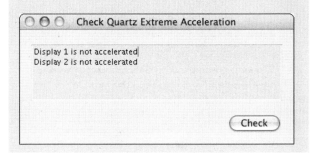

Technique 7

Speedy Keyboard Navigation

Save Time By

✓ Understanding how the different modifier keys are symbolically represented

✓ Finding your way around the Finder window

✓ Moving around the Desktop

✓ Mastering the easiest ways to get other places on your computer

If you read only one Technique in this entire book, make it this one. If you read only two, read the next one, too. Both of these chapters discuss keyboard shortcuts: quickly gettting around and doing stuff with your fingers firmly placed on the keys. **Remember:** Every time that your hands have to leave the keyboard to access the mouse, you lose seconds that could be better spent typing (or playing games).

We've divided all the requisite keyboard navigation techniques into two broad categories: moving around within Finder windows and the more specific "Getting Places" section, which discusses how to get yourself to different spots on the computer and your network. The first and longest section of this chapter covers all the ins and outs of navigating windows, which are the basic unit of the Finder. This is preceded by a brief introduction to the various keyboard shortcut symbols that you find in Panther — a sort of Rosetta stone for these commands. We also cover the Desktop because not everything you do takes place inside a window. The final section is something of a catch-all that shows you how to quickly access different parts of your Mac. These shortcuts can be used inside or outside of Finder windows.

Keyboard Characters

Many of the keyboard navigation techniques can be found onscreen, for example, in the Go menu (see Figure 7-1). To use these shortcuts, you have to first know what the different symbols mean. In case you never knew or simply forgot, Table 7-1 shows how Panther symbolically refers to the modifier keys (⌘, Option, Control, Shift, and Del):

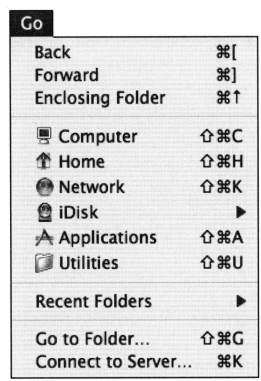

Go	
Back	⌘[
Forward	⌘]
Enclosing Folder	⌘↑
🖥 Computer	⇧⌘C
🏠 Home	⇧⌘H
● Network	⇧⌘K
◉ iDisk	▶
🅰 Applications	⇧⌘A
🗂 Utilities	⇧⌘U
Recent Folders	▶
Go to Folder...	⇧⌘G
Connect to Server...	⌘K

• **Figure 7-1: The Go menu can help you navigate with the mouse and it lists the keyboard equivalents.**

TABLE 7-1: COMMON MAC MODIFIER KEYS

Symbol	Key
⌘	Command
⌃	Control
⇧	Shift
⌥	Option
⌦	Del

To really learn and master the shortcuts in this Technique, practice them on your computer while you're reading the book.

Moving Around in a Finder Window

Navigation, manipulating, and otherwise using the Finder windows is such an integral part of getting the most out of Panther that we devote this and the next three Techniques to covering it. In Panther, the windows are highly customizable so that users can tweak them to their own particular preferences.

If you really, really, really want to be able to use your Mac faster, learn to type well. Knowing how to type is infinitely quicker than hunting and pecking. It'll also improve the speed benefits of these keyboard shortcut chapters.

The Finder has many different shortcuts, which might leave beginning users a bit overwhelmed at first. The shortcuts can vary depending on what view mode you're using. The Finder supports three view modes:

- Icon view
- List view
- Column view

In this Technique, we discuss some keyboard shortcuts that work regardless of the view mode and then cover those that work only in a particular view mode.

While in a window, use ⌘+1 to switch to icon view, ⌘+2 to go to list view, and ⌘+3 for column view.

Navigating in any view mode

These navigational tips apply regardless of the view mode being used:

- Type a letter to go to the first item whose name begins with that letter.

- If multiple items begin with the same letter, type two or more letters to be more selective.

- Press Tab repeatedly to jump alphabetically through a window's contents.

- Hold down Shift while pressing Tab repeatedly to scroll backwards alphabetically through a window's contents.

- Press ⌘+[or] to move backward or forward, respectively, like how clicking the Back and Forward buttons in a Web browser works. This even includes returning to previously used view modes.

 A Finder window can contain any combination of files, applications, folders, network links, and even volumes (hard drives, removable drives, discs). We use the generic *items* to collectively refer to all these things. (In other words, *items* means *things you might find in a Finder window.*)

- Use ⌘+~ (the tilde, found in the upper-left corner of the keyboard) to toggle among the open windows and the Desktop.

- Use the arrow keys (left, right, up, down) to move as you would expect (namely, left, right, up, or down).

 Which view mode you use is best determined by context and personal tastes. Technique 10 discusses the merits of each individually and helps you decide when you should use which.

Navigating in icon view

The icon view mode (see Figure 7-2) shows the window's contents as, well, icons. Although icon view also shows each item's name, you mostly see the icons themselves. The basic shortcuts described in the previous section also work in icon view.

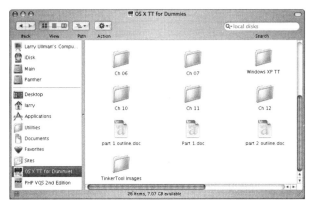

• Figure 7-2: Icon view mode is familiar to every Mac user, although yours may look slightly different.

 Use ⌘+1 to switch to icon view.

In addition, here are some ⌘ options that you can use to navigate in icon view:

- Press ⌘+↑ to go up one level (to the *parent* folder, as Panther describes it).

- Use ⌘+↓ to go into the selected folder (see the Ch 10 folder in Figure 7-3).

• Figure 7-3: In icon view, a folder is marked as selected when the name is highlighted in the selection color.

✔ Press ⌘+O to go into a selected folder.

 ⌘+O is the keyboard shortcut for opening items in general. You can use it to navigate by opening a folder, to start an application by "opening" its icon, or to open a file.

✔ Press ⌘+Shift+O to open the currently selected folder in a new window.

Would You Like a New Window with That?

If you really like windows, you can set the Finder to open all directories in their own new window. To do so:

1. **Press ⌘+, (a comma) to bring up the Finder preferences panel.**

2. **Select the Always Open Folders in a New Window check box.**

3. **Press ⌘+W to close the Finder preferences panel.**

If you enable this option, Panther opens up a new window every time you open a directory. We find that this habit creates a very busy work environment, so we prefer to simply use ⌘+Shift+O to manually request a new window when we need one.

Navigating in list view

The list view (see Figure 7-4) shows the contents of a folder as an itemized list. It always lists the names of the items, but may also display various other properties. (You can customize what properties are shown. For more information, see Technique 10.)

• **Figure 7-4:** The list view mode.

 Use ⌘+2 to switch to list view.

Here are some basic commands for navigating through list view:

✔ Use the up and down arrows to move up and down the list.

✔ Press the right arrow on your keyboard to expand a selected folder (see Figure 7-5). This is the equivalent of clicking on the little right-pointing triangle next to an item's name with your mouse pointer.

✔ Use the left arrow to close an expanded folder, assuming that it's selected. This is the equivalent of clicking on a down-pointing triangle with your mouse.

• **Figure 7-5: Expand a selected directory by using the right keyboard arrow.**

On top of these basic commands, all the ⌘ keyboard shortcuts that work for the icon view also work in the list view. For a refresher on those, refer to the section, "Navigating in icon view."

Navigating in column view

The column view mode is the most complex of the three. It works a little like the list view mode but also allows you to navigate forward and backward by viewing the hierarchy as a series of columns within the Finder window (see Figure 7-6).

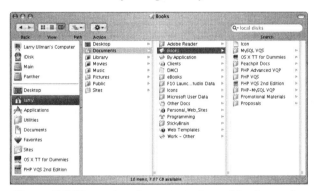

• **Figure 7-6: The curious but extremely useful column view mode.**

 Use ⌘+3 to switch to column view.

Here are some frequently used shortcuts for column view:

✔ Use the up and down arrows to move up and down within a column.

✔ Press the right arrow to move one column to the right (see Figure 7-7).

• **Figure 7-7: The right arrow moves you into a subfolder's listing column.**

✔ Use the left arrow to move one column to the left.

 When in column mode, the currently selected item is highlighted using your selection/highlight color (blue in these images). The gray highlight in preceding columns indicates which folder's contents are listed in the current column. For example, in Figure 7-7, the currently selected item is the folder called OS X TT for Dummies, which is highlighted in the selection color. The items listed in this column are all in the Books folder, which is highlighted in gray in the previous column.

 The quickest way to navigate through columns is to type the initial letter of an item to select it, and then press the right arrow to move to the next column. Repeat until you find the item or directory you are looking for.

Panther offers you the choice of using column view as your default view mode. To do so:

1. **Get yourself over to the Finder by clicking the Desktop or the Finder icon in the Dock.**

2. Press ⌘+, (comma) to bring up the Finder preferences panel.

3. Click General if it's not already selected.

4. Select the Open New Windows in Column View check box (see Figure 7-8).

• **Figure 7-8:** Use the Finder's preferences panel to set column view as the default.

5. Close the preferences panel by pressing ⌘+W.

Navigating the Desktop

The Desktop has some keyboard navigation tricks of its own, most of which will get you to a Finder window. Some of these options will be limited based upon how you've customized your Desktop (for example, what disks, servers, and devices will appear there). The basics are

- ✔ Pressing the arrow keys works as expected, moving you up, down, left, and right.
- ✔ Pressing the Tab key moves you alphabetically from item to item.
- ✔ Pressing Shift+Tab moves you reverse alphabetically from item to item.
- ✔ Typing the first letter or two of any item's name selects that item.

 Within Open/Save dialogs, ⌘+D is the shortcut to your Desktop.

The following four shortcuts all require the everpopular ⌘ key:

- ✔ ⌘+N creates a new Finder window showing the default directory.

 Use the Finder's preferences to determine which directory a new window should open (refer to Figure 7-8).

- ✔ ⌘+Shift+↑ takes you to the *boot disk drive* on the Desktop (the volume on which the running operating system is installed; see Figure 7-9).
- ✔ ⌘+O opens a folder, volume, file, or application.
- ✔ ⌘+↓ opens a folder or volume.

 Exposé, covered in Technique 13, brings with it its own keyboard shortcuts.

• **Figure 7-9: Pressing ⌘+Shift+↑ on the Desktop highlights the boot volume.**

Getting Places

The final type of navigational shortcut that we discuss shows you how to get to important spots on your Mac. These work whether you are in a Finder window or just on the Desktop itself. The first three are the most critical:

 Most of these keyboard shortcuts are duplicated — and listed — in the Finder's Go menu (refer to Figure 7-1).

- ✔ ⌘+Shift+A takes you to the Applications directory.
- ✔ ⌘+Shift+U goes to the Utilities directory.
- ✔ ⌘+Shift+H moves you to your Home folder.

These are also handy typing tips, but many users might never need them:

- ✔ ⌘+Shift+K brings up the window displaying available networks.

- ✔ ⌘+K brings up the Connect to Server prompt.
- ✔ ⌘+Shift+I mounts your iDisk (for .Mac users only).
- ✔ ⌘+? retrieves the Help Viewer application. (This is technically ⌘+Shift+/ because you need to press the Shift key to get the question mark.)

 One of the shareware applications that we discuss most often in this book is LaunchBar, created by Objective Development (www. obdev.at; $39 for businesses, $20 for personal use, free for limited use). Use LaunchBar to quickly and easily get to applications, send e-mails, open Web pages, and more without ever leaving your keyboard. In fact, that's the entire point: LaunchBar lets you do many common tasks just by typing short abbreviations. See Techniques 21, 30, and 33 for specific examples.

Another method of getting around your computer is to use Full Keyboard Access. Full Keyboard Access enables you to use the Tab, arrow, and other keys to select onscreen items. To enable this:

1. **Open System Preferences.**

2. **Click Keyboard & Mouse.**

3. **Click the Keyboard Shortcuts tab of the Keyboard & Mouse panel that appears.**

4. **Select the Turn on Full Keyboard Access check box (see Figure 7-10).**

5. **Under Description, click any of the right-pointing arrows to expand a section.**

6. **Mark the box next to a shortcut or shortcut group to enable or disable it.**

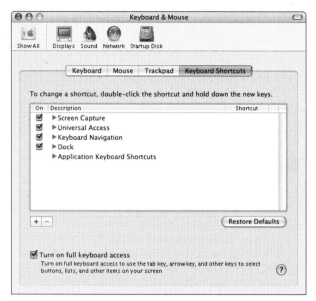

• **Figure 7-10: Use the Keyboard Shortcuts tab to enable Full Keyboard Access.**

The Keyboard Shortcuts panel is a potent tool for those who know how to use it. You can even use it to add your own customized shortcuts. See Technique 8 for some further examples.

The default keyboard shortcuts, listed in the Shortcut column of Figure 7-11, primarily use the Control key in conjunction with your function keys. Under the Keyboard Navigation heading in Figure 7-11, you'll see that:

✔ Control+F2 takes you to the menu bar. (It's just like clicking the menu bar with your mouse.)

✔ Control+F3 takes you to the Dock.

To change any of the default shortcuts, double-click the shortcut and hold down the shortcut keys that you would prefer. Click the Restore

Defaults button to return all shortcuts to their original settings.

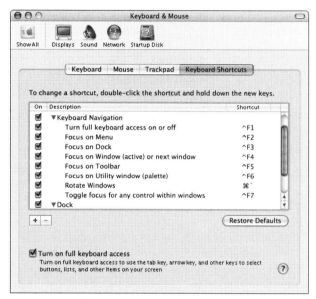

• **Figure 7-11: The Keyboard Navigation shortcuts can really minimize the need to use the mouse.**

After you select the Dock by pressing Control+F3, you can toggle from icon to icon by using the left and right arrow keys or Tab and Shift+Tab. Press Return to select a highlighted icon.

Pressing Control+F4 repeatedly rotates you through every open window in every open application. Control+F5 takes you to the toolbar of the currently active window.

When you're in the toolbar of a window, use Tab and Shift+Tab to move around. You can use the spacebar to select an item, just like clicking it with your mouse.

Using Go To Folder

In the Finder, the ⌘+Shift+G keyboard shortcut brings up the Go To Folder dialog, which you can use to quickly navigate to specific directories.

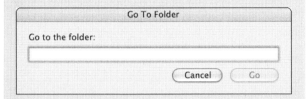

Using the Go To Folder dialog offers the following benefits:

✔ A new Finder window is opened if one isn't open already.

✔ If a Finder window is open, Go To Folder operates within it.

✔ Tab completion (which allows you to type just a few characters and then press Tab to complete the entry) saves you from typing in long names.

✔ The Go To Folder dialog is case-insensitive.

✔ For those familiar with the cd command, the Go To Folder dialog works identically to it.

The only trick to using Go To Folder is that you need to know the path name for that destination. A *path name* is the path of folders that you must follow to find something on the computer. For example:

✔ The base (root) level is /.

✔ Apple's e-mail client is in /Applications.

✔ A file on Larry's Desktop would be under /Users/larry/Desktop (where larry is the short username that he registered with).

✔ Larry's Desktop could also be written in shorthand as ~/Desktop, where ~ (the tilde) represents the current user's Home directory.

✔ A folder on a secondary volume would have a path name of /Volumes/*volumename*/*foldername*.

This might seem like more trouble than it's worth, but if you have a basic understanding of where things are on your computer, Panther will really help you out.

To start:

1. **Bring up the Go menu prompt by pressing ⌘+Shift+G.**

2. **Start typing the path name with either**

   ▸ ~/ (refers to your Home directory)

   ▸ / (refers to the root or base level of the computer)

3. **Begin typing the first letter or first few letters of the directory that's next in the path name.**

   For example, if something is in your Documents folder, type **Do** or **Doc** after the ~/. If it's on your second hard drive, type **/Vo**.

   ```
   Go To Folder
   Go to the folder:
   ~/Do
                    Cancel    Go
   ```

4. **Press the Tab key to have Panther complete the directory name.**

   Or, if you wait just a moment, the directory name is automatically filled in.

   ```
   Go To Folder
   Go to the folder:
   ~/Documents/
                    Cancel    Go
   ```

5. **Repeat Steps 3 and 4 until the full path name of the folder that you want to explore is written out.**

(continued)

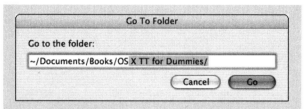

6. **Press Return or click Go to load that directory in a Finder window.**

All in all, Go To Folder is a really smart way to quickly hop to specific destinations on your computer. Further, getting comfortable with this system makes the transition to using the Terminal for command line tasks less daunting. (And most power users eventually get around to taking the Terminal for a spin.)

Technique 8

Essential Keyboard Shortcuts

Save Time By

✔ Mastering the essential keyboard shortcuts that every Mac user should know

✔ Learning some application-related keyboard shortcuts

✔ Finally getting to know those little F keys at the top of the keyboard

✔ Making your own keyboard shortcuts

In the preceding Technique, we discuss and demonstrate most (if not all) of the keyboard navigational techniques that you can use to get around in Finder windows specifically and the operating system as a whole. In this Technique, we follow with a discussion of the other keyboard shortcuts.

We begin with a hodgepodge of keyboard combinations that you ought to know if you don't already. These combinations cover a number of common tasks. Then we go over application-related shortcuts: those key combinations that are used to navigate among open applications and those that work within all applications. Finally, this Technique covers the function keys and how to set your own keyboard shortcuts.

The Most Essential of the Essential Keyboard Shortcuts

This and the preceding Technique present a cornucopia of useful and worthy keyboard shortcuts, but you might have difficultly memorizing them all. These, therefore, are the most important all-purpose shortcuts:

✔ Pressing Return is the same as clicking OK, Yes, Continue, or whatever the default action is for a button in a prompt (see Figure 8-1).

• **Figure 8-1: The Return key is the same as clicking the highlighted button.**

✔ Pressing Esc is the same as clicking Cancel.

✔ ⌘+A selects everything in the currently used directory or document.

✔ ⌘+C copies the selected (or highlighted) text or image to the Clipboard.

✔ ⌘+X deletes the selected (or highlighted) text or image and stores it on the Clipboard.

✔ ⌘+V pastes the current contents of the Clipboard into the current document, window, or other location.

✔ ⌘+Z undoes the previous action, whatever it is.

 Most people know that the ⌘+Z trick works in applications to undo the last action, but it also functions in the Finder. You can use this shortcut to undelete a deleted (but not trashed) file, or to unmove something. Pretty much whatever you just did can be undone with ⌘+Z.

✔ ⌘+O opens anything (folders, files, volumes, or applications).

✔ ⌘+F brings up the Find prompt (see Figure 8-2 for an example of a Find prompt; this one is from Safari).

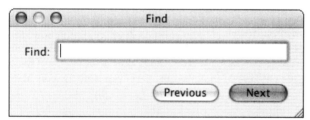

• **Figure 8-2: Safari's Find prompt.**

✔ ⌘+Option+N creates a new folder within the current directory.

✔ ⌘+N creates a new Finder window.

 In the Finder Preferences panel, you can use the New Finder Windows Open drop-down box to set in which directory each new Finder window automatically opens (see Figure 8-3).

Bring up this panel by selecting Preferences from the Finder menu and clicking the General tab.

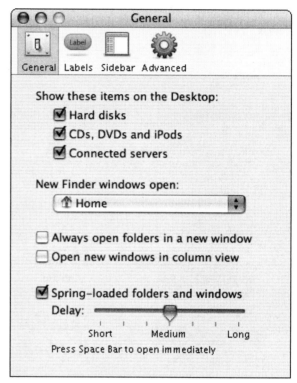

• **Figure 8-3: Use the Finder's preferences to adjust a new window's default behavior.**

✔ ⌘+Delete sends an item to the Trash.

✔ ⌘+Option+Delete takes the Trash to the curb (which is to say, empties it).

Those are the most critical keyboard shortcuts, but here are a few more that are easy to remember and quite useful:

✔ ⌘+W closes the active window.

✔ ⌘+Option+W closes every open window.

✔ ⌘+M minimizes an open window.

✔ ⌘+Option+M minimizes every open window.

✔ ⌘+P prints a document.

✔ ⌘+I brings up the Get Info prompt, where you can find information about (as well as control) some of the properties of a file, a folder, or an application.

✔ ⌘+J brings up a window's (or the Desktop's) view options.

✔ ⌘+Shift+Q lets you log out.

The previous shortcuts work in the Finder and some of them also function within applications (particularly those by Apple). These shortcuts are more particular to the Finder:

✔ ⌘+D duplicates the currently selected item or items.

 If you can't or don't want to remember that ⌘+D duplicates items, you can always select the item, copy it by pressing ⌘+C, and then create the duplicate by pasting the copied item with ⌘+V.

✔ ⌘+L makes an alias to the currently selected item or items. An alias (what Windows calls a *shortcut*) is a reference to an item. These are discussed in Technique 15.

✔ ⌘+R locates an original file that an alias or a pointer represents.

 The ⌘+R shortcut is most useful in two specific instances. In the Finder, if you select an alias, it takes you to the item that the alias points to. In iTunes, if you select a particular track, ⌘+R takes you to the physical file on your computer.

✔ ⌘+T adds the selected item to the window's sidebar (see Technique 10 for more).

✔ ⌘+E ejects the selected disk or disc. (This disc could be an external FireWire hard drive, a Zip or floppy disk, a CD-ROM or DVD, or a mounted disk image.)

Universal Access

Panther users with special needs should seriously consider using *Universal Access,* which is a special set of accessibility tools for improving the standard Panther interface. Universal Access information can be found in the Universal Access System Preferences panel, and most of the relevant shortcuts are repeated under the Keyboard Shortcuts section of the Keyboard & Mouse panel.

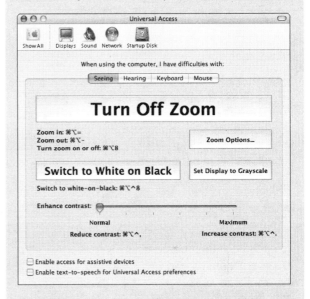

For starters, Universal Access provides keyboard shortcuts to useful visual tools, such as zooming in and out, toggling between color and black and white, and adjusting the contrast. Furthermore, you can set Universal Access to help use the keyboard by conforming to your typing abilities. For example, Panther can be set to consider a sequence of modifier keys the same as pressing all the keys simultaneously (for example, pressing ⌘ followed by Option and then O would be equated with ⌘+Option+O).

Application Shortcuts

Pretty much everything that you do on your Mac takes place within an application (technically, *everything* you do takes place within an application because the Finder is considered an app). Most Panther users have several applications open at any one time. Although Part IV of the book really covers applications in all their glory, here are the highlights that ought to be second nature.

 Technique 22 addresses application switching in greater detail, discussing several different shareware applications that can be used expressly for this purpose. These include **LiteSwitch X** (www.proteron.com/liteswitchx/, **$15**) and **App Switcher** (www.mikeash.com/software/appswitcher/, **free**).

Here's an easy way to switch applications:

1. **Begin by holding down the ⌘ key and then pressing Tab to bring up a palette listing the currently open applications, with the most recently used application automatically selected (see Figure 8-4).**

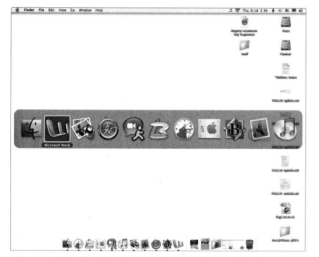

• **Figure 8-4: The list of currently running applications.**

2. **While holding down the ⌘ key, continue pressing Tab to move between the application icons until the desired application is selected.**

Press ⌘+Shift+Tab to go in reverse order.

3. **Release the ⌘ key to bring up the selected application.**

 Safari, Internet Explorer, and a few other applications all have a command similar to ⌘+Tab. You can use ⌘+~ (tilde) to toggle among the open windows.

Working with many applications and windows has two primary considerations: switching among them and clearing out the clutter. Knowing how to hide current and background applications goes a long way towards creating a neater workspace and giving you better peace of mind.

✔ Use ⌘+H to hide the current application.

✔ Use ⌘+Option+H to hide all the background applications.

 Exposé, Panther's new window management tool, creates special mouse and keyboard commands to access all the open windows for the current application or the whole operating system. Get thee over to Technique 13 to find out all about it.

Getting Fancy with ⌘+Tab

Strange is it might seem, you can also use your mouse (or other input device) in conjunction with ⌘+Tab. After you bring up the palette, you can hover your cursor over an application's icon to select it and then release the ⌘ key to travel there. You don't even need to click the mouse for this to work.

This means that you can perform drag-and-drop actions with ⌘+Tab and your mouse or other input device:

1. **In an open application, select the text, image, or whatever you want to copy elsewhere.**

2. **Click and hold the selection.**

3. **While continuing to hold your mouse click, drag the selection slightly off in any direction.**

4. **Press ⌘+Tab to bring up the open application's pallete.**

5. **Use either your cursor or Tab to select the destination application (while continuing to hold both the mouse button and the ⌘ key).**

6. **Release the ⌘ key to bring up the destination application.**

7. **Position your cursor in the appropriate location in the new application.**

8. **Release the mouse key to complete the move.**

This process might seem foreign at first, but it's remarkably effective and a good alternative to copying and pasting.

Function Keys

The purpose of the function keys changes dramatically based on whether you're using a desktop or a laptop Mac. Desktop Mac users have no default function key purposes, although many of them are taken by existing applications and Finder shortcuts.

 Laptop users might need to hold down the fn button to use the function keys for other than their default purposes.

Laptop users, on the other hand, ought to familiarize themselves with using these default functions:

- ✔ F1 dims the display.

- ✔ F2 brightens the display.

- ✔ F3 mutes the sound.

- ✔ F4 lowers the sound volume.

- ✔ F5 increases the sound volume.

- ✔ F6 engages the number lock feature, turning the keypad into a number pad.

 piDog Software (www.pidog.com), the maker of some pretty snazzy Mac OS X software, puts out an application called SimpleKeys ($15). SimpleKeys allows you to program the function keys to automatically insert customizable text into documents. This might conflict with some of the many other uses of the function keys, but if you do find yourself repeating paragraphs of text over and over again (in e-mail perhaps), you might want to consider it.

Programming Your Own Keyboard Shortcuts

The Macintosh has supported programming the function keys in many ways over the years, but now Panther includes a beautiful new tool that does even more. From the Keyboard Shortcuts panel, you can create your own keyboard shortcuts that call menu commands. These shortcuts can work in a particular application or all of them. Here's a primer on how to use it:

1. **Open the System Preferences panel.**

2. **Click Keyboard & Mouse (under Hardware).**

3. **In the Keyboard & Mouse panel, click the Keyboard Shortcuts tab to bring up that panel (see Figure 8-5).**

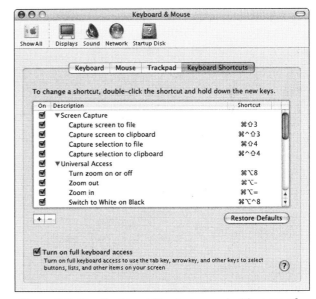

• **Figure 8-5: The Keyboard Shortcuts panel with some of Panther's default shortcuts.**

 Even if you never want to create your own keyboard shortcuts, the Keyboard Shortcuts panel is still great for reminding you of many of the existing shortcuts that you can use.

4. Click the plus sign in the lower-left corner to add a new shortcut.

5. In the drop-down sheet that appears (see Figure 8-6):

1. Select what application you want the shortcut to apply to in the Application drop-down box.

2. In the Menu Title text box, enter the name of the menu command that you want to assign the shortcut to.

3. Immediately enter the keyboard shortcut by pressing the key combination.

• **Figure 8-6:** The panel for adding shortcuts.

6. Click Add, which becomes a clickable button after you've met all the criteria in Step 5.

7. After you log out and log back in or restart your computer, the new shortcut is available (see Figure 8-7).

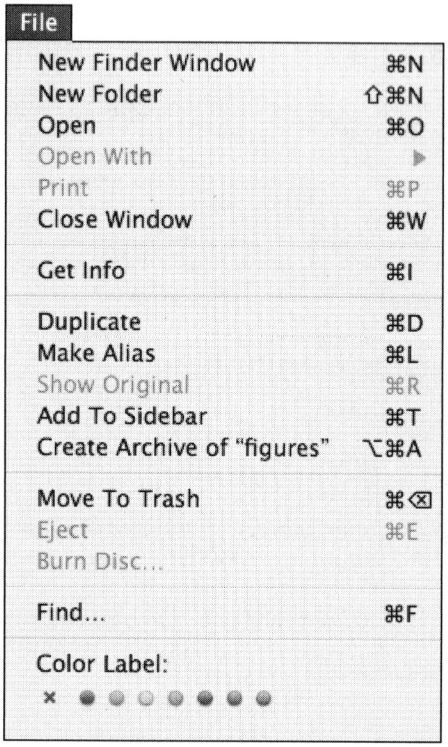

File	
New Finder Window	⌘N
New Folder	⇧⌘N
Open	⌘O
Open With	▶
Print	⌘P
Close Window	⌘W
Get Info	⌘I
Duplicate	⌘D
Make Alias	⌘L
Show Original	⌘R
Add To Sidebar	⌘T
Create Archive of "figures"	⌥⌘A
Move To Trash	⌘⌫
Eject	⌘E
Burn Disc...	
Find...	⌘F
Color Label:	

× ● ○ ○ ○ ● ● ○

• **Figure 8-7:** The new keyboard shortcut has been added to the Finder's File menu.z

Technique 9

A Faster Finder

Save Time By

✔ Setting the Finder preferences to fit the way you use your Mac

✔ Finding out about shortcuts for your mouse or other input device

✔ Getting the most out of the Finder's various menus

✔ Using some of the available Panther shareware

The Mac OS X Finder is a frequently used, yet often underused, application. It is the main interface for you to access files, applications, CD-ROMs, and more. Being familiar with it and knowing how to customize its behavior to suit your tastes is critical to saving time on your Mac.

This Technique begins with the various Finder preferences that can be set within Panther. Included after this section is a treatment of the Finder's many menus. Then a number of the input-device-related shortcuts are covered (the "clicking" equivalent of many of the keyboard shortcuts listed in the preceding two Techniques). Finally, we introduce and discuss some of the shareware and freeware applications that you might want to use to improve your Finder.

Finder Preferences

The Finder has two main areas that can be customized (aside from the Finder windows themselves, which are an entirely other topic; see Technique 10): one specifically for the Desktop; and another, more general, set of preferences. To bring up the Finder preferences panel, either

    ✔ Press ⌘ + , (comma).

or

    ✔ Click Finder on the menu bar and then select Preferences.

 To customize the Desktop, press ⌘+J or go to Show View Options in the View menu. This topic is covered in Technique 14.

The preferences panel (see Figure 9-1) is divided into four sections: General, Labels, Sidebar, and Advanced.

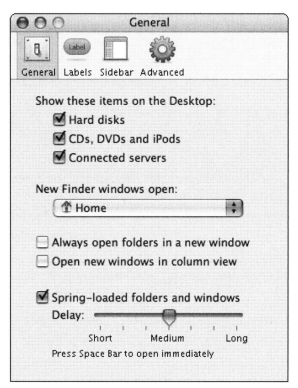

• **Figure 9-1: The Finder's preferences panel.**

General

The General section has a few important controls:

✔ **Show These Items on the Desktop:** We recommend marking all these check boxes, which makes accessing these items and knowing what's connected or mounted to your computer easier.

✔ **New Finder Windows Open:** Use this drop-down list to determine what folder is the default folder when opening new windows. Setting this value saves you a navigational step (for example, hopping over to your Home directory) with each new window.

 If you keep your Home directory organized as Apple recommends and you use it accordingly, set the Finder to open all new windows in the Home directory, where every document that you need is stored.

✔ **Always Open Folders in a New Window:** Selecting this check box is useful only if you really, really like having lots of open windows around.

✔ **Open New Windows in Column View:** Column view is the only view mode that can be set as the default view for new windows.

✔ **Spring-Loaded Folders and Windows:** Spring-loaded folders and windows pop open when you drag something onto them. If you start dragging a file and hold it over a folder, that folder springs open so that you can place the file within a subfolder. You can even continue to spring open subfolders, allowing you to place a file several directories into your hard drive without navigating there first.

Labels

After dropping off the radar in earlier versions of Mac OS X, Labels — OS 9's color-coded decorating tool — has made a triumphant comeback in Panther. In fact, it's better than ever. Labels allow you to mark items with a special highlight color, each color having its own particular meaning. To assign what the different colors represent, do the following:

1. **Open Finder's preferences panel by pressing ⌘ + , (comma).**

2. **Click the Labels button (see Figure 9-2).**

3. **Highlight a color name and change the text to whatever label makes the most sense to you.**

4. **Tab to the next label and change that text.**

   Repeat until a label name is set for each color.

5. **Close the Finder's preferences panel.**

To use the Labels, follow these steps

1. **Select the item or items in a Finder window.**

2. **Control+click the item to bring up the contextual menu (see Figure 9-3).**

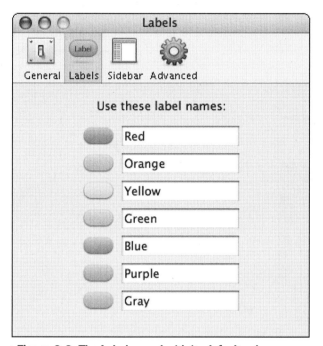

• **Figure 9-2: The Labels panel with its default values.**

_3._ **Under the Color Label heading on the contextual menu, click the appropriate color.**

When you click each color, the contextual menu shows the label associated with each color to make the selection easier and more accurate (in Figure 9-4, the label reads *"Urgent"*).

In icon view mode, the item's name is highlighted in the label color (see Figure 9-5). In list and column view mode, the entire line is highlighted. After you've begun using labels, you can add the Label column to the list view windows (see the section "Show View Options" later in this chapter for instructions) and then sort by using this value (see Figure 9-6).

Sidebar

The Sidebar preferences panel (see Figure 9-7) affects which items appear in a window's sidebar.

The top half of the Sidebar preferences panel dictates what appears in the top half of the window sidebar, whereas the bottom half controls whether three specific folders — the Desktop, your Home directory, or the Applications folder — appear in the bottom half of the window sidebar.

• **Figure 9-3: Add a label to an item from its contextual menu.**

 Enable or disable those items in the Sidebar preferences panel that you will not use or access on a regular basis.

 The Sidebar panel is the only place where you can customize the top half of the window's sidebar. The bottom half can also be customized manually. See Technique 10 for more.

• **Figure 9-4:** When selecting a label color, the contextual menu shows the corresponding text label.

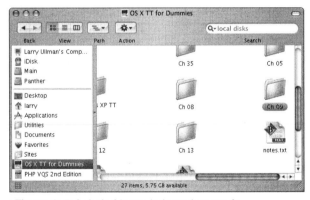

• **Figure 9-5:** Labeled items in icon view mode.

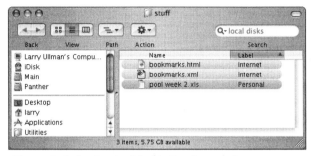

• **Figure 9-6:** Sorting by label in list view mode.

• **Figure 9-7:** The Sidebar preferences panel.

Advanced

The Advanced panel of the Finder preferences panel has just three options in the current version of Panther (see Figure 9-8). If you're most comfortable dealing with files in this manner, you can set the Finder to always show the file extensions. (***Note:*** A file's icon will also imply its extension, most of the time.) You can also set whether you see those pesky warnings when taking out the Trash.

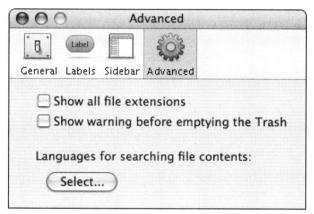

• **Figure 9-8: The Advanced section of the Finder's preferences panel.**

 If you trust your trashing capabilities, disable the Show Warning Before Emptying the Trash option in the Advanced panel.

The third option under the Advanced panel, which allows you to select the language for searching file contents, is often overlooked. In Technique 16, we show you the how's and why's of using this setting to improve the efficiency of your Finder searches.

Show View Options

You can access the Finder's second area of customization by

🗸 **Clicking the View menu and then selecting Show View Options.**

or

🗸 **Pressing ⌘+J.**

The View Options settings apply to the currently active window, if one is open and active. If no

window is open and active, the View Options panel applies to the Desktop.

When you apply the View Options to the Desktop (see Figure 9-9), you control only how items *appear* on the Desktop. (View Options can affect Finder windows more dramatically.) The first three settings — Icon Size, Text Size, and Label Position — do what you'd expect: control how big an item's icon is in pixels, adjust the point size for the item's name, and position the item's name either underneath or to the right of the item's icon.

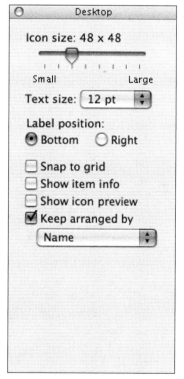

• **Figure 9-9: The View Options panel controls both windows and the Desktop.**

 If your monitor is set at a high resolution (see Technique 6), you can increase the size of your icons and label text to accommodate this.

The final four check boxes in the View Options dialog affect how items are arranged on the Desktop and what information is revealed. The most important of these is Keep Arranged By, which allows you to maintain order in an otherwise chaotic universe (or Desktop). Mark this check box and select to arrange your Desktop by Name, Date Modified, Date Created, Size, Kind, or Label.

 If you select the Show Item Info check box, image sizes are displayed along with their names, and volumes sizes (including remaining space) are listed below their names. The Show Icon Preview check box turns an image's icon into a miniature representation of the actual image (in icon view only).

Menus

The Finder, like any other application, has a series of menus across the top of the display where you can access commonly used features. The Finder's menus are located in two areas:

- ✔ **In the upper-left corner are the standard menus (see Figure 9-10).**

- ✔ **In the upper-right corner are extra and third-party menus (see Figure 9-11).**

• **Figure 9-10: The standard Finder menus.**

• **Figure 9-11: The extended Finder menus, including third-party additions.**

The standard menus include

- ✔ **Apple:** The Apple menu is the catch-all for Panther. Including system tools such as Software Update and System Preferences, it allows you to change the Dock settings and your network location, and it also lists the most recently used items. The bottom half of the Apple menu is for force-quitting applications, shutting down, restarting, putting your Mac to sleep, and logging out. (Read more on some of these in Technique 5.)

- ✔ **Finder:** The Finder menu gives you access to its preferences panel (see earlier in this Technique), controls the showing and hiding of applications, and links to Services (see Technique 27).

- ✔ **File:** The File menu is for basic file-management stuff (such as opening and closing) and includes most of the often-used commands and keyboard shortcuts.

- ✔ **Edit:** The Edit menu, like any application's Edit menu, gives you access to editing shortcuts, the keyboard equivalents of which ought to be second nature to any power user. Two interesting features here show you the contents of the Clipboard (useful if you forget what you pasted there) and bring up the Character Palette to access special characters.

- ✔ **View:** The View menu is mostly useful with respect to windows (see Technique 10). Most of the options are grayed out (unusable) unless you're in a Finder window. The remaining choices will affect the Desktop.

 The View menu lets you customize a selected Finder window or the Desktop. Conversely, the Window menu lets you control windows: You can switch among open windows, minimize a window, and bring all windows to focus.

- ✔ **Go:** The Go menu is a nice little navigational tool, giving you links and the keyboard equivalents for quickly accessing common places. We prefer the keyboard shortcuts ourselves, but the menu option is nice to have, and you'll find the keyboard shortcuts listed there as a reminder.

- ✔ **Window:** The Window menu controls the open Finder windows (much like an application's Window folder gives you access to the open documents in that application). Although it does give you an easy way to handle the mess of multiple windows, you might find Exposé to be an easier solution.

- ✔ **Help:** Need help? Use this menu to bring up the Help View application.

The right side menu area is a more flexible place; what's there depends upon what you've enabled. For example:

- ✔ The Fast User Switching menu appears here if Fast User Switching is enabled under Accounts.

- ✔ The system clock reveals itself if set in the Date & Time control panel.

- ✔ The display menu makes an appearance if set in the Displays panel.

- ✔ The volume control appears here if set in the Sound panel.

- ✔ The Character Palette button shows up after you've selected Special Characters in the Finder's Edit menu.

- ✔ Laptop users find their battery status here if chosen in the Energy Saver panel.

Furthermore, different extensions and applications add menus here. Just a few highlights include

- ✔ **Virtual PC** (www.microsoft.com/mac/products/ virtualpc/virtualpc.aspx?pid=virtualpc), for running other operating systems on your Mac

- ✔ **iMote** (www.mkd.cc/products.html), for controlling iTunes (see Technique 42)

- ✔ **wClock** (www.wolfware.com/wclock/), which is a clock application that also has a built-in calendar

- ✔ **LaunchBar** (www.obdev.at/products/ launchbar/), a utility for accessing files, applications, bookmarks, and e-mail addresses

 To rearrange or remove an item from the right-side of the menu bar, hold down the ⌘ key while clicking on the icon. Then you can either drag the item off to remove it (it will disappear in a cloud of smoke) or drag it side to side to move it (the other icons will move out of its way).

AppleScript's Script Menu

If you're not already familiar with it, *AppleScript* is a powerful automating tool that has been part of the Mac operating system for years. It's so easy to work with that even non-programmers can grasp its concepts, and yet potent enough that seasoned programmers will be pleased. Not only does Panther come with literally dozens of pre-built AppleScripts, but it even comes with a tool for easily accessing them: *Script Menu*.

To enable Script Menu and add a menu icon for it

1. **In the Finder, navigate to Applications⇨AppleScript.**

2. **Double-click the Install Script Menu icon.**

3. **Click the new AppleScript logo located on the right side of the Finder menu.**

   The logo looks like a stylized S, or a scroll.

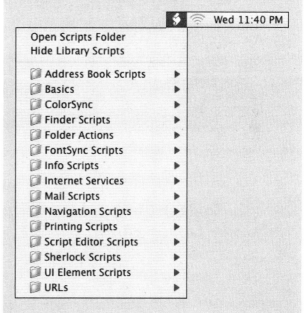

4. **Browse through the folders of scripts and select any script to run.**

You can also download and install other scripts created by Apple:

1. **Go to** www.apple.com/applescript/script_ menu/.

(continued)

2. **Download any of the extra scripts listed at the bottom of the page.**

3. **Open the downloaded archive(s).**

4. **Select Open Scripts Folder from the AppleScript Script Menu.**

5. **Drop the downloaded scripts into the Scripts folder window that was opened in Step 4.**

The new scripts will now be available at the bottom of the Script Menu.

Using Your Input Device

Your input device, be it a trackpad, mouse, trackball, or graphic tablet, has some pretty impressive power built into it. Using input devices with the Finder automatically brings with it a slew of useful timesaving techniques, much like the keyboard shortcuts highlighted in the previous two chapters.

Here are some basic mouse moves that any Mac maven must memorize:

- ✔ Click any item to select it.

- ✔ Click and drag to select multiple items.

- ✔ Double-click any file to open it in its default application.

- ✔ Double-click any folder to open it.

- ✔ Double-click any application's icon to launch it.

- ✔ Click and hold a Dock icon to bring up a menu.

- ✔ Double-click a window to minimize it.

- ✔ Drag an item over a folder or volume to make it pop open (assuming that you have the spring-loaded feature enabled under General preferences).

You can accomplish even more with your mouse by clicking in combination with various modifier keys, such as Control or Option:

- ✔ Control+click any item to launch its contextual menu.

- ✔ Control+click a Dock icon to bring up its menu.

- ✔ ⌘+Option+click a Dock icon to switch to that application and hide every other window.

- ✔ ⌘+Option+click the Finder in the Dock to go to the Finder and hide all the open applications. (This will also open a new window if no windows are open already.)

- ✔ Option+click on the Desktop or the Finder icon in the Dock to go to the Finder and hide the current application.

- ✔ Option+click the red button of any open window to close every open window.

- ✔ Option+double-click to minimize all open windows.

- ✔ Option+click the yellow button of any open window to minimize every open window.

- ✔ Option+drag a file to duplicate it.

- ✔ ⌘+Option+drag a file to make an alias.

- ✔ ⌘+click to select non-contiguous items.

- ✔ ⌘+click to deselect one of multiple selected items.

- ✔ Press the spacebar while dragging an item onto a folder or volume to make it pop open immediately (assuming that you have the spring-loaded feature enabled under General preferences).

 If you repeatedly Option+click an application's Dock icon, the system toggles back and forth between that application and the previously used one.

Freeware and Shareware

We've said it before: One of the best things about Mac OS X is the amount of freeware and shareware available for the platform. This is partly thanks to the UNIX infrastructure, which allows open source software to run on a Mac. It's also thanks to the many easy-to-use tools for developing OS X software, such as REALbasic, AppleScript, and Xcode. We'll quickly mention a few Finder-related tools that you might want to consider.

TinkerTool

TinkerTool (www.bresink.de/osx/TinkerTool.html, free) is not only an innovator in Mac customization, it's also free. TinkerTool is so popular than many of its features eventually get added to the operating system itself.

Some of the highlights of what TinkerTool can do include

✔ Reveal hidden files and folders in the Finder.

✔ Add to the customization options for the Dock.

✔ Further customize the scroll bars in windows.

✔ Determine the different system fonts and adjust the smoothing of them.

✔ Reset all the "tinkered" settings back to the Panther defaults.

For more information on working with TinkerTool, see Technique 53.

wClock

wClock (www.wolfware.com/wclock/, free) is a system clock replacement program with just a couple of extra features. The clock's formatting is customizable, and if you click it in the menu bar, a browseable calendar appears (see Figure 9-12).

 A more potent alternative to wClock is iClock (www.scriptsoftware.com/iclock/index.html, $20). Although it's not free, it comes with many more features than either the system clock or wClock.

• **Figure 9-12: wClock's calendar pops up when you click wClock in the menu bar.**

Changing Themes

Another way to customize your Finder is to adjust what theme it uses. By default, the Finder uses the Aqua theme, which controls the appearance of windows, buttons, alerts, fonts, and more. (Basically everything that gives the operating system a consistent look from application to application is set in the theme.)

Changing your theme isn't for the faint of heart (Apple generally discourages the practice) and, arguably, has a minor payoff. But those of you who like to tinker should head over to www.ResExcellence.com/themes to download different themes and find links to useful shareware. You'll probably want one of the following:

✔ ShapeShifter (www.unsanity.com, $20), which lets you change themes in the least intrusive way possible.

(continued)

✔ Duality 4.0 GT from www.conundrumsoft.com, which allows you to change the themes (they call them schemes). Duality is available in both free and professional (cost) versions.

✔ ThemeChanger (http://sourceforge.net/ projects/themechanger/), which will also change themes.

Menu tools

A handful of shareware applications build on the usefulness of the Finder menus. The most popular titles are

✔ **piPop (**www.pidog.com**, $20 suggested), from piDog Software:** This application creates menus underneath your cursor whenever you want (on the Desktop or in windows), granting access to applications, mounted volumes, and directories.

✔ **FruitMenu (**www.unsanity.com/haxies/ fruitmenu/**, $10), from Unsanity:** FruitMenu allows you to customize your Apple and contextual menus.

✔ **Classic Menu (**www.sigsoftware.com/ classicmenu/index.html**, $10), from Sig Software:** Classic Menu re-creates the old (OS 9 and earlier) Apple menu's ability to list applications and hierarchical folders.

Technique 10

Customizing Windows for Your Convenience

Save Time By

- ✔ Determining which view mode to use
- ✔ Customizing the windows
- ✔ Using the Actions button
- ✔ Navigating among open windows

The Finder window is the basic currency of the operating system. You use the Finder to access applications and files, move items around, organize your data, and much, much more. Previous versions of OS X introduced some new window features, and Panther has raised the bar even more dramatically.

In this Technique, we start by discussing the three different view modes that you can use in your Finder windows: icon, list, and column, each of which has its own benefits. Then we show you how to customize the window's appearance and features. Part of a window's feature set is the new Actions feature, which can expedite many commons tasks. We briefly discuss these before concluding with how to navigate among multiple open windows.

Understanding the Different View Modes

The Finder's window can display the items in a folder in three different view modes: icon, list, and column. Each has its own benefits (and keyboard shortcuts, see Technique 8), so you should take some time to figure out which view mode works best under what circumstances. Mostly, this is a matter of taste, but certain principles can help you make the best decision.

 To switch between the view modes, use ⌘+1 for icon, ⌘+2 for list, and ⌘+3 for column. If you have trouble remembering these shortcuts, they correlate to the order of the icons in the window's toolbar, from left to right (as shown in Figure 10-1).

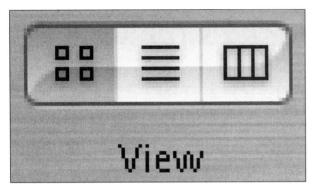

• **Figure 10-1:** Click the icons to change view modes or use the keyboard shortcuts.

Icon view

Icon view is familiar territory for almost everyone and is the default view mode for mounted CD-ROMs and disk images. Icon view (see Figure 10-2) is best when you're dealing with a directory containing only a few items or if you just prefer the look and feel of icons. Many people find selecting a group of items (using the mouse to click and drag) an easy and natural task in icon view.

• **Figure 10-2:** A directory displayed in icon view mode.

 This is a cool but less usable tip: In icon and list view modes, Option+⌘+clicking any blank window space turns the cursor into a hand, allowing you to move the window contents around as if it were a piece of paper on your desk. Release the keys and the mouse button when you've finished scrolling about.

Icon view is limiting if you're dealing with a directory containing lots of items or if you'll be running through multiple subfolders.

 If you're viewing a directory of images, turn on Show Icon Preview in the View Options panel and then use icon view. This displays thumbnails of the window's contents. (After you've selected a window, press ⌘+J or select Show View Options from the View menu to bring up the View Options panel.)

 If Snap to Grid is enabled (meaning that icons are arranged along imaginary grid lines instead of free-form), icon view shows a small grid icon in the lower-left corner of the window (refer to Figure 10-2).

Windows Backgrounds in Icon View

Icon view mode is the only mode that allows you to customize the background of the window. Although this feature might seem like nothing more than eye candy (and it certainly can be), it has its advantages as well. The best way to use the background is to set a different background color or image for different folders. That way, when you minimize them, you can more easily know which window is which by looking at the window's icon in the Dock.

This allows you to distinguish between them more easily. To set a background:

1. **Open the window in question.**

2. **Bring up the View Options panel by pressing ⌘+J or by selecting Show View Options from the View menu in the Finder.**

3. **Within the View Options panel, select the This Window Only radio button (at the top) so that the changes only affect this window.**

4. **At the bottom of the window, select either the Color or the Picture radio button.**

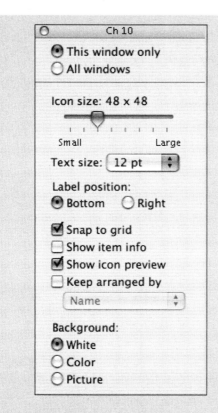

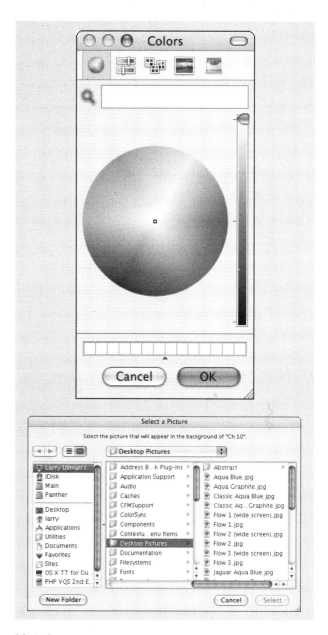

5. **If you select Color in Step 4:**

   1. Click the color block that appears next to the word *Color* to bring up the Colors palette.

   2. Click the color that you want to use.

   3. Click OK.

6. **If you select Picture in Step 4:**

   1. Click the Select button that appears next to the word *Picture* to bring up the Select a Picture dialog.

   2. Use the Select a Picture dialog to navigate to the desired picture.

   3. Click Select to close the dialog.

7. **Press ⌘+J to close the View Options panel (or click the little red circle in the upper-left corner).**

List view

List view is an easy-to-use-and-understand format for pretty much any user. It has two primary advantages:

✔ Items are displayed as a sortable list.

✔ Different details on an item are displayed simultaneously (see Figure 10-3).

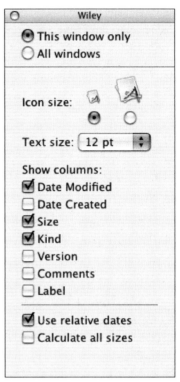

• **Figure 10-3:** The same directory from Figure 10-2, now in list view mode.

Because of these considerations, list view is the obvious choice if you need to sort a folder's contents or view any information (such as size, modification date, kind, creation date, and label). Also, if you need to compare contents of subfolders, list view is great because you can show multiple subfolders within the one window by expanding them.

To get the most out of list view, you must know how to customize and use the column headings. In an open window:

1. **Press ⌘+J to bring up the View Options (see Figure 10-4).**

2. **Use the radio buttons at the top to make these options apply to this window only or to all windows.**

> To create a default window setting for all your windows, select All Windows in the View Options dialog before customizing the settings.

3. **Set the icon and text sizes.**

The icon and text sizes can be increased to make up for a high monitor resolution, or these can both be reduced to make list view windows show more in a smaller space.

• **Figure 10-4:** View Options displays different choices based on the current view mode.

4. **Select which columns you want list view to show.**

See the guidelines below for more information.

5. **Press ⌘+J to close the View Options dialog (or click the little red circle in the upper-left corner).**

Here are some good rules for what you might want to include in list view:

✔ **Date Modified:** The Date Modified option is most useful for sorting your windows by modification date. Doing so brings the most recently altered file to the top.

✔ **Date Created:** The Date Created option is slightly less useful than the Date Modified option but works the same way.

✔ **Size:** The Size value is quite handy, particularly if you're looking for small (such as text documents) or large (like Photoshop files) items. This column can also be used to help you discern between multiple versions of the same file.

 Sizes are not calculated for folders unless the Calculate All Sizes check box is enabled in the View Options panel. Keep in mind that it will take some time to calculate large directories, so those values do not immediately appear in a window.

✔ **Kind:** The Kind attribute of the list view is rarely illuminating. The information that it lists (for example, Folder, Microsoft Word document, TIFF document) can normally be ascertained by the item's name and icon. It does, however, allow you to sort by the file's type.

✔ **Version:** Frankly, we haven't turned on a window's Version option in years. We can't imagine why you would, either.

✔ **Comments:** Listing an item's Comments is very, very useful — if you use comments, that is. If you don't (like most of us), leave it unmarked. You might use comments to note a text file's contents or information about an image.

 You can add comments to any item by opening Get Info using the ⌘+I keyboard shortcut or the File menu.

✔ **Label:** Viewing the Labels, like Comments, is great if you use them. Frankly, Panther's Label system is definitely worth your consideration. See Technique 9 for information on using Labels to your advantage.

After you've established what columns to use, you should understand these facts:

✔ The default view is to sort the items by name in ascending order.

 You can control the sorting of your files by adding special characters to a file's name. Filenames that begin with a space always come first; filenames that begin with symbols always go last. Just don't start a filename with a period or it will become hidden.

✔ Click any column heading to sort the contents of list view by that column in ascending order.

✔ Click again on the current sort column to sort the contents by that column in descending (reverse) order.

✔ You can rearrange the columns by dragging them, except for the Name column, which is always in view and is always listed first.

 The quickest way to see a long filename (which can be cut off in list and column view modes) is to hover the cursor over the filename. After a brief moment, the file's full name appears. To make it appear immediately, hold down the Option key while you hover the cursor above the file (see Figure 10-5).

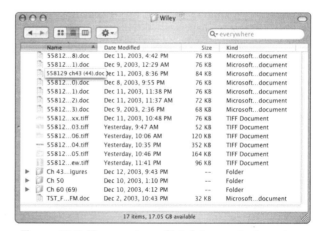

• **Figure 10-5: You can view a file's full name by hovering your cursor above it.**

Column view

Column view mode is unique. It shows a list of a folder's contents, like the list view, but without any of the extra details. Further, column view opens subfolders in columns (opening a folder moves you one column to the right; closing a folder moves you one column to the left). For these reasons, column view mode is the fastest for quickly navigating through multiple directories. You can even set the Finder to use column view mode by default by enabling the appropriate check box in the Finder preferences pane.

 To save space in column view mode, disable Show Icons in the View Options panel.

The trick to using column view mode is knowing how to change the different column sizes. Here are some tips:

- ✔ Click and drag the bottom-right corner of a window to expand it.

- ✔ Click and drag the two vertical lines separating columns to adjust one column's width. The column to the left of the vertical lines will be resized.

- ✔ To adjust every column's width, hold down the Option key while clicking and dragging any two vertical lines.

 One of the best benefits of column view is that it previews different file types for you. You can use it to view images, listen to sounds, and play movies, as shown in Figure 10-6. You can enable or disable this feature using the View Options panel.

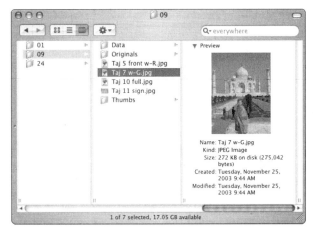

• **Figure 10-6: Column view mode can show an image or a movie or play a sound.**

Customizing Windows

Aside from the different view modes that you can use, you can customize the Finder's windows in many ways. The view modes themselves customize the window's content area, but you can also customize the toolbar along the top, the Sidebar along the side (appropriately enough), and even tinker with how the scroll bars appear and function for larger windows.

Toolbar

The toolbar along the top of the window has been around and customizable for a while now. Panther has added to it by adding the Action pop-up (see the "Using Actions" section later in this Technique) and the search box. To customize the toolbar:

1. **Control+click the toolbar (see Figure 10-7).**

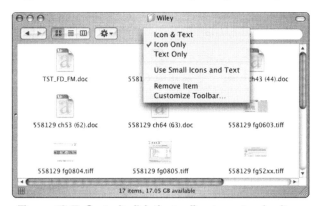

• **Figure 10-7: Control+click the toolbar to customize it.**

2. **Select Customize Toolbar from the contextual menu that appears.**

This is the equivalent of selecting Customize Toolbar from the View menu in the Finder. A Customize Toolbar palette appears.

3. **Add items to the toolbar by dragging them from the palette to their desired location on the toolbar (see Figure 10-8).**

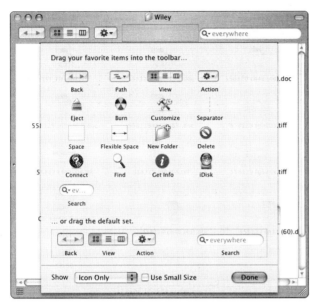

• **Figure 10-8: The Customize Toolbar palette.**

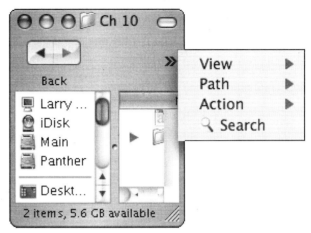

• **Figure 10-9: The double arrows create a menu of hidden toolbar options.**

4. Remove items from the toolbar by dragging them off the window.

5. Use the drop-down list and check box at the bottom of the window to dictate how much information should be shown in the toolbar (Icon & Text, Icon Only, or Text Only) and whether it should be in small size.

The best way to customize the toolbar depends upon how you use it. Some options — Get Info, iDisk, Connect, and Customize — are rarely used and could be omitted. Others — Burn and Eject — will also be an option in the Sidebar if you have volumes mounted there. Finally, almost all the icons have keyboard equivalents or can be re-created by Control+clicking.

Here are some other toolbar tips and shortcuts that you should be aware of:

✔ If your window becomes too small to show all the toolbar features, double arrows appear. Click them to see the hidden options (see Figure 10-9).

✔ Click the oval button in the upper-right corner of the toolbar to switch between a fancy Panther window and a plain version. Strangely enough, you can also use Shift+click, Control+click, or Option+click to do the same thing.

✔ ⌘+clicking the oval button toggles among very subtly different versions of the window.

✔ You can also access the Path by ⌘+clicking the window's title bar. A folder's path indicates where the folder is on the hard drive, like `/Users/larry/Desktop/Stuff`.

 ⌘+clicking the window's title bar is a good trick to remember. Many other applications also use this technique to show you the file path (BBEdit) or your browser's history (Safari).

✔ Hold down the ⌘ key while clicking and dragging to move or remove toolbar items without using the Customize Toolbar panel.

✔ Drag any icon from the Desktop or a Finder window to add it to the toolbar.

✔ Control+click the toolbar to switch view modes. Control+click a toolbar icon or tool to remove it — or just ⌘+drag (it off).

You can add a **Delete** button to the toolbar so that you can delete a file by selecting it and then clicking **Delete**. You can also trash a file by dropping it on the **Delete** toolbar button.

Sidebar

The Sidebar (see Figure 10-10) is new to Panther and contains two separate parts. The top section lists volumes, mounted disk images, discs, and so forth. This can be customized under the Sidebar panel of the Finder's preferences panel. Anything listed in the Sidebar can be accessed with a single mouse click. (These items don't need to be opened with a double click.)

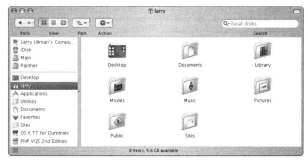

• **Figure 10-10:** The side panel on the left of the window is new to Panther and customizable.

 Resize the Sidebar width by clicking and dragging the dividing line between it and the window's contents.

Here are some things that you can do in the top part of the Sidebar:

✔ Easily access any disk drive.

✔ Access your iDisk without formally connecting to it. iDisk is covered in Technique 41.

✔ View mounted disk images and discs without going to the Desktop.

✔ Eject mounted disk images and discs.

✔ Burn CD-Rs and DVD-Rs.

✔ See what servers you are currently connected to.

Using the Window's Icon to Move Folders

In the title bar of a window, the folder icon that appears next to the window's name is the listed folder's icon. Therefore, this icon is the same as the icon for the directory that you would find it in its parent folder. By clicking and holding the window's icon, you can move this entire directory around without going up one folder. For example:

1. **Open two different folders in two different windows in the Finder.**

2. **Click and hold the title bar icon of the folder that you want to move.**

   You'll need to click and hold for just a second to get the system to engage.

3. **Drag this icon into the other window.**

4. **Release the mouse button.**

You'll now see the first window as a subdirectory in the second. However, the first window is still open; only its location has changed.

 The contents of the Sidebar will also appear in Open/Save dialogs, thus saving you time navigating around the computer.

The bottom section of the Sidebar is partially customizable from the Finder's preferences panel. This area should be used to access frequently used directories, such as

✔ Your Home folder

✔ The Desktop

✔ The Applications folder

✔ Your Documents folder

Select any object and press ⌘+T to instantly add it to your Sidebar. Similarly, you can drag an item to the Sidebar to add it or drag it off to remove it. Sidebar items can also be rearranged by clicking and dragging them.

The ⌘+T shortcut used to add an item to your Favorites directory but now adds items to the Sidebar. There is no longer a shortcut to add items to the Favorites directory.

Scroll bars

One final area of customization with respect to windows involves the scroll bars that appear on the right side of the window when the window is too small to display every item. These settings are adjusted in the Appearance panel of System Preferences (see Figure 10-11). You can set the scrol arrows to appear like the following:

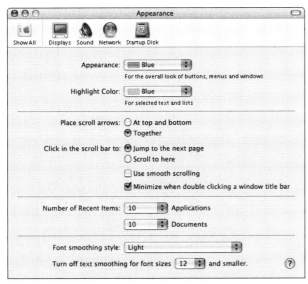

• **Figure 10-11: The Appearance panel also controls the Finder window scroll bars.**

✔ Separate, at the top and bottom of the window

or

✔ Together at the bottom of the window

While you're at it, you can tweak how clicking in the scroll bar area affects the window or document. Select one of the following radio buttons:

✔ **Jump to the Next Page:** Moves a page at a time

or

✔ **Scroll to Here:** Moves to a particular location

Both of these settings are more for personal taste than anything, but you should understand what you're getting when you make your selections. (For the record, we tend to keep our scroll bars together and set clicking in the scroll bar to move one page at a time.)

 If you install the free TinkerTool (see Technique 53), you have even more scroll bar options, including having both together at the top and bottom of the window.

The last two settings that you can enable are smooth scrolling and minimizing windows on double-clicks. The first makes your scrolling look pretty, but it really drags down your productivity. Turn off smooth scrolling for a faster window response. As for double-clicking windows to minimize them, that's handy, but you can also minimize a window by single-clicking on the yellow button or by using ⌘+M.

Using Actions

Actions are a new feature to Mac OS X's windows. They provide a button access point to contextual menu-like behavior. To access the Actions menu, click the toolbar button with a gear pictured on it. If you're in a directory with nothing selected, the default Actions are New Folder, Get Info, and Show View Options (see Figure 10-12).

 Use the Get Info Action when in a directory with nothing selected to get the size of that directory's contents.

If you've selected an item or items, the Actions menu is much a like contextual menu (what you'd get by Control+clicking the items), with the addition of the New Folder option and the subtraction of the Folder Actions options (see Figure 10-13).

• **Figure 10-12: The Actions as they apply to a directory.**

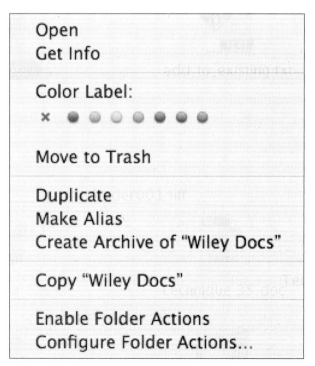

• **Figure 10-13: The Actions as they apply to a selected item.**

Actions are still new to Panther and are therefore a little underwhelming in their current incarnation. We expect this to change when Apple builds more features into the Actions part of a window.

 Another type of actions, Folder Actions, are discussed in Technique 12.

Moving Windows Around

Despite the fact that Exposé (see Technique 13) has greatly facilitated moving about open windows, there are still plenty of other tips and tricks to be learned. Window management is critical to using the operating system efficiently, particularly if you open every folder in a new window. Here are the best tips:

- ✔ Finder windows use three standard buttons in the upper-left corner. They are color-coordinated to represent what they do: red (close), yellow (minimize), and green (maximize).

- ✔ Option+click the yellow button to minimize every open window.

- ✔ Option+click the red button to close every open window.

- ✔ If you place the mouse cursor over an inactive window's buttons, they light up, allowing you to close, minimize, or maximize a window without it being in front (and therefore active).

- ✔ You can move background (non-active) windows by holding down the ⌘ key and clicking them with the mouse.

- ✔ Double-click the toolbar to minimize a window, if enabled.

 The Appearance panel allows you to turn on the window minimizing feature when double-clicking the window's title bar or toolbar.

- ✔ You can directly access any particular window by clicking Window in the menu bar and selecting from the list of windows.

✔ The shortcut ⌘+→ scrolls you forward through the open windows. ⌘+← rotates you backwards.

✔ Minimized windows are stored in the right-hand side of the Dock.

✔ By placing your cursor over a window's Dock icon, you can see the name of the window (see Figure 10-14).

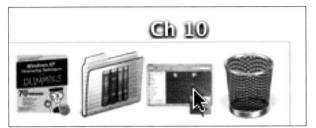

• **Figure 10-14:** A window's title reveals itself when you hover over its icon in the Dock.

Technique 11

Establishing an Efficient Dock

Save Time By

✔ Customizing how the Dock looks and behaves

✔ Organizing your Dock for maximum productivity

✔ Reviewing the various keyboard and mouse shortcuts that you'll use with the Dock

✔ Investigating Dock-related shareware

The *Dock,* that curious little bar at the bottom of your screen, is such a particular aspect of your operating system that it merits its own Technique. A new concept to Mac OS X, the Dock has been much maligned in its various incarnations, but we feel that with the right treatment, the Dock can be an important ally in the war for productivity.

We begin this Technique with a discussion on customizing and organizing the Dock, with the focus on making it as useful as possible. Then we demonstrate the myriad ways that different mouse and keyboard short-cuts can be used to work with the Dock more efficiently. Finally, we intro-duce a couple of the more popular shareware applications that add to or mimic the Dock's purpose and behavior.

Customizing the Dock

The Dock is like a pet: You need to take care of it. Okay, it's really nothing like a pet, but you should still spend a bit of time doing two things: cus-tomizing its behavior and organizing its contents and layout. You can customize the Dock's behavior from the Dock panel of System Preferences (see Figure 11-1).

• **Figure 11-1: Use the Dock System Preferences panel to set the Dock's behavior.**

Dock	
Show All	Displays Sound Network Startup Disk

Dock Size: ──────○────── Small ⟷ Large

☐ Magnification: ──────────○ Min ⟷ Max

Position on screen: ○ Left ● Bottom ○ Right

Minimize using: [Genie Effect ⧨]

☑ Animate opening applications
☐ Automatically hide and show the Dock

You can adjust much of the Dock's behavior from the Dock submenu of the Apple Menu (see Figure 11-2). It gives you immediate access to the Dock preferences panel without forcing you to navigate through System Preferences.

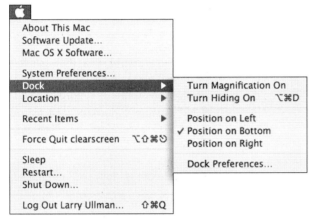

• **Figure 11-2: The Dock submenu is located under the Apple menu.**

You can adjust the following Dock properties, some of which are just cosmetic and some of which are actually useful:

- Size

- Magnification (whether it's on and how potent it is)

- Position on the screen (left, bottom, or right)

- The effect used when windows and documents are minimized into the Dock (Genie and Scale are your choices)

- Whether opening applications are animated

- Whether the Dock automatically hides and shows itself

The size, position, and hiding features of the Dock all directly relate to how you interact with your computer — and therefore, can have an effect on your productivity. That being said, how you set them is largely a matter of taste. Here are some general suggestions:

- Automatically hiding and showing the Dock is a good way to keep your screen clear if you have a smaller monitor (like 15" or less) or a laptop.

- Placing the Dock on the side makes more sense if you have a widescreen display (where you have more screen space on the sides than you do on the top and bottom).

- If you use the Desktop a lot and have folders, volumes, and other icons automatically arranged (meaning that they're located on the right side of the screen), don't put the Dock on the right, or it'll always be in the way.

- Adjust the size of the Dock so that it's as small as reasonable while still allowing you to read it.

 The Dock's size will automatically shrink if the number of items in the Dock makes it too large to fit onscreen. In System Preferences, you can also make the Dock really small, but use magnification to see the items more clearly (see Figure 11-3).

• **Figure 11-3: Magnification increases an icon's size as your mouse goes over it.**

The minimizing effect, the animation of opening applications, and (to a lesser degree) the magnification are cosmetic. Turn them on to impress or annoy your friends; turn them off if you think it'll make things happen faster (it really won't).

The free TinkerTool freeware application (`www.bresink.de/osx/TinkerTool.html`) lets you customize your Dock in other ways. This includes positioning the Dock at the top of the screen, adjusting the alignment (left/top, center, right/bottom), making the Dock icons for hidden applications transparent, and adding a Dock shadow. It also adds a "Suck In" minimize effect for those of you who appreciate eye candy.

Organizing the Dock

The Dock is divided into two sections: the left side (where applications live) and the right side (where you'll find documents, folders, and the Trash). The two sides are divided by a separator bar: A vertical line that runs the height of the Dock.

To add any item to the Dock, drag its icon there. To remove any item (except the Finder and the Trash, which are permanent), drag its icon off the Dock. The Dock always shows every icon that you add to it as well as other currently running applications (which are marked with an upward-pointing black triangle; refer to Figure 11-3).

To organize your Dock:

1. **Remove any of the default icons that you won't regularly use; just click and drag them off the Dock.**

    Apple likes to give you immediate access to every Apple application that comes installed on your Mac, so your Dock has iMovie, iPhoto, iCal, Mail, the Address Book, and other applications by default. If you won't frequently use some of these (like iMovie), drag the icon off the Dock to make it disappear in a puff of smoke.

     You cannot remove these two Dock icons: the Finder, which is always on the far left (or the top, if the Dock is on the side), and the Trash, which is always on the far right (or bottom).

2. **Add every application that you use on a daily basis to the left side of the Dock by dragging their icons from the Finder onto the Dock.**

3. **Add frequently accessed folders to the right side of the Dock by dragging their icons from the Finder onto the Dock.**

    We recommend putting your Favorites folder (which links applications and files that you use less frequently), your Home folder, and perhaps your Documents folder on the right side of the Dock. You should also consider dragging the folders for your current projects and documents there. If you want, add the Desktop folder there to immediately access Desktop items.

     Use customized icons for your Dock folders (before adding them to the Dock) to make it easier to distinguish among multiple folders stored there. See Technique 15 for instructions and resources.

4. **Organize your applications so that those used in conjunction are placed together.**

    For example, if you regularly use multiple Web browsers, place these next to each other. If you use BBEdit (a text editor) with Fetch or Transmit (FTP applications), line them up.

     Icons placed in the center of the Dock are the most stable because they're less affected by the expansion and contraction of the Dock. As your Dock grows, applications found near the center of your Dock will remain near the center of your screen. Conversely, items on the ends of the Dock will be moved closer and closer to the end of the screen, making them slightly harder to get to.

Keyboard and Mouse Shortcuts for the Dock

To get the most out of the Dock, you must be able to customize it properly and also use it with ease. This comes down to understanding the various keyboard and mouse shortcuts that you can use to perform common tasks.

With your mouse (or other input device), here are the basics that you should know:

✔ Click any application's icon to bring it to the front.

✔ Click any folder's icon to show that folder in a Finder window.

✔ Click the Trash icon to see what's in the garbage.

Hierarchical Pop-Up Menus in the Dock

Clicking an icon in the Dock takes you to that application, but clicking folders in the Dock can give you different behavior:

✔ When you click a folder's icon, that directory is opened in a new Finder window.

✔ When you Control+click or click and hold a folder's icon, a hierarchical menu is created of the folder's contents, as shown in the following figure.

Both of these features are quite useful and an easy way to access your documents. The second method allows you to navigate directly to a subfolder or document buried deep inside — the hierarchy of folders is revealed while you navigate. In previous versions of Mac OS X, you were limited to only a handful of submenus, but now you can literally fill your screen up with menus to reach the file that you want, as shown in the following figure.

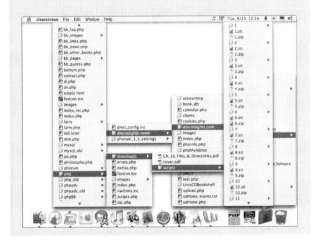

✔ Click a Dock item to make that item active, open it if it's not already open, and reshow minimized documents or windows.

✔ Click and hold a Dock icon to bring up its contextual menu (or a hierarchical menu for a folder).

✔ Use the contextual menu to quit, hide, and go to the item's location in the Finder.

✔ Check the contextual menus for different applications to see what options they provide.

For example, the Mail application gives you the option to check your e-mail (see Figure 11-4). Many others, such as BBEdit, allow you to preselect which open document (in that application) you want to view (see Figure 11-5).

• **Figure 11-4: The Mail contextual menu in the Dock.**

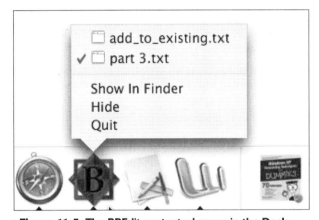

• **Figure 11-5: The BBEdit contextual menu in the Dock.**

✔ Click and drag the Dock's separator up and down to adjust the Dock's size.

✔ You can eject disk images, CDs, DVDs, floppy disks, Zip disks, and external hard drives by dragging their icons onto the Trash icon, which turns into an Eject button.

When using only the keyboard, you are fairly limited by what you can do with the Dock, but to start:

1. **Make sure that Full Keyboard Access is turned on in the Keyboard & Mouse panel of System Preferences (under Keyboard Shortcuts).**

2. **Press Control+F3 to access the Dock (see Figure 11-6).**

• **Figure 11-6:** Pressing Control+F3 highlights the Finder icon in the Dock.

 Laptop users might have to use fn+Control+F3 to access the Dock.

3. **Use the arrow keys to move left and right (you can also Tab+→ and Shift+Tab+←).**

4. **After an item is highlighted, press the spacebar to make it active.**

5. **Use the up- or down-arrow keys to launch the contextual menu for that item (see Figure 11-7).**

6. **Press Return to select an option highlighted in the contextual menu.**

7. **Press Esc at any time to leave the Dock.**

 Another keyboard shortcut that you should remember is pressing ⌘+Option+D to show or hide the Dock.

What you can do with the mouse — or the mouse and keyboard together — is much more impressive:

✔ Control+click a Dock icon to bring up its contextual menu. You can also just click and hold to see it.

✔ Option+Control+click to change the contextual menu's Quit option to Force Quit.

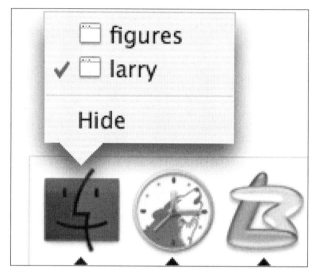

• **Figure 11-7:** Use the arrow keys to navigate the contextual menus in the Dock.

 To empty the Trash by using the Dock and your mouse, click and hold (or Control+click) the Dock's Trash icon and then select Empty Trash from the menu that appears.

✔ ⌘+Option+click a Dock icon to hide all the other applications.

✔ ⌘+click a Dock icon to reveal the icon's original file in the Finder. This is the same as selecting Show In Finder from the contextual menu.

You can also control many of the Dock's settings by using your input device and the modifier keys. For starters:

✔ Control+click the Dock separator (the line between the left and right sides of the Dock) to access the Dock's preferences (see Figure 11-8).

✔ Press Option+click while dragging the Dock separator to change the Dock's size to standard icon sizes.

✔ Pressing ⌘+Shift+click while dragging the Dock's separator bar left and right allows you to move the Dock around the screen (from left to bottom to right).

✔ An application's contextual menu allows you to add the item to the Dock. You can also accomplish this by moving a Dock icon, which makes it a permanent addition.

• **Figure 11-8:** The Dock's preferences can be adjusted from the Dock's contextual menu.

 You can open a file by dragging it onto an application's icon in the Dock. The problem is that the Dock may mistake your intentions and frequently move the application icon out of the way so that the file can be added to the Dock. To make the Dock behave itself, hold down the ⌘ key when dragging the file. To force an application to attempt to open a file, use ⌘+Option while you're dragging the file onto the Dock icon.

Shareware for the Dock

After you get the hang of the Dock, investigate some of the shareware applications that either add to its functionality or otherwise duplicate its utility. Here's a quick summary of the popular candidates:

✔ **DragThing** (www.dragthing.com, $25) gives you the ability to have a *tabbed* Dock (one Dock with multiple subpanels, each of which can contain its own items). It's a very popular application and consistently reviewed well by Mac users.

✔ **Drop Drawers** (www.sigsoftware.com/dropdrawers, $20) is a lot like DragThing with an extra emphasis on storing stuff (text, images, and the like) in a Dock drawer.

✔ **DockSwap** (www.pidog.com/OSX/, $12 suggested) also allows you to have multiple Docks, switching easily back and forth among them.

✔ **Snard** (www.gideonsoftworks.com/snard.html, $10) is a launcher program, quickly bringing up applications, folders, files, and System Preferences. It can exist as a dockling, pop-up menu, or menu bar extension.

 A *dockling* is a special type of application that resides in the Dock and adds extra functionality to your computer. It's unlike other Dock items in that you'll never really use it as a standalone application.

✔ **DockExtender** (www.codetek.com/php/dockext.php, $20) also launches applications, accesses Web pages, and provides contextual menus. Highly customizable, it can work as a dockling, a pop-up menu, or as a menu bar tool.

Technique 12

Saving Steps with Contextual Menus

Save Time By

- Understanding the benefits of contextual menus

- Getting to know some third-party contextual menu software

- Seeing how you can use AppleScripts with contextual menus

Contextual menus have been part of the Macintosh operating system for several incarnations now, and yet still many people underuse them, or don't use them at all. Contextual menus provide an immediate listing of options; usually frequently performed tasks for a file, folder, image, and so forth. Although contextual menus exist in both applications and the Finder, they differ greatly across applications. Therefore, this Techique specifically addresses the Finder's contextual menus (often abbreviated as just *CMs*).

First we cover a smattering of the basics about contextual menus, including the new contextual menu features found in Panther. Then we discuss, in greater detail, some of the specific contextual menu items that you can add to your system. These include many common third-party and shareware applications.

Grasping the Basics of Contextual Menus

When you Control+click an item, whether it's a window, the Desktop, or an icon, a contextual menu appears, listing the things that you can do with that item. Different objects in your system offer different options. For example, here are the CMs for a folder (Figure 12-1), a file (Figure 12-2), and a window (Figure 12-3).

• **Figure 12-1: The default contextual menu for a folder.**

If you use contextual menus a lot — and you really should — and you have a programmable input device (such as a trackball or mouse), you must program one of the buttons to act as a Control+click. Doing so saves countless hours because you can access common features more easily.

The Get Info option is common to all three of the listed CM examples. A window has the fewest number of options, by default, whereas files generally give you the most. Some common uses of the contextual menu include

• **Figure 12-2: The default contextual menu for a file.**

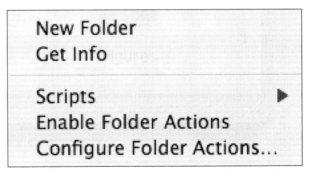

• **Figure 12-3: The default contextual menu for a window.**

If you want to know what CM options are available to you in any application, including the Finder, Control+click to investigate. Get in the habit of Control+clicking within windows, on icons, and in the toolbar of windows.

✔ Creating a new folder within a directory, in case you get tripped up with the ⌘+Option+N shortcut.

✔ Adding, deleting, or changing the Label.

✔ Sending the selected item to the Trash.

✔ Opening a file with a specific application (see Technique 23).

✔ Archiving an item.

> New in Panther is the ability to create an *archive* — a zipped (compressed) version — of a file or folder. This replicates the DropZip feature that users of StuffIt Deluxe have had for years.

✔ Duplicating or just copying the item.

✔ Creating an alias.

> Items in the Dock and the Dock itself have their own contextual menus if you Control+ click a Dock's icon or Control+click the Dock. (This menu differs depending on whether you click on the Dock separator or in a blank area.)

Opening Your Packages

For the more techie user, another nice use of a contextual menu is that it allows you to view the contents of *packages* (special bundles of information presented as one cohesive item). These are used frequently in Mac OS X, but you can only view a package's contents in the Terminal unless you use the Show Package Contents CM.

1. **Control+click a file with the** `.pkg` **extension to bring up the file's contextual menu.**

2. **Choose Show Package Contents from the CM.**

3. **A window of the package's contents appears. In it, you will commonly find**

   ▸ **Two text (XML) files that store version and other information about the package**

▸ **An archive file**

▸ **A resources directory**

These files can then be examined, copied, or (if you know what you're doing) modified. This concept is not unlike using a resource editor like ResEdit back in earlier versions of Mac OS.

As you explore this concept, you'll notice that the `/Library/ Receipts` folder tracks what was installed by creating packages. Also, many installers will come in a package form. Even most of Panther's default applications, like Mail, are packages whose contents can be viewed.

Using CMs with Third-Party Applications

Many third-party applications, including commercial apps, shareware, and freeware, take advantage of Panther's contextual menus. Here are a few:

✔ Rainer Brockerhoff (www.brockerhoff.net) provides, for free, a useful contextual menu application called Zingg!. It replicates Panther's Open With functionality that allows you to open a file with an application other than the default application. It takes this principle a small step further by allowing you to set certain applications, such as Preview, Photoshop, or BBEdit to always appear, and for others to never be listed as an option. Also, you can disable Classic applications as an option if Classic is not open.

✔ The DesktopPictureCM tool from Azine Software (www.azinesoftware.com, free) sets a selected image as the Desktop picture without having to go through System Preferences.

✔ PicturePopCM from setnan.org (www.setnan.org/ mac/, free) quickly displays a preview of a selected image or images without using another application.

✔ QuickAccessCM from Abra Code (http:// free.abracode.com/cmworkshop/, free) grants you immediate access to commonly used folders, files, and even applications. With it, you can move, copy, or even make an alias of a selected item in another directory.

 Abra Code provides a slew of handy contextual menu scripts. They're all free and available at free.abracode.com/cmworkshop/.

✔ StuffIt Deluxe (www.stuffit.com, $80) comes with several contextual menu options. The popular utility (see Figure 12-4), whose main use is for compressing and decompressing files and folders, creates CM tools to immediately archive or open pretty much anything. You can also access StuffIt's preferences through the CM and use sequential tools like Archive and Mail.

✔ StickyBrain 2 (www.chronosnet.com, $40 or potentially free for .Mac users) is the Stickies application on steriods, providing you with an amazing asset for managing information. This application creates contextual menus that incorporate StickyBrain into nearly any other application. See Technique 16 for more information on StickyBrain.

 Search Google or www.versiontracker.com for more contextual menu applications that you can use.

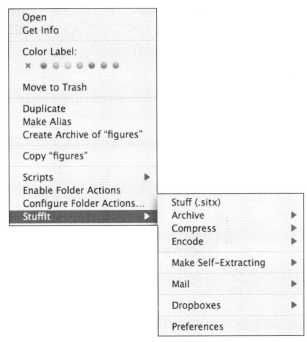

• **Figure 12-4: StuffIt Deluxe adds many useful items to the contextual menus.**

AppleScript, Contextual Menus, and You

A special subsection of contextual menus exist thanks to AppleScript. *AppleScript,* in case you aren't aware, is a programming tool for the Mac. Because it's very easy to use but still powerful, it's remained a popular application over the years. Without too much work, you can trigger (or run) AppleScripts in contextual menus.

 Apple has a vast supply of ready-made AppleScripts available for download. They're organized by application at www.apple.com/ applescript/apps/.

Folder Actions

Folder Actions are Apple-supplied tools that allow you to associate actions to folders. These actions, in the form of AppleScripts, can be run whenever the folder is opened, closed, or moved, or when items are added to or removed from the folder. To use Folder Actions, you must first enable them:

1. **Control+click any folder to bring up the contextual menu.**

2. **From the resulting contextual menu (see Figure 12-5), choose Enable Folder Actions.**

• **Figure 12-5:** You must enable Folder Actions for the system before you can use them.

3. **Find the AppleScript that you want to run.**

   If you know how, you can write your own AppleScripts. Or, you can download one of the many free AppleScripts from Apple's Web site and other online resources. A third option is to use one of the built-in scripts, found in the /Library/Scripts folder.

4. **Save the AppleScript in the** `~/Library/ Scripts/Folder Action Scripts` **folder.**

5. **Bring up the contextual menu again by Control+clicking a folder.**

   It can be any folder.

6. **Choose Configure Folder Actions from the contextual menu.**

7. **In the Folder Actions Setup window (see Figure 12-6), click the plus sign in the left column.**

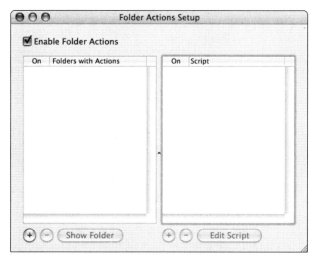

• **Figure 12-6:** The Folder Actions Setup window lets you associate AppleScripts with folders.

8. **Navigate to and select the new AppleScript.**

9. In the right column, click the plus sign.

10. Navigate to and select the folder that you want this script to apply to.

 Go to `www.apple.com/applescript/folder_actions/` **to find tips for writing AppleScripts that work with Folder Actions.**

Big Cat

Big Cat, created by Ranchero Software (`www.ranchero.com`), is a free application that adds the ability to run AppleScripts from contextual menus. It's kind of like Panther's Folder Actions, only broader in scope. Big Cat creates two separate categories of scripts:

✔ **Text:** For example, you can copy, open a selection in TextEdit, or search with Google (see Figure 12-7).

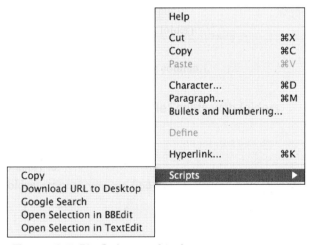

• **Figure 12-7: Big Cat's textual tools.**

✔ **Files:** These include scripts such as Copy Path and Make Alias on Desktop (see Figure 12-8).

• **Figure 12-8: Big Cat's file tools, available as a contextual menu.**

Which options you see depend on what's being selected when the contextual menu is brought up. (Hence the name *contextual* menu.) To install and use Big Cat:

1. Download the latest version of Big Cat from `http://ranchero.com/bigcat/`.

2. Double-click it to open the downloaded file, called something like `BigCat1.0.sit`.

3. Open the resulting folder, called something like Big Cat 1.0.

The contents should resemble Figure 12-9.

• **Figure 12-9: The contents of the Big Cat folder.**

4. Move the Big Cat Scripts folder to `~/Library/Application Support`, **where ~ refers to your Home directory.**

5. Move the file BigCat.plugin to the ~/Library/ Contextual Menu Items **folder, again where ~ refers to your Home directory.**

 If you don't already have either an Application Support or a Contextual Menu Items folder in your Library directory, create one.

6. **Log out of your computer and then log back in.**

 In this case, you cannot use Fast User Switching to log out because that does not close your session.

7. **When you log back in, you should now have the Big Cat options listed under Scripts.**

8. **To install your own AppleScripts to use through Big Cat, drop them into the text or file subfolder of the** ~/Library/Application Support **directory (see Figure 12-10).**

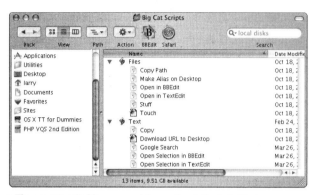

• **Figure 12-10:** You can add any AppleScripts that you want to the appropriate Files or Text folder.

9. **If you really like Big Cat, consider making a donation to the cause via the links at the Web site (**www.ranchero.com/bigcat**).**

 After you realize the benefits of Big Cat, you might want more. The Ranchero Software Web site has other scripts that you can download and install as well as tutorials to teach you how to write your own.

Technique

13

Easily Managing Windows with Exposé

Save Time By

- ✔ Setting System Preferences for Exposé
- ✔ Navigating windows with Exposé
- ✔ Using Exposé without the mouse

Brand new to Panther is a window mangement system called *Exposé*. Exposé allows you to access and switch among open windows either throughout the entire operating system or just in the current application. It also gives you immediate access to the Desktop.

In this Technique, we introduce you to Exposé and all the benefits that it has to offer. We also show the default mouse and keyboard shortcuts for using Exposé and how you can alter these. Finally, we demonstrate a few techniques that you can use, thanks to Exposé. Knowing how to switch documents within an active application, how to drag and drop files more quickly, and how to use Exposé without the mouse will go a long way towards helping you speed through routine tasks.

Introducing Exposé

You enable and control Exposé from the Exposé panel, which is found under the Personal section of System Preferences (see Figure 13-1).

• **Figure 13-1: Exposé is classified as a Personal setting.**

1. Open System Preferences by going to the Apple menu or clicking its icon in the Dock.

2. Click Exposé.

3. In the Exposé panel that appears (see Figure 13-2), set the corner activation settings for Exposé as follows:

Exposé, like a screen saver, can use a feature called *hot corners*. Hot corners are just the corners of your screen that have been assigned special meaning. Moving the cursor into a certain corner activates a function; moving it out of the corner deactivates that function. For example, if you are in Safari, moving into one corner might reveal the Desktop. When you move the cursor back out, Safari is revealed again. Before you can use any hot corner, though, you need to assign functions to them, in the Exposé panel.

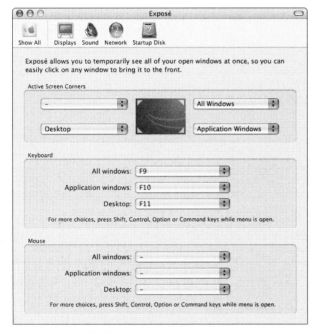

• **Figure 13-2:** The Exposé panel.

▶ You can set one corner to show every open window (All Windows).

▶ You can set another corner to reveal every open window for the currently active application (Application Windows).

▶ You can set another corner to access the Desktop (Desktop).

 The drop-down lists in this dialog correspond to their positions onscreen. In other words, the upper-left drop-down list controls the upper-left corner of your screen, and so on.

4. Also in the Exposé panel, you can use the drop-down lists in the Keyboard section to set your function keys for these same purposes.

 The Exposé panel also allows you to set hot corners to start and disable the screen saver. These controls are duplicated — even for Exposé — under the Desktop & Screen Saver Control Panel.

You might find all these options intimidating. Here are our best rules for customizing Exposé:

✔ You might want to skip setting a Desktop shortcut in Exposé because you can also access the Desktop by clicking on it or by clicking the Finder icon in the Dock.

✔ Because the All Windows and Application Windows features are very similar, place the hot corners on the same side of the screen and use contiguous function keys for them.

✔ If your function keys aren't readily accessible (or, as with laptops, require the use of the fn key to work), avoid setting the function key shortcuts.

✔ If your function keys are already being used for other purposes, skip setting the function keys and just use the hot corners instead.

✔ If your function keys are already being used for other purposes, you can add a modifier key to the keyboard shortcut by holding down the Shift, ⌘, Option, or Control key while you select the corresponding function key (see Figure 13-3).

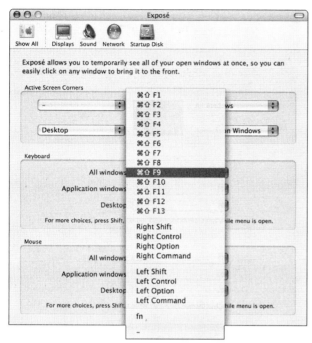

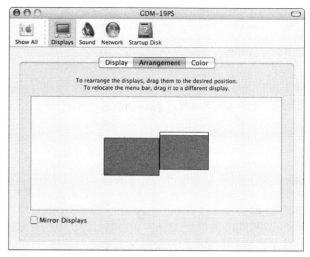

• **Figure 13-4:** The arrangement of your displays dictates how many corners your system has.

• **Figure 13-3:** Exposé can also be triggered by using the function keys and a modifier key.

✔ Users with multiple displays (see Technique 6) probably still only have four corners, even though it might seem that you physically have eight.

 Strange as it might seem, some multiple-display users might have five or more screen corners. If the two displays aren't aligned exactly, there can be an extra corner or two between the two displays, as shown in Figure 13-4. This isn't necessarily a problem or an asset but just a curiosity you should be aware of.

✔ If you have a Mac with a small display (like an iBook or the 12-inch PowerBook), you might find the hot corners a nuisance. They tend to do funny Exposé things when your cursor (even accidentally) nears a corner.

✔ If you have a multi-button input device, you can set the extra buttons to trigger Exposé, with or without modifier keys (see Figure 13-5).

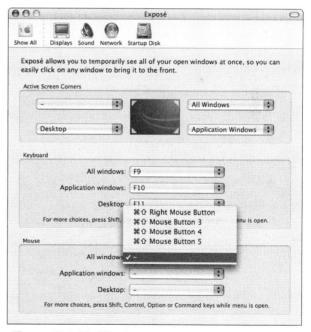

• **Figure 13-5:** Modifier keys and extra mouse buttons can be set to use Exposé.

The most natural way to trigger Exposé is probably to use the hot corners with the mouse. For many people, the function keys aren't as easy to access and use as the mouse is.

How to Get the Most out of Exposé

After you get Exposé set up the way you want it, you need to know how to get the most out of its potential. Aside from revealing the Desktop, Exposé either displays all the open windows (including Finder windows, Web browser windows, and documents) or all the open windows for the current application. Here are the basics for using Exposé.

To switch to a different document within the current application:

1. **Depending on how you've set your System Preferences, press either the keyboard short- cut or move your cursor into the hot corner to bring up all the open windows for the current application (see Figure 13-6).**

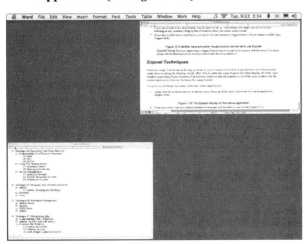

• **Figure 13-6: The Exposé display for the active application.**

2. **Place your cursor over each window (the rest of the screen will be dark) to view its title. (See the upper-right corner of Figure 13-7.)**

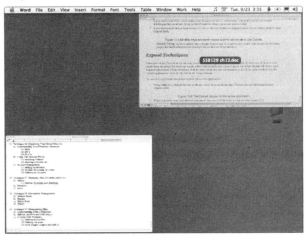

• **Figure 13-7: Exposé shows a window or document's title when you hover the mouse over it.**

 Exposé shows only *open* windows. Minimized documents in the current application are not revealed.

3. **Click the desired window to make it active.**

 You can always press Esc to leave Exposé with- out switching windows or applications.

To switch to a document in another application:

1. **By using either the keyboard shortcut or the hot corner, bring up all the open windows.**

Check out the party in Figure 13-8 (and that's not even a particularly busy day).

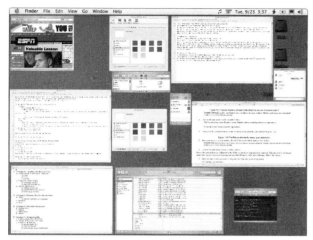

• **Figure 13-8:** The Exposé display for every open
   application.

2. Place your cursor over each window (the rest
   of the screen will be dark) to view its title.

3. Click in the appropriate window to make it
   active.

 This tip's just too cool for school: After you
use Exposé to show all the open windows and
documents, you can access all the windows or
documents for specific (open) applications by
pressing the Tab key. The end result is much
like rotating through Exposé's current application listing without actively switching from one
application to another. If you have a lot of
clutter or want to view a particular window or
document in a larger size, this is the way to go.

Dragging and dropping with Exposé

Although the current incarnation of Exposé is not
quite chock-full of features, it does have some neat
tricks and plenty of room here for future additions
as Apple receives feedback on this new tool. One of
the coolest features of Exposé is that you can use it
for drag-and-drop purposes, like when you want to
quickly add an attachment to an e-mail or copy and
paste some text from one application to another.

This might not be obvious to many users on first
exposure (insert groan here), but it's a really cool
technique. Here's the skinny:

1. Select the item or items that you want to drag
   and drop from the point of origination (see
   Figure 13-9).

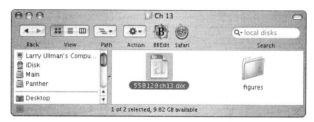

• **Figure 13-9:** To attach a document to an e-mail, first
   select it in the Finder.

For example, you can select:

▶ A file in the Finder to attach to an e-mail

▶ Text in an e-mail to drop into BBEdit

▶ An image in Photoshop to view in your Web
   browser

▶ Text in a Word document to copy into another
   Word document

▶ Files to duplicate or move from one Finder
   window to another

2. Begin dragging the selected item by clicking
   with the mouse and moving your cursor slightly.

3. While continuing to hold down the mouse button, use Exposé to show either all the currently
   open windows or all the open windows for the
   current application.

   Do so by either moving the cursor into the
   correct hot corner or pressing the associated
   keyboard shortcut to engage Exposé.

4. While continuing to hold down the mouse
   button, select the appropriate window or
   document by moving the cursor over it (see
   Figure 13-10).

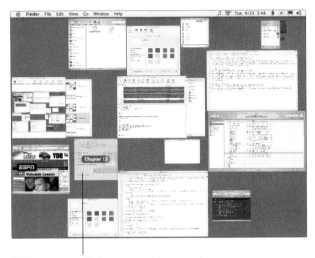

Select the e-mail's image to add an attachment.

• **Figure 13-10:** To add an attachment to an e-mail, select the e-mail's image.

5. While (still!) continuing to hold down the mouse button, activate the highlighted window or document by pressing the spacebar.

Exposé also automatically switches over to a document or window if you hover the cursor over it for a couple of moments.

6. While (of course) continuing to hold down the mouse button, move the cursor within the window or document to where you want to drop the selected item (see Figure 13-11).

7. Release the mouse button to complete the drop.

See the results in Figure 13-12.

8. Apply hot and cold compresses to your tired, aching, mouse-clicking finger as needed.

• **Figure 13-11:** Before releasing the mouse button, move the cursor to where you want the file dropped.

• **Figure 13-12:** The completed drag-and-drop attaches the file to the e-mail.

Using Exposé without the mouse

The last technique that we demonstrate is for those hard-core keyboard users. You know who you are: You never take your hands off the keys, and you use the mouse as a toy for your cat. Exposé can be used without the mouse at all, although the drag-and-drop technique that we cover in the preceding section goes to waste.

1. **In the Exposé panel, make sure that you have the keyboard shortcuts enabled.**

2. **Press the appropriate keyboard shortcut to launch Exposé.**

By default this is

▶ F9 to see all open windows

▶ F10 to view all the current application's open windows (or documents)

▶ F11 to head to the Desktop

3. **Use the arrow keys to select the window or document that you want.**

The arrow keys will move you around the window listings as you would expect: left, right, up, and down.

4. **Press the spacebar to make that window or document active.**

5. **If you brought up all the active windows in Step 2, you can rotate among the windows of the different active applications by pressing Tab. Use the arrow keys to select a window and the spacebar to make it active.**

Part III

Handling Files (And Other Stuff) Quickly

The 5th Wave   By Rich Tennant

"I tell you, it looks like Danny, it sounds like Danny, but it's NOT Danny!! I think the MAC has created an alias of Danny! You can see it in his eyes - little wrist watch icons!"

Technique 14

Organizing Your Home Directory

Picture this: You're sitting there reading this book. You've got a lovely Macintosh in front of you. Panther — Apple's latest and greatest operating system — is purring along. You might have read Part II of this book and picked up some navigation tips, discovered how to work the Finder, organized your Dock, toyed with contextual menus, and (hopefully) begun using Exposé. But the real question haunting your mind is this: What do I do with all my stuff? That's what we tell you in this Technique.

This chapter is all about your stuff: you know, those files and folders that are in your Home directory, most of which were created by default, and some of which you might have added. The first section of this chapter is a primer on the Home directory, how it's organized, and how you should most efficiently use it. We then take you on a brief tour of your Library folder, which is a special area for special files. The third section delves into the Desktop: what you ought to know about it, and some good ideas on how to use it. Finally, we discuss the Dock in brief, just to make sure that you've really started using it.

Your Stuff, Your Home Directory, and You

Mac OS X revolutionized the way files are managed on the hard drive (for Mac users, at least). This is largely thanks to the more secure, multi-user environment. All users have their own directory, located within the Users directory on the boot operating system's hard drive, as shown in Figure 14-1. Each user's directory is named after the user's *short name,* as entered when the account was created.

• **Figure 14-1:** The Users directory and its contents.

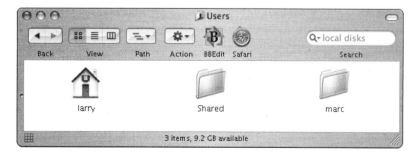

In the Users directory, the current user's Home folder is always marked by a little house icon. (See the folder named *larry* in Figure 14-1.)

Although separating the users this way might seem like a hassle, here are some benefits:

- ✔ **It's more secure:** Each user can only access his or her own files (assuming that folks log in as themselves).

- ✔ **It's safer for the operating system:** Because your stuff is no longer interspersed with the operating system's stuff, you're far less likely to do something that messes up your whole computer. Granted, you can still do something to mess up *your* stuff, but we cover how to avoid doing that, too (see Technique 19).

- ✔ **It's easier to back up:** If you manage your stuff properly, using the format suggested by Apple, you can back up every important item — all your e-mail, documents, pictures, music, and even application preferences settings — simply by backing up this one directory.

- ✔ **It's easier to restore:** Should a disaster ever strike, you can fully recover all of your stuff as long as you have backed up your Home directory. Whether you use backup software or just copy the entire directory to an external drive, restoring your files is never that complicated.

- ✔ **It's easier to transfer:** If you want to move your files from one computer or hard drive to another, copying over the contents of your Home directory does the trick.

- ✔ **Operating system upgrades are less intrusive:** Whereas previous Mac OS upgrades could affect your data, OS X upgrades avoid touching the Users directory altogether, making these transitions less painful.

 The ~ (tilde) within a path name refers to the current user's Home directory. For example, if Marc is logged in, ~ refers to /Users/marc. If Larry is logged in, ~ means /Users/larry. Thus, ~/Documents can stand for either /Users/larry/Documents or /Users/marc/Documents, but it is always the *current* user's Document folder.

By default, your Home directory consists of what you see in Figure 14-2:

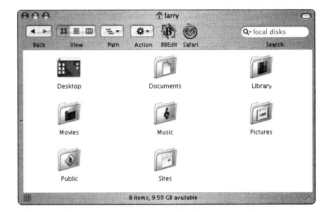

• **Figure 14-2: The standard user's Home directory.**

- ✔ **Desktop:** The Desktop folder contains all the files and folders stored on the Desktop. Even though the Desktop might also show volumes, CDs, DVDs, disk images, and more, those aren't actually in the Desktop folder.

- ✔ **Documents:** The Documents folder was created as a place for you to store your, um, documents (like your Word files, work related projects, downloaded stuff, and more). Things you'll look at, edit, read, delete, create, and so forth all go in the Documents directory.

 The Documents directory should be the folder that you work with the most!

✔ **Library:** The Library could actually be the most important part of your Home folder (or second most important after the Documents folder). The Library stores everything that the operating system needs to know about you. This includes

  ▶ Address Book records

  ▶ iCal calendars

  ▶ Favorites

  ▶ Keychains

  ▶ The Mail application's data

  ▶ Preferences files

  ▶ Web browser bookmarks

  ▶ Stickies contents

Because the Library folder is so important, we discuss it a bit more later in this chapter.

✔ **Movies:** The Movies directory was intended as the default directory for creating movies in iMovie. It's one of the few optional folders in the Home directory.

✔ **Music:** The Music directory is the iTunes equivalent of the Movies directory. It's intended to store your music collection and the text files that iTunes uses to manage that collection.

✔ **Pictures:** The Pictures directory is the iPhoto equivalent of the Movies and Music folders. The iPhoto application uses it by default, but it's also a logical place to store any graphics that you have.

✔ **Public:** The Public folder is a special case. It's designed to provide a storeroom for files that will be accessible by other users on your Macintosh or on your network. Within the Public folder is a Drop Box folder so that others on your Network or Mac can give you files (see Figure 14-3).

 If a number of files need to be accessible by everyone on your Mac (such as your iTunes music), place them in the Shared folder, within the Users directory. Every user can read from and write to this folder, making it a great document management tool.

• **Figure 14-3: Other users can place files in your Drop Box to pass them to you.**

✔ **Sites:** The Sites folder is for Web pages, which can be accessed by going to `http://localhost/~username/` or `http://your.ip.address/~username/` (see Figure 14-4).

• **Figure 14-4: The Sites folder holds Web pages that can be accessible through browsers like Safari.**

Here are our top ten tips for organizing and using your Home directory:

✔ **Don't delete or rename any of the existing folders.**

 As a general rule, you can *add* folders or files to your Home directory, but you should not delete or rename any of the default folders. In particular, tinkering with the Desktop or Library folders would be a grave mistake.

✔ **Use the Desktop as a temporary storage place.**

See "A Cluttered Desktop Is a Sign of a Cluttered Mind," later in this chapter.

✔ **Use the Documents folder for all your documents.**

Go wild with it. Organize your documents as logically as possible, creating subdirectories for files by type (or application), purpose (personal, school, work), and so forth.

 Most applications use the Documents folder as the default place to save or open files. Go with the flow on this point: It will save you endless time spent wandering around your computer in search of a file.

✔ **If you have enough disk space, go ahead and place all your music, movies, and pictures in the appropriate media folders.**

 As you'll see in later Techniques, Apple's iLife applications (iTunes, iPhoto, iMovie, iDVD) can use directories outside of your Home directory for their files.

✔ **If you create Web sites, place all the associated files within the Sites directory, not split between both Sites and Documents.**

✔ **If an application gives you the option of installing it system wide or just for your use, install it just for your use.**

If you install it for yourself, the files go into your Home directory and are retained through any operating system transitions that follow.

✔ **Store smaller-sized software that you simply must have — such as drivers for an input device or printer — in your Home directory so that they'll be easy to find if you need to reinstall them.**

 Create an Installs or Software directory within your Documents folder to store small applications that you will probably need to install again. For example, the driver for your mouse may only be 2MB in size and needs to be reinstalled with every major operating system upgrade. Keeping a copy of the installer saves you a trip online the next time you need to install it.

✔ **Create a text document listing all the software and corresponding serial numbers that you use on your computer — and then store it in your Home folder.**

Print this document out for reference as well (see Technique 20 for tips on recording serial numbers and installed software).

✔ **Add fonts, contextual menu items, AppleScripts, screen savers, and other add-ons to the operating system in the corresponding folders of your Library, not the system library.**

✔ **Back up your entire Home directory frequently, often, regularly, consistently, without fail, and on a regular basis. See Technique 48 for backup utilities and best practices.**

Checking Out Your Library

Most OS X users know little about their Library folder. The Library is, in some ways, the most important item in your Home directory. It contains all the information about you and how you use the computer. Here's a rundown of some of the Library's important folders and how they relate to your use of the computer:

✔ The Application Support folder contains critical files for many applications (check it out in Figure 14-5), including

  ▶ Your Address Book data

  ▶ iCal information (other than calendars)

  ▶ Extensions to the Terminal application

Third-party applications also use the Application Support folder for various reasons:

▶ The LaunchBar utility keeps its settings there.

▶ The Camino Web browser stores preferences and bookmarks.

▶ Big Cat stores AppleScripts for contextual menus.

▶ The Fire list of accounts and preferences is saved here. (*Fire* is an instant messaging application.)

• **Figure 14-5: Many applications add items to your Application Support directory.**

✔ Extra system alert sounds can be added to the Sounds subfolder of the Audio directory.

✔ The Calendars directory stores all your iCal data (see Technique 44).

✔ The ColorSync folder has your ColorSync profiles (see Technique 6).

✔ Contextual Menu Items contains your added CM tools (see Technique 12).

✔ The Favorites folder is where aliases to favorite applications, documents, and folders are kept (see Technique 15).

✔ You can install your own fonts by adding them to Fonts.

✔ Additional plug-ins and tools for iMovie can go in the iMovie folder.

✔ Additional plug-ins and scripts for iTunes can go in the iTunes folder (see Technique 42).

✔ The Keychains folder stores your *keychain,* which contains your passwords (see Technique 52).

✔ The Mail folder has all your Mail application's data.

✔ The Preferences folder contains the preferences files for almost all your applications and even your operating system as a whole.

✔ Safari stuff is stored in the Safari directory (see Figure 14-6).

• **Figure 14-6: The** ~/Library/Safari **folder keeps your bookmarks, viewing history, and more.**

As you can see, pretty much everything except for your applications and your files (images, documents, and what-not) gets stored in the Library directory. For this reason, you should treat it with respect and include it in your daily backups. (You are doing daily backups, right?)

 Aside from backing up your Library folder and possibly adding a few things to it, don't mess around with it unless you really know what you're doing. If you delete something you shouldn't, you can cause yourself a lot of pain.

How Many Libraries Does One Computer Need?

Your Macintosh actually has several Library folders on it . . . three at least. You'll find a Library folder in the root of the system disk (/Library), one under the System folder (/System/Library), and one for each user (~/Library). Strange as this might seem, these libraries all serve approximately the same purpose. The main differences are the priority and scope that each Library has.

The /System folder is basically for Apple and only Apple usage. The /Library folder is primarily for third-party applications and other developers to install items for all users. During OS upgrades, Apple won't mess with the /Library folder but has carte blanche with /System. For example, each of these Libraries might have a Contextual Menu Items folder. Items in your CM folder will only be available to you. Those in the /System/Library CM folder are available to every user on the computer and were probably put there by Apple. In future versions of the operating system, those CM items might be upgraded. Those in the /Library folder are available to all users and should remain unharmed by upgrading the OS. In case you're the curious type, note that the contents of the various libraries are loaded in this order: /Library, /System/Library, ~/Library.

One important consideration with the Libraries is that things stored in either /Library or /System/Library might be replaced with every new installation of an operating system. If you perform an Erase and Install, an Archive and Install, or even an Upgrade, these contents will likely be replaced or overwritten. The contents of your Library folder will remain though, making it a good place to store all your stuff!

A Cluttered Desktop Is a Sign of a Cluttered Mind

The Desktop exists in two worlds. First, it's the base level of the Finder, appearing on your screen underneath everything else (as shown in Figure 14-7). Second, it's another folder within your Home directory that can be used to store your stuff (see Figure 14-8). Yes, that's right: The Desktop is both a dessert topping *and* a floor wax.

• **Figure 14-7: The Desktop as viewed in the Finder.**

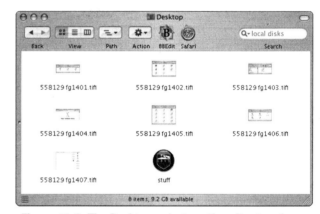

• **Figure 14-8: The Desktop as just another directory in a Finder window.**

The main difference between the Desktop and your other folders is that the Desktop's contents are pretty much always visible because it's the bottom layer (so to speak) of what's on your monitor. On the bright side, anything that's stored there is readily accessible. But if you've got a lot going on there, it can quickly become overwhelming.

Because the Desktop is almost always visible and can become cluttered quickly, we strongly advocate that you use it primarily for temporary storage and to access hard drives, CD-ROMs, and the like. You might even want to create subfolders on the Desktop for longer term (yet still temporary) storage to cut down the mess.

Aside from tinkering with how much stuff is lingering on your Desktop, you can customize its behavior in three ways:

✔ **Use the Desktop & Screen Saver panel of System Preferences (see Figure 14-9).**

This panel allows you to set what color, graphic, or picture is used as the backdrop of the Desktop. Although it's an aesthetic decision, having a visually-pleasing Desktop goes a long way toward preserving your sanity.

To change your Desktop:

1. Control+click the Desktop to bring up the contextual menu.

2. Select Change Desktop Background from the contextual menu.

3. In the resulting window (see Figure 14-9), select a broad category from the left-hand column.

   Only one of the options behaves uniquely: If you click Choose Folder, you are given an Open dialog to find a folder on your hard drive. After you find the folder you want, click Choose or press Return.

4. Click one of the options that appears in the right-hand column to select a specific color or image.

5. Quit the System Preferences panel.

 If you really like eye candy, set the Desktop panel to rotate its picture every so often by using the Change Picture drop-down list. You can also do a hack to make screen savers run as the background to your Desktop. It's a very processor-intensive thing to do, slowing down your computer noticeably, but it's soooo cool. See Technique 61 for instructions and helpful tools.

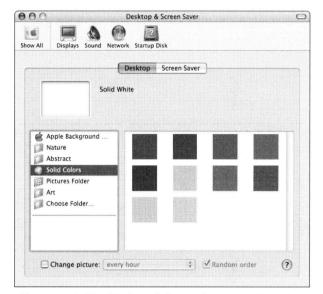

• **Figure 14-9:** The Desktop & Screen Saver panel sets the graphical appearance of your Desktop.

✔ **Use the Finder preferences panel (Figure 14-10), under General.**

Here you can indicate whether you want hard drives, CDs, DVDs, iPods, and connected servers to appear as icons on your Deskop.

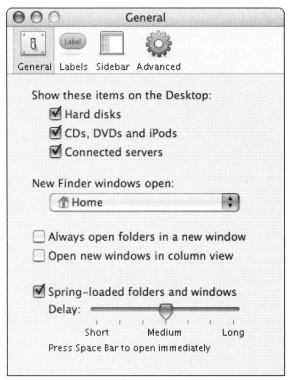

• **Figure 14-10: Use the Finder's preferences to dictate what volumes are mounted on the Desktop.**

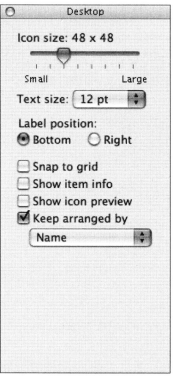

• **Figure 14-11: If no window is selected, the View Options control the Desktop.**

✔ **Use the Show View Options panel (see Figure 14-11), from the Finder's View menu.**

For how your Desktop looks and functions, the Show View Options panel is the most critical of the settings panels. Here you can set

▶ The default size of icons (in pixels)

▶ The default text size for names of items

▶ Whether an item's name (called "label" in this panel) should appear below or beside (to the right of) an item

▶ Whether you want to see an item's info (for example, the dimensions of an image or the size of a hard drive)

▶ Whether you want to see a thumbnail preview of images as their icon

▶ How files should be arranged, if at all

You'll want to set the icon and text sizes so that they're easy to view but don't take up too much space. The arrangement of items is the most important consideration. If you keep them arranged by name, your hard drives, discs, and such appear in the upper-right corner. Remaining items are listed in alphabetical order, just as you'd see them in the list or column view of a Finder window.

Revisiting Our Friend, the Dock

We give a good amount of attention to our friend, the Dock, in Technique 11. Now that you're more familiar with your stuff, we'd like to revisit (or visit, if you haven't read that other technique yet) one aspect of organizing the Dock.

The Dock has two sides: the left, where applications are docked, and the right, which contains the Trash and any folders or files that you choose to dock there. After you get your stuff organized is a good time to add the key components to the Dock. Some of our best recommendations for what should be placed on the right side of the Dock are (see Figure 14-12)

• **Figure 14-12: Larry's Dock, with current projects, his Home folder, and his Favorites all docked.**

✔ Your Home folder itself

✔ Your Documents folder

✔ The folder for any current projects

✔ The Desktop folder, if you really use the Desktop

You can access any directories that you add to the Dock in hierarchical form by Control+clicking the directory's icon (see Figure 14-13). This trick gives you fast access to those files that you'll use the most.

• **Figure 14-13: Control+clicking a docked folder brings up a menu of its contents.**

Technique

15

Managing Aliases, Favorites, and Icons

Save Time By

✓ Working with aliases to establish shortcuts to popular files, directories, and applications

✓ Using Favorites to quickly get to your favorite things

✓ Customizing the icons used for files and folders

The preceding Technique is all about managing your stuff — the files, folders, and miscellaneous junk that clutter a computer — but this one deals with aliases, Favorites, and icons: all the things that give you quick access to the files and folders that you use most.

This chapter has three main sections, each of which takes a tangential approach to the contents of your computer. In the first section, we talk about aliases: what they are, how you create them, and how you'll want to use them. In the second, we go into *Favorites,* which are a specific grouping of aliases. In the final part of this chapter, you find out about icons, which are the visual representation for your stuff.

Also Known As: Working with Aliases

Your computer is loaded (perhaps overloaded) with many different things such as files, folders, and applications. Each of these items is located in a specific spot on your hard drive, represented by an icon and a filename. An *alias* is a secondary pointer to the same item. It can be (and normally is) located in another location; it can have a different name; and it can even have a different icon. However, by default, an item's alias uses the same icon as the original except for the addition of a little, black arrow in the lower-left corner (see the bottom icon of Figure 15-1). The alias is also created with the same filename except that the word *alias* is also appended to the end under most circumstances.

Aliases offer the following benefits:

✓ They allow you to have virtually the same item existing in many locations.

✓ They are relatively small in size. For example, the alias of a 6MB MP3 file might only take up a few KB.

✓ They enable you to create groups of aliases to related items without shuffling around the original items.

They are very easy to create, manage, and delete.

They make accessing files, folders, and applications easier without undermining any organizational structures.

Picture 2

Picture 2 alias

• **Figure 15-1: An alias looks like the original file save for the black, curved arrow.**

Here's how aliases work:

Opening an alias of a file has the same effect as opening the original file.

Opening an alias of an application is the same as opening the application by using its original icon.

Opening an alias of a folder opens the original folder.

Deleting an alias has no effect on the original item at all.

 An alias is *not* a copy of an item. If you open and edit the alias of a file, the effect is the same as if you open and edit the original file. But if you delete an alias, the original remains.

After you select an item, you can create an alias in any of four ways:

Press ⌘+L.

Hold down the Option and ⌘ keys while dragging the item with your mouse.

If you use this method, the cursor turns into the little, curved alias arrow.

 If you use the Option+⌘+drag method to make an alias, it adds the word *alias* to the file's name if you drop the file within the same folder as the original (because a folder cannot contain two items with the same name). If you create the alias in another folder, it does not add the word *alias*. In either case, the curved, black arrow is added to the icon, indicating its alias status.

Go to the Finder's File menu and choose Make Alias (see Figure 15-2).

File	
New Finder Window	⌘N
New Folder	⇧⌘N
Open	⌘O
Open With	▶
Close Window	⌘W
Get Info	⌘I
Duplicate	⌘D
Make Alias	⌘L
Show Original	⌘R
Add To Favorites	⇧⌘T
Create Archive of "ch_14_new_images.zip alias"	
Move To Trash	⌘⌫
Eject	⌘E
Burn Disc...	
Find...	⌘F
Color Label:	

• **Figure 15-2: The Make Alias command is located in the Finder's File menu.**

The operating system makes use of aliases all over the place. Items in the Dock, in the left side of a Finder window, and some menu items are aliases. You may not be aware of these aliases and they may not have the little black, curved arrows, but the principle remains.

✔ **Control+click the item and select Make Alias from the resulting contextual menu.**

To find the original item for an alias, select the alias and do one of the following:

✔ Press ⌘+R.

✔ Choose Show Original from the Finder's File menu.

✔ Control+click the alias and choose Show Original from the contextual menu (see Figure 15-3).

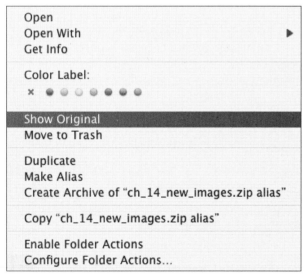

• **Figure 15-3:** You can use an alias' contextual menu to make aliases or find an alias' original file.

Remarkably, aliases continue to work no matter what you do with either the alias or the original file as long as you don't remove either from the volume where it was created. If an alias cannot find the original file, you see a prompt (as shown in Figure 15-4) that allows you to reselect the original or delete the alias.

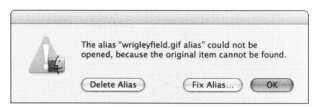

• **Figure 15-4:** Opening an alias whose original file cannot be found generates this prompt.

A UNIX Alias: Symbolic Links

The Macintosh alias is the equivalent of the UNIX *symbolic link* (and the Windows shortcut, too, but who cares about Windows?). A *symbolic link* is just a secondary pointer to the original file, application, or folder. Because Mac OS X is based upon the FreeBSD version of UNIX, you can also make symbolic links in it by using the Terminal application.

The syntax for linking to a file is `ln -s alias_name original_file_name`. If you're not in the same directory as both the original and the alias or if you otherwise want to be exact, you'll probably want to include the path to both the link and the original file: `ln -s /path/to/original_file_name /path/to/alias_name`. If you want to create an alias to a folder, the same syntax applies: for example, `ln -s /Users/larry/Sites /Users/larry/Desktop/Sites_alias` or simply `ln -s ~/Sites ~/Desktop/Sites_alias`. As with standard aliases, a symbolic pointer is created by this command, pointing to the original item.

Like UNIX, with the Mac you can create either hard or soft links. The `-s` option creates a soft link, and omitting it creates a hard one. A *soft link* is exactly like an alias. A *hard link* is like having another copy of the data itself and also has the restriction that hard links cannot traverse volumes. You really should stick to soft links because hard links are likely to cause problems in one way or another.

One advantage that the Mac's aliases have over symbolic links is that you can move an alias from one location to another, and it still works — it finds the original just fine. Conversely, symbolic links can never be moved. They must be deleted and re-created instead.

These are a few of my Favorites things

In Mac OS X, Apple introduced *Favorites:* a collection of aliases for your favorite things. By default, your Favorites were linked as a folder in your Dock, allowing you to access those items by Control+clicking (or clicking and holding) the icon (see Figure 15-5).

• **Figure 15-5: The Favorites folder in the Dock.**

In previous versions of Mac OS X, the ⌘+T shortcut added the selected item to your Favorites, but this feature has been eliminated. (In Panther, that shortcut now adds the item to the Finder window's Sidebar.) But we still like the idea of Favorites, so here's the easiest way to add items to your Favorites:

1. **Open a Finder window.**

2. **Navigate to the Library folder in your Home directory (~/Library).**

3. **Select the Favorites folder (see Figure 15-6).**

• **Figure 15-6: Your Favorites folder is located in your Library.**

4. **Press ⌘+T to add the Favorites to the window's Sidebar (see Figure 15-7).**

 These first four steps add the Favorites folder to the Finder window's Sidebar. You only need to follow these steps once.

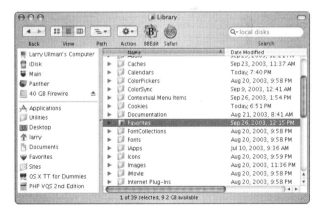

• **Figure 15-7: Your Favorites appear in the Sidebar with a heart-shaped icon.**

5. **From the Finder window, navigate to the item that you want to add to your Favorites.**

6. **Select the item.**

7. Begin dragging the selected item toward the Favorites icon in the Sidebar.

8. While still dragging but before reaching the Favorites icon, hold down the Option and the ⌘ keys so that the Make Alias icon appears with your dragged selection.

9. To confirm that the item was added to your Favorites, click the Favorites icon in the Sidebar to bring up the directory (see Figure 15-8).

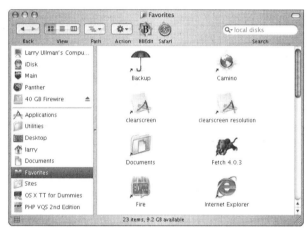

• **Figure 15-8: A Favorites folder, with aliases for applications and directories.**

 Whether you use Favorites is up to you, but the idea of collecting, organizing, and accessing a collection of aliases to your favorite applications, documents, and files is one worth pursuing. After you place items in your Favorites folder, you can quickly launch applications, open files, or find directories using the Favorites link in the Sidebar or the Dock.

 You don't have to limit yourself to only one Favorites folder. Create a second or a third Favorites folder and then add these folders to your primary Favorites directory. This way you can have subgroups of applications by use or files by project. Many sequences of steps that you frequently take can be expedited by using aliases and Favorites.

If you can, icon

An *icon* is the visual representation of an item, and it tells you a lot about the item in question. Knowing how icons work and how to manipulate them goes a ways toward more productively using your computer. Here are some basics:

✔ All folders use a default icon that looks like a, well, folder.

✔ Files use an icon showing what application they're associated with.

✔ Applications normally use their own custom icon.

How your computer treats icons is dictated by the View Options panel (see Figure 15-9). You can bring this up by pressing ⌘+J or choosing Show View Options from the View menu. The View Options menu controls these icon settings:

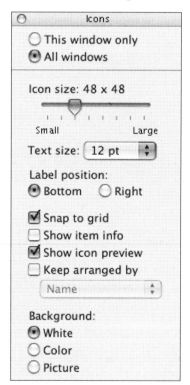

• **Figure 15-9: The View Options panel controls icon settings, among other things.**

✔ The icon size in pixels

✔ The size of the text associated with an icon (the item's name)

✔ Where the item's name (called the "label" in the Show View Options panel) appears (underneath or beside the icon)

✔ How icons are arranged on the Desktop or in a window

In icon view mode only, you can dictate if and how icons are automatically arranged. Your options are by: Name, Data Modified, Date Created, Size, Kind, and Label.

 Select the Show Icon Preview check box under the View Options panel to have all images represented by a thumbnail of the actual image. This feature is nice but can slow down your computer when you open directories with lots of images.

 The View Options panel is also discussed in Technique 10, which covers how to customize the Finder windows.

In all likelihood, you're not going to change the default icons for your files or applications, but you could (and frequently should) use new icons for your folders. Doing so helps you more easily recognize a particular folder, whether it's in a Finder window or the Dock. You can create your own icons by using Adobe Photoshop, the open source The Gimp application, or other graphics software (see the sidebar "Making Your Own Icons"), or you can download icons that others have made. Check out these sites:

✔ **The Iconfactory:** www.iconfactory.com

✔ **Xicons.com:** www.xicons.com

✔ **ResExcellence:** www.resexcellence.com

Making Your Own Icons

If you're graphically inclined, you can make your own custom icons without much effort. Two popular tools for doing so are Folder Icon Maker X (http://homepage.mac.com/niteowl169, $5) and IconBuilder Pro (www.iconfactory.com/ib_home.asp, $70), an add-on tool for Adobe Photoshop. A free alternative is Viou (http://perso.wanadoo.fr/prime). We haven't used this last application ourselves but the price is right and it looks promising.

Here, for example, is how to use Folder Icon Maker X to create a custom folder icon for Microsoft Word documents:

1. **Launch Folder Icon Maker X.**

   You'll see its main window with a generic folder icon already loaded.

2. **Find the Microsoft Word application in your Applications folder.**

3. **Drag the Microsoft Word icon into the lower-right quarter of the folder icon of Folder Icon Maker X (as shown in this figure).**

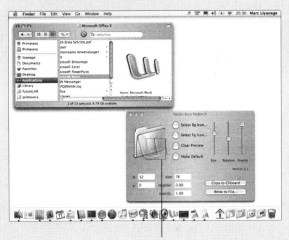

Drag the icon to be customized here.

(continued)

4. **Move the Word icon around and resize it until it fits your taste (check it out in the figure).**

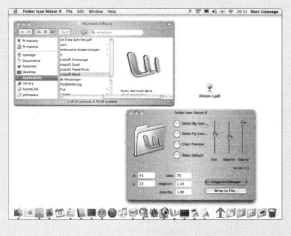

5. **Click the Copy to Clipboard button.**

6. **To use this new icon for an existing folder, follow the steps that we give for changing an icon.**

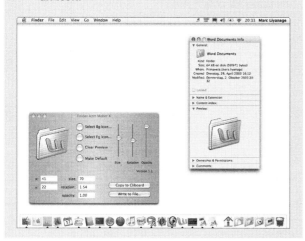

To change an item's icon:

1. Create or find the new icon image that you want to use.

2. Select the new icon.

A border appears around it, as shown in Figure 15-10.

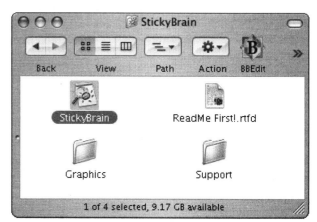

• **Figure 15-10:** To change an icon, first select a replacement image.

3. Press ⌘+I to bring up the Get Info panel (see Figure 15-11) for the new icon.

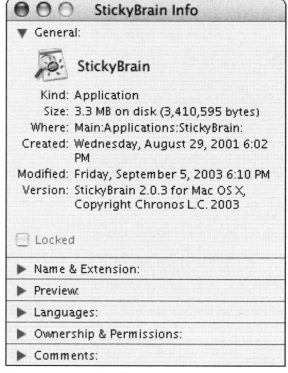

• **Figure 15-11:** Use the Get Info panel to copy or change an item's icon.

4. Click the icon in the General part of the Get Info panel to select it.

5. Press ⌘+C to copy the icon.

6. Select the item whose icon you want to replace (see Figure 15-12).

7. Bring up the Get Info panel again.

8. Select the icon in the Get Info Panel and press ⌘+V to paste in the new icon (see Figure 15-13).

• **Figure 15-13:** The same folder with its new image.

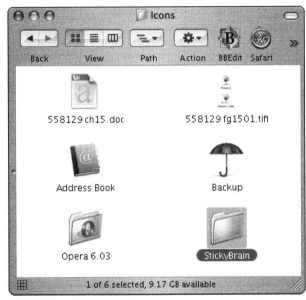

• **Figure 15-12:** Selecting the folder whose icon will be changing.

To restore an item's icon to its default:

1. Select the item whose icon you want to restore.

2. Bring up the Get Info panel (press ⌘+I).

3. Select the icon in the Get Info panel.

4. Press the Delete key to delete the icon.

Technique 16

Managing Information Effectively

Save Time By

✔ Making the most of the Address Book

✔ Knowing what applications are available for storing and accessing tidbits of information

In this Technique, we delve into the applications that you'll use to manage your information. This Technique helps you organize that conventional desk drawer crammed with a traditional address book and a thousand slips of paper.

The first application to discuss is the Address Book, which is much more useful and important than you might think. It "only" manages a list of people and contact information, but that's a pretty big task. Secondly, we list a few scrapbook-like applications such as Apple's Stickies, Chronos's StickyBrain, and Omni Group's OmniOutliner. Each of these can be used to manage and organize sporadic bits of information, sort of like an electronic Post-it note.

Getting to Know the Address Book

The Address Book has been around since the beginning of OS X, although the new features added in Panther make it even more useful than ever. Those features include

✔ The ability to print mailing labels

✔ Autoformatting phone numbers

✔ Creating your own default templates for records

✔ Listing relations, friends, and associates for the people in your Address Book

BuddyPop (projects.tynsoe.org/en/, $6) creates a pop-up window for Address Book records. You can use it to navigate to and display records as a pop-up window underneath the menu bar (see Figure 16-1).

• **Figure 16-1:** BuddyPop gives you access to Address Book records without opening up the Address Book.

One good reason to use the default applications that Apple includes with the operating system (like the Address Book, Mail, and iTunes) is how well they work together. Take the Address Book, for example. If you use it to store and manage your contacts, you'll appreciate how nicely it works with Mail. Most of what the Address Book does is self-explanatory, so in this Technique, we cover a few techniques and habits that you might not be aware of . . . but might find useful.

 If you use the Address Book a lot, make sure that you back up the contents just in case of disaster. The Address Book database will be stored in your Home directory (in the Library folder), but you can manually back it up by choosing Back Up Database under the Address Book's File menu.

 If you have Bluetooth and a Bluetooth-enabled cellular phone, you can dial phone numbers by using the Address Book (see Technique 54).

Customizing the Template

When you add contacts to your Address Book, you're given a default template with set fields of records that can be entered for each contact, such as name, e-mail address, and so on. In all likelihood, these preset fields and formats don't adequately reflect the information that you want to record or use. The first thing that you should do with the Address Book is to customize this default template.

 Taking the time once to create a default Address Book template makes adding or editing records easier and more efficient. Also, understand that changing the template does *not* delete nor change any previously existing records. The template only determines what fields are part of *new* records — not what information is recorded or displayed.

To customize the default Address Book application:

1. **Open the Address Book application.**

2. **Choose Preferences from the File menu or press ⌘+, (that's a comma).**

3. **In the Preferences dialog that appears, click Template (see Figure 16-2).**

• **Figure 16-2:** The Template panel allows you to customize the Address Book's default template.

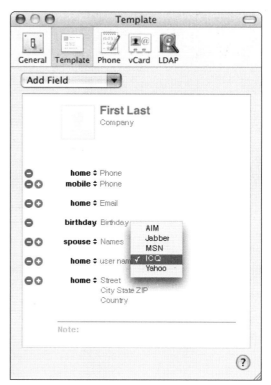

• **Figure 16-3:** You can access more options by clicking the up and down arrows to create this pop-up menu.

4. **Begin by changing any existing fields that you don't like to ones that you will use.**

For example:

▶ If you want the template to have a home phone field by default but no work phone, change the work phone listing by clicking the word *work* next to Phone and selecting *home* from the pull-down menu that appears.

▶ If you want to list a person's spouse instead of friend or assistant, click the word next to Names (this is "spouse" by default) and select the appropriate alternative from the pull-down menu that appears.

▶ If AOL Instant Messenging (AIM) isn't the instant messaging application that you use most often, change it to another from the drop-down menu, as shown in Figure 16-3.

5. **Delete all the fields that you won't be using by default by clicking the red minus sign next to an item to remove it.**

 Your Address Book records must have the First (name), Last (name), Company, image, and Note fields. These are the only ones that cannot be deleted.

6. **Add multiple fields of the same type using the green button with the plus sign on it.**

If you want to have several phone options or e-mail listings in your default template, click the green plus button to add another field of that type. Then select a description from the pull-down menu. For example, add another e-mail address by clicking the green button next to

Email (marked as "home"). Then choose "work", "other", or "custom" from the new field's pull-down menu.

7. **Use the drop-down menu at the top of the window to add any additional fields that you desire.**

Use the top menu (see Figure 16-4) to add new fields (like a birthday or nickname) or standard ones that you've removed (e-mail addresses and phone numbers).

• **Figure 16-4:** Use the Add Field menu to add fields not currently listed in the template.

8. **When you finish creating the template, close the Preferences window by clicking the Close button or pressing ⌘+W.**

 After you finish defining the Address Book template, go to the Phone panel, where you can establish the default format for phone numbers (see Figure 16-5). If you check the Automatically Format Phone Numbers box, those numbers that match the default format are formatted, while others (like international numbers) are safely left alone.

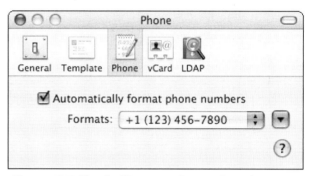

• **Figure 16-5:** Use the Phone panel to set the default format for phone numbers.

Creating Your Own vCard

The Address Book uses the *vCard* format, which is the default format for personnel records. If you create your own record in the Address Book (the application creates a record for you automatically), you can export the record as a vCard and e-mail it to friends or co-workers. They can then import it into their own contacts application, whether they use Address Book or another such as Mail or Microsoft Entourage, which saves them the trouble of typing in the information.

1. **Open the Address Book application.**

2. **Navigate to your record by choosing Go to My Card from the Card menu (you can see one in Figure 16-6).**

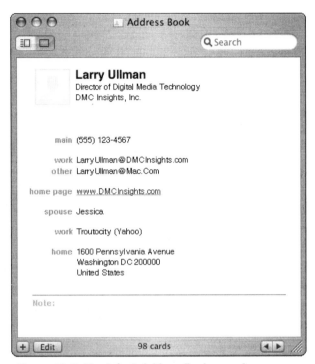

• **Figure 16-6: My default Address Book record.**

 You can have more than one record for yourself (or anyone), but you can only mark one as your official record in the Address Book. This way, you can make different records for personal or business purposes.

3. Click the Edit button at the bottom of the card panel.

 You can toggle between edit and view mode with the ⌘+L keyboard shortcut.

4. Edit your information, adding, changing, and removing fields as necessary.

 You can add other fields to the card by using the Add Field option under the Card menu.

5. Add your image — if you want — by double-clicking the image icon.

Double-clicking the image icon in the edit mode brings up the image panel (see Figure 16-7). With it, you can

▶ Drag an image file from the Finder into the window.

▶ Use an attached video camera to take a snapshot of yourself.

 If you have a FireWire video camera connected to your computer — like one you would use for video conferencing with iChat — your mug appears in this window. You can capture yourself by clicking on Take Video Snapshot.

▶ Click the Choose button to navigate to and select the image to use.

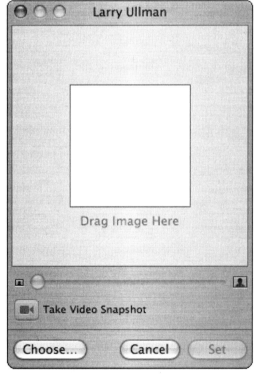

• **Figure 16-7: The image panel lets you add a graphical or pictorial representation of yourself to your card.**

After you select your image, click Set to apply the changes. Then you return to the Card panel, where you can continue editing your record.

6. **When you're done editing your record, click the Edit button to complete the changes.**

7. **Choose Export vCard from the File menu.**

8. **Save the vCard (see Figure 16-8).**

   You'll most likely want to use your name as the name of the file (with no file extension) and save it in your Documents or other subfolder of your Home directory.

• **Figure 16-8: Export your vCard to your Documents directory.**

After you create your vCard, you can attach it to e-mails so that people will be able to add your record to their virtual Rolodex (whether they use Address Book or not). If fact, adding and editing your own card is a great way to feel comfortable with the process and the application for when you start adding other people's information.

You can also access the Export vCard option by Control+clicking your record and choosing Export vCard from the contextual menu that appears.

If someone e-mails you a vCard, add it to your Address Book by dragging and dropping it onto the application.

Technique 33 shows how using the ⌘+Y shortcut, within the Mail application, creates an Address Book entry for the sender of the currently selected (or viewed) e-mail.

Creating and Using Groups

The final Address Book technique that we demonstrate is how to create a group. Every record in your Address Book can also be a member of one or more groups. (They don't have to be, though; a record can be independent of all groups.) Defining groups brings you three main benefits:

- ✔ Better organization for finding a record
- ✔ Ability to send an entire group (like your family) updated contact information with the click of a button
- ✔ Ability to send e-mails to a defined set of people, such as everyone in your department, by referring to the group name in the Mail application

You can create a group in three ways: by using the New Group From Selection tool, manually, or by duplicating an existing group.

Using the New Group From Selection tool

The fastest way to create a new group is to choose New Group From Selection from the File menu.

1. **Click All under Groups to display every record.**

2. **⌘+click the names listed in the Names column to select the group members.**

3. Choose New Group From Selection from the File menu (see Figure 16-9).

• **Figure 16-9:** The New Group From Selection option eases the group creation process.

4. Enter the new group's name.

After Step 3, a new group is created in the Group column. This new group's name ("Group Name" by default) is highlighted, ready for you to start typing the new name.

5. Press Return to complete the transaction.

Creating a group manually

To create a group manually:

1. Make sure that you're in Card and Columns view mode by selecting it from the View menu or by pressing ⌘+1 (see Figure 16-10).

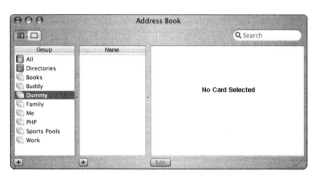

• **Figure 16-10:** Card and Columns view mode is easier to navigate than Card mode.

2. Click the plus sign in the lower left-hand corner to create a new group.

3. Type the new group's name in the new, highlighted field that appears (see Figure 16-11).

• **Figure 16-11:** When you add a new group, it's given a default name that you can easily change.

4. Search or browse through the Address Book names, adding people to the new group by dragging their card onto the group name.

5. To delete a group member, select the member's name from under the group listing and then press the Delete key.

Press Return at the prompt that appears (see Figure 16-12) to remove the user from this group only and not from the Address Book as a whole.

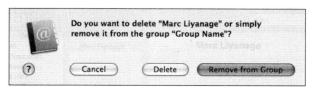

• **Figure 16-12:** Deleting a user from a group asks you to clarify just what your intentions are.

Duplicating an existing group

If you want to create a new group that contains some of the members of an existing group, you might want to simply duplicate the existing group and edit members accordingly. Here's how:

1. **Select the existing group in the group listing in the left-hand column.**

2. **Choose Edit⇨Copy or press ⌘+C.**

3. **Choose Edit⇨Paste or press ⌘+V to create a copy of that group.**

4. **Rename the new group (called *Old Group Name* copy) by clicking the group's name.**

5. **Edit the group's members by using the steps outlined in the preceding section.**

Other Cool Address Book Tricks

Apple put a lot of thought into the Address Book, and it has its fair share of cool tricks. Here are the ones that you should know, in case you don't:

- ✔ If you change your contact information, use the Send Updates option (under the File menu) to automatically e-mail your new information to others. By selecting among the groups you have already created, your friends and family can be notified every time you move or change Internet providers.

- ✔ Click the address link for a home page to go to that site.

- ✔ Click a person's e-mail address to be given a prompt to e-mail them (see Figure 16-13).

• **Figure 16-13:** The pop-up menu for e-mail addresses in the Address Book.

- ✔ Click a person's phone number to see it in large type.

- ✔ Add a phonetic field to records to remind yourself how a name is pronounced. (It's up to you to master the International Phonetic Alphabet.)

- ✔ Click an address to be given the option of seeing a map for that address via MapQuest (see Figure 16-14).

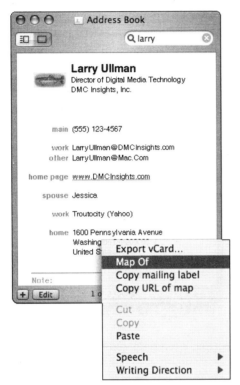

LDAP Servers

Many organizations, especially larger ones, store information about people (such as employees, customers, and suppliers) in central LDAP (Lightweight Directory Access Protocol) directories. *LDAP* is a protocol for querying directories capable of holding information about millions of people, and Apple's Address Book is able to look up people in such directory services. The Directories group in the Groups column in Address Book was created for this purpose.

You add new directories by using the LDAP tab in the preferences panel. There, you can add servers by clicking the plus sign at the bottom of the window. This brings up the Add a Directory panel, as shown in this figure.

In the Name box, give the directory any name you want. The server name, which you enter in the Server box, is the most important consideration. This will be something like `ldap.company.com`. Some servers require you to authenticate yourself with a username and password as well, so those values can be entered by using this interface. Check with your network administrator (or whomever controls the LDAP server) for what the proper connection values should be. When you enter all the required fields (including Search Base, Port, and Scope), click Save.

To search for people in a directory server that you configured this way, open the Directories group and then click the name that you gave your directory. Type a few letters of the name or e-mail address of the person whom you're looking for into the Search text field in the top-right corner of the window. You will get a list of all entries containing these letters, as shown here.

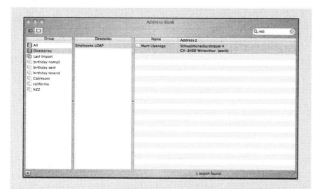

Double-click one of the entries to view that person's record. If you know that you'll need the contact information again, drag the list entry over to your All group to create a local copy in your Address Book. This way, you have access to the information even when you're not connected to a network.

Organizing and Prioritizing Information

If you're like us, you have lots of little bits of information floating around your head, office, and computer. The ability to find little things — like a person's name, a quote, a computer command, your to-do list, or whatever — determines whether you'll be productive or struggling to keep your head above water in a sea of chaos. We'll briefly discuss the many applications that you can use for these purposes.

Storing random bits of data as Stickies

If you're not already using *Stickies* — an Apple application that comes with the operating system — you're missing out on a useful little tool for storing little tidbits of stuff. Stickies are essentially small text files with Post-It Note–like behavior. Unlike using Text Edit, with Stickies you can create color-coded notes, quickly make a note using Services (see Technique 27), and keep a note at the front of your screen while you're using another application.

Some good Stickies tips include the following:

- In the Finder and any other Carbon application (like Mail, Safari, TextEdit, and the Address Book), create a new Stickie note out of highlighted text by pressing ⌘+Shift+Y.

- Use different colored Stickies for different purposes (see Figure 16-15). You can change a note's color using the Color menu and the fonts using the Font menu or the Font palette (accessible by pressing ⌘+T).

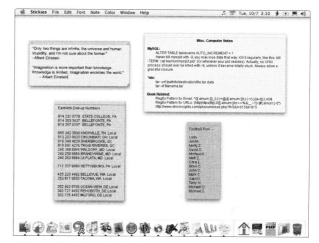

• Figure 16-15: Each Stickie note uses a color that helps you remember whether it's personal, work related, and so forth.

- After you find a note color and style that you like, choose the Use as Default option under the Note menu to have your Stickies created in that format by default.

- Check the spelling in a note from the contextual menu (Control+click a note) or choose Edit➪ Spelling.

- Stickies support Services (see Technique 27), meaning that you can access many different shortcuts from within the Stickies application (see Figure 16-16).

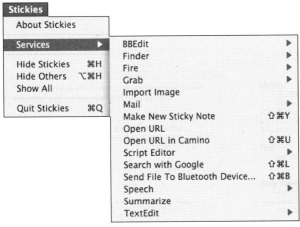

• **Figure 16-16:** Services provide quick access to common tasks.

✔ Have a Stickie float above other applications by clicking it and pressing ⌘+Shift+F or choosing Floating Window from the Note menu. A floating Stickie will never be hidden by other applications (it always appears at the "front" of the screen).

✔ Stickies can also store images, videos, and sounds. This capability makes Stickies much like the long-gone Scrapbook application.

 If you like Stickies, you'll really like StickyBrain, from Chronos (www.chronosnet.com, $40). StickyBrain takes the idea behind Stickies and turns it into a full-fledged, potent application. It includes graphic backgrounds, different types of lists, a search feature, and much, much more.

Prioritizing with to-do lists

If you really need an application for managing your to-do lists — and you want something more advanced than just Stickies or a text application — well, have we got some suggestions for you! Here are two solid shareware applications whose main purpose is to create and manage to-do lists:

✔ **Check Off** (www.ricciadams.com, $5) places a to-do list in the menu bar where you can add to it and mark items as completed.

✔ **BurnoutMenu** (www.clichesw.com, $6) also places a to-do list in the menu bar. Further, it manages multiple to-do lists and works with *iCal*, which is the calendar application that comes with Mac OS X.

Getting organized with outlining applications

Outlining applications are tools to create lists with a structure. Unlike TextEdit or even Microsoft Word, outlining applications make it easier to stay organized, come up with game plans, and stay on top of your information. Whether you are planning a Web site, developing software, or writing a book, an outlining application manages your information for you, making you more productive and keeping key ideas from slipping through the cracks.

 Obviously, you can create outlines with almost any application, from Stickies or TextEdit to Microsoft Word or QuarkXPress. The main benefit of a formal outlining application is the ease with which it sorts, structures, and manages your content.

✔ **OmniOutliner** from the good people at Omni Group (www.omnigroup.com, $30) is Marc's favorite outlining application, possibly his favorite application of all. It can be a very basic tool, but it also expands to fit your needs. It even performs calculations for you.

✔ **Inspiration** (www.inspiration.com, $70) is higher priced than OmniOutliner but more advanced. For example, Inspiration can create visual (graphical) outlines and flowcharts.

Technique 17

Working with Files

Save Time By

- ✔ Comprehending how Panther treats files
- ✔ Working with the Get Info panel
- ✔ Troubleshooting common file problems

This, the third part of the book, is all about your stuff: where to put it, how to file it, and what to do with all the things that fill up a computer. In this technique, we talk about files (as opposed to folders or applications) and Panther. We should, therefore, talk a little bit about how the operating system treats your stuff. Being able to comprehend and make the most of this relationship (between the operating system and your files) goes a long way towards being able to use your computer more readily.

We begin by discussing a file's properties. This includes Panther's naming conventions, locking files, how to add comments, and more. Then we conclude with how to solve some common file problems that most users encounter eventually. In the process, we get a little technical but not overwhelmingly so. After all, the benefit of owning a Mac is that you don't need to be a rocket scientist to use it.

Understanding a File's Properties

The files on your computer have many properties, such as name, extension, size, and type. You'll work with filenames more than any other property, but understanding and manipulating the other file properties effectively is also important. Doing so can make the time that you spend on your computer more efficient and secure.

 Most of a file's properties can be parameters for advanced searches (see Technique 18).

You can discern some file properties, such as name, extension, size (depending upon how the window is customized), type, and default opening application, just by looking at the file in the Finder (see Figure 17-1).

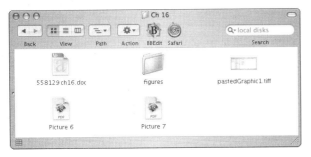

• **Figure 17-1: You can tell a lot about a file just by looking at its name and icon in the Finder.**

These and other properties are not only viewable but also editable in the Get Info panel. If you're not familiar with it, it's about time to become so. After you select a file, you can bring up the Get Info panel by

- ✔ Control+clicking and choosing Get Info from the contextual menu.

- ✔ Pressing ⌘+I.

- ✔ Choosing Get Info from the File menu.

We discuss the Get Info panel extensively in this Technique (and you use it often in day-to-day Panther usage), so you really should get to know your way around it. In this Technique, we go through its subparts and how they relate to you and your stuff. Note that each item on the Get Info panel has a right-pointing arrow next to it: Click that arrow to expand its section and see more information, as shown in Figure 17-2.

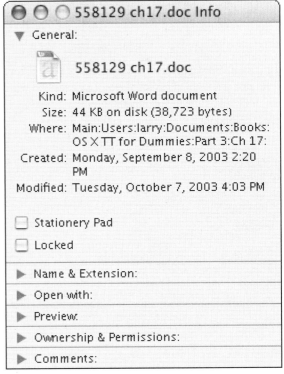

• **Figure 17-2: Most of the Get Info panel's subparts are hidden until you expand them.**

The General panel

The General panel shows you the basics, almost all of which can appear in the list view mode of the Finder window. The only two things that you can change here are

- ✔ **Stationery Pad:** If you select the Stationery Pad check box, the currently selected file becomes a template with its own special icon (see Figure 17-3). When you open a Stationery Pad file, Panther creates and opens a copy of it, allowing you to work with the copy without altering the original.

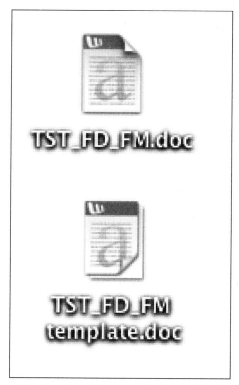

• **Figure 17-3:** Template files use a slight modification of the default file type.

✔ **Locked:** If you enable the Locked check box, the file is safeguarded against changes or incidental deletions. A locked file's icon features a small padlock (see the bottom file icon in Figure 17-4). Locked files can be opened but not deleted nor altered.

Lock a file to protect it from being changed or removed.

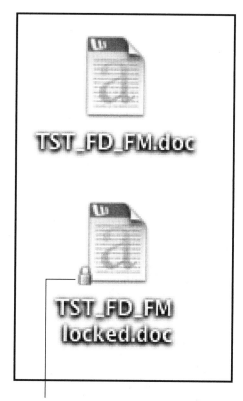

The locked icon

• **Figure 17-4:** Locked files have a little padlock on their icon.

The Name & Extension panel

You likely know what a file's name is and what it means. (If you don't, perhaps it's time you pick up Bob Levitus's *Mac OS X Panther For Dummies,* Wiley Publishing, Inc.) You can change a file's name by these three methods:

✔ Click the filename in the Finder and type the new name.

✔ Select the item, press Return, and type the new name.

✔ Type the new name in the Name & Extension box of the Get Info panel (see Figure 17-5).

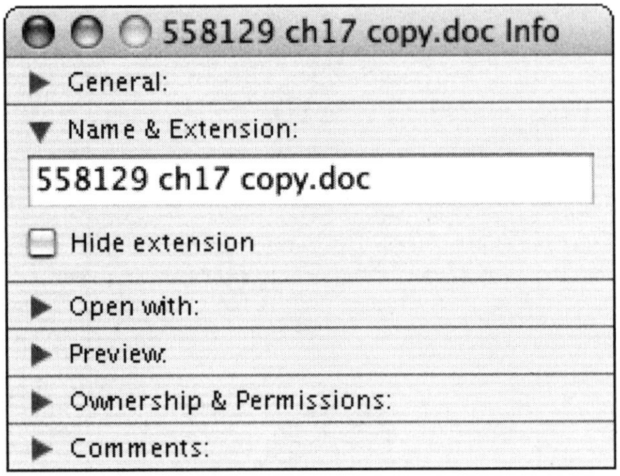

● ● ○ 558129 ch17 copy.doc Info

▶ General:

▼ Name & Extension:

558129 ch17 copy.doc

☐ Hide extension

▶ Open with:

▶ Preview:

▶ Ownership & Permissions:

▶ Comments:

• **Figure 17-5:** The Name & Extension section of a file's Get Info panel.

Panther has very few rules for how to name a file, except for these:

- ✔ Filenames cannot begin with a period.

- ✔ Filenames cannot contain a semicolon.

- ✔ Filenames should not contain a slash.

- ✔ The maximum filename length is 255 characters, although you might not be able to see a filename this large under many conditions.

- ✔ Two files within the same directory cannot have the same name.

 Strangely enough, you can change the name or even the location of a file without disrupting the Recent Documents listing in the Finder and applications. This is because the operating system uses a secret, hidden method of referring to files rather than the more obvious name and location.

How Panther Identifies a File

Instead of relying upon name and location to identify a file, as you or we might, Panther assigns identifying numbers to them. These values never change regardless of what you do to the file, short of deleting it. (This is very similar to the way Panther assigns identifying numbers to running applications, or, technically, processes.)

The beauty of this system is that it allows you to make all sorts of modifications to a file without concern for causing problems or rendering the file unusable.

Although a file's extension is an issue that has been mostly hidden from Mac users over the years, it's critical for many reasons. The file's extension (and kind, which is related) dictates what application is used by default to open it (see "The Open With panel" section next). You can change a file's extension by

- ✔ Changing the file's name in the Finder, if the extension is also shown

 Hide or show a file's extension by checking the appropriate box in the Name & Extension panel (refer to Figure 17-5).

- ✔ Typing the filename and its new extension in the Name & Extension part of the Get Info panel

When you change a file's extension, Panther displays a prompt (see Figure 17-6) confirming whether you truly want to make this change because it will affect what application is used to open it. Unfortunately, you can't avoid this prompt — Panther is trying to behave in your best interest. Most commonly, you might change the extensions on text files, Web pages, and downloaded files. Doing so is not really a problem — primarily it just affects what application will open the file by default — and you can also change the file's extension back, if necessary.

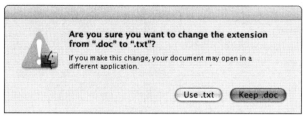

• **Figure 17-6:** Before you can change a file's extension, you must confirm the action through this prompt.

 Deleting a file's extension in the Finder is the same as selecting the Hide Extension check box in the Get Info panel. Hiding or deleting an extension does not affect which application the file is associated with.

The Open With panel

The Open With panel shows you what application opens a file by default. The pull-down menu also allows you to change this setting for a particular file. The Change All button lets you enact the change for every file of this type. See Technique 23 for more.

The Preview panel

The Preview panel, as you might expect, shows you a preview of the file. For many file types (text files, spreadsheets, Web pages, and more), you see only the file's icon (see Figure 17-7). For image file types, this panel shows a thumbnail of the image itself (see Figure 17-8). With movies and sound files, you can actually play them by clicking the Play button of the preview (the right-pointing triangle, Figure 17-9).

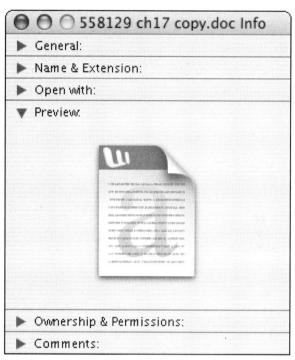

• **Figure 17-7:** The preview of a Word document.

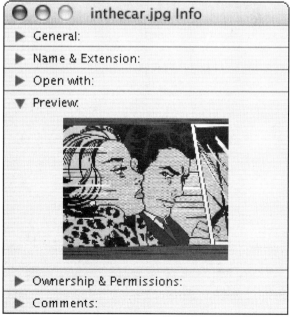

• **Figure 17-8:** The preview of an image file.

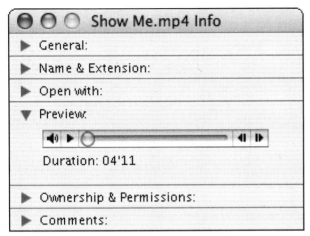

• **Figure 17-9:** The preview of an MP3 allows you to play the sound file.

 The Preview panel of the Get Info panel is replicated by the column view mode of a Finder window, where the final column is used for the preview.

The Ownership & Permissions panel

The Ownership & Permissions panel of the Get Info panel is its most complex panel because it's based upon a UNIX concept (see the "UNIX Permissions" sidebar if you really want to know more). The first rule for this area is not to mess with it unless you really know what you're doing.

 Permissions are a sticky subject. Toying with them without fully understanding the ramifications can affect the security and operability of your system.

UNIX Permissions

The UNIX operating systems have an elaborate set of permissions for files and folders based upon who owns a file and who can do what with it. It all starts with the owner and the group.

By default, the owner of a file is whoever created it — in Panther, that means your short username for most of your stuff. Permissions are also based upon groups. Again, by default, this will be the group that the owner is a member of. Of course, a user can be part of many different groups, too, in which case one of those groups will be used.

The UNIX command for changing an owner — which must be entered using the Terminal — is

    chown *owner filename*

Of course, you'll need to be an administrative level user in order to do this. To change the group, you would use

    chgrp *group filename*

or, conversely,

    chown *owner:group filename*

The second file permissions issue is who can do what with the file. The options are read, write, and execute (for a file) or search (for a directory). Each of these options can be specified for the owner, for the group, or for everyone. The options for a specific file are represented in the Terminal by a string of eight letters, as shown in the figure here. Starting from the left, the first letter represents owner write, and the string is read across in the following order: read, execute; group write, read, execute; and everyone write, read, execute. A *w* means writable, *r* means readable, and *x* means executable/searchable. A dash means that the permission is not granted, and an initial *d* indicates that the file is actually a directory.

```
000                    Terminal — bash (ttyp1)
Larry-Ullmans-Computer:~/Documents/Books/OS X TT for Dummies/Part 3/Ch 17 larry$ ls -al
total 184
drwxr-xr-x   6 larry  larry   204  7 Oct 16:40 .
drwxr-xr-x  12 larry  larry   408 30 Sep 11:55 ..
-rw-r--r--   1 larry  larry  6148 24 Sep 17:31 .DS_Store
-rw-r--r--   1 larry  larry 36864  7 Oct 16:06 558129 ch17 copy.doc
-rw-r--r--   1 larry  larry 39936  7 Oct 16:40 558129 ch17.doc
drwxr-xr-x   3 larry  larry   102 24 Sep 17:28 figures
Larry-Ullmans-Computer:~/Documents/Books/OS X TT for Dummies/Part 3/Ch 17 larry$
```

In the figure, for example, the file `558129 ch17.doc` has read permissions for everyone and write permissions for `larry`. The owner is `larry`, who is part of the group `larry`.

Assuming that you have the permission to do so, you can change permissions by using `chmod`. The syntax is

    chmod *permissions file*

The permissions are assigned by using a three-digit number (although they can also be adjusted by using an alphabetic system). The first of the three numbers represents the owner's permission, the second is the group, and the third is everyone else (others). Each number is made by adding up the write permissions (worth 4), read permissions (2), and search/execute permissions (1). A file with 777 permissions is writable, readable, and executable by everyone. To give yourself write and read permissions and everyone else just read permissions on a file, use

```
chmod 622 filename
```

For more information on any of these tools, type **man chmod**, **man chgrp**, or **man chown** in the Terminal.

The Comments panel

Adding comments to files, folders, and applications has been part of the Mac operating system for years, although most people don't use them much. Panther has added a feature — the ability to show comments in a Finder window — that can make them more useful. As an example:

1. Select the file in the Finder.

2. Press ⌘+I to bring up the Get Info panel.

3. Click the arrow for the Comments box if it's not currently pointing down.

4. In the box, type any comments that you want to add (see Figure 17-10).

5. Close the panel by clicking the red Close button in the upper left-hand corner.

6. Set your window to list view by clicking the icon in the toolbar or by pressing ⌘+1.

7. Customize the window settings by choosing Show View Options from the View menu or by pressing ⌘+J.

8. In the list of options, enable the check box next to Comments.

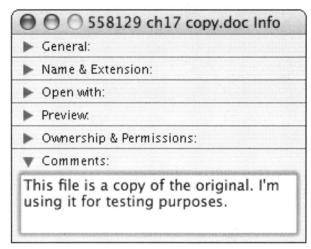

• **Figure 17-10:** Add comments to a file by using the Get Info panel.

9. Close the View Options panel by pressing ⌘+J or clicking the red Close button.

You should now see your comments in the Finder window (see Figure 17-11).

• **Figure 17-11:** With Panther, you can show comments in the list view mode.

 You can use comments to remind yourself of the purpose or contents of a file. If a comment is too long to view in the window, hover your cursor over it to view the whole thing in a popup window (as shown in Figure 17-12).

• **Figure 17-12:** Long comments, like long filenames, can be seen by hovering the cursor over them.

Shareware Alternatives

If you really, really get into manipulating a file's properties (you know who you are), check out these shareware applications to facilitate the process.

✔ Bare Bones's Super Get Info (www.barebones.com, $20) makes altering a file's type (or kind) easier. It also lets you work with invisible files and empty the Trash even when the Finder says you can't.

✔ piDog Software's InfoDog (pidog.com/infodog/, $10 suggested) is similar to Super Get Info but also has a file browser built into it.

✔ Marc likes File Buddy (www.skytag.com/filebuddy/, $38), which is like a Get Info tool and file utility all in one. It not only helps you manage individual files but also provides system-wide features and troubleshooting techniques.

Solving Common File Problems

You likely won't have too many problems when dealing with files in your operating system, but they will occur occasionally. Here's your file-specific troubleshooting guide:

 You'll minimize some problems by using the Repair Disk Permissions tool in the Disk Utility. Run this monthly on the disk volume that contains the operating system for smoother sailing.

Deleting locked files

As a security feature, locked files cannot be trashed. There is absolutely no keyboard shortcut to override this. The only way to delete a locked file is to unlock it first.

1. Select the file in the Finder.

2. Press ⌘+I to bring up the Get Info panel.

3. Select the Locked check box to unlock it.

4. Close the panel by clicking the red Close button in the upper-left corner.

5. Go ahead and delete the file as you normally would.

 If you don't want to see the confirmation prompt every time you go to empty the Trash, disable Show Warning Before Emptying the Trash under the Finder's Advanced preferences (see Figure 17-13).

• **Figure 17-13:** The show warning option is an extra level of protection or annoyance, depending upon your tastes.

Ejecting stuck disk images

A somewhat common occurrence is that you cannot eject a disk image (whether a mounted hard drive, a CD-ROM, or whatever). This usually happens because Panther thinks that the disk is currently in use. Even if you promise Panther that it isn't, your options are limited. Here are three good ways of solving the problem:

✔ Quit all open applications and try again.

✔ Log out and log back in using the Apple menu or ⌘+Shift+Q (but not by using Fast User Switching).

✔ Ignore the problem for now. The next time you reboot, you'll be able to eject the image without issue.

Similarly, a file cannot be deleted if it's currently in use. This is almost always because the application that the file was being used in is still running (and the file itself might still be open). Close the file and application and try again.

Finding the original for an alias

If Panther cannot find the original file that an alias refers to, it gives you a prompt (see Figure 17-14) with three options:

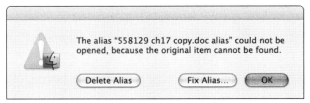

The alias "558129 ch17 copy.doc alias" could not be opened, because the original item cannot be found.

(Delete Alias)   (Fix Alias...)   (OK)

• **Figure 17-14:** The error prompt for when Panther cannot find an alias's original file.

✔ **Delete Alias:** Obviously, this option gets rid of the alias, which fixes the problem.

✔ **Fix Alias:** If you select what's behind door number two, you'll be presented with a window (see Figure 17-15) so that you can select a new original for this alias.

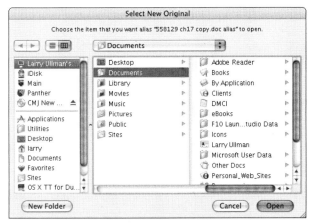

• **Figure 17-15:** You can use this dialog to navigate to the file an alias should point to.

✔ **OK:** If you click OK or press Return, nothing happens.

You can also select a new original for an alias (whether there's a problem with it or not) by clicking the Select New Original button under the Get Info's General panel (see Figure 17-16).

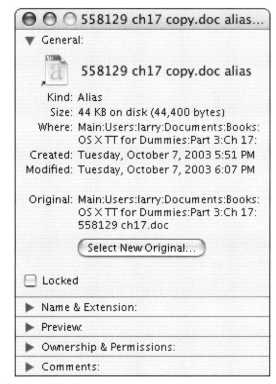

• **Figure 17-16:** You can change the original for an alias by pulling up Get Info while the alias is selected.

Sharing files with another OS

This last technique isn't really a problem-solver for Mac users — because Panther's such a great operating system — but rather for those less fortunate souls not running Mac OS X. While sharing files on other operating systems (whether through a network or a disc), you can ease potential conflicts by abiding by these rules:

- ✔ Use filenames that are shorter than 32 characters in length.

- ✔ Stick to alphanumeric characters in a filename.

- ✔ Avoid using spaces in the filename. (***Hint:*** Use an underscore instead.)

- ✔ Keep the file's extension as part of the filename.

 Many operating systems used to or still do rely on a file's extension to know what application should be used to open it.

Technique 18

Finding Files in the Finder

Regardless of how well you organize your stuff and how on top of things you stay, you'll inevitably go looking for a file that you just can't find. Old-school Mac users might be familiar with Sherlock (the file detective), but Panther has converted Sherlock to an Internet-based search tool, replacing its role in the Finder with two separate tools: the Search box and Find tool.

The search method that you'll use most often is the Search box, present in the Finder windows. This is an easy and fast way to locate what you need. On a more advanced level, you can use the Finder's Find tool, which brings to the table the capability to do more exacting searches as well as the ability to search for specific content. Finally, to wrap up this Technique, we discuss some of the ways you can improve the effectiveness and speed of your searches.

Finder Window Searches

For simple searches, you can't beat the Finder windows. Although the search features have been part of the Finder window for some time, Panther has added some new features, particularly in the speed and response of your searches. The Search box, by default, appears in the upper-right corner of the Finder window (see Figure 18-1).

• **Figure 18-1: The Finder window Search box.**

Use the Search box to perform a case-insensitive search on the names of the folders, files, and applications located on your hard drives. The Finder window search turns up any match found anywhere in a name. For example, searching for *cat* brings up files such as *Cat*alog.pdf, sub*cat*.php, or Pictures of My *Cat*s.

If you can't see the Search box because the window is too narrow — but you know it's there — click the double right-facing arrows in the upper-right corner and then select Search from the menu that appears (see Figure 18-2).

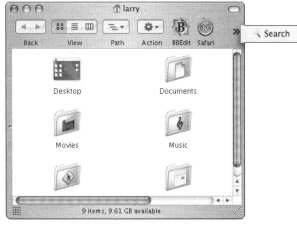

• **Figure 18-2:** If the Search box disappears, you can retrieve it with the double arrows.

To use the Search box:

1. Click in the Search box and begin typing the name of the file or folder that you want to locate.

Alternatively, you can use the ⌘+Option+F keyboard shortcut to select the Search box.

If you don't have a Search box in your window's toolbar, you can customize the toolbar to add it (see Technique 10). If the current window doesn't have a toolbar at all, press ⌘+Option+ or choose Show Toolbar from the View menu.

The Finder instantly begins searching your hard drive. Even so, you can continue to type in the full file or folder name.

The window Search box lets you specify where you'd like the search to look. The options are discussed at the end of this chapter, but you can change this setting by clicking the magnifying glass icon in the Search box (see Figure 18-3).

Click to cancel a search.

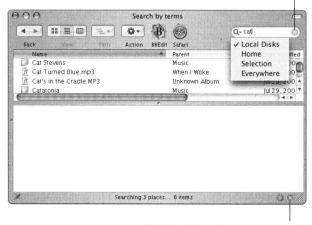

Click to halt an in-progress search.

• **Figure 18-3:** Use the magnifying glass to limit your search to specific areas of your computer.

2. If you see the file that you are looking for before the search is finished, click the Stop button (which bears an X) in the lower-right corner of the window to stop the search.

While the Finder continues its search, it shows the results in the top panel and the status in the bottom of the window.

3. To cancel the search, click the Stop button (X) in the Search box.

Clicking the Stop button in the Search box stops the search, wipes out any results, and returns the Finder window to its previous directory.

4. After the search is completed or you've stopped it, scroll through the results to see which files matched the search.

Attempting to scroll through the search results, let alone open one of these files, while the search is still going is a pain because the window and its contents keep changing. We recommend either stopping the search if you see what you were looking for or waiting for it to complete.

5. To more quickly browse through the search results, click the list headings to sort them (see Figure 18-4).

No matter which view mode you use for your window when the search begins, the results will always be shown in list view.

• **Figure 18-4:** Sort the results via the column headings to browse more efficiently through the results.

6. To learn more about a particular result, click it once to select it (see Figure 18-5).

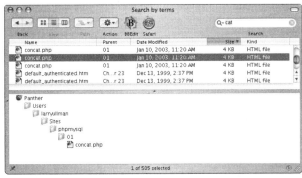

• **Figure 18-5:** Selecting a returned item in the results window displays that item's path in the bottom window.

7. Open the file by double-clicking it.

If you didn't find the file you want, try a different search term or use the Find window for a more advanced search.

 Hold down the Option key while opening the file to close the search window at the same time.

Using the Find Window

For more sophisticated searches, you'll need to leave the windows behind and make use of Finder's built-in Find command. This has replaced Sherlock's Find Files feature and is accessible by using the universal ⌘+F keyboard shortcut or by choosing Find from the File menu in the Finder.

The Find tool (see Figure 18-6) is to the Finder's Search tool what the Stealth bomber is to a paper airplane. The main difference is that the Find tool lets you establish multiple parameters for your search, beyond just the file's name. You can even use ranges and conditionals with many of the parameters, greatly expanding the possibilities.

Use the Search In drop-down list of the Find dialog to choose what parts of the computer should be searched. The default options are

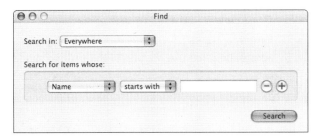

• **Figure 18-6:** Panther's Find application.

✔ **Everywhere:** Includes all mounted volumes like CD-ROMs and even mounted servers.

✔ **Local Disks:** All the hard drives on the computer.

✔ **Your Home directory**

✔ **Specific Places:** The most potent. As a default, it enables you to select among the available volumes (see Figure 18-7), but you can also permanently add other search locations to the list.

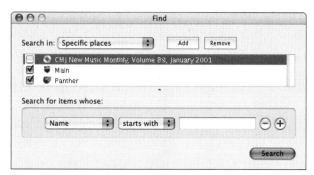

• **Figure 18-7: The Specific Places search box.**

1. **Select Specific Places from the pull-down menu in the Find tool.**

2. **Click the Add button.**

3. **Navigate to the directory that you want to add and then press Return.**

Remember that there's no need to mark your Home directory or the local volumes because these have already been flagged by Find.

4. **Select check boxes to use or not use a specific search location (see Figure 18-8).**

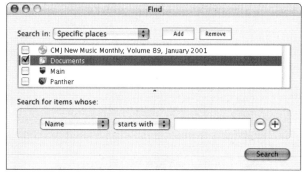

• **Figure 18-8: Add your Documents directory to the list of specific locations.**

 One of the benefits of the specific locations option is that you can permanently add locations to the search list but use only certain ones by marking the check box next to its name.

The Search for Items Whose section is the most powerful part of the Find tool. With it, you can set one or more search criterion. When you first bring up the Find tool, two criteria are shown (Name and Content). You can get rid of an item by clicking the minus sign button or add more criteria by clicking the plus button. For each item, you use the pull-down menu to select your first criteria. Then, more pull-down menus or text boxes appear, letting you add more details to that search (for example, a part of a name or a range for a date).

The available criteria include

✔ **Filename:** Unlike the window search, the Name field gives you the secondary option of selecting whether the entered text should start, end, exactly match, or simply be in a matched filename (see Figure 18-9). With this, you can more effectively fine-tune the returned results.

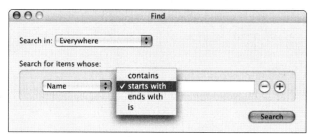

• **Figure 18-9: The pull-down menus let you further limit a search.**

✔ **Content:** The Find by Content feature searches through the contents of a file (for example a Word document, a plain text file, or even an HTML page) for matching text. This is clearly the most exhaustive search that you can execute.

 When using the Find by Content feature, try to limit the scope of your search as much as possible. If you don't, you might as well take the day off while Panther looks through every word of every file on your Mac.

✔ **Date Modified or Date Created Dates:** If you have a sense of one of these two dates as they relate to the desired file, this is a great way to locate it. In the Find tool, use the first pull-down menu to select which date you want to work with, use the second menu to decide whether the file should have a specific date or fall within a range, and use the third menu (if given the option) for setting that range. Using dates, you can search for a file whose modified or created date is

▶ Today

▶ Within a certain time period relative to today (see Figure 18-10)

▶ Before a particular date

▶ After a particular date

▶ A particular date

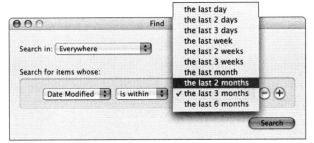

• **Figure 18-10: The date search fields are very flexible, allowing you to specify specific dates or a range.**

✔ **Kind:** The Kind search field lets you limit the search to whether the file is of a certain type. The list of types comprises alias, application, folder, document, sound (audio file), image, or movie.

✔ **Label:** If you use Labels, you can also search over whether the file has a particular label.

✔ **Size:** If you know the approximate size of the item in question, you can add a *size is greater than* or *size is less than* search criterion.

Unfortunately, you cannot add two size options at the same time to create a range of acceptable values.

 The size field is listed in kilobytes. If you need something in bytes, divide the bytes by 1,000 (or 1,024 to be precise) and use that number. If you need something in megabytes, multiply the megabytes by 1,000 (or 1,024) to find the kilobyte value to use.

✔ **Extension:** The extension for a file is its (normally) three-letter indicator of its application association. Whether you have the system set to show file extensions or not, you can still search with this criteria. Unlike Kind (which is more general), with Extension, you can find a specific file format, such as a TIFF as opposed to a GIF.

✔ **Visibility:** Unbeknownst to many, oodles of hidden files are lurking around your computer. This is largely thanks to the UNIX infrastructure that remains hidden from novice users. You can use the Visibility parameter to look for visible files, invisible (hidden) files, or both file types (Figure 18-11).

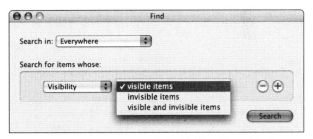

• **Figure 18-11: You can search for hidden files with the Find tool.**

✔ **Type:** The file's Type refers to an old system that the Macintosh used where each file had a four-letter type code. Because Apple seems to be moving away from Types — and you'd have to be pretty advanced to use them anyway — we recommend just skipping this category.

✔ **Creator:** A file's *creator* is the application used to originally make the file, which could differ from the file's extension association. This, like the Type, is an advanced concept you're better off not muddling with.

As a little example of how you might use the Find tool, here's how to create a search that locates the largest files in your Home directory, so that you can delete those you don't need any more to clear up some space.

1. Open the Find tool by pressing ⌘+F in the Finder or by choosing Find from the File menu.

2. Select Home from the Search In menu (see Figure 18-12).

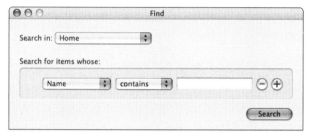

• **Figure 18-12: Your Home directory is a default search realm.**

3. In the Search for Items Whose section, select Kind, Is Not, and Folder from the first, second, and third parameter menus (respectively).

This excludes folders from the search. Because you want to find the largest *files* (not folders), eliminate folders (which can be quite large) from your search.

4. Click the plus button to add another search criterion.

5. To eliminate results smaller than about 10MB, select Size and Is Greater Than from the first two parameter menus, and then type 10000 in the KB box (see Figure 18-13).

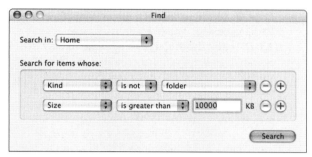

• **Figure 18-13: Two search criteria have been added.**

6. Press Return or click the Search button to begin the search process.

7. When the search is complete, click the Size column heading to list the returned items by size in descending order (see Figure 18-14).

• **Figure 18-14: Sorting results by size shows the largest files returned first.**

8. Select each individual item and view its location in the bottom panel to get more information.

9. Press Delete to delete any selected files that you decide you don't need.

 You can delete an item from the Search box, but — and here's the confusing part — it remains in the search results listing. The only difference is that its location will change to the Trash.

 The File Buddy application (www.skytag.com/filebuddy/, $38) has a great search capability built into it. If you're already using this application for other purposes, be certain to check out its Find tool.

Incorporating Better Search Techniques

You can improve the quickness and effectiveness of your searches in many ways, whether you're using the Finder windows or the Find prompt. Here are some of the best tips and techniques:

🖊 The Finder window's search box allows you to specify where the search should run. Your options are

 ▶ **Local Disks:** All the hard drives on the computer

 ▶ **Your Home directory**

 ▶ **The Current Selection:** In other words, the directory shown in the current window

 ▶ **Everywhere:** Includes all mounted volumes

 Making this selection — before you start typing the search characters — greatly improves both how fast the search is executed as well as how useful the returned results are.

🖊 Pressing ⌘+J in the search window results panel (whether you use the window or the Find tool) brings up the Search Results View Options panel allowing you to customize all Search results windows (see Figure 18-15).

🖊 If you use the Find by Content search feature, minimize the number of languages that the Finder is considering to speed it up considerably. Do so by following these steps:

 1. Make the Finder active.

  Of course, you can do this by clicking the Desktop, clicking the Finder's icon in the Dock, or by pressing ⌘+Tab to toggle over.

 2. Bring up the Finder preferences by pressing ⌘+, (comma) or by choosing Preferences from the File menu.

 3. In the Preferences panel, click Advanced.

 4. At the bottom of the Advanced panel (see Figure 18-16), click the Select button.

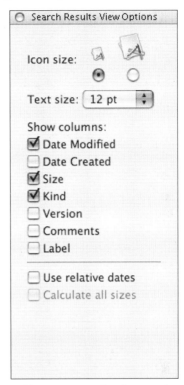

• **Figure 18-15:** You can customize the search results just like any other window.

• **Figure 18-16:** The search languages can be selected in the Finder's preferences.

5. In the resulting window (see Figure 18-17), deselect every language that you won't be searching through.

• **Figure 18-17: The Find by Content should only use those languages that you regularly use.**

6. Click OK to close the languages window, and then click the red button to close the Preferences panel.

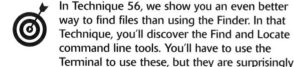
In Technique 56, we show you an even better way to find files than using the Finder. In that Technique, you'll discover the Find and Locate command line tools. You'll have to use the Terminal to use these, but they are surprisingly fast and effective.

✔ If you use the Find by Content feature, you can improve the speed of the search by maintaining an index of your content. Such an index is just like the index at the back of this book: a cataloged reference of where things can be found. If you have well-maintained indexes, Find by Content can use this to quickly return results.

1. Select a folder or volume in the Finder that you want to index.

The operating system can index any directory, whether your Home folder, your Documents folder, or a whole hard drive.

2. Bring up the Get Info panel.

3. Show the Content Index panel by clicking the arrow next to this heading (see the results in Figure 18-18).

• **Figure 18-18: The Get Info panel has a Content Index subsection when applied to folders.**

4. Click the Index Now button to begin the indexing process.

5. As desired, repeat these steps for other, commonly searched (by content) directories.

6. Repeat the indexing process on a regular schedule (like weekly) if you do a lot of Find by Content searches.

7. Use the Get Info panel to delete a directory's index if you find yourself not using it.

 Although indexes greatly improve the speed of your Find By Content searches, they also take a while to create and take up a considerable amount of disk space. Don't go crazy with indexes, particularly if you never make use of them, or else you'll quickly clutter up your file system.

Technique 19

Slimming Down Your Hard Drive

Save Time By

✔ Avoiding installing unnecessary applications

✔ Manually deleting junk from your hard drive

✔ Using third-party applications to remove the deadweight

✔ Understanding what not to throw away

It never fails to happen: All that extra space you thought you'd never fill up is suddenly gone. It's a sad fact that's just as true whether you're talking about a new house or an apartment or that 60GB hard drive that you believed would allow you to download the whole Internet to your computer. Eventually the time comes to either clean house or upgrade.

Knowing what you can get rid of and how to do it saves you the time and expense of upgrading a hard drive (and makes your computer perform slightly better). This begins with doing nothing: that is, not installing applications and files that you won't use. After that, you should look at getting rid of the files on your hard drive that are no longer needed. You can do this manually with a little prudent knowledge. Third-party applications that help you remove the hidden system files you no longer need are also available. Finally, we send up some warning flares to remind you of those things you absolutely, positively shouldn't get rid of.

Avoiding Unnecessary Installations

If you've read Technique 1, you know that during the Panther installation process, you can customize your installation so that only those features you need are installed. A new Panther installation can take anywhere from a few hundred megabytes to two whole gigabytes.

Because you cannot easily uninstall parts of Panther, you're better off not installing them in the first place — assuming you won't need them, that is. The worst offenders, in terms of disk space, are

✔ **Printer drivers:** Panther supports many common printers — which is great — but it does so at a huge cost of disk space. Installing all the printer drivers would take nearly a gigabyte. This is definitely one area where you should use some judgment about what to install and what to leave out. Three good options are

▶ If you don't have a printer, don't install any printer drivers.

▶ If you do have a printer, see whether the manufacturer provides a driver for your specific model by checking the support, software, or drivers section of its Web site. That driver might be only a few megabytes in size and therefore much smaller than the one-size-fits-all driver provided by Apple for that manufacturer's printers.

▶ If neither applies to you, install only the drivers for your make of printer.

✔ **Language Translations:** Language Translations allow your Mac to display system controls (menus and such) in languages other than English. Although it's great that Apple recognizes the global, multilingual community, if all the people using your computer speak the same language, avoid Language Translations. These take up nearly 400MB.

✔ **Fonts:** In a similar vein, Panther can also install fonts for you to use a dozen non–Indo-European languages with your Mac. These fonts enable you to read Japanese, Chinese, Korean, and other languages in your applications. Naturally, if you don't see that happening, you don't need to install these fonts.

You should also be prudent when installing applications. Most installers give you the option of customizing the installation process (as Photoshop does in Figure 19-1) so that unnecessary pieces don't clutter up your computer. As a general rule, hard drive-hogging applications — for example, Adobe Photoshop or Apple's Final Cut Pro — give you more flexibility to customize installation.

 Many installers, including Panther, allow you to dictate what gets installed. If you won't use something, don't install it. If you later realize that you need something you didn't install, you can always add it by running the installer again.

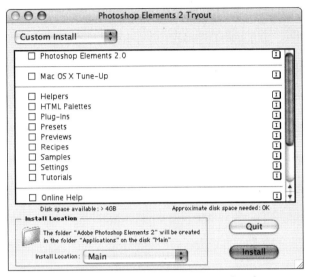

• **Figure 19-1:** Many installers let you customize the installation itself.

Weeding Your Hard Drive: Manually Deleting Files

As a general rule, Mac OS X does not use uninstallers for either the operating system or for individual applications. Thus, after you've installed the junk . . . er, files . . . on your computer and realize that you no longer need them, you must delete them manually. You might want to do some judicious weeding in these four general areas: your Home folder, the Applications folder, the System folder, and other volumes.

 Use ⌘+Delete to send a selected item (or items) to the Trash.

 Be certain to back up the contents of your computer before going hog-wild deleting items that you believe to be unnecessary. A good backup makes restoring items a snap if you inadvertently delete something important in your housecleaning frenzy. See Technique 48 for everything you need to know about backups.

Pruning your Home directory

Your Home directory is where you're most likely to get rid of extraneous stuff. Fortunately for you, it's generally the safest place to make cuts as well. Here's what you can do:

- ✔ Clean up the contents of your Desktop folder.

- ✔ Delete anything that you no longer want in the Documents folder.

- ✔ Free up some space in the Movies, Music, and Pictures folders.

- ✔ Get rid of anything that you don't want in the Public folder *unless* it's still needed by others on your computer or network.

- ✔ Remove files from the Sites directory. The Sites directory is where you store Web pages. As any Web developer knows, these directories become easily cluttered with old versions of files. Remove them to save some room here and there.

 If the contents of the Movies, Music, or Pictures folders are managed by iMovie, iTunes, or iPhoto, you'll be better off deleting these files from within those applications because they have associations with the physical files.

Thinning out no-longer-required applications

Applications can take up a huge amount of space on your computer. If you're actually using the applications, it's no big deal. But after you've stopped playing a certain game or found a better alternative to an application, you might want to get rid of it. Because you normally won't find an uninstaller for an application, here are the steps you'll want to take:

 Personally, we don't install shareware or demos of applications that we don't reasonably expect to buy. Doing so only wastes time and clutters up your hard drive.

1. **Locate the application's file or folder within the Applications directory.**

Simple applications are wrapped in a single icon, which can be deleted (like Internet Explorer). More involved applications have their own folder (for example, Netscape Navigator).

2. **Move the file or folder to a temporary location.**

Instead of deleting the files immediately, we recommend temporarily setting them aside as a just-in-case measure. You can create a folder on the Desktop for this purpose or move them onto an external driver or CD.

3. **Open the Library folder of your Home directory.**

If you really want to clean house, you should also get rid of the corresponding application stuff that was placed within your directory. This includes supporting materials and preferences.

4. **Check the Application Support folder for files associated with the application and move any applicable items to the temporary folder.**

Only a few applications have files here, but if you want to be thorough, it's worth checking out.

5. **Repeat Step 4 for the Preferences directory.**

Pretty much every application adds at least one file to your Preferences folder. Although these files are small, they're still worth getting rid of.

6. **Wait a few days. Then, if you don't see any problems caused by moving these files, delete the temporary folder.**

 If you installed an application, it should be safe for you to remove it. Applications installed by Panther shouldn't be messed with. This includes items in the Applications folder such as System Preferences and Internet Connect.

Cleaning out your System and Library folders

If you check out the size of your system files, stored both in the Library and the System folders, you'll see that they take up a lot of space (in Figure 19-2, see how two folders take up a gig). That being said, you don't want to go traipsing through there to remove files. The reward for clearing up some room is slight, while the risk that you take will be grave. As the worst case, it's possible that you would trash something that renders your computer inoperable. For the most part, you're better off leaving these files as-is.

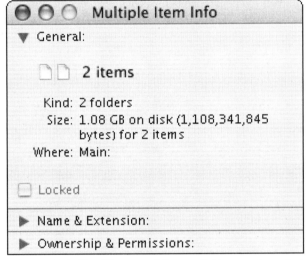

• **Figure 19-2: The Library and System folders are huge but off-limits!**

However, here's one thing that you can do with system files: If you performed an Archive and Install installation of Panther, the installer creates a Previous Systems folder to store the old system files. If everything's running okay with the new operating system, you can delete this entire folder.

Don't remove anything (anything!) from the System or the Library folders unless you really, really know what you're doing and have backed up the entire computer.

Cleaning other volumes

Most computer users have already established multiple volumes for their computer. This is accomplished by either installing extra hard drives or partitioning larger hard drives into separate volumes. If you've done this, you're probably using the other volumes purely for storage purposes (because the main volume is running the operating system and should have your Home directory). Your other volumes, therefore, are a good place to get rid of no-longer-needed files.

Classic and OS 9

If you're still running Classic or dual-booting into OS 9 (gasp!), you have another area where you can trim down files. Some considerations include the following:

- Drop OS 9 applications for which there are good OS X alternatives. There's no reason to keep two applications that do the same thing.

- If you're using Classic, there are many system extensions you won't be using. For example, if you won't be using QuickTime or a printer within Classic, you can drop many megabytes of deadwood. Getting rid of these will save space and make Classic launch faster.

- Keep all your files within your OS X Home directory. You can still access them from OS 9.

- Best of all, get rid of OS 9 and Classic as soon as possible, and then delete all those files!

Diet Tools: Third-Party Applications

If you'd rather spend your weekend cleaning the attic and not your hard drive, you can invest in one of many third-party applications that facilitate the process. (The process of cleaning up your hard drive, that is. You're on your own when it comes to cleaning up the attic.) In truth, these applications make more of a quantitative than a qualitative deci-sion. Whereas you might know that you no longer need a particular document or no longer like a par-ticular song (an MP3 file), these tools earmark files whose size and lack of use might merit removal.

✔ **OmniDiskSweeper,** by the good people at the Omni Group (www.omnigroup.com, $15), offers a good bang for very little buck. It basically repli-cates the process of going through the Finder and removing large files but gives you a nicer interface. It also warns you about deleting potentially critical files.

✔ **Cocktail** (www.macosxcocktail.com, $10) offers many system utilities to your operating system, including the ability to clean up unnecessary files such as system logs.

✔ **MacJanitor** (personalpages.tds.net/~brian_hill/macjanitor.html, free) provides the routine maintenance tasks that your computer would naturally do if you left it on 24 hours per day. Because many people don't do this, MacJanitor does the cleaning up for you. You can also run it if you just want to manually clear up some space.

 Panther runs some utilities between 3 a.m. and 5 a.m. to delete system files that are no longer necessary. If you don't leave your com-puter on overnight, use a tool like MacJanitor to clean up unnecessary system files.

Hands-Off: What Not to Trash

Now that you've mastered how to get rid of files, we should go over what you don't want to do. You might be the type who'll gladly spend a day tinkering just to clear up a little space, but here are some rules that you should never break:

✔ **Do not delete or rename the Applications or Utilities folders.**

✔ **Do not delete or rename your Home folder.**

✔ **Do not delete or rename the Desktop or Library folders in your Home directory.**

✔ **Do not touch the System or Library folders.**

Part IV

Improving Application Performance

The 5th Wave   **By Rich Tennant**

Arthur inadvertently replaces his mouse pad with a Ouija board. For the rest of the day, he receives messages from the spectral world.

YOU WILL FORGET YOUR PASSWORD. YOUR HARD DISK WILL CRASH AAAHAHAHAHA

Technique

20

Managing Applications

In this Technique, we don't cover anything specific about a particular application, but rather we discuss general techniques that apply to almost every application.

We tell you everything you ought to know about installing, moving, and uninstalling applications. Although you might not do these things frequently, understanding what each step does and how it affects your computer goes a long way toward helping you master Panther. We also show you a brilliant strategy to save you untold hours the next time that you begin working with a new computer or a new hard drive.

Installing Applications

Okay, you've probably installed applications on your own already. In fact, you probably did a fine job of it, too. But did you really comprehend all the possibilities available, and did you really prepare yourself for future installations? There's more to installing applications than just double-clicking an installer and following the prompts.

 Before you install any commercial application, make sure you've got your serial number for that application handy.

Consider these two important factors when installing an application:

✔ Where should you install the files?

✔ How can you customize the installation?

By default, an installer normally tries to place the new installs in the Applications directory (as shown in Figure 20-1), and you should let it! That's the purpose of the Applications folder, after all. We discuss the merits of organizing the Applications directory in the next section.

• **Figure 20-1:** You should let installers place applications in the default location.

Older versions of Mac OS X also created an Applications folder within each user's Home directory. Even if you have this, you should probably not use it. Apple has moved away from the idea (which is obvious by the fact that this feature has disappeared in Panther) and recommends that you use the Applications folder in the root of your computer (/Applications in formal terms) instead.

 You don't necessarily need to install an application in order to use it. You can run some applications from a CD-ROM.

The customization process is critical because it affects both what features are available and how much disk space the application takes up. As a rule, the larger the application, the more room there is for customization. For example, Microsoft Office (see Figure 20-2) and many Adobe products are highly customizable, and their installation can take up to several hundred megabytes if all options are

installed. Such applications often include megabytes worth of sample files, templates, and tutorials, which you may or may not ever need.

• **Figure 20-2:** Microsoft Office comes with scads of extras.

A few special pieces of software have a secondary level of customization. Drivers, preference panels, and contextual menu items can normally be installed on a user or system-wide level. This includes stuff like TinkerTool (as in Figure 20-3) and Big Cat from Ranchero software.

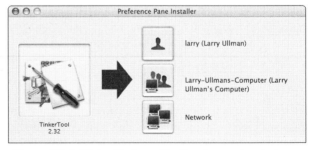

• **Figure 20-3:** TinkerTool specifically asks you in what scope the utility should be installed.

If you choose to install these things for yourself, they'll be added to the Library folder within your Home directory. The benefit of this is that they'll be backed up and easily moved because they travel with the rest of your stuff. Of course, other users (when they log in as themselves) won't be able to take advantage of the new tools. This could be a good or a bad thing, depending on how you feel about the other people sharing your computer.

Nontraditional Applications

Many applications (such as drivers and UNIX apps and tools) do not follow the normal Mac OS X installation process. Drivers — special software that adds capabilities to your computer — may run in the background or be installed as a System Preferences panel. Many UNIX applications and tools do not come with a GUI (graphical user interface). Therefore, they won't have an icon in the Applications folder or launch from the Finder. In these cases, you really should let the installers place everything where they want to and then leave well enough alone. Nontraditional applications like these break easily, so attempting to use settings other than the defaults is a bad idea.

X11 (www.apple.com/macosx/features/x11), which provides a GUI for UNIX software, uses its own installation procedures. The easiest way to install software is to use the FinkCommander (http://finkcommander.source forge.net) utility. It provides a list of available applications and quickly installs them for you. Installed software is placed in a secret location (either a folder called sw or a hidden directory) and is accessible through X11. Again, don't toy with these settings unless you like trouble or really know what you're doing.

Tracking Installed Applications

Installing applications on your computer is more complicated than just running an installer. Although following through those steps gets you the results you want (namely, the application on your computer), that's about all it does. We've hinted at this in other techniques, and now we'll be more explicit: Prudent Mac users maintain a collection of the software they've installed, and we're not talking about a

drawer full of discs! Following these steps saves you, without exaggeration, *hours* should you buy a new computer, get a new hard drive, or have to reinstall everything after some sort of disaster.

 Panther records what files where installed using packages in the /Library/Receipts directory.

Here's what we recommend that you do:

1. **Set aside the CD-ROMs for commercial applications in a common place.**

 Saving the gigantic two-disc Microsoft Office installers on your hard drive is a waste of space, so instead, just try not to lose these discs.

2. **Store copies of all the software you've installed in a new directory.**

You should save copies of shareware items that you've downloaded from the Internet as well as freeware stuff like the Camino Web browser on your computer. Doing so not only reminds you of what you've installed but also saves you the hassle of re-downloading the file later.

 If you have a slow Internet connection, save copies of the files that you download. This saves you the time of finding the items online again and the drag of waiting for them to be downloaded.

3. **Organize the software directory so that it parallels the structure of your Applications directory.**

Create separate subdirectories to reflect the drivers, games, utilities, and UNIX software that you've installed.

4. **Use TextEdit to create a master text file that lists every application that you installed.**

Beyond storing and listing the files themselves, maintaining a text list of the applications that you use is a good idea because it'll remind you of what applications you use and give you a central repository for every serial number. Making this list in TextEdit means that any Mac will be able to read it (whereas you couldn't read a Microsoft Word document until you've installed Word).

5. **Add the serial numbers — with the corresponding software version number — to the text file.**

Tracking serial numbers for the many different applications that you use is really difficult. If you store them all in one text file, the next time you have to install an application, you can just refer to your master list rather than hunt through variously shaped cards and manuals. Be certain to also note the version number of the software because serial numbers normally correspond to a specific version of the application.

6. **Add to your master text file the URLs of the Web sites from where you downloaded files.**

If you want to search the Web for the latest version of something you use, place the URL (and maybe even the current version number) for downloaded software in your text file. Then, the next time you go to install these things, a quick check suffices to let you know whether a newer version is available for download.

7. **Store this text file within the software directory that you created.**

8. **Print out a copy of the text file and put the current date on it.**

If you get a new computer or reformat your hard drive, you might not immediately have a printer working. While you can still use the digital copy of the file, having a hard copy available makes entering in serial numbers during installations easier (rather than switching back and forth between the installer and TextEdit). By adding a date to this file, you can rest assured that you are using the most current version of the document.

9. **If you can, burn the software directory to CD or DVD (see Figure 20-4).**

Alternatively, move the software directory to an external source (such as a Zip drive or external hard drive).

• **Figure 20-4: Use a CD to store and help track all the software that you use on your computer.**

10. **Store the CD or DVD, along with the printed text file, in a safe, memorable location.**

Rather than keeping all of your well-organized files and data on your hard drive — where it both takes up space and has the potential to be lost — store it elsewhere for safekeeping.

11. **When using a new disk drive, a reformatted drive, or a new Mac, use your software disk and the backup of your Home directory (see Technique 48) to recreate your previous environment.**

 A well-thought-out CD or DVD with all (or most) of your software and the corresponding serial numbers can help you out tremendously the next time you are looking at a brand-new hard drive.

Working with Packages

The Apple Installer application installs *packages,* which are a special file format. Although the process works smoothly, and you normally don't need to think much about it, the Mac power user might appreciate a couple of additional tricks.

After the Installer works its magic (installs a package), you can get a detailed list of what files were installed by using the `lsbom -f` command in the Terminal. Apply it to the appropriate `.bom` (Bill of Materials) file inside the package receipt directory in `/Library/Receipts` to get a detailed list of the files that were installed by a particular installation:

1. **Open the Terminal application.**

2. **Move to the** `/Library/Receipts` **directory by using the command** `cd /Library/Receipts`.

3. **List the receipts by typing** ls **and pressing Return.**

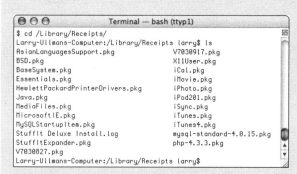

4. **Move into a specific directory with the command** `cd ReceiptName/Contents` **(for example,** `cd BSD.pkg/Contents`**).**

5. **View the installed files with** `lsbom -f Archive.bom`.

You might also investigate a cool little tool called *Pacifist* (`www.charlessoft.com`, $20), which allows you to (if you know what you're doing) to selectively install single files out of a big package. This can be a big timesaver if you know what you're looking for.

Moving Installed Applications

You might need to move an application from one volume to another someday for various reasons. These include

- ✔ You've backed up the hard drive, reformatted it, and are trying to restore it to its previous condition.

- ✔ You've bought a new hard drive and want it to be usable without formally installing every application.

- ✔ You have a new computer.

Here's how:

1. **For starters, move the application's folder (the top images in Figure 20-5) or the application itself (the bottom images in Figure 20-5) to the destination volume.**

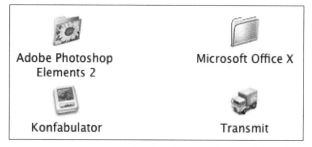

Adobe Photoshop Elements 2

Microsoft Office X

Konfabulator

Transmit

• **Figure 20-5: Some applications have their own folder, but others are represented by an icon.**

2. **Check the Preferences folder within the Library directory of your Home folder for associated files.**

   Most applications store at least one Preferences file in your Home directory. If you fail to move a Preferences file, the application will most likely build you a new one, but you'll lose all the application preferences that you've set, of course.

3. **Check the Application Support folder with the Library directory of your Home folder for corresponding files.**

Many applications add files to your Application Support folder (see Figure 20-6). You'll also need to transfer these.

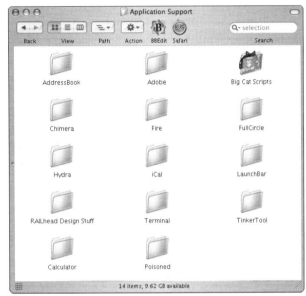

• **Figure 20-6:** A user's Application Support folder, with tools required by some software.

 Applications that you installed via an installer almost always place files in several locations, including Application Support. Applications that you installed simply by dragging a folder or icon into your hard drive most likely only have a Preferences file.

4. **Move the files found in Steps 2 and 3 to the appropriate folders in the new Home directory.**

5. **Search the rest of the hard drive for other related files.**

See the next section, "Uninstalling Applications," for information on how to effectively search your hard drive. You might find other Application Support files within the /Library and /System/ Library directories.

6. **Move the files found in Step 5 to the corresponding directory in the new location.**

 Moving the Apple applications (those that come with the operating system and those that the operating system relies upon) is not a good idea. You might not create problems by doing so, but why take the risk?

Moving applications is not really an exact science, but it is feasible. (In fact, it's much easier for Mac users than it is for those poor Windows people.) As a worst-case scenario, if an application acts funny after being moved, you should probably just trash it and install a fresh copy from the original installation media.

Organizing the Applications folder

Like the files in your Home directory, you have some leeway as to how you organize the Applications folder. Apple gives you just a Utilities subfolder. If you leave it this way, however, your Applications folder can quickly become unwieldy. You are welcome to add folders to this directory (for example, a Games folder), but you should do so *before* you begin installing applications.

Your safest option for organizing the Applications directory is to leave it as is. Instead of fuddling around in there, make judicious use of aliases, Finder windows, the Dock, and Favorites to access your applications with ease.

OS 9, Classic, and You

If you came to Panther from using OS 9 or otherwise had installed OS 9 along the way, you can get rid of plenty of applications. For starters, trash every OS 9 application for which there is already a good Mac OS X alternative. (See the section "Uninstalling Applications," later in this Technique, for more on how to delete an application that you no longer want cluttering up your hard drive.) You have no reason to keep these old, outdated pieces of software around.

You can uninstall OS 9 applications by trashing the application's icon or folder. But, unlike OS X files, OS 9 applications store extra files in the /System/Preferences folder and/or the /System/Extensions directory. While these files are small, they can and should also be deleted.

If you decide to keep OS 9 and some of its applications, be certain to keep them separate from your OS X software! By default, your OS 9 applications should be in the *Applications (Mac OS 9)* folder, not the Mac OS X *Applications* folder. Keeping these separate insures that you don't inadvertently launch the wrong version of an application or go into Classic when you didn't mean to.

Uninstalling Applications

If you find yourself no longer using an application, or you desperately need to clean up some disk space, you can uninstall applications. Unlike Windows, the Mac has no uninstaller application built into the operating system. And, for that matter, few, if any, Macintosh applications come with an uninstaller. Therefore, to get rid of an app, you'll have to do it manually, like so:

1. Select the application's icon.

2. Bring up the Get Info panel using ⌘+I (as shown in Figure 20-7).

3. Make note of the application's full name and creation date.

4. Using the Finder, delete the application's folder or icon.

5. Open up the Finder's Find tool by pressing ⌘+F or choosing Find from the File menu.

6. Search your entire hard drive for files that

► Contain the application's name in its name

► Have the same creation date

► Contain the manufacturer's name in its name

► Have a location that, in some way, corresponds to the application itself

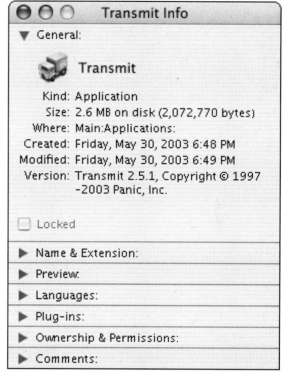

• **Figure 20-7: An application's Get Info panel reveals many useful bits of data.**

 If an application came with a README file or created an installer log, you can use this document to help guide your manual uninstallation process. README files often indicate what will be installed where and installer logs specifically list what *was* installed where.

7. Delete any files that meet any of the criteria in Step 6.

 The largest percentage of space is taken up by the application itself. Getting rid of the extraneous files clears out only a minimal amount of space, but you risk getting rid of something you shouldn't. Be extra careful when doing so or skip Steps 5 through 7 entirely.

8. **Empty the Trash and kiss that application (and hopefully not too much more) goodbye.**

 Aladdin Systems, the maker of StuffIt (among other software), offers the Spring Cleaning application (www.aladdinsys.com, $50). It records what was installed for particular applications, making thoroughly uninstalling an app easier and safer.

Launching Applications Fast

Y ou might think that opening (or launching, starting, or however you want to say it) an application is so simple that you couldn't possibly improve on it. But surprisingly, you can use many techniques and tools to improve on this common procedure. Putting some time and effort into mastering the easiest ways to open applications goes a long way towards expediting how you use your computer.

The first timesaving technique is to have Panther automatically open an application when you log into the computer. Then we go over the multitude of ways you can launch applications (such as from the Finder or Dock), some of which you probably already know. Finally, you read about a couple of shareware tools designed to open applications in easier ways.

Auto-launching with the Accounts Panel

The Accounts panel, which is part of your System Preferences, does more than just allow you to manage the computer's users. Individual users can also pop open the Accounts panel to adjust some of the computer's behavior for their account. The relevant subsection with respect to opening applications is the StartUp Items panel. To access this, select System Preferences from the Apple menu, and then click Accounts under the System heading. Click your account in the left column and then click Startup Items in the right column (see Figure 21-1).

• **Figure 21-1:** Use Startup Items to automatically launch applications.

be hidden when you log in. Essentially it will be as if you opened the application and then selected Hide *application* from the application menu. This is a good option for behind-the-scenes utilities that you don't need to be aware of.

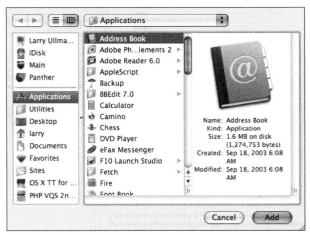

• **Figure 21-2:** This is the slow way to add applications to Startup Items.

To make a program launch automatically when you log in to your computer, add it to the Startup Items list. You can add items to the Startup Items list in two ways:

- ✔ By clicking the plus button at the bottom of the page, navigating to the application, and then clicking Add to access an Open dialog (Figure 21-2).

- ✔ By dragging an application's icon from its folder onto the Startup Items panel.

 The quickest way to add applications to the Startup Items panel is to drag them there from the Finder.

After you add an item to this listing, you can choose to have it open in hidden mode by marking the check box next to its name (as shown in Figure 21-3). Hiding a Startup Item just means that the application will

• **Figure 21-3:** Enable its check box to hide an application while it's opening.

To remove an application from the Startup Items panel, you have only one method:

1. **Select the item in the list by clicking it.**

2. **Click the minus button at the bottom of the window to remove the item.**

You might be wondering, "How do I decide what applications to automatically start?" The answer to this depends, obviously, on what kind of computer you have and how you use it. Primarily, if you have a laptop — meaning that you frequently run off battery power and change your computing habits often — you probably don't want to overdo it with Startup Items. But, in general, abide by these rules:

✔ Add utilities and shareware that provide perpetually necessary services (for example, LaunchBar or system clock replacements).

✔ Add applications that you'll always use first thing on your computer (such as Mail or Eudora).

✔ Include applications that you use every day (like Safari or iTunes).

✔ Add utilities that should be run on a daily basis (maybe Virex or Backup).

✔ Add applications that take a long time to load (like Photoshop) if there's a good chance you'll use it on a nearly daily basis.

 Many applications, such as Virex, have options within their Preferences panels (see Figure 21-4) that have a similar effect to adding the application to the Accounts panel Startup Items listing. You are best off using the Preferences panel to add these to your Startup Items list (because, in this particular case, the item being added is the VirexLogin utility, not Virex itself).

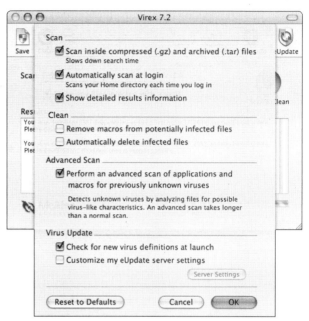

• **Figure 21-4: Virus utilities can be set to automatically scan at startup.**

Launching with the Finder

Even though you can launch applications in the Finder, knowing all your options can go a long way toward speeding up this very common task.

 The fastest way to open an application is to never shut it down. Because of the way Mac OS X handles memory, you'll notice very little performance loss by keeping applications open, and you'll never have to wait for the application to launch again. This applies both to individual applications as well as the operating system as a whole.

The most common (but not necessarily the most convenient) way of opening an application is to use Finder windows. You can either navigate your way to the Applications directory or set up your preferences so that the Applications folder is automatically listed in the Finder window's left-side section (Figure 21-5). Refer to Technique 10 for instructions on customizing the Finder windows and Sidebars.

• **Figure 21-5:** Among the locations that can be linked in the Finder window Sidebar is the Applications directory.

After you've found your way to the application and selected its icon, you can launch the application in many ways. Here are your options, listed from easiest to most time-consuming:

✔ Double-click the icon.

✔ Press ⌘+O.

✔ Press ⌘+↓.

✔ Control+click the application and choose Open from the contextual menu.

✔ Choose Open from the Finder's File menu.

 If you add an application's icon to the Finder window's toolbar (such as BBEdit and Safari in Figure 21-6), you can launch the application by clicking the icon, which will now appear in every Finder window by default. You can place applications in the toolbar by dragging their icons from the Finder onto it (see Technique 10).

• **Figure 21-6:** Add icons for critical applications to your Finder window's toolbar.

 You can also launch an application by opening a file that uses that application as its default. Furthermore, dragging the file onto the application's icon or using the contextual menu's Open With prompt achieves the same result. Techniques for opening files are discussed in great detail in Technique 23.

Here's a common sequence for easily opening an application by using only the keyboard:

1. Navigate to the Finder by pressing ⌘+Tab.

2. Press ⌘+Shift+A to bring up the Applications directory.

3. Type the first few letters of the application's name to highlight it.

4. If necessary, press Tab to go to the next application (if it wasn't highlighted in Step 3).

5. If you need to open the application's folder, press ⌘+O (in icon view mode) or ⌘+→ (in list and column view modes).

6. After you select the application, press ⌘+O to open it.

Launching with the Dock

Although Technique 11 covers the Dock in great detail, it's worth repeating some of the content here. The Dock can serve many purposes (such as linking files and folders or displaying the Trash), but the left side of the Dock is strictly for your applications. This area is where open applications reside (flagged by an upward-pointing triangle, as shown in Figure 21-7), as well as any other application that can be permanently linked there.

• **Figure 21-7: The Dock indicates open applications with a black triangle.**

You can dock an application in many ways, each of which is covered in just a couple of pages. Skip ahead to that section if you can't remember the methods.

Here are two things to consider with respect to applications and your Dock:

✔ What applications to dock there

✔ How best to arrange the docked items

As a general rule, dock every application that you use on a frequent basis. Considering all the ways you have to access applications, making sure the right applications are docked is less critical for most users. What's more important is the organization scheme you choose. Larry prefers to organize his Dock this way, as shown in Figure 21-8:

• **Figure 21-8: Larry's Dock (in case you're curious).**

✔ Keep perpetually running, but infrequently accessed, utilities on the far left.

✔ Keep applications with similar uses grouped together (like Web development tools or multimedia software).

✔ Place the applications that you use most often as close to the middle of the Dock as possible.

Items in the center of the Dock seem to have a more stable location. When the Dock expands and contracts, these items move around less on your screen.

Marc, for a different opinion, has the following suggestions (see Figure 21-9):

• **Figure 21-9: Marc's Dock.**

✔ Dock a select few items that are always running, such as System Preferences, CPU Monitor, and LaunchBar.

✔ Next dock the essential iApps from Apple: Safari, iCal (whose Dock icon also reminds you of today's date when the application is open), Mail, and Address Book.

✔ Next add the productivity applications, depending on what kind of work you do with your Macintosh. Because Marc is a software engineer, the productivity applications that he uses most often are the Terminal, BBEdit, Xcode, and so forth. If you're a graphic designer, you'd probably have things like Photoshop, Illustrator, or InDesign here instead. If you're working with the bread-and-butter applications, it's the place for Word, Excel, PowerPoint, and so on.

✔ Finally, place entertainment applications like iPhoto, iTunes, iChat, and so on.

Marc's main goal is to have stable positions for the items that he needs to reach most often. After a while, you get a feeling for where in the Dock a particular application is located, and you'll be able to find it instinctively with the mouse, just like menu items in the menu bar.

Here's what you need to know about working with the Dock:

✔ To dock an item, drag its icon to the Dock from the Finder.

When you do so, the other Dock items make way for their new roommate.

✔ To remove any Dock item — particularly all those that Apple installs there by default — drag its icon off the Dock (while it's not running).

✔ You can add any currently running application to the Dock by dragging its icon from one location to another.

✔ The Finder icon will always be on the far-left side of the Dock. It cannot be moved nor removed. The same applies to the Trash on the far right.

✔ Running applications that are not always part of your Dock will be added to the right side of the Dock.

 If you remove an icon from the Dock while the application is running, the item will be removed from its permanent location in the Dock even though it will look like it's still there (because it's running).

Other Ways to Launch Applications

Although the Finder and the Dock are the most frequently used way of launching applications, they certainly aren't your only options. Favorites, aliases, and Recent Items are all timesavers for this task.

Favorites and aliases

Another way to launch your applications is to create aliases of them and place those aliases in convenient locations. This is the principle behind Favorites, a concept deprecated in Panther but still worth using (check out Technique 15 for coverage of Favorites and aliases).

If you add a slew of applications (perhaps organized by purpose) to your Favorites, you can then dock your Favorites folder and quickly launch these apps (see Figure 21-10).

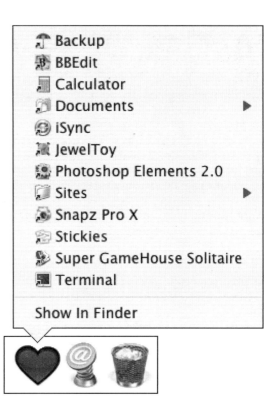

• **Figure 21-10: The Favorites folder functions as a hierarchical menu in the Dock.**

Recent Items

Finally, after you've recently closed an application, you can always reopen it from the Recent Items submenu under the Apple menu (see Figure 21-11). To adjust how many items are listed here, use the Appearance panel under System Preferences.

Opening Applications in the Terminal

The more techie Mac user might like to know that you can launch applications from the Terminal application. Although this isn't a practical way to open an application as a rule, if you're already in the Terminal, it's a nice feature to use. Here's how:

1. **Open the Terminal.**

2. **Type** cd /Applications **and press Return to move to the Applications folder.**

3. **If necessary, move to a subfolder by typing** cd *subfoldername* **and pressing Return.**

4. **Type** open, **followed by a space.**

5. **Type the first couple of letters of the application's name.**

6. **Press Tab to have the Terminal complete the application's name.**

7. **Press Return to launch the application.**

You can shorten this whole process by typing **open /Applications/*Appname*** as one command. You can also use the Tab completion technique at any point. These steps will launch the application outside the Terminal, as if you had opened it in the Finder.

Some applications can be opened without even navigating to the Applications folder with this command: open -a *ApplicationName*. You should be able to use this trick no matter what directory you're in.

BBEdit fans will appreciate the ability to open text files in it from the command line, just as you might use vi, pico, or emacs. To use this technique

1. **Open the preferences panel in BBEdit.**

2. **Click Tools in the left-hand column.**

3. **Click the Install "bbedit" Tool button.**

4. **Open a new Terminal window.**

5. **Type** bbedit */path/to/filename* **and press Return.**

This opens the file in question in the BBEdit application.

• **Figure 21-11: Recently used applications are listed in the Recent Items menu.**

Launching with Shareware Tools

Many third-party applications are in existence explicitly for the purpose of launching applications. Our favorite is LaunchBar — which we'll demonstrate momentarily — but here are some other options:

- ✔ **menuCommence** (http://mysite.verizon.net/vze35vrv/projects.htm, free) creates a menu bar icon that lists every application on your computer in alphabetical order.

- ✔ **Yadal** (http://orane.org.free.fr, free) provides an organized menu of applications from your Dock, much like using the Favorites folder this way.

- ✔ **XBar** (http://macosx.syr.edu/spottedsoftware/XBar.html, free) is like a mini-Dock whose sole purpose is to launch applications.

✔ **DragThing** (www.dragthing.com, $29) also duplicates the Dock but on a very advanced level.

✔ **F10 Launch Studio** (http://chronosnet.com, $29) is strictly an application launching utility but automatically finds your applications and has a beautiful interface.

Using LaunchBar

LaunchBar (www.obdev.at/products/launchbar, $20 for personal use, free for limited use) is a utility designed to always run on your computer. The first time it runs, it logs every application on your hard drive (along with your files, Safari bookmarks, Address Book contacts, and more). To launch an application, you simply

1. **Press ⌘+spacebar to bring up LaunchBar.**

2. **Type the keyboard shortcut for the application in question.**

   For example:

   ▶ **M** for Mail

   ▶ **ME** for Microsoft Excel

   ▶ **S** for Safari

   ▶ **BB** for BBEdit

   ▶ **PH** for Photoshop

3. **Select the application that you want to launch from the list if it's not already highlighted (see Figure 21-12).**

4. **Press Return to launch the application.**

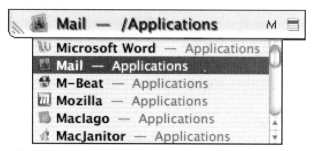

• **Figure 21-12: LaunchBar presents a list of potential candidates.**

You can manually configure LaunchBar's keyboard shortcuts by editing the AbbreviationHabits.plist document found within the ~/Library/Application Support/LaunchBar folder. To indicate the associations between keys and actions, it uses records like this:

```
<key>AB</key>
<dict>
    <key>/Applications/Address
    Book.app</key>
    <integer>2</integer>
</dict>
```

In this example, AB launches the Address Book. By editing these values, you can change the settings for the next time LaunchBar is started. The values you'll want to alter are the keys, which map an abbreviation to an application (or e-mail address or bookmark). The integer marks the priority given to an application, in case the same abbreviation has been associated with multiple items (the higher the integer, the bigger priority).

 Viewing the AbbreviationHabits.plist **file is also a good way to remind yourself of what abbreviations you've already used.**

Technique 22

Switching, Hiding, and Quitting Applications

Save Time By

✔ Switching among open applications

✔ Hiding open applications

✔ Delving into all the ways to quit open applications

Understanding how to launch applications (see Technique 21) is useful — but still something you'll probably only do once a day per application. What most Mac users spend a lot of their time doing is switching among open applications, hiding them, and (when the time is right) quitting them.

In this Technique, we take you through the best, fastest, and easiest ways to work with your open applications. We begin with switching: how to effectively toggle from one application to another. After that, we quickly address hiding open applications (which overlaps a bit with switching) and quitting them.

Switching among Open Applications

Because pretty much every Mac user has a half-dozen or so applications open at all times, being able to quickly switch from one to another is a critical skill to master. Several different methods for application switching are built into the operating system, and you can also make use of third-party tools to expand the possibilities.

Switching apps with Panther

Perhaps the best way to switch from one open application to another is to use the ⌘+Tab keyboard technique. We cover this in other techniques, but it bears repeating:

1. **Press and hold down the ⌘ key.**

2. **While continuing to hold down the ⌘ key, press the Tab key once to bring up the list of open applications (as shown in Figure 22-1).**

• **Figure 22-1: Pressing ⌘+Tab presents you with a list of open applications.**

3. While still holding down the ⌘ key, press Tab to sequentially highlight each open application (see Figure 22-2).

In Figure 22-2, the Finder is highlighted.

• **Figure 22-2:** The currently highlighted icon is surrounded by a white border and displays its name beneath it.

 Using the ⌘+Tab technique cycles through the open applications in the order of most recent usage. The application that you were using prior to the current, active one will be highlighted first . . . then the one before that and so forth. If you just want to switch back and forth between two applications, quickly press and release ⌘+Tab once.

4. To go back one application, press Shift+Tab (while continuing to hold down the ⌘ key).

5. After you've highlighted the application that you want to switch to, release the ⌘ key to make it active.

6. To abort the application switching, press the Escape key at any time while still holding down the ⌘ key.

The Finder also has a nice variation on the ⌘+Tab trick that uses the mouse.

1. Press and hold the ⌘ key.

2. While continuing to hold down the ⌘ key, press the Tab key once to bring up the list of open applications.

3. While still holding down the ⌘ key, move your cursor over the application that you want to switch to (it will be highlighted).

4. Release the ⌘ key to make that application active.

5. Again, you can abort the application switching by pressing the Escape key at any time while still holding down the ⌘ key.

 Use the cursor in conjunction with ⌘+Tab to quickly access another application. If you have a dozen or so applications open, this could be the fastest method to use.

The other preferred method for switching among open applications is to use Exposé. This tool — new to Panther — is covered in detail in Technique 13, but here's what you really need to know:

✔ Exposé shows all the windows (either documents or Finder windows) for every open and unhidden application with just one keystroke combination or hot corner. (The keystroke or hot corner varies, depending on how you've set your preferences.)

✔ Exposé shows all the windows for the currently active application with a different keystroke and hot corner.

✔ A third key combination or hot corner takes you to the Finder.

Although Exposé focuses on windows and documents, it can easily be used to switch from one application to another. Just do this:

1. Trigger Exposé by using the key combination or hot corner to bring up every non-hidden document or window (see Figure 22-3).

2. Move the cursor over each document image to view its name (see Figure 22-4).

3. After you've selected the document in the application that you want to switch to, click the document with your mouse button or press the spacebar.

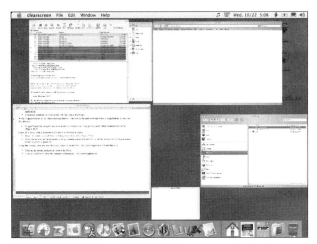

• **Figure 22-3:** Every visible document and window is revealed by Exposé.

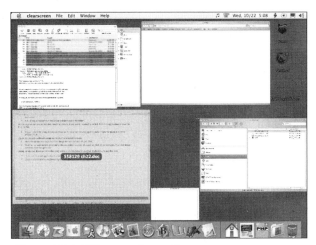

• **Figure 22-4:** When you hover the mouse over a document, its name becomes visible.

By using the mouse, two other easy ways to switch from the current application to another are available:

✔ Click the second application's icon in the Dock.

✔ Click a visible window (for example, a document) in the second application.

Switching apps with shareware

If you want validation that switching among open applications is a critical concept, just look at the number and variety of third-party applications designed for this very purpose. A quick search on VersionTracker will return many utilities, like LiteSwitch X (`www.proteron.com/liteswitchx/`, $15).

This next group of applications aren't necessarily switchers: In fact, they're actually advanced launching tools that allow you to assign keys to open particular applications. Because of this, though, they can also be used to switch to another application:

✔ **LaunchBar** (`www.obdev.at/products/launchbar`, $20 for personal use, free for limited use)

✔ **DragThing** (`www.dragthing.com`, $29)

✔ **Keyboard Maestro** (`www.keyboardmaestro.com`; free for the Lite version, $20 for the full)

✔ **QuicKeys** (`www.cesoft.com`, $100)

 These programs and others are discussed in more detail in Technique 21, particularly LaunchBar.

Hiding Applications

Being able to hide an application is a more important concept than you might initially think. Hiding or minimizing an application that you're temporarily not using makes for a less cluttered Mac, which, in turn, makes for a more productive user.

 Hidden applications appear in the ⌘+Tab application listing but not in Exposé.

Here are several ways to hide active applications:

✔ While the application is active, press ⌘+H.

✔ While the application is active, choose Hide *ApplicationName* from the application's menu (see Figure 22-5).

• **Figure 22-5: Every application should have a Hide option.**

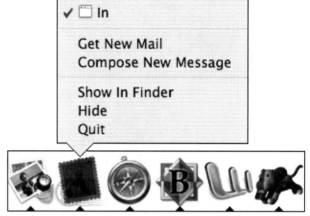

• **Figure 22-6: You can hide applications that aren't even active just by using the Dock.**

✔ While in any application, click and hold on another application's Dock icon (see the Mail icon in Figure 22-6). Then choose Hide from the contextual menu that appears.

✔ While in any application, press ⌘+Option+H to hide every other application. You can also hide every other application using the Hide Others option in the application menu (refer to Figure 22-5). Hiding every application but the currently active one really cleans up your screen and is very helpful when your active application has a lot going on (like many windows, palettes, and documents).

If you're switching to another application, you can hide the application that you're currently in by holding down the Option key while clicking the second application's Dock icon or document window. If you hold down both the ⌘ and Option keys while clicking, every other application will be hidden.

✔ Press and hold down the ⌘+Option keys while clicking the Desktop or the Finder icon in the Dock to go to the Finder and hide every other application.

You can also hide an application using the ⌘+Tab switching technique:

1. **Hold down the ⌘ key and press Tab once to activate the switcher.**

2. **While still holding down the ⌘ key, press Tab (or press Shift+Tab) until the target application is highlighted.**

   Alternatively, you can highlight the target application by putting the cursor over the icon.

3. **While still holding down the ⌘ key, press H.**

4. **Release the ⌘ and H keys simultaneously.**

Quitting Applications

You might be thinking to yourself: Why do I need to read about quitting applications? I *know* how to do that. Although you probably know at least one way to quit your applications, you might not know the easiest or best way. Here's a quick rundown of your options:

✔ While the application is active, press ⌘+Q.

✔ While the application is active, choose Quit from the application's menu.

✔ While in any application, click and hold the application's Dock icon (see Figure 22-7). Choose Quit from the contextual menu that appears.

• **Figure 22-7: Every application provides a Quit option in the Dock's contextual menu.**

You can also quit an application using the ⌘+Tab switching technique:

1. **Hold down the ⌘ key and press Tab once to activate the switcher.**

2. **While still holding down the ⌘ key, press Tab (or press Shift+Tab) until the target application is highlighted.**

Alternatively, you can highlight the target application by putting the cursor over the icon.

3. **While still holding down the ⌘ key, press Q.**

4. **Release the ⌘ and Q keys simultaneously.**

Force Quitting

If an application is stuck, quitting it the usual way simply won't work. Instead, you'll need to use Force Quit. You can force-quit an application in either of two ways:

✔ Press ⌘+Option+Escape to bring up the Force Quit menu.

✔ Alternatively, hold Option+Control and then click the Dock icon. Or, click and hold the Dock icon and then press the Option key. Both of these methods bring up the contextual menu, from which you can choose Force Quit.

Fortunately, applications rarely freeze up, so you shouldn't need to use these techniques very often.

Logging Out and Shutting Down

The most drastic way to quit every application is to log out, restart, or shut down your computer. If you choose one of these options, Panther automatically closes every open application, assuming you do not have unsaved documents still open.

✔ Pressing ⌘+Shift+Q logs you out but asks you for confirmation (see Figure 22-8).

✔ Pressing ⌘+Option+Shift+Q logs you out without asking for confirmation.

If you log out with Fast User Switching, all your applications remain open.

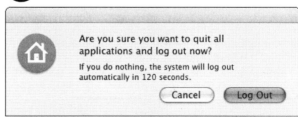

• **Figure 22-8: The confirmation prompt can be avoided by holding down the Option key when logging out.**

Technique 23

Opening Files Faster

Save Time By

- ✔ Opening files with the Finder
- ✔ Opening files with specific applications
- ✔ Using LaunchBar
- ✔ Opening files within an application
- ✔ Recalling recent items
- ✔ Setting the default application for a file

The Macintosh operating system allows for many ways to open your files efficiently, and this number increases tenfold if you add third-party tools such as LaunchBar to the mix. In this Technique, you see a number of ways to achieve the same end result. Like most timesaving techniques, many options are available; it's really up to you to determine which works most efficiently for your computing habits.

Opening Files with the Finder

As you probably already know, you can open any file by double-clicking it, in which case it automatically opens by using the default application for that particular file type. If you'd rather open the file without your hands leaving the keyboard, press ⌘+O instead.

 The slow way to open a file is to select it, go to the File menu, and then select Open. If this is the method that you use, there's room for improvement, and you should definitely keep reading!

 If you use an input device with programmable buttons (for example, a trackball or a multibuttoned mouse), program one of the buttons to behave as a double-click. Doing so saves a step (literally a click) whenever you need to open a file. Check the software or manual that came with your input device to see whether it's programmed — and if so, how.

Entering a File?

Here's one place where we think Windows users have an advantage. To open a file in Windows, a user simply selects the file and then presses Enter (the Mac Return key equivalent for PC users). When Mac users press Return, they can rename the file. This makes little sense because frankly, files are opened much more often than renamed. But we'd be surprised to see Apple make this change — and the concessions to Microsoft — at this late date.

Opening Files with Specific Applications

Double-clicking a file in the Finder works just fine for opening files the majority of the times, particularly when the file is set to open in the application of your choosing. Frequently, however, the default application is not the one that you want to use in a specific instance. For example, you might normally open HyperText Markup Language (HTML) files in Safari, but maybe you want to edit a particular HTML file in BBEdit. Likewise, images open in Preview by default, but maybe you want to use Adobe Photoshop to tweak a particular image. Here are some steps to automatically open files with a specific application. At the end of this Technique, we reveal how to set the default application for a file or a file type. This is helpful if you find yourself frequently needing to change the application used to open a type of file.

Using the Window navigational bar to open files

In Technique 10, we demonstrate the how's and why's of tweaking the default window setup. One recommended addition is to put the most commonly used applications there (see Figure 23-1). When you do, opening a file with that application is a simple case of dragging and dropping the file onto the icon.

• **Figure 23-1: By placing an application in the window's navigational area, you can quickly open a file by dragging it onto the icon.**

 The applications that you store in the navigational area should be selected judiciously. They should not be applications that are always running or remain in the Dock because you already have access to those. As a concrete suggestion, we recommend leaving Preview in the Dock but placing Photoshop in the navigational area.

 A neat trick that results from Panther's new window structure is that the folders in the Sidebar spring open if files are held over them. Therefore, you can drag a file onto the Applications icon, which in turn opens the Applications directory. Then you can drop the file directly onto the appropriate application.

Using the Dock to open files

Another easy method of opening a file with a particular application is simply to drag the file onto the application's icon in the Dock. However, for this method to work, the application must either permanently reside in the Dock or currently be open.

 In Technique 11, we provide guidelines for organizing an efficient Dock.

 Out of kindness (or maybe insolence), the Dock tries to make room for the files that you drag there, moving your application's icon out of the way in the process. To prevent this behavior, hold down ⌘ while dragging your files, and the Dock with remain motionless.

Using Favorites to open files

If you've already read Technique 15, you've probably already set up your Favorites folder to contain your most frequently used applications (and possibly files and folders, too). If you place a link to your Favorites in the window's navigational area, you can pop that open and find your favorite application, just like we suggest you can by using the Applications folder.

 The spring-loaded folder technique works with folders in the Sidebar but not with those in the Dock. So although you might keep the Favorites folder docked, trying to drag a file onto it doesn't work.

 If you haven't yet customized your Favorites folder, run — don't walk — to Technique 15 to do so now.

Opening files with a contextual menu

This method of opening a file in a specific application is perhaps the best. Control+click a file's icon, and you'll be prompted by a contextual menu that offers a list of common possible things that you might want to do with said file, such as get info about it and archive the file (see Figure 23-2).

One of these menu items, Open With, gives you immediate access to other applications with which you might want to open the file. The resulting submenu (see Figure 23-3) lists the current default application at the top along with the other potential candidates. If the application that you're looking for isn't listed, select Other (at the bottom) and navigate your way to it.

 If you have a programmable input device, we recommend programming one of the buttons as a Control+click, allowing you to access a contextual menu with just the one hand.

• **Figure 23-2: A contextual menu provides quick access to a wealth of common tasks.**

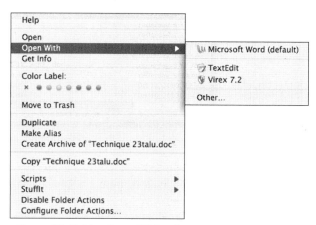

• **Figure 23-3: The Open With submenu lists logical choices for handling a file.**

Using LaunchBar

LaunchBar (www.obdev.at) is far and away one of our favorite third-party applications for the Macintosh. Its ease of use, impressive speed, and very reasonable cost ($20 for personal use; free for limited use) make it a must-have in our minds, particularly for users looking to shave seconds off common tasks. In Technique 21, we introduce LaunchBar for the purposes of accessing applications; but by following these steps, it can be similarly used to quickly open files in the appropriate application:

1. **Press ⌘+spacebar to activate LaunchBar.**

2. **Enter the shortcut for the application that you want to open a file with.**

   In this example, the letter *B* represents BBEdit (see Figure 23-4).

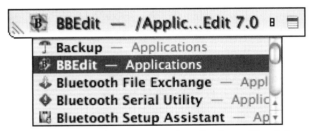

• **Figure 23-4:** The first two steps in using LaunchBar bring the required application to the launch pad.

3. **From the Finder, drag the desired file onto the launch pad.**

4. **From the drop-down menu, select Open with** *<Application>* **(in this case Open with BBEdit; see Figure 23-5).**

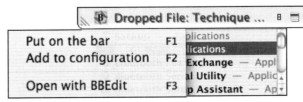

• **Figure 23-5:** LaunchBar offers three choices of actions after you drop a file onto it.

Set LaunchBar to automatically open a file dropped onto it instead of presenting a list of options.

Opening Files within an Application

If you have an application open, you can expedite opening files from within it. For starters, every application uses the ⌘+O shortcut to bring up the Open dialog (see Figure 23-6).

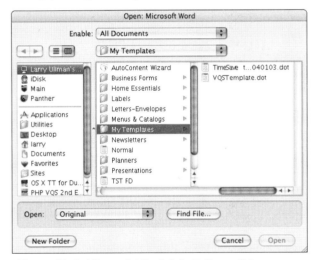

• **Figure 23-6:** Microsoft Word default Open dialog.

The standard navigational keyboard shortcuts (such as ⌘+D for the Desktop) work within the Open dialog. Further, you can click the folders and files in the navigational toolbar on the left for immediate access to commonly used directories.

If using list view is more natural to you than column view, click the list view icon in the dialog. Unlike Finder windows, Open dialogs don't offer an icon view option.

A few shareware applications allow you to set the default folder for applications to use (such as Default Folder X; www.stclairsoft.com/ DefaultFolderX/index.html, $35). Using one of these saves you from navigating to the appropriate folder when opening or saving a file.

Many OS X applications include their own tools for finding files more quickly. In Microsoft Word, you can click the Find File button at the bottom of the Open dialog (refer to Figure 23-6) to bring up a search mechanism. BBEdit provides an Open File by Name option (under File) that locates files for you.

Recalling Recent Items

After you access a file, it becomes much, much easier to bring it up again because Panther has (or can have) a memory of your actions in the Recent Items menu, found in the Finder and in many applications.

Recalling files from the Apple menu

The Apple menu has gone through many changes over the years, and since OS X, has been more or less off-limits to customization by the user. However, one tweak-able feature that remains is the Recent Items submenu (see Figure 23-7).

The number of items listed here can be set from the Appearance System Preferences panel (see Figure 23-8). You can have your Mac show anywhere from 0–50 recent documents and 0–50 recent applications. Notice that the Apple menu keeps each separate and also lists them alphabetically (not by date or time).

If you don't use many applications and have your Dock, window navigational area, and Favorites well organized, you probably won't have the need to recall recently used applications. If that's the case for you, set this value to 0 in the Appearance System Preferences panel and save the valuable Recent Items real estate solely for files.

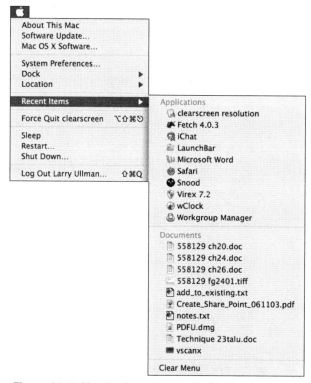

• **Figure 23-7: The Apple menu can track recently used applications and files.**

If your Recent Items menu is getting too cluttered (or you don't want others to see what you've been up to), select Clear Menu at the bottom of the Recent Items submenu.

Recalling files from application menus

It might be a chicken-or-the-egg type of debate, but either the Apple menu inspired similar behavior in many applications or vice versa. Regardless, most of Panther's commonly used applications include their own Recent Items menu. Examples include BBEdit, Acrobat Reader, and Photoshop. As a rule, you find the recent items listed under the File menu. Some applications, like the Microsoft Office products, retain this information at the bottom of the File menu instead.

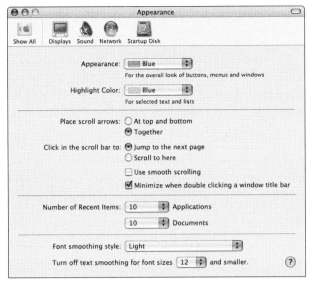

• **Figure 23-8:** Set how many recent files and applications (if any) are remembered from the Appearance panel.

Setting the Default Application for Files

In case you haven't figured out by now, the default application to be used when opening a file is indicated by the file's icon in the Finder. Each application has its own, unique look for corresponding files. As you can see at the beginning of this Technique, double-clicking (or using the keyboard equivalent, ⌘+O) automatically opens the file in the assigned application. But what if you want to change the default application? In Panther, you can manage file types using the ubiquitous Get Info panel, following these steps:

1. Select the file in the Finder.

2. Click the file and press ⌘+I (or choose File⇨ Get Info) to bring up the Get Info panel (see Figure 23-9).

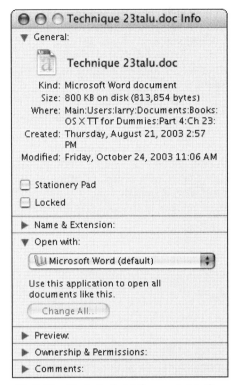

• **Figure 23-9:** The Finder's Get Info panel details — and allows you to administer — a file's properties.

 Reach the Get Info panel by Control+clicking the file and selecting Get Info from the contextual menu that appears.

3. Click the arrow next to Open With to expand that subpanel, if it's not already visible.

4. Select the default application to use from the pull-down menu.

If the application is not already listed, select Other at the bottom and navigate to the appropriate application.

5. If desired, click the Change All button to set this application to always open files of this particular type.

If you have only a file or two that should always be opened with a specific application (for example, a really large PDF that you want opened with Acrobat Reader instead of Preview), don't click Change All in the Get Info panel.

A few applications — Adobe Acrobat Reader and Microsoft Internet Explorer, just to name two — can automatically associate certain file types with themselves, if desired. Peruse through the application's Preferences for the appropriate setting.

24 Technique

Saving and Printing Files

Save Time By

✔ Saving your files quickly

✔ Comprehending the options for printing documents

✔ Creating PDF documents instead of printing

T his part of the book is all about your applications — not what they specifically do, but those common elements that you'll run across in every application. This includes saving and printing your documents.

Although you probably know what you're doing when it comes to these issues, in this Technique, you might find a better way to do those common tasks. We begin by discussing how to navigate and use Save dialogs quickly. Then we go into printing your documents. Finally, we cover how to turn any document into a PDF file, which is a widely accepted file format for sharing documents on Macs and PCs alike.

Saving Files

Regardless of what application you're using, when you go to save an untitled document, you'll be presented with a Save dialog. (See one in Figure 24-1.) The Save dialog appears as a sheet, meaning that it drops down from the top of the document window.

• **Figure 24-1: Panther's Save As sheet as it appears in Microsoft word.**

The keyboard shortcut for save is ⌘+S. Some applications have a shortcut of ⌘+Shfit+S for Save As.

Panther uses a different Save dialog format than previous versions of OS X, which is very similar to the new Finder window format. The top section is for the document's name, and the down-arrow button enables you to display or hide (see Figure 24-2) your other options.

Save As: 558129 ch24.doc
Where: OS X TT for Dummies
Format: Microsoft Word document
Append file extension
Options...
Cancel
Save

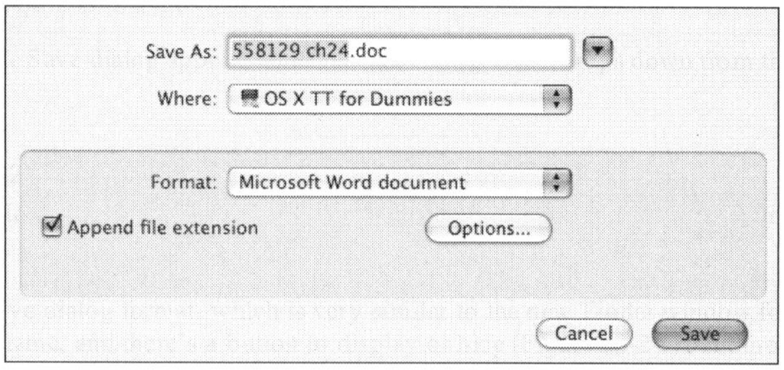

• **Figure 24-2: Save dialogs can be this minimal, or you can click the down arrow to see more options.**

Some applications, like Microsoft Word (refer to Figures 24-1 and 24-2), provide an Options button linking to that application's Save preferences panel and a drop-down menu that allows you to save the document in another file format (see Figure 24-3). What is available in an application's Save preferences panel (if it has one) can vary but normally it will let you select a default file format and how often to perform automatic backups.

The left side of the fully expanded Save dialog displays volumes at the top and your favorite places at the bottom. This is the same setup that you'll find in your Finder windows.

Because the Save dialog uses the same format as your Finder windows, customizations made to the Finder windows are reflected in your Save dialogs. (See Technique 10 for customization tips.) Placing some of your favorite directories in the Finder's Sidebar will improve your ease of using both Finder windows and Open or Save dialogs.

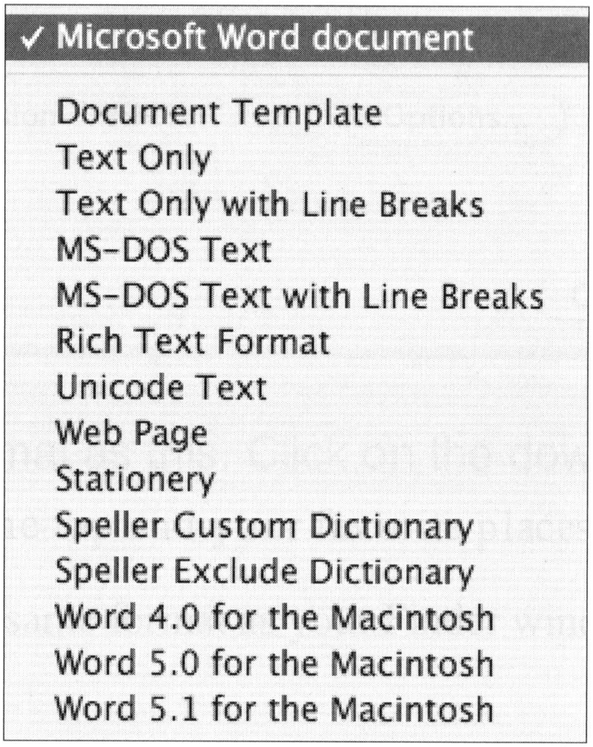

✓ Microsoft Word document
Document Template
Text Only
Text Only with Line Breaks
MS-DOS Text
MS-DOS Text with Line Breaks
Rich Text Format
Unicode Text
Web Page
Stationery
Speller Custom Dictionary
Speller Exclude Dictionary
Word 4.0 for the Macintosh
Word 5.0 for the Macintosh
Word 5.1 for the Macintosh

• **Figure 24-3: Some applications allow you to specify a file format other than the default.**

Another nice feature of the Save dialog is that you can use it in either list (as shown in Figure 24-4) or column mode. In fact, the Finder keyboard shortcuts — ⌘+2 for list view or ⌘+3 for column view — work in your Save dialogs!

Save your documents in the most logical place. (See Technique 14 for organizing your Home directory.) If you're looking for a quick, temporary storage location, use the Desktop.

Here are some tips for getting the most out of your saves:

- Use the Sidebar navigation area to quickly access your favorite common areas.
- Press ⌘+D to go to the Desktop.

• **Figure 24-4: The same Save dialog as Figure 24-1 but now in list view mode.**

• **Figure 24-5: Use the pull-down menu to access parent or recently used folders.**

 The **Default Folder X** shareware program (www.stclairsoft.com/DefaultFolderX/index.html, $35) brings many useful features to the Save dialogs. For example, with it you can save documents to open Finder windows or delete and rename existing folders and files without exiting your application.

✔ Press ⌘+Shift+H to go to your Home directory.

✔ Use the Tab key to move forward from one area of the Save dialog to another.

✔ Press Shift+Tab to move backward from one area to another.

 The Tab and Shift+Tab keyboard shortcuts move you from the document title window to the Sidebar to the main window area. The currently active area is indicated by a colored box.

✔ The pull-down menu at the top lists the hierarchy for the current folder.

✔ The pull-down menu at the top also lists the most recently used folders (check it out in Figure 24-5).

✔ Click and drag the lower-right corner to resize a Save dialog.

✔ Most of the keyboard shortcuts that function in a Finder window also work inside Save dialogs, including

▶ ⌘+[(opening brace) to move back (in list view)

▶ ⌘+↑ to move up one folder (in list view)

▶ ⌘+↓ to move into a selected folder (in list view)

▶ ⌘+← to move back one folder (in column view)

▶ ⌘+→ to move into a selected folder (in column view)

✔ The Save As dialogs work exactly the same as the Save dialogs.

 Save your work frequently! Although your Mac will rarely crash, there's no need to risk it. Also get in the habit of saving your work before switching applications, printing, leaving your computer, and so forth.

Marc's cool trick for navigating in Save dialogs

If you don't like trying to navigate all over your computer system to save a file or if you're frequently saving multiple files to the same area (like if you are, um, writing a book), here's a cool trick:

1. **Bring up the Save or Save As dialog for the application that you're working in.**

2. **Go to the Finder.**

3. **Open the folder where you want to store the document in a Finder window.**

 This trick makes the most sense (time-wise) if you already have the destination folder open in a Finder window.

4. **Click and hold the folder proxy icon in the Finder window (see the sidebar "Proxy Window Icons").**

The *proxy icon* is the representation of that folder at the top of the Finder window, next to the folder's name.

5. **Drag the folder icon onto the Save dialog.**

The dialog now shows that folder as the destination for the file being saved.

If you like this technique, you can really speed it up by using a drag and drop in conjunction with Exposé (see Technique 13) or the Finder's ⌘+Tab trick (see Technique 9) to quickly go back and forth between the Finder and the primary application.

 You can drag folders *and* files from the Finder. The Save dialog moves to the new location, and the name of the file that you dragged is entered into the filename text field, saving you some typing if you want to overwrite an existing file.

Proxy Window Icons

The proxy icon is a great thing, and not just in Finder windows. Because the window title bar can be used both for moving the window as well as for initiating a drag of the proxy icon, Apple had to find a way to distinguish between the two actions. Because window title bar proxy icons were added quite late in the development cycle, and every Mac user was used to moving windows by grabbing and moving them quickly, Apple added the requirement that the user has to hold the mouse still for about half a second after clicking the mouse button over the icon. This indicates to the system that the user wants to drag the proxy icon and not move the window.

The great thing is that the proxy icon functionality of allowing you to move the folder works in almost every application. Each document has a proxy icon next to the document's name at the top of the window. This icon can also be dragged to move the file to a new location, attach it to an e-mail, and more!

Overwriting existing files

As you might notice, existing files in Save and Save As dialogs appear in gray, indicating that you cannot use that filename without overwriting another document. In the past, to force a used name upon the document that you were saving, you had to type it manually. Now, selecting a grayed-out file automatically enters that filename as the saved document's name.

 Be careful when you use an existing filename in Save dialogs. Doing so wipes out the previous document, with no recourse for recovery.

Printing

After you've got your printer set up, you can use some timesaving techniques regardless of the printer connected.

The following examples use Larry's printer, but the thrust of these tips should still apply to whatever printer you're using.

Customizing print settings

Many print drivers come with the ability to create and save your print settings. This is very useful if you frequently need to print documents in certain ways. For example, you might adjust

- The number of copies to print
- What pages to print
- The quality of the printing
- Whether to use two-sided printing (if possible)

Larry has a few different settings created already. One is for printing a lower-quality draft of something double-sided. This is great for spitting out large documents that don't require the best quality. On the opposite end of the spectrum, Larry uses a setting for printing photos in color and on glossy paper.

For most printers, arranging this is a matter of following these steps:

1. **Select Print in any application.**

 The keyboard equivalent of Print is ⌘+P.

2. **In the Print dialog that appears, adjust all the settings as desired. (See your choices in Figure 24-6.)**

3. **Select Save As from the Presets menu.**

4. **In the Save Preset dialog that appears, choose a distinctive and descriptive name for these settings, like One Page Draft (see Figure 24-7) or Color Photo.**

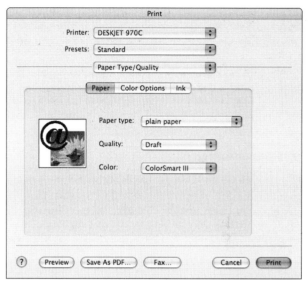

• **Figure 24-6: Go through your printer's options and adjust each accordingly.**

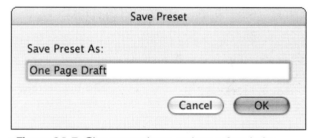

• **Figure 24-7: Give your printer settings a descriptive name.**

The next time you want to print something with these preset settings, you can select them in the Print dialog from the Presets drop-down menu.

Previewing your documents

Using the Preview option turns a document into a PDF (Portable Document Format) and sends it to the Preview application. From there, you can scroll through the multiple pages, print it, save the file as a PDF, or convert it to another format. This functionality works in any OS X application that can print. To learn more, see "Creating PDFs" later in this chapter.

 Using the operating system's Preview tool is often a better choice than the default preview feature built into an application (if it even has one).

Desktop printing

In short, desktop printing is the ability to print documents (or start the print process) using the Finder instead of an application. It works by creating an alias to your printer. When you drag a file onto this alias, Panther will

✔ Print the file if its format is readable by Preview (images and PDFs)

✔ Launch the file's default application and then print the file if its format isn't readable by Preview (Microsoft Office documents, as an example)

Using desktop printing can save you a lot of time if you frequently need to print documents that you might not be currently viewing or editing — in other words, if you print documents separately from working with them.

To create a desktop printer, follow these steps:

1. **Launch the Printer Setup Utility, found in the Applications⇨Utilities folder.**

2. **Add your printer to the list of available printers, if it's not already listed.**

Click the Add button and follow the prompts to add a printer already connected to your Mac. See Technique 39 for adding a networked printer.

3. **Select your printer by clicking on its name in the list of available printers.**

4. **Choose Create Desktop Printer from the Printers menu.**

5. **In the Save dialog that appears, give your printer a descriptive name and save it to your Desktop.**

6. **If you want, move the printer alias from the Desktop to your Dock so it's more readily available.**

After you create a desktop printer (even if you Dock it), just drag any document from the Finder onto the Desktop Printer icon to print it.

Creating PDFs

One of the coolest features of OS X is that it uses the Portable Document Format as a standard technology. The benefits of this are

✔ Easy viewing of PDFs via *Preview,* which is the OS X default media viewing application

✔ Easy creation of PDFs without the need for expensive software

With little fanfare, a cool feature called PDF Workflow was added to the Mac OS X operating system. With PDF Workflow, you can broaden your PDF options. Instead of saving a document as a PDF, you could

✔ Save it in a specific folder without prompting

✔ Attach the PDF to an e-mail

✔ Open the PDF in Adobe Acrobat Reader

After you turn on PDF Workflow, the Save as PDF button will turn into a drop-down menu of options (see Figure 24-8). To enable PDF Workflow, follow these steps:

1. **Open up your Home directory in a Finder window.**

2. **Navigate to the Library folder.**

3. **Create a new folder called PDF Services.**

The PDF Services directory is Panther's link to PDF Workflow functionality. It will be used to add all the different features you want to the PDF Workflow menu.

 PDFU, from If Then Software (www.ifthensoft. com, free), automates the PDF Services directory creation and adds several useful starter services for you.

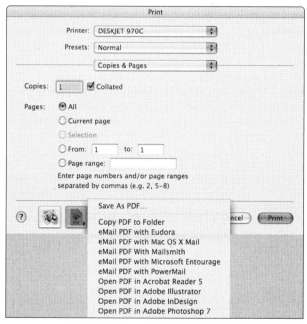

• **Figure 24-8: The Save As PDF button can work as a pull-down menu instead.**

After you've created this folder, here's what you can do with it:

✔ **Add aliases to other folders there, giving you a very quick way to save a PDF file to that folder.**

✔ **Add aliases to applications there.**

For example, if you drop an alias to the Mail application into the PDF Services directory, selecting Mail from the pop-up menu creates a PDF that is then immediately attached to a new, blank message in Mail. You simply have to add a recipient and subject to the message, and then you can fire off the PDF.

✔ **Advanced users can add both AppleScripts and UNIX scripts to the folder, which can be run — using the created PDF — when selected.**

For example, you could create an AppleScript that moves the PDF onto a network server or performs some type of post-processing.

Technique 25

Cut, Copy, Paste

Save Time By

- ✔ Memorizing the shortcuts for cutting, copying, and pasting
- ✔ Understanding how to use the Clipboard
- ✔ Expanding the Clipboard with shareware

You might be thinking to yourself, "Why is a whole Technique devoted to cutting, copying, and pasting? I already know how to do that just fine." True, but the topic is so important that you really ought to make sure you know every possible option and method available.

In this Technique, we give you everything that you absolutely must know about editing a document: cutting, copying, and pasting (with a little selecting thrown in). This begins with the basic and not-so-basic shortcuts. After that, we discuss the Clipboard itself: what it is, how it works, and how this affects you. At the same time, we introduce a couple of new tools that expand on the functionality of the Clipboard. Finally, we show you a few other related tricks and get into Panther's Find Clipboard.

Copying and Pasting with the Keyboard and Mouse

Editing is so common in everything that you do on computers these days that if you haven't already learned or mastered the editing shortcuts, you're selling yourself short. The options in the Edit menu are fairly common whether you're talking about the Finder (see Figure 25-1) or BBEdit (see Figure 25-2).

• **Figure 25-1: The Finder's Edit menu is rather basic.**

Edit	
Undo Copy of "558129 ch25.doc"	⌘Z
Cut	⌘X
Copy "558129 ch25.doc"	⌘C
Paste item	⌘V
Select All	⌘A
Show Clipboard	
Special Characters…	

Edit	
Undo Paste	⌘Z
Redo Typing	⇧⌘Z
Cut & Append	⇧⌘X
Copy & Append	⇧⌘C
Paste Previous Clipboard	⇧⌘V
Clear	
Select All	⌘A
Select None	⇧⌘A
Select Line	⌘L
Select Paragraph	⌥⌘L
Insert	▶
Auto-Complete Glossary...	
Insert Glossary Entry...	
Show Clipboard	
Previous Clipboard	^[
Next Clipboard	^]
Text Options...	⌥⌘;
Printing Options...	⇧⌘;

• **Figure 25-2:** BBEdit's Edit menu is more involved.

The Edit items apply to whatever you have selected, including

- ✔ Files, folders, icons, or applications in the Finder
- ✔ Text
- ✔ Images
- ✔ Pretty much anything else you can think of

Of the Edit menu options, the most important considerations are

- ✔ Select All
- ✔ Copy
- ✔ Cut
- ✔ Delete

- ✔ Paste
- ✔ Undo
- ✔ Redo

Many of the editing tools rely upon the *Clipboard*, which is a place for temporary storage on your computer. A single selection can be stored in the Clipboard. (To be clear: The Clipboard can store multiple files or lots of text, but only if they are selected at the same time.) Also, the Clipboard's contents are erased when you restart, shut down, or log out (if you don't use Fast User Switching).

Both Copy and Cut place a copy of the selected item on the Clipboard, but the latter also removes the selected item from its original location. (Think of Cut like a Copy followed by a Delete.) Delete removes the selected item (although not files and such in the Finder, which must be deleted by using the Option and Delete keys together), whereas Paste puts the Clipboard's contents in the current location. Undo, well, undoes the last action, and Redo redoes the last thing that you undid.

 If you cut something (for example, text in a document), you can always put it back by using Paste. If you delete it, however, it might be gone forever (depending upon the application in use). Conversely, cutting something takes up more memory because the cut item must be stored, if only temporarily. Unless you've selected something really large, this is rarely an issue.

Everywhere you go in your Mac, you'll find these keyboard shortcuts:

- ✔ **Select All:** ⌘+A
- ✔ **Copy:** ⌘+C
- ✔ **Cut:** ⌘+X
- ✔ **Paste:** ⌘+V
- ✔ **Undo:** ⌘+Z

You really, really, *really* must memorize these if you haven't already. These keyboard shortcuts are also duplicated in Edit menus (as mentioned) and in contextual menus (as shown in Figure 25-3), if you prefer sticking with the mouse.

Help	
Cut	⌘X
Copy	⌘C
Paste	⌘V
Character...	⌘D
Paragraph...	⌘M
Bullets and Numbering...	
Define	
Synonyms	▶
Hyperlink...	⌘K
Scripts	▶

• **Figure 25-3:** The Edit options are frequently available within contextual menus.

Most, but not all, applications use the ⌘+Shift+Z shortcut for Redo. Others use ⌘+Y.

You can also use your mouse for some neat editing tricks. After you select an item, click it and begin dragging, and then

- ✔ Drag the item anywhere else to perform a cut and paste.

- ✔ Drag the item to the Trash to delete it.

- ✔ Hold down the Option key while you drag to create a copy of the selection in a new location (copy and paste).

- ✔ Move the item to a new volume (in the Finder) or document (in an application) to create a copy in the new location.

- ✔ Hold down the ⌘ key to move the item to a new volume without copying it (in the Finder).

- ✔ Hold down the Control key before you release the mouse button to be given options when moving the selection from one document to another within an application. After selecting some text, say in a Word document, begin dragging it to another location. After you arrive at your destination, press the Control key and release the mouse button to see a menu of options (see Figure 25-4).

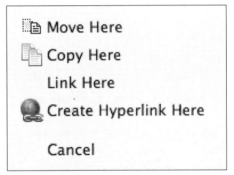

• **Figure 25-4:** Contextual menus work within the Finder and other applications while dragging stuff around.

All these tricks work with text and other content in documents.

You can also select items (in the Finder or in an application) by using these techniques:

✔ Select a range of contiguous items by continuing to hold down the mouse button while dragging around a group of items.

✔ Click to mark the beginning and then Shift+click to mark the end to select a range of items.

✔ Press ⌘+click to add an item to the current selection (like another file in a Finder window).

✔ You can also press ⌘+click to deselect a selected item (for example, to deselect one item from a range of already selected items).

Understanding the Clipboard

The Clipboard has been a part of the Macintosh operating system for a good long time and is a simple and essential tool. The *Clipboard* is an area of memory that stores the most recently copied or cut stuff. Here are some basic rules of how it works:

✔ **The Clipboard can only contain one selected item at a time.** The Clipboard has no history. It can remember a group of files or a paragraph of text or whatever, but it can only ever store one level of copying or cutting.

✔ **The Clipboard's contents are remembered across the entire operating system and every application.** Even if you quit or open an application, the Clipboard's contents will remain.

✔ **The Clipboard's contents are changed only when you cut or copy something else.** The Clipboard is not emptied by any other option, including pasting, deleting, and so forth.

✔ **The Clipboard's contents are dropped when you log out, shut down, or restart your computer.**

 You can always view the current contents of the Clipboard by choosing Show Clipboard from the Finder's Edit menu. See an example in Figure 25-5.

• **Figure 25-5: If you forget what's on the Clipboard, view its contents in the Finder.**

The main limitation of the Clipboard is its single-storage nature. In the next section, you find out about a couple of tools that make up for this.

Copy and Paste Tips and Tricks

To wrap up this Technique, we want to discuss a few editing tips and tricks that you ought to be familiar with. This includes both shareware tools and general techniques than any Panther user can try.

Clipboard shareware options

The Clipboard is nice, but limited. You don't need to be a power user to be hindered by its lack of history and single-use nature. For those of you wanting just a little bit more, here are some more potent alternatives.

✔ **CopyPaste-X** (`www.scriptsoftware.com/copypaste`, $20) provides you with a Clipboard that can automatically store ten items and also includes a Clipboard Editor to alter the stored contents.

✔ **XShelf** (`http://homepage.mac.com/khsu/XShelf/XShelf.html`, free) is more like Mac OS 9's Scrapbook but can be used in lieu of the Clipboard. Instead of using Cut, Copy, and Paste, you drop selected items onto the application (shelve them for later). When it's time to use the stored text, image, or what-have-you, drag it off of the shelf and into it's new location.

✓ **iPasteboard** (http://ipasteboard. brunoblondeau.com, $15), like CopyPaste-X, is closer to the old Scrapbook utility from OS 9 and earlier. It provides multiple Clipboards whose contents are retained even after restarts.

✓ **ClipboardSharing** (www.lagercrantz.ath.cx/ software/clipboardsharing, free) lets you share a Clipboard's contents from one Macintosh to another over a network.

Copying items within the Finder

You can use Copy and Paste to copy an item in the Finder to another location without cluttering up the Desktop with windows. Here's the skinny:

1. **Open a new Finder window.**

2. **Select the item or items that you want to duplicate.**

3. **Press ⌘+C to copy your selection.**

4. **Navigate within the same window to the destination folder.**

5. **Press ⌘+V to paste the copied items there.**

 If you duplicate an item within a folder, the Finder automatically adds the word *copy* to its name. This is because two items within the same directory cannot have the same name. If you duplicate an item multiple times, the word *copy*, followed by sequential numbers, is added to the duplicates' names.

Using the Find Clipboard

One of the interesting new editions in Panther is the *Find Clipboard,* which is an independent Clipboard that stores text for which the user has been searching. The great thing is that it is also system-wide and works in every Apple application plus a few others (you'll need to experiment to be certain) while still leaving your Clipboard contents unchanged.

Often, people copy a word from a document and then open up the Find panel and paste the word there. This replaces any other text in the Clipboard, which might still be needed. With the Find Clipboard, you can do the same thing much quicker and without ever opening up the Find panel. Here's how:

1. **In an application like Safari, Mail, or TextEdit, select some text.**

2. **Press ⌘+E.**

   ⌘+E is the keyboard shortcut for Use Selection for Find.

3. **Open the Find panel for that or any other application.**

   If the current application supports this feature, this text will automatically be in the Find dialog, and you can simply press Return to begin the search.

4. **Or, instead of using the Find prompt at all, use ⌘+G to search for the selected text automatically.**

   Strange as it might seem, with the Find Clipboard and the ⌘+E shortcut, you can actually use Find Again to find text even If you haven't run the search previously. This is another timesaving benefit of the Find Clipboard!

 ⌘+G is the keyboard shortcut for Find Again.

As you'll see, having two separate Clipboards speeds up the workflow considerably. The Clipboard text being accessible system-wide means that you can search for a string in one application and then switch to another one and continue the search there. For example, you can select some text in a Mail message, press ⌘+E, and then switch to Safari. Press ⌘+G to search the current Safari window for the exact same text without ever opening a Find panel.

Managing Fonts

Save Time By

↙ Understanding how Panther deals with fonts

↙ Adding fonts to your operating system

↙ Accessing and viewing fonts

↙ Managing your fonts with Font Book

Either because of a lack of need or because of a lack of good, inexpensive tools, font management has long been a terrain where everyday Mac users did not tread. While graphic designers used high-priced applications to manage their fonts, the rest of us were left out in the cold. Now, thanks to the Font Book application, any Mac user can add wacky fonts to their Word documents or, more importantly, make their applications load faster by enabling and disabling fonts as needed.

In this Technique, we cover pretty much everything you'll need to know about fonts and your computer, including installing, viewing, and managing your fonts. Along the way, we show you our own special tricks for working with fonts in the easiest way possible.

Fonts Support in Panther

To get the most out of fonts on your system, you should fully understand how Panther deals with fonts, particularly because this has changed significantly in OS X.

Panther supports several types of fonts:

↙ **Cross-platform fonts**

▶ TrueType: `.ttf`

▶ TrueType font collections: `.ttc`

▶ OpenType: `.otf`

These types of fonts were originally made by Microsoft. They are very common and provide good results on the monitor and in lower quality (DPI: dots per inch) printings.

↙ **PostScript fonts**

PostScript fonts, created by Adobe (and also called Type 1 fonts), look great at even high quality (professional level) printings.

✔ **Data fork suitcase fonts:** .dfont

Similar to OpenType fonts, data fork fonts are new to Mac OS X. Theoretically, these fonts have the best qualities of both Microsoft's TrueType and Adobe's PostScript fonts.

✔ **Mac TrueType fonts**

Mac OS 9 and earlier used various TrueType and bitmapped (think "crude" and "jagged") fonts.

That's a pretty broad range of options, meaning that you have an enviable list of options. Fonts from Windows computers work on your Mac, as do your old OS 9 fonts that you might still use in some documents.

Installing Fonts

Although your Mac comes with a few dozen fonts out of the box, you can — and probably should — add more. You can find fonts by purchasing them (either online or in a good software store) or by downloading free ones from the Web. Some of the better online font resources include

✔ **Font Freak:** www.fontfreak.com

✔ **Adobe:** www.adobe.com/type/main.jhtml

✔ **MyFonts.com:** www.myfonts.com

✔ **Fonts.com:** www.fonts.com

To install a font, all you need to do is drop the font file into the appropriate location. Fonts can be installed in any of the following places:

✔ ~/Library/Fonts (where ~ refers to your Home directory; see Figure 26-1)

✔ /Library/Fonts

✔ /System/Library/Fonts

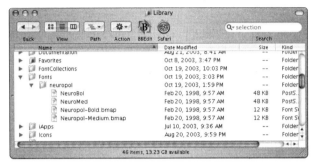

• **Figure 26-1: Add fonts to your system by placing them within your personal Fonts folder.**

 Fonts used by your Classic system are stored in the /System Folder/Fonts directory where your OS 9 installation resides. The great thing about this is that OS X automatically finds and supports fonts that are installed in OS 9.

Any fonts that you install are recognized the next time an application is opened. (For the Finder, this means that the font is recognized after you restart your computer, log in and log out, or manually quit and restart the Finder.)

 If you install fonts into your Home directory (specifically ~/Library/Fonts), they'll be easy to back up and move from one system to the next. On the downside, other users on your Mac will not be able to use them.

To uninstall any font, just delete its file from the Fonts folder in which it resides. Of course, you can also install and delete fonts by using the Font Book application, as you'll soon see in the section titled "Font Book" later in this Technique.

 If you delete a font, any document that uses that font will be forced to find a substitute. You may not like the results, particularly when it comes to graphics. For this reason alone, we recommend you use Font Book for managing your fonts, which is covered later in this chapter.

Viewing Fonts

After you install your fonts, you have several options for viewing them. Although every individual application will (or should) show you a list of available fonts, Panther's tools go a step further by showing you what the fonts look like and providing more powerful levels of tinkering. The operating system offers three tools for looking at your fonts: Character Palette, the Font panel, and Font Book.

Character Palette

Character Palette was new in Jaguar and replaced the old Key Caps utility. It is like Font Book but has the added advantage of being accessible via the menu bar at the top of the display. To set up your preferences so that you can activate Character Palette from the menu, just follow these steps:

1. **Bring up System Preferences and select the International panel.**

2. **Click the Input Menu tab and then select the check box next to Character Palette, as shown in Figure 26-2.**

• **Figure 26-2: The Input Menu panel controls palettes, keyboards, and input methods.**

3. **Select the Show Input Menu in Menu Bar check box at the bottom of the window.**

Following these steps creates an icon in the menu bar. Clicking it brings up the Character Palette (as shown in Figure 26-3). Character Palette is a useful tool for accessing particular characters. For example, use Character Palette if you want to insert a symbol (such as a star, asterisk, and so on) into a Word document or add a character with an umlaut or tilde in an e-mail. Character Palette provides a much faster interface for hunting down these peculiar items.

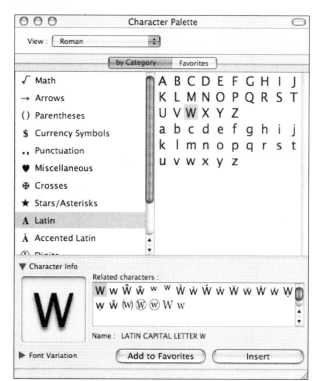

• **Figure 26-3: Panther's Character Palette.**

To find a particular character, just follow these steps:

1. **Within Character Palette, use the View drop-down list at the top of the panel to select the appropriate view.**

   You'll most likely want to use Roman, unless you have a need to access Japanese, Korean, or Chinese characters. The Unicode View shows many other symbols and characters such as mathematical symbols, signs of the zodiac, and Cyrillic letters.

2. **Either keep the By Category tab highlighted or click the Favorites tab to immediately access predefined favorite characters.**

    Use the Add to Favorites button at the bottom of the Character Palette window to add a frequently used character to your list of favorites. Then you'll be able to quickly insert these into documents.

3. **If you're browsing by category, use the menu at the left to select a category.**

4. **In the panel on the right, find the character that you're looking for and click it to highlight it.**

5. **If desired, click the arrow next to Character Info to learn more about the highlighted character and to see related characters.**

   For example, if you are looking for a special accented character, you would choose Roman for the View and Accented Latin as the Category, which brings up the list of possible characters. The top right column shows primary options and the Character Info shows variations for each option (uppercase, lowercase) and similar characters.

6. **If desired, click the arrow next to Font Variation to see the character in other fonts.**

7. **To use Character Palette to insert a special character within the current document, just double-click the character that you want to insert.**

 Character Palette can also be accessed by choosing Edit⇨Special Characters from the Finder.

Font panel

The Font panel is a solid tool for viewing, selecting, and tweaking fonts. It's available in all Cocoa (native to Mac OS X) applications, like Stickies, TextEdit, Mail, and Safari.

 Applications that support the Font panel, like Mail, Stickies, and TextEdit, often use the ⌘+T keyboard shortcut for accessing the Font panel.

 The Font panel's options change based upon how big the Font panel window is. Adjust the window's size to see more information.

The primary purpose of the Font panel is to allow you to select and customize the font used in an application. The basic view (as shown in Figure 26-4) shows the different font collections, families, and sizes available. Set the font face and size to use by clicking on a Collection, then a Family, and then a Typeface (navigate the Font panel like you would a Finder window in column view mode). Enter a value or use the slider to adjust the size.

If you're looking for a particular font but you're not sure which collection or family it belongs to, use the Search button at the bottom of the window to find it.

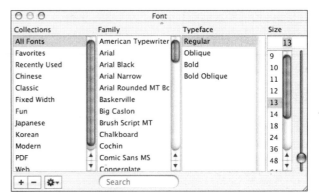

• **Figure 26-4: The Font panel exists in all Cocoa Panther applications.**

The slider on the far right side of the Font panel adjusts the font size. Move the slider up to increase the font size; move it down to decrease the font size.

The Font panel's greatest asset is the *Actions button* at the bottom left (the thing that looks like a cog or a gear with a downward-pointing arrow next to it), which creates a menu of useful options (see these in Figure 26-5). The effect of the options change depending upon whether you've already selected a font, but your choices include

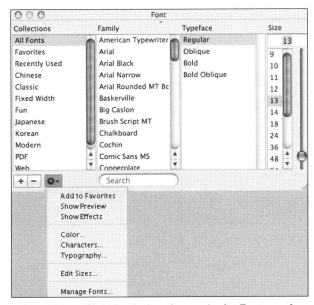

• **Figure 26-5: Click the Actions button in the Font panel for more font options.**

✔ **Add to Favorites:** If you add a font to your Favorites (Font Favorites, not the other Favorites that your system uses), you can easily access it in any application. Any Favorite font you've established will be listed when you select Favorites from the Collections column in the Font panel. The wonderful thing is that the Favorites doesn't just recall the font itself, but also its size and any special effects applied. So if you like a certain style for an e-mail or a heading in a text document, it can be quickly retrieved time and again.

 Make good use of the Font Favorites tool to save yourself time when accessing frequently used fonts and styles.

✔ **Show/Hide Preview:** This Action option toggles a Preview window that shows the font name in its font to demonstrate its appearance. Use the Preview option while you're tweaking a font's settings.

✔ **Show/Hide Effects:** This setting reveals and hides the toolbar of font effects, which lets you customize your fonts. Using the different font effect tools, you can adjust these font attributes:

▶ *Underline* (none, single, double, or color)

▶ *Strikethrough* (none, single, double, or color)

▶ *Font color*

▶ *Font background color*

▶ *Shadow* (opacity, blur, offset, and angle)

Unfortunately, the effects are not reflected in the Preview section of the Font panel, so you'll need to select the text in the document (to which you want to apply the effects) to see how the different adjustments look.

 Thanks to the Font panel and the Effects section in particular, you can now perform fancy text manipulations in TextEdit. Fliers and signs that used to require sophisticated applications like Adobe Pagemaker can now be made in the free (and simple to use) TextEdit.

✔ **Color:** This brings up the Color Palette, a separate window of color choices. The Color Palette is used all over the operating system and has several subpanels, each of which lets you find a color in a different way (using a color wheel, a box of Crayons, an image).

✔ **Characters:** The Characters option brings up the Character Palette, which we discuss in the preceding section.

✔ **Typography:** Panther includes many new options for precise typographical control, but the availability of advanced typographical options varies from font to font. Commonly you can tweak a font's ligatures (how two characters joined together are spaced) and glyphs (special characters). Some fonts also have tweaks for managing em (or wide) dashes, hyphens, case, and spacing.

✔ **Edit Sizes:** The Edit Sizes menu allows you to set the default sizes available for your fonts.

✔ **Manage Fonts:** This last option brings up Font Book.

Font Book

The *Font Book* utility can be used to view and manage your fonts. Font Book consists of a window that lists the groupings or categories of fonts in the left column, the specific fonts for that grouping in the middle column, and a preview of the font in the right column (although the preview can be disabled).

 If you double-click any font in the Finder, it opens in Font Book, where you can view and manage it (see Figure 26-6). You can also access Font Book from within your Applications folder or from the Font panel.

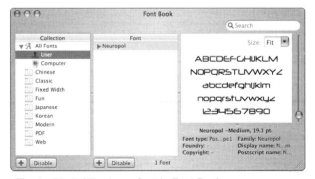

• **Figure 26-6:** Viewing a font in Font Book.

To preview any font, follow these steps:

1. **Start by clicking the appropriate collection in the left column.**

2. **Select the font family in the middle column.**

3. **If desired, click the arrow next to the font's name to expand the font listing.**

4. **If desired, select a specific subfont from the family.**

5. **Adjust the view size in the third column by moving the slider or using the Size pull-down menu.**

If you want, you can have Font Book preview a font by using specific text. After you select your font, choose Preview⇨Custom or press ⌘+3. In the third column (which has now highlighted the alphanumeric preview of the font), type the text that you want to use as the sample (see Figure 26-7).

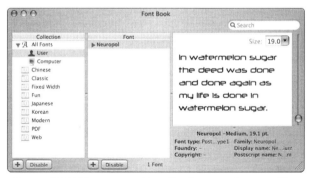

• **Figure 26-7:** You can use Font Book to preview specific text in a font.

 Font Book has a Search box in its upper-right corner, which allows you to quickly find a font by name or family.

 The Show Font Info option (under the Preview menu or accessed by pressing ⌘+I) displays a technical description of the font being previewed.

Managing Fonts

You can always install and uninstall fonts simply by manually removing them from a Fonts folder and then replacing them when needed. Although this is effective, it's unnecessarily slow and cumbersome. Instead, use Font Book to manage your fonts. With Font Book, you can

- ✔ More quickly install fonts
- ✔ View every font on your Mac at once (a time-saver because fonts may be found in many locations)
- ✔ Disable fonts without having to delete them (which makes applications load faster)
- ✔ Create font groupings so that particular applications (like Adobe Photoshop) have access to fonts not required by other applications
- ✔ Uninstall fonts without searching all over your hard drive for the actual files

 Use Font Book's Preferences (accessed by pressing ⌘+,) to adjust how the application behaves. You can set it to install fonts for you or for everyone on your Mac and adjust how disabling a font collection works. If you're worried about Font Book messing up a nicely organized system of fonts, enable the Always Copy Font Files When Installing option. This will keep Font Book from moving the original font.

To create a collection

1. **Click the plus sign at the bottom of the Collection column.**

   In the Collection column, a new listing appears with a name like "New-0" already highlighted for you.

2. **Type a name for the collection (see Figure 26-8).**

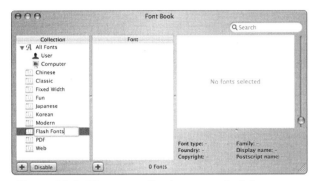

• **Figure 26-8: Give your collection a meaningful name.**

3. **In the Collection column, click All Fonts to view every font.**

4. **Drag each font you want to add from the Font column onto your new collection.**

 Use the Disable/Enable buttons to deactivate or activate fonts and collections as needed. Deactivating fonts and collections make your applications load faster (because it doesn't have to access all those fonts) and makes it easier to select a font to use (because you'll be searching through a smaller list).

Although Font Book is sufficient for the typical Mac user, those who work a lot with different sets of fonts (such as graphic artists) might find third-party tools to be a better alternative. The best candidate is Suitcase (www.extensis.com/suitcase/, $100), which has been with Mac users for a long time. It can interact with some applications like Adobe InDesign or Illustrator directly, meaning that fonts are opened automatically as soon as a document needs them. An alternative, Font Reserve, has just been purchased by Extensis (the makers of Suitcase), so its status is unclear at the time of this writing.

Technique 27

Getting to Know Services

Save Time By

✔ Figuring out what Services are

✔ Finding out about some of the best ways to use Services

✔ Seeing what extra Services are available

Services have been around since the introduction of OS X, but surprisingly few Mac users know about them or use them with any regularity. Services are like the geeky younger brothers of contextual menus: not as impressive at first, but pretty cool after you get to know them. The minutes you spend reading this chapter will greatly improve your productivity, as Services cut to the chase in performing many common tasks.

In this Technique, we give you the all-in-one treatment for Services. We begin with a quick introduction to the concept: what they are, how you use them, and where they work. Then we present a more advanced coverage of the topic, going over our best tips and techniques. Finally, we point you toward some resources for adding to your currently available Services.

What Are Services?

Services are little tools, usually chosen from a menu or keyboard shortcut, that are essentially a part of the operating system, which makes them available in many of your applications. Services work by providing the functionality of one application as an option in a second application. Some common examples of what Services can do are

✔ Open a file

✔ Send selected content in an e-mail

✔ Create a new Stickie note from selected text

✔ Have your computer speak selected text

✔ Open a URL in your Web browser

✔ Search in Google for selected text

Services are normally applied to the current selection. Most often, this is text, but it could also be a selected file or folder in the Finder. You'll also find that what services are available (unavailable Services appear in gray text) depends upon the application you are using and the content you have selected.

An application's Services are listed as menu choices in its application menu, whether the Finder (as in Figure 27-1) or Safari (like Figure 27-2). Because of their unique nature, Services function only in certain applications — specifically Cocoa applications and some Carbon applications (see the sidebar, "Cocoa and Carbon Applications").

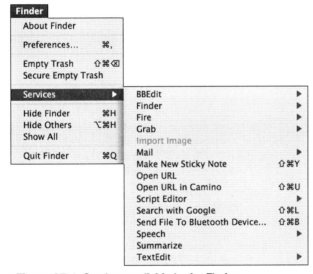

• **Figure 27-1: Services available in the Finder.**

At the time of writing, all these applications (and many more besides) support Services:

- ✔ Finder
- ✔ Mail
- ✔ Safari
- ✔ iTunes
- ✔ BBEdit

- ✔ Stickies
- ✔ StickyBrain (a Stickies-like utility)
- ✔ Camino (a Web browser)

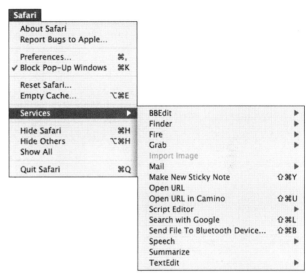

• **Figure 27-2: Services available in Safari.**

 To tell whether an application supports Services, select some text in a document or window and then peruse through the Services menu. If all the options are in gray (folders will not be in gray although their contents will be), the answer is no (see Figure 27-3). If any of the options are selectable, you're good to go!

• **Figure 27-3: The current version of Microsoft Office does not support Services.**

Your Mac comes with a good dozen of Services right out of the box, and you can add more with shareware as well (see the upcoming section, "Adding On Services").

Cocoa and Carbon Applications

Two Mac OS X terms that you might hear with some frequency are *Cocoa* and *Carbon*. These came about in part to ease the transition from OS 9 to OS X. *Carbon applications* are normally OS 9 tools that have been modified to work in OS X: for example, BBEdit. *Cocoa applications* are written specifically for OS X and take advantage of its technology (Safari, iTunes, and others). Although both of these application types run in OS X — and you don't really need to know whether an application is Cocoa- or Carbon-based — remember that all Cocoa applications support Services, whereas only some Carbon applications do.

Grasping the Best Services Techniques

The world of Services is still expanding, but good, useful Services are already available. Here is a quick tour of our favorites. Remember that Services are provided by one application to other applications that support Services. In each of these cases, we focus on what functionality an application provides:

✔ **BBEdit:** BBEdit offers a service that opens a selected file in that application. For example, select any file in the Finder and then choose Open File from the BBEdit Services menu (see Figure 27-4). It automatically opens that file — even if it isn't a standard BBEdit file type — in the popular text editor. Alternatively, BBEdit's Open Selection Service creates a new document using selected text. You can use this to take HTML code or text from a Web page and start a new BBEdit file with it.

 The BBEdit Open Selection Service has the added functionality of placing the path name of a selected file in a new BBEdit document.

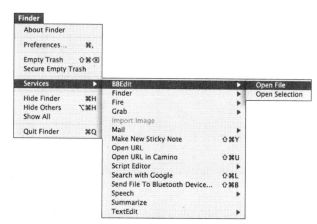

• **Figure 27-4: The BBEdit Services menu has two useful tools.**

✔ **Grab:** The Grab utility is useful for taking screen shots and it can run independent of any other application (see Technique 45). Grab also provides a highly specific, and frankly odd, Service. The Grab Service can also be used to perform screen captures — but because Services can't create files, you can only use the Grab Service to place a screenshot within another document. Figure 27-5 shows a screenshot of a Finder window placed inside of a TextEdit document.

✔ **Mail's Send Selection and Send File:** Two Mail Services let you send selected text or files as part of an e-mail. For example:

1. Select a file in the Finder.

2. Choose Finder⇨Services⇨Mail⇨Send File.

3. This brings up the Mail application, with a new e-mail already created and the file attached.

or

1. Select some text in any application that supports Services.

2. Choose *Application Menu*⇨Services⇨Mail⇨ Send Selection.

3. This brings up the Mail application, with a new e-mail already created and the selected text in the body.

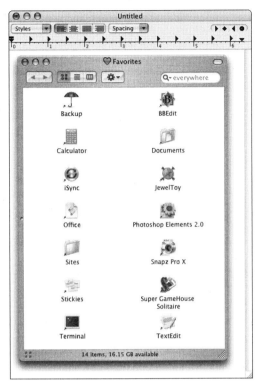

• **Figure 27-5:** No, you're not seeing double: Grab places a screenshot of a document within a document.

🗸 **Mail's Send To:** A third Mail Service automatically creates a new e-mail message addressed to the selected text, which would presumably be an e-mail address.

🗸 **Make New Sticky Note:** The Make New Sticky Note Service creates a new Stickie note from selected content (be it text or an image; see Figure 27-6).

 You can also trigger the Make New Sticky Note Service with the ⌘+Shift+Y keyboard shortcut.

🗸 **Search with Google:** This Service searches Google (in your default Web browser), using selected text as the search terms.

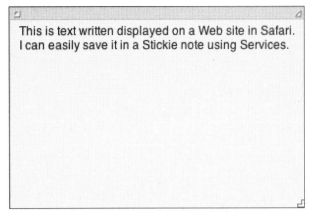

This is text written displayed on a Web site in Safari. I can easily save it in a Stickie note using Services.

• **Figure 27-6:** The Make New Sticky Note Service takes a selected image and makes a new Stickie with it.

🗸 **TextEdit's New Window Containing Selection:** This Service, similar to Make New Sticky Note, launches TextEdit and creates a new document using the selected text.

🗸 **Open URL:** The Open URL Service opens the selected URL in a new browser window in your default Web browser, saving you these steps:

1. Copying the URL to the Clipboard.

2. Navigating your way over to the Web browser.

3. Opening a new browser window.

4. Highlighting the browser's address/ location bar.

5. Pasting the URL.

6. Pressing Return to load the page.

The most important tip regarding Services is that, as with contextual menus, you should get in the habit of actively checking what options are available. New Services can be added without your knowing it (when applications are installed), or you might just forget how useful a tool they really are. Services provide huge timesaving potential for any Mac user. The next time that you have a few minutes to kill, play with the Services menu!

Bluetooth is a wireless technology that works over a limited range. It's discussed in good detail in Technique 54.

Services and Their Keyboard Shortcomings

Services have one drawback: An application's keyboard shortcuts have precedence over those used by the Services menu. This means that unlike the rest of the Mac OS X user interface, these shortcuts are really unstable.

For example, the Search with Google Service, activated by the ⌘+Shift+G keyboard shortcut, might work in one application but not another: That second application might already use ⌘+Shift+G for something else. Frankly, we think that Apple's Services should take precedence, but no one at Apple is returning our calls on the issue.

Just be aware of this issue when you use Services . . . and understand that's the cause if a shortcut fails to act predictably in certain applications.

Adding On Services

As you might imagine, you can obtain a few shareware applications that add to and improve upon the default set of Services. Unlike the Services discussed in the previous section of this chapter (which are added when applications are installed), these Services add functionality independent of any application. For example:

✔ **DEVONtechnologies** offers several free Service tools (www.devon-technologies.com/freeware.php). These include

  ▶ *AntiWordService*, which allows you to open up Microsoft Word documents in any Cocoa text editor

  ▶ *BlueService*, which enables you to send text to a Bluetooth device (assuming your computer is Bluetooth-enabled and the device is nearby)

  ▶ *CalcService*, which performs calculations

  ▶ *EasyFind*, which is a search tool

  ▶ *HotService*, which allows you to use Devon's Services through a keyboard shortcut

  ▶ *WordService*, for doing common conversions of text (like changing the case or switching between straight and curly quotation marks)

✔ The **SearchGoogle** Service (http://gu.st/proj/SearchGoogle.service/, free) automatically searches Google (using your default Web browser) for the selected text. Despite its name, the Service can also perform searches at Amazon.com and the iTunes Music Store.

✔ **CleverKeys** (www.cleverkeys.com, free) looks up definitions and synonyms online and links to Amazon.com for shopping purposes. It installs as both a Service and a contextual menu, so it works even in Carbon applications that don't support Services.

✔ **ICeCoffEE** (http://web.sabi.net/nriley/software/, free) adds a number of Services but also makes all of your Services available as contextual menus (in applications that support Services).

Most of these tools come with their own installers, but those that don't can be installed by dropping them in the /Library/Services directory. Most Services require you to log out and log back in for them to take effect.

Part V

Cranking Up Your Internet Activities

The 5th Wave   By Rich Tennant

"Look, I've already launched a search for 'reanimated babe cadavers' three times and nothing came up!"

Surfing with Safari

Whether you're surfing the Web for personal or business use, having the right tools and knowing how to get the most out of them goes a long way toward improving your experience. *Safari* is Apple's default Web browser and should be the preferred tool of choice for your browsing needs. Not only does it come free with Panther, but it's also a pretty good browser in its own right.

In this Technique, you'll find out most everything you need to know about using Safari quickly and easily. (Everything, that is, except searching with Google and managing bookmarks, each of which merit their own Techniques.) Although Web surfing is largely a mouse-driven activity, we begin with some useful keyboard shortcuts that you ought to know. Then we cover the different Safari preferences settings and why and how you should set them. After that, you read about the *AutoFill tool,* which saves you countless time spent filling out Web forms. Finally, we mention the customization tools available for tweaking the default appearance and behavior of Safari.

Navigation Shortcuts

Although you *can* surf the Net without using an input device (your mouse, trackball, or whatever), realistically, the Web is still a primarily mouse-driven world. Despite that, here is a smattering of navigation-related keyboard shortcuts that you might find useful:

✓ ⌘+N: Creates a new browser window.

✓ ⌘+T: Opens a new tab in the current window.

 Safari supports *tabbed browsing,* which is the ability to open multiple Web pages within a single browser window. We discuss this in detail in "Working with tabbed browsing."

✓ ⌘+[(opening brace): Goes back one page.

✓ ⌘+] (closing brace): Goes forward one page (to a page you have previously visited).

Back and forth navigation is represented by two sets of keyboard shortcuts. The standard Mac shortcuts that use brackets ([and]) work like they do in the Finder. The standard shortcuts for other browsers (using the left and right arrow keys) also function.

✔ ⌘+L: The ⌘+L shortcut — Open Location — highlights the address bar (or location window) and places the cursor there. If no browser window is open, this command opens a new browser window and places the cursor in the address bar (see Figure 28-1).

• **Figure 28-1: Use ⌘+L to access the address bar.**

✔ ⌘+. (period): Stops a page from loading.

✔ ⌘+R: Reloads the page.

✔ ⌘+Shift+H: Goes to your home page (as set in Safari's preferences).

✔ ⌘+` (accent grave) or ~ (tilde): Rotates among the open windows.

✔ ⌘+Shift+→ and ⌘+Shift+←: Rotates among tabs within a window.

✔ Tab key: Normally moves from element to element within a Web page.

 Many people don't know this, but for most Web sites, you can skip the *www* at the beginning of the URL without consequence. You can almost always skip the *http://* part. In fact, many common Web sites can be accessed by using a bare minimum of typing: *apple, microsoft, espn, adobe,* and so forth. (Whether this works for you depends on your browsing history, but it's worth trying.)

Standard Shortcuts

Along with the Safari navigation shortcuts, all the common Panther keyboard commands work in Safari as well:

✔ ⌘+O: Opens a file (if you want to open a saved Web page from your hard drive)

✔ ⌘+W: Closes the open window

✔ ⌘+S: Saves a document

✔ ⌘+P: Prints the open document

✔ ⌘+C: Copies selected text to the Clipboard

✔ ⌘+X: Cuts selected text (which is much less useful in Safari than in other applications)

✔ ⌘+V: Pastes Clipboard contents where the cursor is

✔ ⌘+A: Selects everything

✔ ⌘+Z: Undoes the last action

✔ ⌘+Shift+Z: Redoes the last undone action

✔ ⌘+E: Adds a selection to the Find Clipboard

 Read more about the Find Clipboard in Technique 25.

✔ ⌘+F: Brings up the Find dialog (see Figure 28-2)

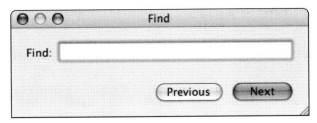

• **Figure 28-2: Safari's Find dialog.**

✔ ⌘+G: Finds something again

✔ ⌘+Shift+G: Goes to the previously found item

✔ ⌘+H: Hides Safari

✔ ⌘+Option+H: Hides every other application

✔ ⌘+Q: Quits Safari

✔ ⌘+, (comma): Brings up the Appearance preferences panel (see Figure 28-3)

• **Figure 28-3: Safari's preferences panel.**

Other Shortcuts

Finally, you should know about a few other miscellaneous-purpose keyboard shortcuts that will come in handy.

✔ ⌘+= (equal sign): Increases text size

 The Increase Text Size keyboard shortcut is technically pressing the ⌘ and + keys at the same time. But because pressing the Shift key to make the plus sign would be inconvenient, you can get away with ⌘+=.

✔ ⌘+− (minus sign): Decreases text size

✔ ⌘+K: Sets Safari to block pop-up ads

✔ ⌘+: (colon; you could also think of this as ⌘+Shift+;): Brings up the Spelling dialog (see Figure 28-4)

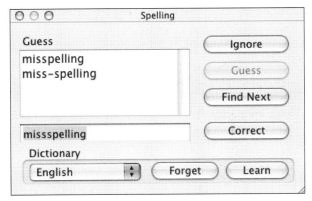

• **Figure 28-4: Apple's spelling tool works in Safari.**

✔ ⌘+; (semicolon): Checks your spelling, separate from the Spelling dialog

 Turn on the Check Spelling as You Type option (under Edit⇨Spelling) to look smarter when you fill out forms. Once enabled, text you enter in forms will be spell checked, just as your typing in a text editor is.

Mice and Safari

Presumably you already know the basics of using the mouse (or other input device) with Safari. Consider a couple of additions, however, to improve on your experience.

For starters, a mouse with a scroll wheel enables you to simply rotate the wheel to move up and down within a Web page. This saves you the time and hassle of switching back and forth between your mouse and the keyboard. Your mice will even scroll sideways within a page if you hold down the Shift key while using the scroll wheel. Some mouse software (like Kensington's MouseWorks) will let you set the scroll wheel to act as a button click if you press down on it.

Second, if you have a programmable mouse, you can set one of the buttons to act as a Control+click, enacting the

(continued)

contextual menus. What you see in the contextual menu will differ based upon what you Control+click on. If you just click on a Web page without selecting any text, you can view the HTML source, save the page, or print it.

View Source
Save Page As...
Print Page...

If you select some text and press Control+click, you can copy that text or use it as a Google search term.

Copy
Google Search

If you Control+click an image or a link, you're given different options, such as opening the link in a new window or downloading the image to your computer.

You can use the mouse in even more innovative ways if you use Cocoa Gestures (www.bitart.com/Cocoa Gestures.html, free). This shareware application lets you associate commands with mouse movements made while holding down the primary mouse button. For example, you can set Cocoa Gestures so that if you hold down the mouse button and move the mouse to the left, Safari goes back to the previous page. Gestures are an odd concept to wrap your head around, but you'll love them once you start using them. They let you perform common tasks without switching over to the keyboard or moving your cursor up to the proper buttons.

Setting Preferences

Adjusting Safari's sparse but potent preferences goes a long way toward improving your Web-browsing experience. Most of the options are easy to comprehend, so we stick to discussing those that most directly improves how quickly and easily you can use the application. Specifically, we focus on those features that you can adjust within the General, Tabs, and Security sections of the Preferences panel. To address the Safari preferences, press ⌘+, (comma) or select Preferences from the Safari menu.

Setting General preferences

The General panel (as shown in Figure 28-5) greatly affects your entire Internet surfing experience. The best timesaving techniques here are

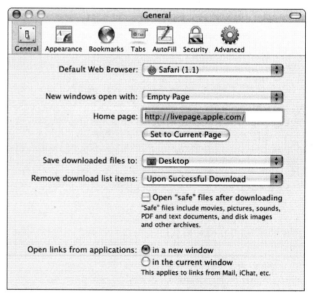

• **Figure 28-5:** Safari's General preferences panel.

> ✔ **Set your default Web browser.** Although Mac users often use many different browsers at once (particularly graphic designers and Web developers), you should identify a primary browser. The

benefit to this is that every URL you click in an e-mail, iChat session, or document will be automatically opened in your preferred Web browser. Strangely enough, this setting is now in the Safari browser rather than in an Internet preferences panel (so, yes, you would use Safari to say that you want Netscape to be your default Web Browser).

✔ **Set new windows to open with an empty page.** Accessing your home page or bookmarks immediately is convenient, but how frequently will you really be doing that? Instead, save yourself the loading time by choosing Empty Page from the New Windows Open With pull-down menu. Every time you press ⌘+N (new browser window), a blank window will be opened, ready for you to type the address. On those occasions when you want to go to your Home page or Bookmarks, just press ⌘+Shift+H or ⌘+Option+B, respectively.

✔ **Set your home page.** Your home page can be anything — not necessarily a traditional, customizable site like Yahoo!, Apple.Netscape.com, or the one provided by your ISP. For example, in the past, Larry set Google as his home page, but now he's just as likely to use www.espn.com (which *must* be checked several times per day).

 Your home page — like your Home directory in the Finder — can be quickly viewed by pressing the ⌘+Shift+H keyboard shortcut. (Both shortcuts only work within each specific application.)

✔ **Set where Safari saves downloaded files.** When your browser downloads a file, you want that to happen with as little interruption as possible. To that end, use the Save Downloaded Files To dropdown list to have Safari automatically download files to the Desktop where you can easily find them. In the Remove Download List Items dropdown list, choose Upon Successful Download to have downloaded items automatically removed after a download is successfully completed. Also clear the Open "Safe" Files After Downloading check box. If you do this, you can easily see and

access your downloaded files by ⌘+Option+ clicking the Desktop (which hides all other applications in the process).

✔ **Set Safari to open links from applications in a new window.** You'll want to select the In a New Window radio button because otherwise every URL that you click in any application wipes out the contents of the current browser window. (If you were to click several links within an e-mail, as an example, each would continually replace its predecessor.) To look through them all, you would need to do some savvy navigation within the same browser window. Avoid the hassle and just have Safari create a new window for each new link. They're easy enough to cycle through (⌘+`) or close (⌘+W) anyway.

 To adjust the appearance of the browser window, you can always show/hide the address bar, status bar, and bookmark bar by using the options under the View menu or by using the keyboard shortcuts (⌘ + | to toggle the address bar off and on, ⌘ + / for the status bar, and ⌘+B for the bookmark bar).

Working with tabbed browsing

Tabbed browsing is a relative newcomer to the world of Web browsers, and it's a most welcome addition. It first came about in lesser-known browsers such as Mozilla and OmniWeb, and has just recently made its way to Safari. For those of you unfamiliar with the concept, *tabbed browsing* allows you to have multiple documents (Web pages) nicely organized and displayed within a single document window. Each page has its own tab that you can then click to access quickly and easily. This helps keep things organized during regular use and allows you to access bookmarks in novel ways.

To set up tabbed browsing:

1. **Click the Tabs icon in Safari's preferences (see Figure 28-6).**

• **Figure 28-6:** Enable tabbed browsing from the Tabs panel.

2. Mark the Enable Tabbed Browsing check box.

3. Make sure that the Select New Tabs As They Are Created check box is not checked.

One of the biggest benefits of tabbed browsing is that you can click links without disrupting the flow of reading through a page, so selecting this option defeats that purpose. If you want to immediately view a tabbed link, hold down ⌘+Shift while clicking a link. Otherwise, leave this check box clear so that each tab appears in the background.

4. Make sure that the Always Show Tab Bar check box is also not checked.

The tab bar automatically appears and disappears as needed, so you don't need to have it always hanging around. (In fact, that just uses up unnecessary screen space.)

 If you find all of these shortcuts hard to remember, just be certain to keep the status bar visible. It will show you what each action will do before you take it. For example, if you hold down the ⌘ key while hovering over a link, the status bar reads Go to *whatever-URL-the-link-is* in a new tab behind the current one. ⌘+click on the link and Safari will do just that.

To use tabbed browsing:

✔ Hold down the ⌘ key while clicking a link to view it in a tab (see Figure 28-7).

• **Figure 28-7:** A browser window with multiple tabs.

✔ Hold down the ⌘ and Shift keys while clicking a link to view it in a new tab immediately. (In other words, open the new tab in front of the existing tab.)

✔ The ⌘+Shift+→ shortcut rotates one tab to the right.

✔ Pressing ⌘+Shift+← rotates one tab to the left.

✔ Hold down the Option key while clicking a link to view it in a new window (as opposed to a tab).

 If tabbed browsing is enabled, holding down the Option key when you click on a link opens that link in a new window, as opposed to a tab. If tabbed browsing is not enabled, holding down the Option key when you click on a link downloads the link to your computer.

✔ Use Option+Shift+click to open a link in a new window in front of the active window.

 The keyboard shortcuts for tabs come down to this: ⌘ means a new tab, and Shift means that the new tab should be selected (opened in front). Option, on the other hand, makes a new window, so pressing Option+Shift makes a new window in front of the others.

Here's a cool little tidbit: If you enter any text in the address bar or Google search bar and press ⌘+Return, the result opens in a new tab. Pressing ⌘+Shift+Return opens it in a new tab at the front.

If a browser window has multiple tabs

- Pressing ⌘+W closes the current tab.

- Clicking the little X icon next to the tab's title closes that tab. (This goes for any tab and not just the active one.)

- Clicking the window's red button in the upper-left corner closes the entire window and every tab in it.

- Control+click a tab's title to see a contextual menu (see Figure 28-8). With this menu you can close that tab or all the others, or reload that tab or every other.

> New Tab
> Close Tab
> Close Other Tabs
>
> Reload Tab
> Reload All Tabs

• **Figure 28-8: Contextual menus work on tabs in Safari.**

Blocking pop-up windows

Pop-up windows, the Web's version of spam, have to be one of the most annoying things around. (Except for maybe Carrot Top's long distance commercials, that is.) Fortunately, you don't have to see pop-ups if you don't want to. We *highly* recommend that you do one of the following:

- While in Safari, press ⌘+K to turn on pop-up window blocking (pressing it again will turn pop-up window blocking back off, if you miss the extra windows).

- In the Security panel of Safari's Preferences, mark the Block Pop-Up Windows check box.

The nice thing about this feature of Safari is that pop-up windows that you request (for example, by clicking a link) still appear, but those requested by the page itself (read: advertisements for travel deals, super-fast weight loss, and phenomenal hair regrowth) never do.

 Setting Safari to block pop-up windows saves you a lifetime of effort spent closing annoying little windows. You're still on your own with the Carrot Top commercials, though!

Cache as Catch Can

Web browsers use two concepts behind the scenes to improve the speed of surfing the Web. The first, history, records places you've visited. You can access them again by using the History menu or by letting the application automatically complete the URL when you begin typing it. A cache is the browser's way of saving text, images, videos, and other content to your hard disk. The benefit of caching is that the next time the page is loaded, some of the content can be recalled from the disk, rather than having to re-download it.

Most browsers allow you to put a limit on how big the cache of Web pages saved by your browser can grow, which keeps your cache from getting too big. Odd as it might seem, Safari doesn't let you adjust the amount of disk space used by its cache. (In fact, Safari provides few of the standard options in terms of refreshing the browser, managing your history, and so forth.) Instead, you can simply empty the cache when you feel like it. To do so, either choose Empty Cache from the Safari menu or use the ⌘+Option+E shortcut. Either of these makes Safari rebuild each page it encounters from the source, without relying upon any cached materials. This is particularly useful if you are creating Web pages and want to insure that Safari is reflecting the most recent changes.

With respect to your history, although you can't set a default number of days or pages to track, you can clear it all by using the Clear History option at the bottom of the History menu.

(continued)

While we're at it, we might as well mention the cookies stored in Safari. These are controlled in the Security tab. There you can adjust how Safari handles cookies, or view stored cookies by clicking on Show Cookies. In the resulting window, you can delete any cookies by selecting them from the list and clicking Remove (or by clicking Remove All to really sweep away the cookie crumbs).

Saving Time with AutoFill Forms

Surfing the Internet, to a large degree, comes down to filling out forms. Passwords, search boxes, order pages, and other forms require you to constantly enter the same information again and again. To save yourself the tedium and much time in the bargain, familiarize yourself with Safari's AutoFill Forms feature.

Select the check boxes of the AutoFill panel of the Preferences dialog (as shown in Figure 28-9) to enable three types of AutoFill:

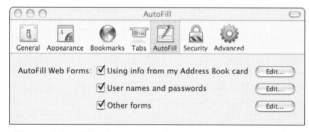

• **Figure 28-9: The AutoFill preferences panel.**

✔ **Your personal information:** This option allows Safari to fill in your name, company name, e-mail address, phone number, and mailing address, using the information you've established in your Address Book record. Checking this AutoFill option is the most important in terms of saving time and involves the least amount of security risks.

 Safari's AutoFill tool is another reason to use your Address Book: That's where Safari gets its information from, after all. Furthermore, if you move, you only need to change your address record in the Address Book, and Safari's AutoFill values are automatically updated.

✔ **Usernames and passwords:** There are two types of username/password combinations Safari can help with. First, and most common, are those associated with login forms, like when you log into Amazon.com or NewYorkTimes.com. The second type are those used to limit access to Web pages or sections of a Web page. These use a separate pop-up window (although it's not the same kind of browser pop-up window used by advertisers), not a standard Web-based form. In either case, Safari will — if you let it — remember the proper username and password for each individual Web site.

 The passwords stored by Safari are safe because they cannot be retrieved without a person knowing your system's master password. Safari uses the keychain (see Technique 52) to store these passwords, where they are only visible after revalidating using the account's login password.

✔ **Other forms:** This catch-all records (again, if you want it to) those things you entered in, er, other forms. These values might be for a preferences page of a Web site or an address entered into MapQuest.

After you enable AutoFill, it will automatically fill in values when you encounter personal information forms (assuming that the Web site has form inputs named logically so that AutoFill recognizes them as such). If the AutoFill doesn't immediately engage, use the ⌘+Shift+A shortcut to activate it.

For usernames and passwords, and for other forms, Safari automatically fills these out at a Web site using the values you entered in the previous visit.

 The AutoFill tool marks in yellow those form inputs that it fills out. Also, if you have multiple options for an input (for example, you might have several e-mail addresses), begin typing the first few letters of the one that you want and then select it from the option menu that appears.

Managing Usernames and Passwords

When you first encounter a site that requires a user-name and password, create a username and pass-word and then click Submit. Safari then asks you whether you would like to save this password as an AutoFill entry, giving you three options (check them out in Figure 28-10):

Would you like to save this password?
Saved passwords can be reviewed and removed in the AutoFill preferences.

[Never for this Website]   [Not Now]   (Yes)

• **Figure 28-10: Let Safari manage your usernames and passwords.**

✔ Never for this Website

✔ Not Now

✔ Yes

For almost every instance, choosing to have Safari remember the values is the smart move, saving you the time of re-entering that information upon your next visit. If the site in question is of a particularly sensitive nature (such as your online banking), you might want to ask Safari not to remember the values and never prompt you again. If you aren't certain what to do, opt for door number three (Not Now), and you'll be prompted again the next time that you enter that username and password.

To have Safari forget some remembered values

1. **Click the Edit button next to User Names and Passwords of the AutoFill panel (refer to Figure 28-9).**

2. **In the resulting panel, select the site whose values should be forgotten (see Figure 28-11).**

Website	User Name
http://127.0.0.1/	Passwords Never Saved
http://bluechippick.com/	larry
http://chicagosports.chicagotribune.com/	spiritualized
http://comcast.net/	larryullman
http://discussions.ucxonline.berkeley.edu:808	phpunex
http://dmcinsights.com/	kudzu
http://dotster.com/	larryullman
http://giganews.com/	cc0089024
http://localhost/	Passwords Never Saved
http://projectseed.ed.psu.edu/	lu3906
http://projectseed.psu.edu/	Passwords Never Saved
http://registration.excite.com/	larry-ullman
http://www.amazon.com/	larryullman@mac.com
http://www.bluechippick.com/	larry
http://www.comcast.net/	lullman
http://www.doverafbservices.com/	Passwords Never Saved

(Remove)   (Remove All)   (Done)

• **Figure 28-11: Forget submitted username and password combinations using this window.**

3. **Click the Remove button.**

Do not click Remove All in this window unless you really want to spend the time retyping every username and password everywhere you go.

4. **Repeat Steps 2 and 3 as necessary.**

5. **Click Done when you're finished.**

Marking Pages with SnapBack

A really, really, really great feature in Safari is *SnapBack,* which is kind of like a temporary book-mark. You'll find two different SnapBacks in Safari: one for the main page of a Web site, and another for your Google searches. With SnapBack, you can des-ignate a place as a SnapBack page and then return to that page immediately without being forced to navi-gate back through all the intermediary pages.

An alternative to both the SnapBack and the History features is to use the browser window's title bar. ⌘+click on the title and you'll see a menu of previously visited pages (Figure 28-12), like the path hierarchy of a Finder window.

```
⇧ http://movies2.nytimes.com/gst/movies/movie.html?v_id=278981
⊕ http://movies2.nytimes.com/gst/movies
⊕ http://movies2.nytimes.com/gst
⊕ http://movies2.nytimes.com/
```

• **Figure 28-12:** See, and quickly go back to, places you've been in a Web site by ⌘+clicking on the browser window title.

Safari automatically manages the two SnapBack pages:

✔ **When you go to any site, Safari marks it for SnapBack.** After you browse from there, the orange SnapBack arrow appears. Clicking it returns you to the original page. This also works for bookmarks you load.

Here's an example of how you might use this feature:

1. Open Amazon.com in Safari.

2. Click the Books tab.

   The original URL is now marked for SnapBack.

3. Navigate through the Browse Subjects pages to access the books on, say, Mac OS X.

4. Mark the resulting page for SnapBack by choosing Mark Page for SnapBack under the History menu.

5. View all the books you want and add them to your cart as desired.

   We highly recommend picking up a few copies of *Mac OS X Panther Timesaving Techniques For Dummies* (Wiley, 2004).

6. Return to the original Mac OS X books page (what you set in Step 4) by clicking the orange SnapBack arrow.

✔ **Every Google search page is marked for Snap-Back.** The Google Search box appears next to the address bar (you can show and hide it using the View menu) and has its own SnapBack, entirely independent from the location/address SnapBack.

Here's an example of how you might manually use this technique:

1. **Click in the Google Search box to place your cursor there.**

2. **Enter your search terms and press Return.**

   For example, you can search for "Larry Ullman" or "Marc Liyanage."

3. **Click on any link returned by Google to visit that page.**

4. **If you need to return to the Google search results page, click on the SnapBack icon found in the Google Search box.**

The keyboard shortcuts for working with SnapBack are

✔ ⌘+Option+K: Marks a page for SnapBack

✔ ⌘+Option+P: Goes to the SnapBack page

✔ ⌘+Option+S: Returns to the Google search SnapBack

Safari's Debug Menu

The really techie user out there will appreciate this little trick. You can enact Safari's Debug menu from the Terminal. The Debug menu lets you pretend that you are using a different browser (good for accessing persnickety Web sites), debug JavaScript, import bookmarks from other browsers, and more.

Here's one way to turn on the Debug menu:

1. **Open the Terminal application.**

2. **Navigate to your Preferences folder with the command** cd ~/Library/Preferences.

3. **Type** defaults write com.apple.Safari IncludeDebugMenu 1 **and then press Return.**

4. **Quit and then relaunch the Safari application.**

The Debug menu now appears as an option, letting you do such things as have Safari pose as other Web browsers when visiting sites. Alternatively, you can use the Safari Enhancer (discussed in "Customizing Safari") to do this and more.

Customizing Safari

The techniques in this section won't necessarily save you a lot of time, but you can employ them to customize Safari to your way of thinking, which is still worthwhile. Here are a few of our favorites:

✔ **Use your own style sheet:** If you're comfortable with cascading style sheets (CSSes), create your own style sheet and set Safari to always use it. How much or how little you dictate in the style sheet is up to you. In-depth coverage of CSSes is outside the scope of this book, but if you would like to read up on the subject, check out *Cascading Style Sheets For Dummies,* by Damon Dean (Wiley).

✔ **Investigate a handful of utilities online for changing the theme and appearance of Safari, such as**

▶ **Lioness** (http://w1.864.telia.com/ ~u86428755/superqult_software/lioness. html, free)

▶ **Safari Aquafier and Safari Font** (www.scifience.net, free)

▶ **SafariIcon** (http://homepage.mac.com/ reinholdpenner, free)

▶ **SafariNoBrush** (http://www.macupdate.com/ info.php/id/10525, free)

✔ **Use Safari Enhancer** (www.lordofthecows.com, **free) or Safari Helper** (http://zoffware.com, **free) to change Safari's appearance and some of its behavior.**

✔ **Use PithHelmet** (www.culater.net/osd/Pith Helmet/PithHelmet.html, **free) to have Safari block out advertising images in Web pages. It can also stop sounds from playing and cut out Flash and Shockwave animations.**

Don't forget that your contextual menus and services offer Search with Google and Open URL shortcuts, thanks to Safari. With these, you can quickly start common Safari tasks from within other applications. See Techniques 12 (on contextual menus) and 27 (on Services) for more.

Technique 29

Surfing with Other Browsers

Save Time By

- ✔ Picking up some useful tips for Internet Explorer
- ✔ Finding out a bit about Netscape, Mozilla, and Camino
- ✔ Checking out the commercial browsers available on the Mac

If Microsoft has taught the world anything, it's that using only one browser — and the browser that comes with the operating system in particular — might not be the best move. Although *Safari,* Apple's default browser, is a great product, you should consider using another Web browser, if only as a secondary option. Web developers must have multiple Web browsers in order to test how a Web site will look and behave for different users. We would suggest that the average Mac user have a couple of Web browsers for two reasons. First, you can take advantage of different features that don't exist or aren't consistent across all browsers. Second, some Web pages look and work better in one browser than they do in another.

A handful of other browsers work on Panther, and we discuss most of those here. You're not going to get too much of an introduction to any one browser (they all do the same thing, after all), but you will see the most useful features and techniques of each. Our focus will be on Internet Explorer (IE) and the Netscape/Mozilla/Camino line, with a little attention given to three commercial products: OmniWeb, Opera, and iCab.

 Pretty much every browser you use asks you whether you want to set it as your default browser. You're not permanently beholden to that decision, though, because you can always change this setting through Safari's preferences panel (see Technique 28).

Internet Explorer

Internet Explorer — as you likely know — is the 800-pound gorilla of the Web browser market. Many Mac users began relying upon it during the years of Apple's close contractual ties with Microsoft (also know as *the Dark Ages*). Despite the fact that we're of the anti-IE camp (see the "A Rant against Internet Explorer" sidebar, later in this Technique), we acknowledge that a number of readers still use it. For those readers, we'd like to give you some information to help you get the most out of the application.

In our opinion, you have two main reasons to use IE:

✔ You're a Web developer and want to test a site on one of the more common browsers.

✔ You're accessing a site that requires you to use IE.

 To add to our cause of getting you to not use Internet Explorer, note that it lacks three very useful features that Safari boasts: tabbed browsing, pop-up ad blocking, and the ability to Snap-Back to a page or search results. Also, Microsoft no longer plans to develop IE for the Mac.

Keyboard shortcuts

You don't need to read much of this book to know that we're pretty keen on using keyboard shortcuts whenever possible. Without overwhelming you with all the options, here are some of the most important ones for IE:

✔ ⌘+[(opening brace): Moves you back one page

✔ ⌘+] (closing brace): Goes forward one page (a page you've already visited)

✔ ⌘+. (period): Stops the loading of the current page

✔ ⌘+R: Refreshes the current page

✔ ⌘+D: Adds the current page to your list of Favorites (otherwise known as *bookmarks*)

✔ ⌘+1: Brings up the main IE window

✔ ⌘+2: Shows your Favorites (see Figure 29-1)

✔ ⌘+3: Displays your browsing history

✔ ⌘+4: Reveals the Download Manager

✔ ⌘+~ (tilde): Cycles through all the open windows

• **Figure 29-1: Internet Explorer's Favorites window.**

Favorites

Internet Explorer uses the concept of *Favorites* (the equivalent of a bookmark), which allows you to mark a page and quickly return to it later. Technique 30 discusses bookmarks in greater detail (across all browsers), but here are a few things that you ought to know if you use IE as your primary browser:

✔ Pressing ⌘+D adds the current page to your list of Favorites.

 Unlike many other browsers, when you add a page to your IE Favorites, all the action happens behind the scenes. (That is, you're not given a prompt.)

✔ Press ⌘+2 to view all your Favorites.

When you're in the Favorites window

✔ Click the arrows to expand a folder.

✔ Choose Favorites⇨Organize Favorites⇨ New Folder (see Figure 29-2) to create new folders.

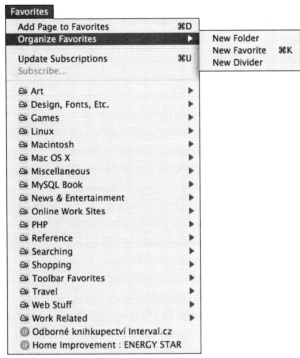

• **Figure 29-2: The Favorites menu assists the bookmark management process.**

✔ Drag and drop Favorites to move them from one folder to another.

✔ Press ⌘+Option+Delete to remove a Favorite without receiving a prompt asking you to confirm your action.

Explorer bar

Internet Explorer puts several of its most useful features in a Sidebar of the browser window called the *Explorer bar* (see it in Figure 29-3).

• **Figure 29-3: The Explorer bar appears on the left side of the browser window.**

 Use the ⌘+T keyboard shortcut to show/hide the Explorer bar.

To view any of the tools, click its tab. In the Explorer bar, you can view the following:

✔ **Favorites:** Use the IE Explorer bar to easily view, create, delete, and organize your Favorites (bookmarks).

✔ **History:** View a log of the pages you have seen so that you can quickly revisit a site.

✔ **Search:** Theoretically you can perform searches in the Explorer bar, but it's a buggy feature with an inclination towards using Microsoft's search engines.

✔ **Scrapbook:** The Scrapbook lets you store images and static versions of Web pages. To add an image, drag it from the Web page into the Scrapbook. To add a Web page, click the Add button in the Explorer bar window. Click any item in your Scrapbook to view it again.

✔ **Page Holder:** The Page Holder lets you place a Web page in the Explorer bar, and all its links open in the main window. This is a good substitute for the tabbed browsing feature that Explorer lacks (and Safari has).

Other features

Unlike Safari, IE has many preferences that can be adjusted. Press ⌘+; (semicolon) to access the Preferences panel, as shown in Figure 29-4. Click a menu item in the left pane to bring up different settings on the right side of this dialog. A lot of the preferences are cosmetic — and some are security- or feature-related — but here are those most useful to the Mac user interested in productivity.

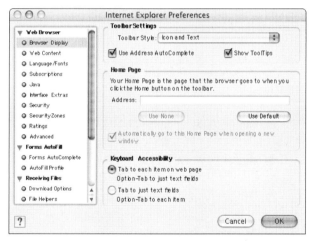

• **Figure 29-4: The Internet Explorer Preferences panel.**

✔ Use the Forms AutoFill panel to set your personal information (such as name, address, and e-mail address) to be automatically entered in Web forms.

✔ Under the Advanced section, adjust the History and Cache policies. A large history lets you quickly access Web pages without retyping entire URLs. Visited URLs are automatically completed as you begin typing them. The Cache dictates how much of the Web site needs to be downloaded with each new viewing. This is particularly useful if you visit the same sites frequently and are on a slow Internet connection.

Furthermore, here are a couple of other tools worth looking into:

✔ Under the Tools menu, check out the Track Auctions feature, which will help your eBay and similar endeavors. This tool notifies you of the time remaining, current bid, and so forth of auctions that you're tracking. Explanations on using it can be found by clicking Help after you bring up the Auction Manager window.

✔ The Related Links option is like a mini search engine that uses the current page as the search term.

✔ Subscriptions track the content of your favorite sites, automatically updating them in your Web browser and notifying you of the update, per your instructions.

A Rant against Internet Explorer

We would be remiss to discuss Internet Explorer without giving a quick rant on how it's been responsible for the downfall of the Internet. Okay, that's an overstatement, but IE has made being a Web developer far more difficult. Whereas most of the other browsers that we discuss in this chapter were developed for any platform supporting existing Web standards, IE chose to go its own way instead. The consequence is that Web developers had to make Web sites compatible for two types of users: those with standards-compliant browsers and those with IE.

Our point: Despite its popularity and decent feature set, throw your copy of Internet Explorer out the door as an act of social conscience or civil disobedience. More than enough good alternatives are available, particularly for use with Panther. And because Microsoft is phasing out its production of IE for the Mac, it's only going to become more dated as time passes.

Netscape, Mozilla, and Camino

Netscape is actually one of the grandfathers of the World Wide Web. Its predecessor, Mosaic, was one of the very first Web browsers. Netscape sadly ended up taking a back seat to the IE behemoth and was then purchased by America Online (AOL). It's still a good and reliable browser, though.

Netscape's main benefit could be the familiarity that most users have with its interface and features. (Netscape 4 was very popular on Mac OS 8 and 9.) But the application does have more to offer than just comfort, including

- ✔ Pop-up ad blocking

- ✔ Tabbed browsing

- ✔ Ability to perform searches from the address bar

- ✔ A fully integrated e-mail client

- ✔ Integration with the AOL Instant Messenger

Mozilla, Firebird, and Camino are all byproducts of the same source code. The makers (www.mozilla. org) took the Netscape source code and expanded upon it. The three have a few differences, but the most significant is that Mozilla includes e-mail functionality and Web development tools, whereas Firebird and Camino are standalone Web browsers.

 Three of the strengths of these browsers are their tabbed browsing, the ability to block pop-up ads, and their leading position in displaying Web content correctly. Plus, Mozilla and Netscape can handle your e-mail, if you'd prefer to keep your e-mail and Web browsing within the same application.

Mozilla has Netscape-like feel to it and therefore isn't much of a leap for most users. Further, Mozilla offers

- ✔ The most complete implementation of today's Web standards of any browser

- ✔ JavaScript and Document Object Model (DOM) debugging tools

- ✔ High-grade security support

 Web developers might find Mozilla to be an indispensable aid in developing effective Web sites. For information and specific examples, see http://devedge.netscape.com/viewsource/ 2003/mozilla-webdev/.

Camino (which used to be called *Chimera*) is Mozilla's baby brother. It skips the e-mail and developer tools, leaving only a speedy little browser. This browser is easy to use and renders Web pages beautifully. Firebird is a new product and differs from Camino mainly in that it's available on all platforms, whereas Camino is Mac-only.

Commercial Web Browsers

Believe it or not, despite the number of free Web browsers available, a few commercial (read: not free) browsers are out there. Each of these has a feature set that should make it worth paying for, and they offer a free trial that you can use while you decide.

- ✔ **OmniWeb** (www.omnigroup.com/applications/ omniweb/, $30): OmniWeb is a beautiful Web browser with many very nice features, such as

  - ▶ Pop-up blocking

  - ▶ Ad blocking (blocks ads which appear within a Web page, like banner ads)

  - ▶ Ability to search through your browsing history

  - ▶ Built-in Google search

  - ▶ Voice recognition (you can control the browser by speaking)

 OmniWeb is a great browser for Web developers because of its many tools. You can control cookies on a sophisticated level, view HTML source code in an easy-to-read layout, and edit HTML in the browser.

- ✔ **Opera** (www.opera.com, $40): Opera claims to be the fastest browser on Earth, partially because of its small size. It also has

  - ▶ E-mail tools

  - ▶ A high degree of Web-standard compliance

- ▶ Keyboard shortcuts for navigating without the mouse

- ▶ Pop-up ad blocking

✔ **iCab** (www.icab.de, $30): iCab is still being developed but looks to have some promising features, including

- ▶ Ad blocking

- ▶ HTML syntax validation (checks that a page uses valid HTML code)

- ▶ HTML editing (lets you edit HTML code within iCab itself)

Technique 30

Managing Bookmarks Better

Save Time By

✔ Managing bookmarks with Safari

✔ Sharing bookmarks across multiple browsers

✔ Discovering other ways to bookmark and access Web pages

Surfing the Internet would be a much more tedious process if it weren't for the advent of bookmarks. *Bookmarks* (or Favorites, as they are also called) are a collection of URLs that you can organize the way you like for easy access. We haven't discussed bookmarks much in previous Techniques because they really merit their own discussion, particularly if you use multiple browsers.

The focus in this chapter is the Safari Web browser, which we recommend you use as your default. We first talk about bookmark management within Safari, and then we go into sharing bookmarks across multiple browsers (which is a good thing whether you actively use multiple browsers or just switched to a different one). Finally, we wrap up with some tips and techniques for bookmark management that you might want to employ.

Managing Bookmarks in Safari

Because we assume that you're using Safari as your primary Web browser, we cover bookmarks in that application most specifically. Safari's bookmarks tools have taken the best qualities from every other browser and wrapped them into one package. With Safari, you have three bookmark locations:

✔ **The Bookmarks Bar** (see Figure 30-1): This is an area intended for your most frequently used bookmarks because they can appear in your browser window at all times, making them the easiest to access. The Bookmarks Bar can display individual URLs (like Apple and Amazon in Figure 30-1), folders of sites (News and Localhost), and it also provides a link to the Bookmarks window (the open book icon on the far left).

Bookmarks Bar

• **Figure 30-1: The Bookmarks Bar appears underneath the address bar.**

✔ **The Bookmarks menu** (see Figure 30-2): The Bookmarks menu lists bookmarks that you can access by selecting a site from the list. Figure 30-2 shows two bookmarks in Larry's menu.

• **Figure 30-2: The Bookmarks menu can list bookmarks.**

✔ **The Bookmarks window** (see Figure 30-3): The Bookmarks windows is the least accessible (it just requires an extra click to access it) but helps to manage all of your bookmarks. The Bookmarks window is where you'll store the majority of your bookmarks, and it's also where you can add, edit, or delete bookmarks that appear in the Bookmarks Bar and Bookmarks menu.

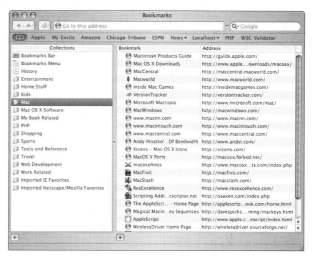

• **Figure 30-3: Use the Bookmarks window to manage and access sites.**

 A fourth, related tool is the History menu. This menu doesn't contain bookmarks per se but is rather a history of pages that you've visited. Those URLs you've been to appear under the History menu and within the Bookmarks window (the third item under Collections in the left column of Figure 30-3). The History menu displays the most recent few pages visited, followed by other pages grouped by the date on which you were there.

To add bookmarks, access the Bookmarks window or Bookmarks Bar, or to create new folders for organizing your bookmarks (in the Bookmarks window), you can use the Bookmarks menu (refer to Figure 30-2) or the following keyboard shortcuts:

✔ ⌘+D: Creates a bookmark for the current page

✔ ⌘+B: Toggles to show and hide the bookmark bar

✔ ⌘+Option+B: Displays the Bookmarks window

✔ ⌘+Shift+N: Creates a new folder within the Bookmarks window

Safari comes with many bookmarks and folders already grouped into News, Mac, Kids, Sports, and more. This is important because creating a folder for each category of Web page that you want to bookmark helps you find your bookmarks faster. Some good folders you might want to add would be Work, Mac OS X Software, Local Interest, and any other types of pages that you visit frequently.

Bookmarking a page

To bookmark a page, follow these steps:

1. **Load the page in your Web browser.**

2. **Press ⌘+D.**

This brings up the Add Bookmark prompt, as shown in Figure 30-4.

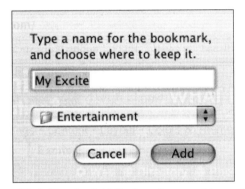

Type a name for the bookmark, and choose where to keep it.

My Excite

📁 Entertainment

Cancel Add

• **Figure 30-4:** Use the Add Bookmark prompt to mark a page.

3. **If desired, enter a new title for this bookmark.**

The default bookmark name comes from the title of the page as it appears in the browser window's title bar. For some pages, this is quite long or not very descriptive, so you might want to devise a new name that makes sense to you.

4. **Use the drop-down list to select the location for the bookmark.**

An important part of managing your bookmarks is to place them in the right folder in the first place. If you've adequately organized your bookmarks, you should already have a folder available to store them in.

 You can immediately add a site to your Bookmarks menu or Bookmarks Bar by choosing the appropriate location from the Add Bookmark prompt's pull-down menu (refer to Figure 30-4). More immediately, you can add a site to your Bookmarks Bar by dragging the site's icon (found just to the left of the URL in the address bar) onto the Bookmarks Bar.

Using the Bookmarks window

The Bookmarks window is a special browser page that you can use to view and manage your bookmarks. The left column (Collections; refer to Figure 30-3) shows the different groupings of bookmarks that you have. These include Bookmarks Bar, Bookmarks Menu, History, the folders that came with Safari, and the folders that you create. When you select an item in the Collections column, its contents are listed in the right side of the window.

Here are some tips and techniques for working with this window:

✔ Create a new folder by pressing ⌘+Shift+N or clicking the + button at the bottom of the window.

 Depending upon which plus sign you click, you can create a new primary folder (by clicking at the bottom of the Collections column) or a new secondary folder (by clicking at the bottom of the Bookmark column). If you click the + underneath the Bookmark column, a new folder will be created within the currently selected Collection.

✔ Alphabetize your folders by dragging and dropping them to reorder them.

✔ Don't mess with the folders named Imported IE Favorites or Imported Netscape/Mozilla Favorites! (See the bottom of the Collections area in Figure 30-3.) Leaving these folders intact allows you to access bookmarks that you've set in those browsers.

✔ Nest related folders inside each other to maintain order without cluttering up the main set of collections. For example, you might want to create a Software folder inside of the Mac folder or add a Movies folder to Entertainment.

✔ Rename a folder by pressing Return after you've selected it.

✔ If you want to copy a bookmark from one location to another (from one folder to another or from the Bookmarks window to the Bookmarks Bar), hold down the Option key as you move it.

Using the Bookmarks menu

The Bookmarks menu is a useful tool, but you should be careful not to place too many bookmarks there because it can quickly become cluttered and less useful. The two ways to add sites to the Bookmarks menu are

✔ Selecting Bookmarks Menu from the pull-down menu in the Add Bookmark prompt (refer to Figure 30-4).

✔ Using the Bookmarks window (drag existing bookmarks into the Bookmarks Menu listing in the Collections section).

To delete a bookmark from the menu, just do this:

1. **Open the Bookmarks window.**

2. **Click Bookmarks Menu in the Collections column.**

3. **Select the bookmark to be deleted in the right column.**

4. **Press Delete.**

While in the Bookmarks window, you can add folders to the Bookmarks menu in order to create an organized, hierarchical menu of favorite sites. Doing so lets you put more bookmarks in the menu without too much clutter.

Working with the Bookmarks Bar

The Bookmarks Bar is a special section of the bookmarks world that can appear as part of the browser window. The Bookmarks Bar has a limited amount of visual real estate, so you must be judicious in selecting Web pages to put there, but you have plenty of configuration options.

You're not really limited to a certain number of bookmarks in the Bookmarks Bar, but if the titles of all the bookmarks run longer than the width of the browser window, some bookmarks won't be shown. Instead, double arrows will appear at the far right side of the bar and you'll need to click them to access the other bookmarks. This behavior is exactly the same as it is with Finder window toolbars if the window is not wide enough to show every tool.

To manage the Bookmarks Bar

1. **Open the Bookmarks window by pressing ⌘+Option+B.**

2. **Click Bookmarks Bar at the top of the Collections column.**

3. **In the right pane, delete any bookmark or folder that you don't want to appear on the Bookmarks Bar by pressing Delete.**

4. **Add any bookmark by dragging it from another location into the Bookmarks Bar listing.**

5. **If you like, create a new folder by pressing ⌘+Shift+N.**

6. **Arrange the bookmarks by clicking and dragging them to suit your preferences.**

You can also add pages to the bookmark bar by dragging the URL directly onto the bar in the browser window. You can remove items by dragging them off, and you can rearrange the order by clicking and dragging the bookmark names.

One of the best features of the Bookmarks Bar is the ability to group bookmarks into folders. For example, Safari already comes with the News folder on its

Bookmarks Bar, containing CNN, *The New York Times,* BBC News, and more. Folders on the Bookmarks Bar are marked with a downward pointing triangle, which displays a pop-up menu of the bookmarks in that folder when you click it, as shown in Figure 30-5.

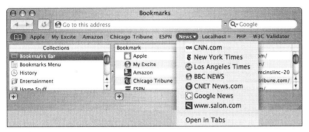

• **Figure 30-5:** Bookmarks Bar folders are presented as pop-up menus.

Here's how to add a folder to your Bookmarks Bar:

1. **Open the Bookmarks window by pressing ⌘+Option+B.**

2. **Click Bookmarks Bar at the top of the Collections column.**

3. **Create a new folder by pressing the ⌘+Shift+N keyboard shortcut or by clicking the + sign at the bottom of the Bookmark column.**

4. **Give the new folder a name.**

5. **Drag all the bookmarks that you want to add to the folder.**

If you hold down the Option key while dragging a bookmark into a folder, a copy of the bookmark will be placed there, and the orignal will remain.

6. **If desired, click the AutoTab box, which will appear between the Bookmark and Address columns.**

The AutoTab feature means that instead of providing a drop-down list of bookmarks in the folder, clicking the folder name in the Bookmarks Bar would automatically open every bookmark at once, using multiple tabs.

Use bookmark folders to create groups of related bookmarks. Use the AutoTab feature to make a collection of related bookmarks to be opened together (see Figure 30-6).

• **Figure 30-6:** AutoTab folders open all at once in a multitabbed browser window.

Setting bookmark preferences in Safari

You can control Safari's bookmarks somewhat by using the Bookmarks preferences panel (see Figure 30-7), accessed by choosing Safari⇨ Preferences and clicking Bookmarks. With it, you can decide whether to add Address Book or Rendezvous bookmarks to any of three places: the Bookmarks Bar, the Bookmarks Menu, or the Collections panel of the Bookmarks window.

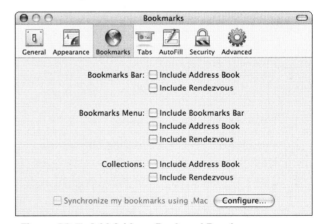

• **Figure 30-7:** Add Address Book and Rendezvous bookmarks automatically using the Bookmarks preferences dialog.

If you mark the Include Address Book check box next to the Bookmarks Bar heading, for example,

Safari loads all the URLs stored in the Address Book as a folder in your bookmark bar. Each URL is accessible through the person's name with whom it's associated.

 You can also tell Safari to include the Bookmarks Bar in the Bookmarks menu. This is worthwhile only if you don't already display the Bookmarks Bar.

Accessing Safari Bookmarks

After you organize and create all your bookmarks, you want to be able to access them with ease. Here's all the information you need to know:

✔ Click a bookmark in the Bookmarks Bar to open it.

✔ Click a folder in the Bookmarks Bar to view the list of bookmarks in it (and then select from the options, refer to Figure 30-5).

✔ ⌘+click a bookmark in the Bookmarks Bar to open it in a new tab.

✔ ⌘+click a Bookmarks Bar folder to open its contents at once in separate tabs.

✔ Use the Bookmarks menu to access bookmarks stored there.

✔ Click the open book icon on the far left of the bookmark bar to access the Bookmarks window.

✔ Choose the Open in Tabs option at the bottom of the Bookmarks menu (refer to Figure 30-2) to open every menu bookmark at once (within a single browser window but in separate tabs).

One of the coolest features of Safari is that it automatically numbers your Bookmarks Bar bookmarks in order from left to right so they're accessible via a keyboard shortcut. For example, in Larry's Bookmarks Bar (as shown in Figure 30-8), the Apple bookmark is launched by pressing ⌘+1, My Excite is launched by pressing ⌘+2, and so forth. Folders are skipped in the numbering sequence so that (again referring to Figure 30-8) PHP is associated with ⌘+6.

• **Figure 30-8: The ⌘ shortcuts for the Bookmarks Bar start with 1 and are numbered from left to right.**

This trick works for all the bookmarks not in folders and even works if no browser window is open!

Sharing Bookmarks across Browsers

The biggest downfall to using multiple Web browsers or switching to a different browser is trying to re-establish all your bookmarks. Fortunately, some of the Web browsers have acknowledged this and can automatically import bookmarks from other applications.

✔ Safari automatically imports Internet Explorer and Netscape/Mozilla bookmarks. (They appear as folders in the Collections panel of the Bookmarks window.)

✔ Camino, Mozilla, and Netscape automatically list Internet Explorer bookmarks.

✔ Opera can import bookmarks from other applications in certain formats.

If you have only a few bookmarks to move around, your best bet is to drag and drop them from one application to the other. Or, you can investigate one of the many bookmark management applications available (most of them are not free) if you're in a serious bookmark quandary. For example, if you are moving from another browser to Safari or want to import someone else's Safari bookmarks into your Safari, Safari Enhancer (www.lordofthecows.com, free) adds an Import Bookmarks option in a Debug menu that the utility can add to Safari.

 In Technique 41, we go over *iSync,* which is an Apple tool. One of its features is the ability to synchronize your Safari bookmarks with your .Mac account, letting you access all your bookmarks online when you're away from your computer. It lets you synchronize Safari bookmarks across multiple computers.

Transferring Your Bookmarks to a New Mac

Different applications can access the bookmarks managed by other applications because bookmarks are stored as text files on your computer. Specifically:

✔ Safari uses an eXtensible Markup Language (XML) file stored in ~/Library/Safari/Boomarks.plist.

✔ Camino uses an XML file stored within your Application Support folder.

✔ Mozilla uses a HyperText Markup Language (HTML) file stored with the ~/Library/Mozilla directory.

✔ Internet Explorer uses an HTML file stored within the ~/Library/Preferences/Explorer directory.

This system has two benefits for you, the end user. First, you can easily transfer all your bookmarks from one computer to another just by copying over the appropriate file. Second, you can manually tweak your bookmarks by editing these files in any text editor.

Bookmark Tips and Tricks

Finally, we'd like to mention a couple of other cool bookmark tips.

First, you can make a bookmark as a file on your computer by dragging the URL from your browser's address bar onto the Desktop (or anywhere else). This will create a special *webloc* file type, which is like an alias to that Web site (see an example in Figure 30-9).

• **Figure 30-9: URLs saved on your computer have a special icon.**

After you do this

✔ Open that file to open the Web site in your Web browser.

✔ Add the file to your Startup Items to automatically load the URL when you log into your computer. (See Technique 2 for more on Startup Items.)

✔ Add the file to your Favorites (see Technique 15) or a docked folder (see Technique 11) to keep it out of the way, yet easily accessible.

One of our favorite shareware applications, LaunchBar (www.obdev.at/products/launchbar; free for limited use, $20 for personal use), can be used to open many things, including your favorite Web pages. As we demonstrate in detail in Technique 21, LaunchBar lets you perform tasks by typing a key combination. For starters, you can use LaunchBar to open or switch to applications, but LaunchBar will also read through and index all your bookmarks, making them only a couple of keys away. To try this, follow the example in Technique 21 but use a logical keyboard combination for one of your bookmarks (like *CT* for *Chicago Tribune*).

Technique

31

Speedy Searches with Google

Save Time By

- ✔ Performing advanced searches in Google
- ✔ Working with Google in the Safari Web browser
- ✔ Checking out some nifty Google tips and tricks

The World Wide Web wouldn't be half as useful as it is if it weren't for the search engines that make its content findable. Throughout the history of the Internet, several search engines have been popular, but the current reigning champ is Google.

Most search engines help you find what you need, but there's a lot to be said for Google in particular. Knowing how to use it and all its options goes a long way towards improving the speed and accuracy with which you find stuff. We start this Technique by going through some more advanced Google navigation tips. Then you discover how Safari and Google work together nicely. Lastly, this Technique mentions a handful of different tips that, although not universally useful, are quite handy to know.

Doing Basic Google Searches

Google is one of those wonderful tools that can be used on a basic or advanced level. In other words, any Joe Bag-o'-Doughnuts can use it for everyday purposes, whereas rocket scientists can really tweak the heck out of it. Basic searches involve typing a few words (or just one) in the Search box and then clicking the Google Search button. Beyond this, here are some rules to follow that you might (or might not) be consciously aware of:

- ✔ **The more words you use, the more specific the search will be.** Too-general searches tend to return an unwieldy number of results.

 Google, by default, only returns results that include all the search words.

- ✔ **Be as specific with your keywords as possible.** It's far, far more likely that Google will return too many results than too few, so you should be as specific as you can when you have a good sense of what you're looking for.

As you might have noticed, Google suggests alternate search terms if you've possibly misspelled a word or words.

✔ **Order your keywords by importance.** The order of your keywords affects the results of the search. Enter the most important terms first.

 If a particular result is very close to what you were looking for, click the Similar Pages text at the end of that record to perform a search on Google for similar sites.

✔ **Skip common words.** Google automatically ignores very common words, such as conjunctions *(and)*, verbs *(are, is)*, or interrogatives *(who, what, why)*, so you might as well save Google the trouble and not use them in the first place.

 Google is a case-insensitive search by default. This means that *word, WORD, Word,* and *WoRd* are all treated the same.

Doing Advanced Google Searches

After you master the basics, here are some fancier tools that you should use:

✔ **Use OR to make a less restrictive search.** Google normally requires that every keyword be in a search result, but you can overrule this behavior by typing **OR** between each word. *Note:* OR should be in uppercase letters, and you'll want to add a space after it.

✔ **Use a plus sign (+) before a word to indicate that the word is required (see Figure 31-1).** Although Google will always search for every word, it skips common terms and numbers. By using the plus sign before a word (without a preceding space), you can insist upon its use.

• **Figure 31-1: The plus sign makes otherwise omitted words required.**

✔ **Use a minus sign (–) to rule out a keyword.** For example, if you want to search for *apples* — the fruit, and not the computers — you could use *apple –computer –mac* as your search terms. *Remember:* Do not include a space between the search term(s) and the minus sign(s).

✔ **Place phrases within quotation marks (see Figure 31-2).** Using phrases is a much more exact way to execute a search. For example, searching for *Larry Ullman* turns up about 40,000 search results, whereas searching for *"Larry Ullman"* returns only 6,000.

• **Figure 31-2: Quotation marks change search words to phrases.**

 If you're bored one day, search for yourself on Google. This is called *Ego Surfing.* Or, if you want a real challenge, try *Googlewhacking* — finding two words which, when searched in Google, return only one record.

✔ **To further limit your searches without relying upon keywords, check out Google's directory feature.** The Google directory, which is accessed via a tab above the search box, breaks the Web down into a series of categories. To limit search results, search within a category.

✔ **Use the *site:* restrictions to search a particular site.** The *site:* keyword restricts a search to a specific Web address or domain type. For example:

   ▶ You can use Google to search Apple's Web site by including *site:www.apple.com*.

   ▶ You can limit your searches to schools with *site:edu*.

   ▶ Search only a particular country realm with *site:ch* (*ch* stands for Switzerland).

 To find the domain name abbreviation for a country (or find what country an abbreviation represents), head to www.iana.org/cctld/cctld-whois.htm. There you can find out that .tv is Tuvalu and the Vatican is .va.

   ▶ Check out U.S. government pages with *site:gov*.

Finally, Google provides an advanced search page that can be accessed by clicking the <u>Advanced Search</u> link. This page has a number of other options, the two best of which are

✔ **In the Date drop-down list, restrict the returned records to a certain date range.**

✔ **In the Occurrences drop-down list, specify where in a page the search should run:**

   ▶ Selecting *In The Title* dictates that the keywords must be found in the page's title.

   ▶ Selecting *In The Text* dictates that the keywords must be found within the page's text (ignoring links and titles).

Doing Specialized Google Searches

Google's default search takes place within the Web, meaning that it looks through Web pages. You can also have Google search for or through the following:

✔ **Images:** http://images.google.com

✔ **Newsgroup postings:** http://groups.google.com

✔ **Mail-order catalogs:** http://catalogs.google.com

✔ **News articles:** http://news.google.com

✔ **Specific technical topics** (like BSD, Apple, and Microsoft): www.google.com/options/special searches.html

✔ **University Web pages:** www.google.com/options/universities.html

Google also has the ability to search for specific file types. You can request a specific type of file by adding the *filetype:type* designation to your search parameters, where *type* is the file extension. You can omit a specific type with *–filetype:type*.

The types of files that Google can search for are

✔ Adobe Portable Document Format (.pdf)

✔ Adobe PostScript (.ps)

✔ Lotus 1-2-3 (.wk1, .wk2, .wk3, .wk4, .wk5, .wki, .wks, .wku)

✔ Lotus WordPro (.lwp)

✔ MacWrite (.mw)

✔ Microsoft Excel (.xls)

✔ Microsoft PowerPoint (.ppt)

✔ Microsoft Word (.doc)

✔ Microsoft Works (.wks, .wps, .wdb)

✔ Microsoft Write (.wri)

✔ Rich Text Format (.rtf)

✔ Text (.ans, .txt)

 We highly recommend that you check out the Google Preferences page (see the same-named sidebar). For fun, set Google to use Elmer Fudd or Bork, Bork, Bork! as your default Google language to help combat the tedium of using your computer.

Google's Preferences Page

Google has its own preferences page, which you really ought to use. Click the Preferences link to access a page where you can set

✔ The default Google language

✔ What languages to search

✔ What level of SafeSearch filtering is applied

✔ How many records to return per page

✔ Whether each search results link should open in a new browser window

By adjusting these settings, you can improve not only what type of results is returned but also how they are displayed and how you'll access them. The 30 seconds that it takes to adjust these pays off in spades as you use the site. *Note:* You must have cookies enabled in your Web browser for this to work.

Searching Google with Safari

One of the coolest features of Safari is how nicely it ties into Google. From the Safari View menu, you can add a Google Search box to the top-right section of the browser window (as shown in Figure 31-3), which in turn offers some other nice features.

• **Figure 31-3:** Add a Google Search box to your browser.

Safari's Google bar has its own SnapBack capability. The SnapBack feature (which we discuss in Technique 28) creates a temporary bookmark of a page so that you can quickly access it again.

1. **Place your cursor in the Google Search box.**

 You can use your mouse to access the Google Search bar directly — or press ⌘+L to move to the address bar — and then press Tab to highlight the Google box.

2. **Enter your search terms.**

3. **Press Return.**

4. **The search results display in the main part of the browser — check out the results all you want.**

5. **When you're done browsing, click the orange arrow in the Google Search box to snap back to the search results page.**

 Alternatively, you can use the ⌘+Option+S keyboard shortcut to go to the Google SnapBack page.

The Google bar even keeps track of recent searches, as shown in Figure 31-4. Click the magnifying glass icon in the Google Search box to view and access recent searches.

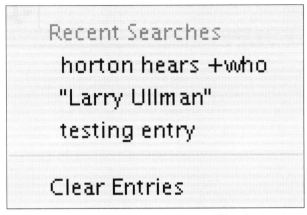

• **Figure 31-4:** Safari remembers your latest Google searches.

Google Tips and Tricks

Google is much more than just a search engine. The fine folks at Google have been continually adding new widgets and features over the years, expanding its capabilities. Here are some of our favorites.

Google, the dictionary

You can use Google to look up a word for you.

1. **Open Google in your Web browser.**

2. **Type** define *word* **or** define *phrase*, **replacing** *word* **or** *phrase* **with the actual word or phrase that you want defined.**

3. **Click the Google Search button.**

If you're using Safari, you can just type **define** *word* or *phrase* in the Google Search bar and then press Return.

4. **You'll find the definition listed first in the search results, by the heading Web Definition (see Figure 31-5).**

• **Figure 31-5:** Google's definition trick retrieves the meanings of words for you.

If you use **define** :*word* (note the colon), Google will instead take you to a page of definitions, without any other search results.

5. **If desired, click the <u>More Definitions</u> link to see, um, more definitions.**

Alternatively, if you do an ordinary search for a single word and Google can find a definition for it, this word is underlined in the blue bar at the top of the Google window (check out Figure 31-6). Click that word to view its definition.

• **Figure 31-6:** Google automatically finds definitions for your search terms, if it can.

Google, the mathematician

Did you know that Google can do your math homework for you? Okay, maybe not, but it *can* perform basic calculations. See Table 31-1 for the operators and terms that you'll want to use. (Most of them are common sense.)

TABLE 31-1: GOOGLE MATHEMATICAL TERMS

Operator	Function	Example
+	Addition	2+2
–	Subtraction	5–3
*	Multiplication	2*2
/	Division	9/3
^	Exponent	2^3
%	Modulus	5%3
% of	Percentage	75% of 300
sqrt	Square root	sqrt(81)
!	Factorial	4!

Plus Google can handle logarithms, trigonometric functions, and more. Here are some other rules to abide by:

✔ **Use parentheses to avoid operator precedence issues.**

✔ **Conclude a statement with an equal sign to indicate what result you're looking for.**

For example, each of the following Google searches will return the desired mathematical result:

✔ **12,908,308,089/4,979 (as shown in Figure 31-7)**

• **Figure 31-7: Google will perform calculations for you.**

 Google's calculator is very flexible (and maybe even a little strange). You can enter long numbers with or without the commas (indicating thousands) and returned results use spaces instead of commas.

✔ **67% of 5,000**

✔ **sqrt(625)**

Google, the unit converter

Do you remember how many pints are in a gallon or how many meters are in a furlong? If not, use Google's measurement conversion feature to help you out. Here are some examples:

✔ **Ten miles in kilometers**

✔ **Teaspoons in a quarter cup**

✔ **One hundred yards in meters (see Figure 31-8)**

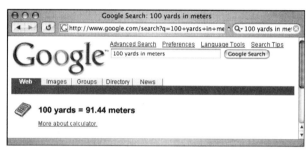

• **Figure 31-8: Try running a 91.44 meter dash instead of a 100 yard dash!**

Google, the linguist

Google can also be your own personal translator.

1. **Click the Language Tools link.**

2. **Enter a selection of text in the Translate Text box.**

3. **Use the drop-down list to select what kind of language conversion to perform.**

Right now, Google's translation service is not as potent as Babel Fish (`http://babelfish.altavista.com`) but is worth considering. As of the time of this writing, you've got these choices:

▶ English

▶ German

▶ Spanish

> ► French
>
> ► Italian
>
> ► Portuguese

4. **Click Translate to see the result.**

Alternatively, you can have Google translate an entire Web page by entering its URL in the Translate a Web Page box.

 Google's Language Tools page also lets you set the default language to use in Google and shows the many Google home pages for various countries around the world.

Google, the investor

Google provides you with stock quotes if you enter ticker symbols in the search box. Alternatively, if a search turns up a company's Web site, Google also provides a link to the stock quote (see Figure 31-9).

> **Apple**
> **Apple** The **Apple** Store iPod+iTunes .Mac QuickTime **Apple** Support Mac OS X. ... Site Map | Search Tips. Visit the **Apple** Store online or at retail locations. ...
> Description: **Apple's** main homepage.
> Category: Computers > Systems > Apple > Macintosh
> www.apple.com/ - 18k - Oct 27, 2003 - Cached - Similar pages - Stock quotes: AAPL

• Figure 31-9: Apple's ticker symbol appears with its link.

Google, the cartographer

If you enter a street address in Google, it will provide you with links to both Yahoo! and MapQuest maps for that address.

Google, the (fill in the blank)

Along with the above, you can check out

> ✔ **Froogle** (`http://froogle.google.com`), an e-commerce tool
>
> ✔ **Google Answers** (`http://answers.google.com`), a pay-for-use consulting resource

 To see what other tools Google has in the works, check out the Google Labs page (`http://labs.google.com`).

Technique 32

Searching the Internet with Other Tools

Save Time By

✔ Seeking answers with Sherlock

✔ Working with *Watson*, a third-party search tool

✔ Finding out what other good search tools are available

In the previous Technique, we discuss the Google search engine in detail, covering the best ways to hunt for things online via your Web browser. But Google isn't the only answer when it comes to looking around for stuff. In fact, in some cases, it's not even the best answer.

In this Technique, you'll find out about some different applications that can scour the Internet for you. The two biggies are Sherlock (from Apple) and Watson (from Karelia Software; www.karelia.com). Each of these is discussed in some length. We conclude with a couple of search tools that are useful yet function on a much more specific plane than Sherlock or Watson.

Searching Swiftly with Sherlock

Sherlock is Apple's application for finding stuff, and it comes free with Panther. Sherlock used to be a combination of a Web search tool and a computer Find tool but is now focused strictly on Internet-based searches. The version in Panther is a slight variation on the greatly improved version that debuted with Jaguar.

Some of the benefits of using Sherlock include

✔ Searching multiple search engines at once

✔ Tracking stocks and eBay auctions

✔ Displaying images, video, and more within the application

✔ Working well with the operating system as a whole

Sherlock uses different channels, each representing a type of search that you can run. For example, you can look up stocks, movie listings (the times when movies are playing in theaters near you), eBay auctions, and word definitions. Through the Sherlock interface (see Figure 32-1), you can access channels by clicking their icons on the toolbar, selecting them from the Channel menu, or by organizing and using *Collections,* which is a concept very similar to Safari's bookmark collections.

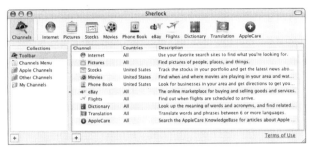

• **Figure 32-1: The basic Sherlock window.**

How you use each channel differs — each has its own interface — but the basic concept is this:

1. **Open Sherlock by double-clicking its icon in the Applications directory.**

2. **Select a channel (for example, Internet).**

   Select a channel by using the toolbar, the Channel menu, or the main Channels window (accessed by clicking Channels in the toolbar).

3. **In the search box, enter your search term or terms.**

   Your search terms will depend upon the channel. It might be a stock's symbol, a flight number, or a word. Almost every channel uses some kind of text box, although some (like Movies and Flights) rely upon pull-down menus instead.

4. **Press Return or use the pull-down menus (if available) to further adjust the search.**

A few of the channels also use pull-down menus (for example, the departure and arrival cities in Flights). Use these as warranted.

5. **If the search results display in columns, click them to sort the results.**

Some of the channels, like the Internet (see Figure 32-2), return a table of results. In these cases, you can click the column headings to sort the results, like you would in any Finder window.

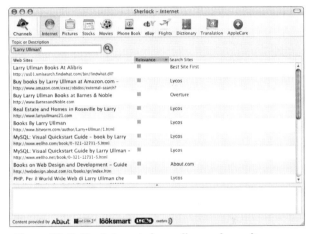

• **Figure 32-2: The Internet channel's search results.**

 Sherlock has a pathetic level of preferences. The only customizing that you can do in Sherlock really comes down to tweaking the toolbar to your tastes. Choose Customize Toolbar from the View menu and then customize it like you would a toolbar in a Finder window.

You can immediately access the different channels by using Sherlock's Dock icon (see Figure 32-3). If Sherlock is running, it's much, much faster to access individual channels by using the Dock icon's contextual menu.

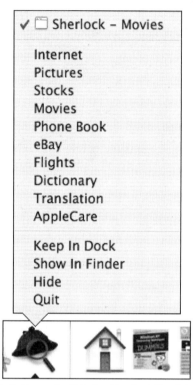

• **Figure 32-3:** Control+click the Sherlock Dock icon to access the specific channels.

You can create multiple searches by opening multiple Sherlock windows (press ⌘+N).

Sherlock employs a feature called *Shortcuts* that allow you immediate access to particular channels. Here's how you might use it:

1. Bring up a favorite channel, like Movies (as shown in Figure 32-4).

2. Choose Select Channel⇨Make a Shortcut or press ⌘+L.

3. In the resulting Save As dialog, give the channel a name.

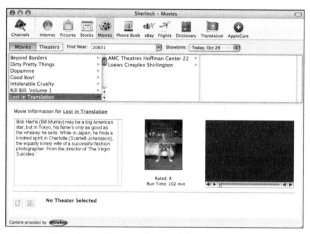

• **Figure 32-4:** The Movies channel shows movies, theaters, and times near you.

4. Choose an appropriate location for the shortcut (see Figure 32-5).

You might want to save the shortcut to the Desktop or your Favorites folder.

• **Figure 32-5:** Save the shortcut in a logical location where it's easy to access.

Click the down arrow next to the Save As box in order to view the more advanced save options. Click the up arrow (refer to Figure 32-5) to hide the more advanced options.

5. **Click the Make button.**

6. **When you want to access that channel, open the shortcut by using any standard method: Double-click it, press ⌘+O, or whatever.**

The shortcut launches Sherlock and selects the channel if the application isn't open. If Sherlock is already running, the shortcut opens the channel in a new Sherlock window.

Searching with Watson

Watson was Sherlock before Sherlock was Sherlock (which is our nice way of saying that most of the best features of Sherlock were, um, *inspired* by Watson). Still, Sherlock is at best a watered-down version of a far superior product. Watson has long been a favorite of Mac users who find its low cost ($29) to be money well spent. Watson is a product of Karelia Software (www.karelia.com/watson/).

Despite the cost, the arguments in favor of Watson over Sherlock are

- ✔ It has more features.
- ✔ It's faster.
- ✔ It makes developing and accessing additional tools easier.
- ✔ It searches Google. (Sherlock does not.)
- ✔ It gives you the good feeling of knowing that you're supporting the people who came up with the idea in the first place.

The general principle of Watson is that it searches the Web for specific items or in specific locations (*channels* in Sherlock terms). A non-exhaustive list includes

- ✔ Recipes
- ✔ Prices for products
- ✔ Weather

- ✔ Movies
- ✔ Amazon.com
- ✔ Words (definitions, synonyms)
- ✔ TV listings
- ✔ Phone numbers
- ✔ Translations
- ✔ Currency exchange rates
- ✔ Stock quotes
- ✔ Images
- ✔ eBay auctions
- ✔ ZIP codes

Like Sherlock, how you use each search differs in Watson — each has its own interface — but the basic concept is this:

1. **Open Watson by double-clicking its icon in the Applications directory (after you've installed it).**

2. **Select a search (for example, Amazon.com).**

You can select a search by using the toolbar, the View menu, or by clicking the Show All button in the toolbar and then clicking the desired search.

3. **In the search box, enter your search term or terms.**

Your search terms will depend upon the type of search being executed. The terms might be a stock's symbol, a dollar amount (for the currency exchange), or a tracking number (like for UPS and FedEx packages). Almost every channel uses some kind of text box and many also rely upon pull-down menus.

4. **Press Return or use the pull-down menus (if available) to further adjust the search.**

Most of Watson's searches also use pull-down menus (for example, a search parameter in Amazon.com). Use these as warranted. You might also find columns of options to help narrow your search (see Figure 32-6).

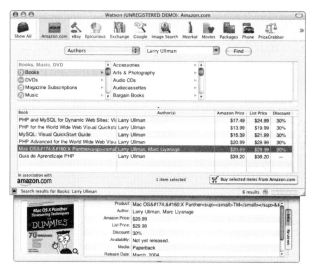

• **Figure 32-6:** The Amazon.com search in Watson.

Watson is really easy to use, but a little customization will help your cause.

✔ **In the Preferences page, choose the Appearance tab and enable the Open Web Pages in Background check box (see Figure 32-7).**

This opens search results in your Web browser behind the scenes, letting you continue to use Watson until you're finished.

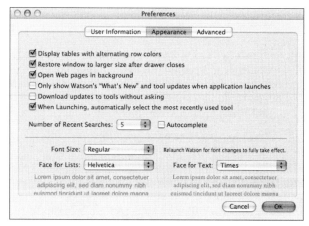

• **Figure 32-7:** Watson's Preferences panel is easy to use and understand.

✔ **On the same tab, enable the When Launching, Automatically Select the Most Recently Used Tool check box.**

Watson has to launch in some state, so it might as well be as you left it. For example, if you last used Watson's Amazon.com channel, the next time you open Watson, you'll see that channel again. This saves you the time of reselecting a popular search channel.

✔ **Customize the toolbar so that it includes the features you use, in the order of most common usage. Just choose Customize Toolbar from the Window menu to bring up a customization palette (see Figure 32-8).**

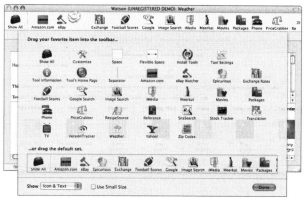

• **Figure 32-8:** Customize Watson's toolbar with the channels that you need.

✔ **Take the time to read the introductory text for each tool (see an example in Figure 32-9). These little blurbs appear the first time you access any search, giving you a guideline to using it.**

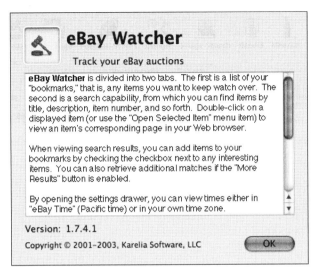

• **Figure 32-9: Each channel includes introductory text for using it.**

 Use Watson's Install More Tools option under the Watson menu to add even more functionality to your Watson. You'll be allowed to install other searches and tools, like sports scores and news browsers.

Watson has a free two-week demo version available, which we highly recommend. You'll be stunned by how nice this tool is and how easily it works.

Other Search Tools

If you don't require all the features and overhead of Sherlock or Watson, a more single-purpose application might be better suited to you. These are our favorites.

CleverKeys

CleverKeys (www.cleverkeys.com/ck.html, free) is a great little piece of software for initiating specific bits of research from within the Finder or any other application. After you install this tool, you can select a word and search one of many resources, such as Dictionary.com, Google, or eLibrary, for it. You can access CleverKeys with

✔ The contextual menu (see Figure 32-10)

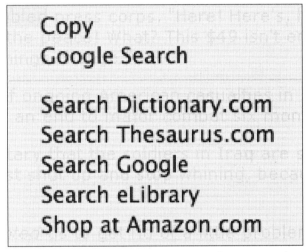

• **Figure 32-10: CleverKeys adds items to the contextual menus.**

✔ The Services menu (as shown in Figure 32-11), in applications that support Services

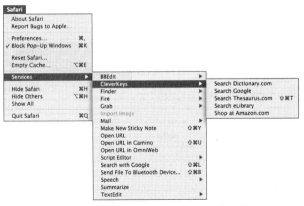

• **Figure 32-11: CleverKeys also works as a Service.**

CleverKeys then returns the appropriate search results in your Web browser.

iSeek

iSeek, from the wonderful people at Ambrosia Software (www.ambrosiasw.com/utilities/iseek, $15), adds a search tool to the menu bar (see Figure 32-12). You can then use this within any application to

- ✔ Search Google.

- ✔ Return definitions and synonyms of words.

- ✔ Get the weather report from weather.com.

- ✔ Find a quotation.

- ✔ Look up an acronym's meaning.

- ✔ Search for software on VersionTracker and MacUpdate.

 If you like iSeek and decide to use it full-time, add the application to your StartUp Items so that it loads automatically when you log in.

Huevos

Ranchero Software's *Huevos* (http://ranchero.com/huevos/, donation) provides a search tool from within any application. Press a key combination that you set to launch the search tool, enter your keywords in the search window that appears, and press Return to have that search performed in your Web browser. Huevos requires no mouse usage and can search 15 different engines out of the box — and you can add more via the Preferences window.

• **Figure 32-12:** iSeek is unique because it runs from the menu bar.

Mastering Mail

Along with surfing the Internet, the ability to send and receive e-mail might be the most common reason people use computers today. Sadly, until the Mac operating system turned over the OS X leaf, there was no such thing as an Apple-made e-mail application. Today's Panther user can rest assured that Apple's solution — *Mail* — is not only available and free, but it's pretty darn good, too.

We've tried to distill the overabundance of information available on Mail into the most critical bundle, with respect to timesaving techniques. You're not going to get much in the way of introductions or basics here except as they apply to using this application more efficiently. This Technique begins with some keyboard shortcuts and then goes into the relevant preferences for our purposes. This is followed by tips on organizing your mailboxes and performing searches within them. Finally, we tack on some information about signatures (the kind you put at the bottom of an e-mail message, not your John Hancock), and a few other useful Mail-related tidbits that didn't fit in elsewhere.

Keyboard Shortcuts

E-mail is overwhelmingly a keyboard-based technology. (Although you *could* probably compose an entire e-mail by using just your mouse and the Character Palette, don't plan on getting anything else done that day.) If you memorize the right keyboard shortcuts and figure out how to navigate around the application, you can get away with barely using your mouse, if at all. Mail has a lot of keyboard shortcuts, most of which are convoluted, so we're sticking to the most useful here.

 If you can't recall what the keyboard shortcut is, just peruse through the menus to remind yourself.

Navigation shortcuts

🗸 **Tab:** Use the Tab key to move from the message window (where your e-mails are listed) to the Preview panel (where an e-mail is displayed) to the Search box.

🗸 **↑:** Use the up arrow to view the previous message (while in the messages window).

🗸 **↓:** Use the down arrow to view the next message (while in the messages window).

🗸 **Page Up:** Use Page Up to go up within a message (while in a message).

🗸 **Page Down:** Use Page Down to scroll down within a message (while in a message).

🗸 **⌘+N:** ⌘+N moves you through the top six mailboxes, where N is one of the numbers below:

▶ 1: Inbox

▶ 2: Outbox

▶ 3: Drafts

▶ 4: Sent

▶ 5: Trash

▶ 6: Junk

Other shortcuts

🗸 **⌘+N:** Creates a new e-mail message

🗸 **Delete key:** Sends the selected message to the Trash

🗸 **⌘+R:** Creates a reply to the selected message

🗸 **⌘+Shift+R:** Creates a reply to all the recipients of a message

🗸 **⌘+Shift+F:** Forwards a message

🗸 **⌘+Shift+V:** Pastes Clipboard text as a quotation (see Figure 33-1)

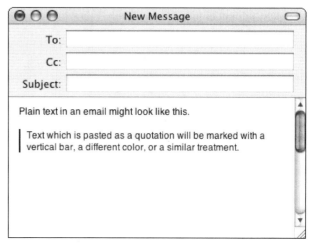

• **Figure 33-1: Mail can paste text as a quotation, which is marked with a vertical bar.**

🗸 **⌘+Y:** Adds the sender of the selected message to your Address Book

🗸 **⌘+Shift+D:** Sends an e-mail

🗸 **⌘+Shift+A:** Attaches a file to the e-mail

🗸 **⌘+Shift+N:** Retrieves new e-mail

🗸 **⌘+Shift+M:** Shows and hides the Mail drawer

🗸 **⌘+K:** Empties the Trash

🗸 **⌘+Option+N:** Creates a new viewer window

 All the standard Mac shortcuts work within Mail as well: ⌘+S (Save), ⌘+W (Close), ⌘+P (Print), ⌘+H (Hide), ⌘+Q (Quit), ⌘+C (Copy), ⌘+F (Find), ⌘+− (makes text smaller), and so forth.

Customizing Mail's Appearance and Behavior

We trust that you can probably make your way through Mail's preferences panel without too much handholding. But because you might not yet appreciate the ramifications of some of the options, we'll give you a heads-up on a few of them.

The Junk Mail and Rules panels — and their usage — are discussed in Technique 34.

General preferences

The General panel (as shown in Figure 33-2) is fairly simple, but here are a couple of things worth mentioning:

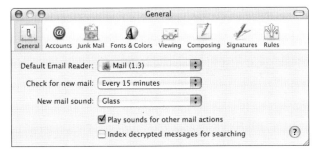

• **Figure 33-2: Mail's General preferences panel.**

✔ Strange as it might seem, you can use the Mail application to set your default e-mail client to be something other than Mail. You probably don't want to do this, though.

✔ Use the Check for New Mail drop-down list to control how often Mail checks for new messages.

 If you have a persistent (always-on) Internet connection, have Mail automatically fetch your new messages, saving you the step. If you use a dialup connection, disable this and do it manually when you're online.

Composing

The Composing panel (see Figure 33-3) sets your preferences for how Mail should behave when you write e-mail. Because you'll be writing messages frequently, it's a good idea to pay attention to these options.

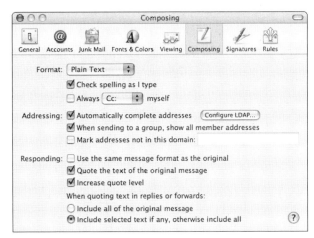

• **Figure 33-3: Mail's Composing preferences affect how you write and reply to e-mail.**

In this panel, you can make Mail do the following:

✔ **Check spelling as you type:** This won't really save you time, but it will make you look more professional, and that's got to be worth something.

 If Mail catches a spelling error, the error is underlined in red. Control+click the underlined word to bring up a contextual menu of options for fixing the boo-boo (see Figure 33-4).

✔ **Automatically complete addresses:** As you type, Mail will look up addresses for you by using your Address Book and/or a Lightweight Directory Access Protocol (LDAP) server, if you have one. With this method, you only need to type a few letters and then select the appropriate address.

 For more on LDAP servers, read through Technique 16.

✔ **Include selected text (if any) when replying:** Assuming that you have marked the Quote the Text of the Original Message check box, you can set up Mail to quote original text in your reply in one of two ways:

➤ Simply replying quotes the entire message in your reply.

➤ Selecting a section of text and replying to the message quotes just that section in your reply.

• **Figure 33-4:** Don't forget about contextual menus in Mail! They're very useful.

Customizing the Mail toolbar

Just like the Finder window toolbars, you can (and should) customize Mail's toolbar so that it sports the features you use most often. To bring up the customize window (see Figure 33-5), do one of the following:

• **Figure 33-5:** Mail's Customize Toolbar window provides oodles of options.

✔ Choose View⇨Customize Toolbar.

✔ Control+click the toolbar and choose Customize Toolbar from the contextual menu that appears (see Figure 33-6).

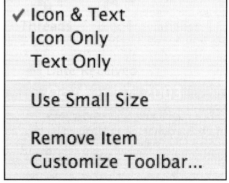

• **Figure 33-6:** Quickly access the Customize Toolbar window from a contextual menu.

The default set gives you an idea of what you want to accomplish. Basically, by dragging and dropping icons onto the toolbar, you can

- ✔ Add items that you use but might not remember the keyboard shortcut for.

- ✔ Organize items into similarly themed groups.

- ✔ Use separators and spaces to divide groups.

- ✔ Place a search bar on the right.

- ✔ Use the Show drop-down list to indicate whether the toolbar should contain the icons, text, or both.

- ✔ Control the size of text and icons from the Use Small Size check box.

 Use the Mail toolbar for a while to see what tools you never use and which ones you keep going to the menus for, and then adjust your toolbar accordingly. Of course, you can tweak the toolbar's settings at any time.

 Using both icons and text in the toolbar provides you with two visual clues as to what a button is. The small size setting lets you put more items in the toolbar.

While we're discussing the toolbar, we should remind you of these universal toolbar shortcuts:

- ✔ Click the oval-shaped white button in the upper-right corner of the Mail application to show and hide the toolbar.

- ✔ ⌘+click the oval-shaped white button in the upper-right corner of the Mail application to rotate among various versions and sizes of the toolbar (icons only, text only, plus different sizes of each).

Customizing the messages window

Another area of the Mail application that you ought to customize is the message window itself, which is

the area where your messages are listed. From the View menu (as shown in Figure 33-7), you can dictate what columns are listed and also adjust the sorting column.

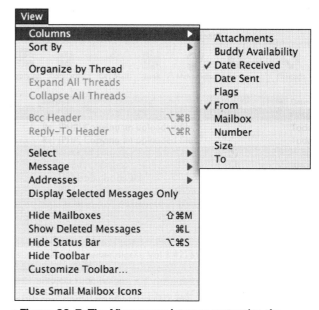

• **Figure 33-7: The View menu lets you customize the message window layout.**

Like with standard Finder windows, you can also adjust how the columns are sorted by clicking the column headers. Further, you can rearrange the columns by clicking and dragging them.

Finally, be certain to use the Organize by Thread option (available under the View menu or by clicking the Threads button on the toolbar), particularly if you use message groups and news lists. If you have this turned on, Mail automatically sorts incoming messages by thread (think of a *thread* as a more formal subject declaration), using the e-mail headers (see Figure 33-8). Even the heated political discussions you have with your uncle will be kept organized, as repeated messages on the same topic are grouped together.

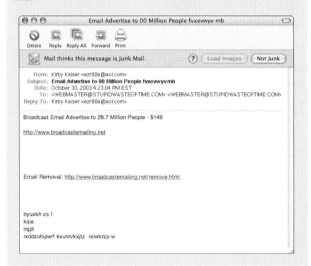

• **Figure 33-8: Threading sorts your messages in an easier-to-follow manner.**

Maintain a neater Inbox by using the Organize by Thread option (under the View menu). Multiple e-mails on the same topic will be listed as one item. Clicking the item shows all the e-mails that are part of that thread.

Understanding and Using Mail Headers

An e-mail actually begins with a hidden series of lines called *mail headers*, which are used for many purposes, including

✔ Identifying the sender

✔ Identifying the recipient

✔ Indicating the subject line

✔ Marking the time and date when the e-mail was sent

✔ Flagging the message as it's handled by mail servers

Panther's Mail — and any other e-mail client — turns most of these headers into a more user-friendly display, like that you see in the messages window or in the Preview panel for a single message. But, you can still get a more techie viewpoint of a message, if you'd like.

To show all the headers for a message, use the ⌘+Shift+H shortcut or choose Long Headers from the Message submenu of the View menu. For example, instead of seeing this:

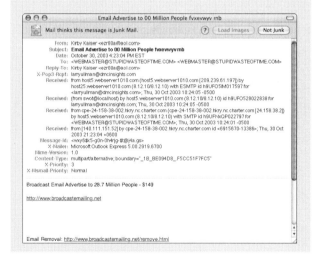

you would get this:

Similarly, you can have Mail display a message as the raw source, invoked by using the Raw Source option under the Message submenu of the View menu or with the ⌘+Option+U keyboard shortcut. The raw source of this same e-mail looks like this:

The raw source view helps you look at messages written in HTML that aren't displaying properly. You can also weed out spam by checking out either the raw source or the long headers. In this example, the message has an @aol.com return address, although it was never sent through an AOL mail server (which means that the address was faked).

Organizing Your Mailboxes

Organizing your mailboxes is as important to efficiently handling your e-mail as organizing your Home directory is to handling your stuff. If you want to be

able to find anything again, you better put it in the right place. By default, Mail has several mailboxes:

- ✔ **In:** Stores incoming messages waiting to be read.

- ✔ **Out:** Stores outgoing messages waiting to be sent.

- ✔ **Drafts:** Stores messages that you're composing. If you save a message before sending it, a copy is placed in the Drafts box. This message remains there until it is sent.

- ✔ **Trash:** Holds messages that you've deleted. Use ⌘+K to empty the Trash, or you can set the Mail application to do this automatically.

 To set how the Mail application handles the Trash, open the Preferences panel and then click Accounts. Select an account from the left column and then click Special Mailboxes in the right column. At the bottom of the resulting page, you dictate how Mail handles deleted messages for that one account.

- ✔ **Junk:** Holds e-mail marked as junk. (See Technique 34 for more on how to use Mail to snuff out spam.)

- ✔ **On My Mac:** Where you should store messages that you want to save. Think of this as the equivalent of your Home directory.

- ✔ **Mac:** Shows only if you have a .Mac account. You really don't need to concern yourself with this one too much.

Most of these boxes are subdivided for your multiple accounts (see Figure 33-9). If you want to view all the messages for all the accounts at once, click the main box icon. If you want to view only all the new or sent or trashed messages for a particular account, click the appropriate subfolder.

• **Figure 33-9:** Click the arrow to access a box's subfolders.

Before you get too heavily invested into Mail, add new folders to the On My Mac box so that you can store and organize the messages you keep. For example, Larry uses mailboxes for

✔ **Books:** Has subfolders for each book

✔ **Clients:** Has subfolders for each client and subfolders within those for multiple projects

✔ **Personal:** Has subfolders for receipts, registration e-mails, and so forth

✔ **Other Work Related:** Has subfolders for things that are work related but don't fall under the *Books* or *Clients* categories

 Creating and maintaining a good organization scheme with your mailboxes makes finding messages — particularly using searches — much, much faster.

All your mailboxes appear in the *Mail drawer*, which is a panel that resides on either the left or right side of the main viewer window. But there's more to the Mail drawer than just a collection of mailboxes. Here are some tips for working with the Mail drawer:

✔ Click the Actions icon at the bottom of the window (it looks like a cog; see the bottom-left of Figure 33-10) to access common tools.

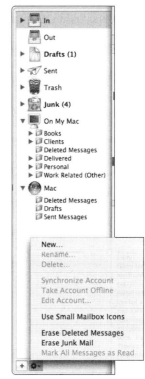

• **Figure 33-10:** The Actions menu lets you create new folders, delete e-mail, and more.

✔ From the Actions menu that appears, choose the Use Small Mailbox Icons option so that the mailbox takes up less room.

✔ The Mail drawer automatically appears on the side of the application with the most room on the screen.

↙ Use ⌘+Shift+M to show and hide the Mail drawer.

↙ You can manually back up any single mailbox or folder by dragging its icon from the Mail drawer into the Finder.

Performing Searches

Inevitably, you're going to need to hunt down that message your boss sent you two weeks ago (in which he changed the project) or the one from your mother (in which she reminded you of her birthday). Fortunately for you, Mail has a sweet little search engine built into the application. Here's the easiest way to use it:

1. **Do not begin by typing anything in the Search window box!**

 As soon as you enter text into the Search box, Mail begins searching. This only slows down the process. Set all your search parameters first and then enter your search terms.

2. **Use the Mail drawer to select a specific mailbox or subfolder to search.**

If you're looking for an e-mail that you sent, begin with the Sent mailbox. If the message was sent from a particular address, select that subfolder instead. If you expect that you would have stored the e-mail in the Jobagadonuts folder under Clients, select that. When you do this, all the messages in that box or folder appear in the messages window. You can also ⌘+click to select multiple mailboxes.

3. **Click the magnifying glass icon and select an area of your e-mail to search (see Figure 33-11).**

• **Figure 33-11: The Search box pull-down menu lets you choose the scope of the search.**

Your search term can be applied to

▶ The entire message

▶ The From address

▶ The To address

▶ The Subject name

You should try to be as specific as possible and select the proper option here first.

 The search pull-down menu has two halves: The top half applies the search to the currently selected mailbox, and the bottom half applies it to every mailbox. First run the search on the selected mailbox. If that doesn't turn up the message that you seek, change the pull-down menu to apply to every mailbox. You can also ⌘+click to select multiple mailboxes, in which case the top half of options apply to selected mailboxes.

4. Enter your search term or terms in the window.

5. Use the search results in the message window to find the right message.

6. If you still didn't find the right message, change the scope of the search or the search terms and try again.

Creating and Using Signatures

Signatures, in e-mail terms, are those footers that appear at the bottom of people's e-mail addresses (Figure 33-12). They are used to add contact information, links to Web sites, or disclaimers (in company e-mails). Here's how you can create and use signatures in Mail:

• **Figure 33-12: A basic e-mail signature.**

1. Open Mail's preferences panel.

2. Click the Signatures icon (see Figure 33-13).

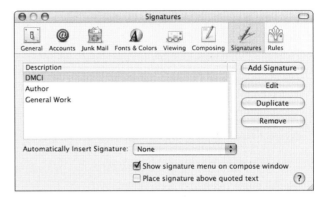

• **Figure 33-13: Mail's Signatures preferences panel.**

3. Click the Add Signature button.

4. In the resulting prompt, give the signature a description (a title).

5. Press the Tab key to move to the text box.

6. Type all the text that you want to use as your signature (see Figure 33-14).

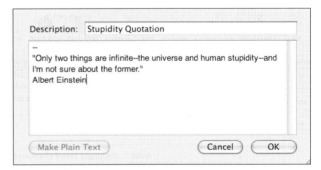

• **Figure 33-14: Add a new signature here.**

You can add as much text as you'd like, separating multiple lines by pressing Return. The signature is meant to be informative and communicative — not showy and bulky — so follow these general rules:

▶ Begin your signature with two dashes and a space (--) on the first line, which helps mail readers understand that your signature is beginning.

▶ Signatures should be plain text.

▶ Restrict yourself to four to seven lines.

▶ Avoid long lines (more than 80 characters).

▶ Resist the urge to create elaborate graphics using spaces and keys.

7. **Click OK when you're finished.**

You return to the Signatures preferences panel.

8. **In the Signatures panel, use the Automatically Insert Signature pull-down menu to decide which, if any, signature should automatically be used (see Figure 33-15).**

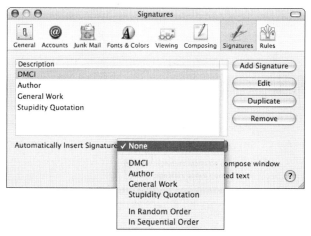

• **Figure 33-15: Mail automatically adds signatures to new messages if you want.**

9. **Alternatively, mark the Show Signature Menu on Compose Window check box.**

If you do, you'll be given a pull-down menu of signatures to add to an e-mail when writing one (see Figure 33-16).

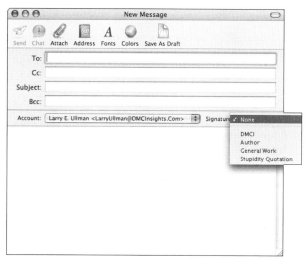

• **Figure 33-16: You can add signatures to messages from this pull-down menu.**

The Best Mail Tips and Tricks

We conclude this chapter with a quick discussion and demonstration of some of the best Mail-related tips and tricks.

Using the Dock icon

The Mail's Dock icon is your friend. Not only will it indicate how many new messages you have, but you can also use it to perform, or at least start, common tasks. After you Control+click the Mail icon to bring up its contextual menu (see Figure 33-17), you can

• **Figure 33-17:** The contextual menu for the Mail icon in the Dock is a wonderful timesaver.

✔ Retrieve new messages.

✔ Create a new e-mail. (You'll be taken to the Mail application, where a new message has been created for you.)

✔ Choose what document to view (for example, the Viewer window or an open e-mail).

 The number of new messages in your Inbox also appears as part of the Mail icon in the application switcher palette.

Sending attachments

You have a choice of many ways to add attachments to an e-mail:

✔ Press ⌘+Option+A to bring up the Open dialog (while composing an e-mail).

✔ Choose Attach File from the File menu.

✔ Click the Attach button in the message toolbar.

 If your message doesn't have an Attach button, customize the message toolbar (see "Customizing Mail's Appearance and Behavior," earlier in this chapter).

✔ Drag and drop a file from the Finder or other application onto the message.

✔ Drag and drop a file from the Finder onto the Mail's Dock icon, which creates a new message with the file already attached to it.

 For a cool technique on dragging and dropping by using Exposé, check out Technique 13.

When sending attachments, you ought to seriously consider compressing anything that you send. This both cuts down on the size of the file and makes it easier for the receiver to distinguish between the message and the attachment. (Some attachments will be displayed inline in the message itself rather than as an icon that the recipient has to click to open.) The easiest way to compress any file or folder is to select it in the Finder and choose Create Archive from the File menu.

Stopping Spam in Its Tracks

Save Time By

✔ Filtering out spam in Mail

✔ Using Rules to add filters to Mail

✔ Minimizing the amount of spam that you get

Spam is nothing short of a pox on the world of the Internet and e-mail. Unwanted and unsolicited e-mail is slowing down networks, costing businesses billions of dollars, and cluttering up mailboxes. Okay, maybe it is or isn't all of that, but it is a pain and a fact of e-mail life. Despite the overwhelming permeance of this plague, you can take steps to fight this time-waster. In this Technique, we put forth two approaches to spam: handling it after you receive it in your mail application, and how to avoid getting it in the first place.

The first two sections of this Technique focus on Apple's Mail program specifically. The concluding section discusses software, techniques, and steps that you can take to take a bite out of the amount of spam that you receive. These ideas will be useful regardless of what application you use for e-mail.

Fighting Spam with the Junk Mail Button

One of Mail's strongest suits is its ability to identify and filter out spam. We cannot think of a single reason why you wouldn't want to use this feature. It's a breeze to get going and, over time, teaches itself how to be more accurate at guessing which messages are spam.

1. **Open the Mail preferences panel.**

You can do this by choosing Preferences under the Mail menu or by pressing ⌘+, (comma).

2. **Click the Junk Mail icon (see Figure 34-1).**

3. **Make sure that the Enable Junk Mail Filtering check box is marked.**

This check box should be enabled in new installations of Panther, and you'll want to keep it that way.

 Junk Mail filtering is enabled by default in Panther. That's a good thing, and you shouldn't mess with it.

• Figure 34-1: Use the Junk Mail panel to adjust spam settings.

4. **Make sure that the Leave It in My Inbox option is selected.**

You'll want to use the training mode for about a month or so (depending upon how much e-mail and junk you receive).

 After about a month of usage, open the Junk Mail preferences and select the Move It to the Junk Mailbox (Automatic) radio button under When Junk Mail Arrives. By having the Junk Mail filter move it to the Junk mailbox (as shown in Figure 34-2), you won't have to look at it anymore, but you still have an opportunity to review the message later.

5. **Mark the check box next to Sender of Message Is in My Address Book to exempt these senders' messages from filtering.**

Presumably people in your Address Book will not be sending you spam, so these messages shouldn't be filtered. They might end up unintentionally sending you viruses (particularly if your friends run Windows), but those can be dealt with by using the Rules feature, which we discuss in the upcoming section, "Creating and Using Rules."

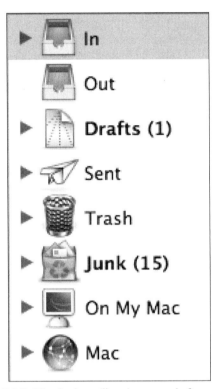

• Figure 34-2: The Junk mailbox is expressly for temporarily storing spam.

6. **Mark the check box next to Sender of Message Is in My Previous Recipients to exempt these messages from filtering.**

Spam is often sent using different permutations on an e-mail address; therefore, you aren't likely to get spam from the same address twice. Enabling this option helps to avoid false positives (incorrectly identifying mail as spam).

7. **Mark the check box next to Trust Junk Mail Headers Set by Your Internet Service Provider.**

Many ISPs use their own software to filter spam. Some providers automatically block those from ever reaching you. Others send the messages anyway but mark them as spam. In those cases, you want Mail to trust the preliminary spam designation. In the worst case, you'll just need to fish non-spam messages out of the Junk mailbox later.

8. **Close the Junk Mail preferences panel.**

9. **If spam still slips through the cracks, select the message and click the Junk icon (see Figure 34-3) on the toolbar to let Mail know that the message is spam.**

Although Mail's spam filter does a really good job, sometimes it needs a little help.

• **Figure 34-3: Use the Junk icon to manually mark a message as spam.**

 Use the Junk icon to help Mail learn what you think qualifies as spam. During the training mode, this button will be your greatest ally. If you just delete spam, Mail will never improve upon its filtering skills. As you continue to indicate what you think is spam, Mail becomes more and more efficient at catching it first.

 If you don't have a Junk button in your toolbar, customize the toolbar by using the steps that we outline in Technique 33.

Read the section "Bouncing spam" to see what to do with all your spam now stored in the Junk mailbox.

What, Exactly, Is Spam?

In case you were curious, *spam* is unsolicited junk e-mail sent to huge numbers of people at once. The content of these messages normally revolves around

✔ Get-rich-quick schemes

✔ Physical enhancement products

✔ Sexually explicit content

✔ Trendy products or ideas

Businesses might send out spam-like messages as well, but these don't qualify as spam if they fit both of these criteria:

✔ Users are given the option of opting out of receiving the messages.

✔ The messages advertise actual products or services.

Generally, such messages also tend to come from a company with which you've had previous interactions.

If an e-mail is spam, you need to fight it by using the methods that we outline in this chapter. If it's an advertisement from a business that seems trustworthy, simply following their opt-out instructions should stop the messages from coming.

Creating and Using Rules

The Junk Mail filter does an admirable job identifying spam, but it's not perfect. Fortunately, it's not the only tool that you have in your arsenal. Mail also includes the Rules feature. To use it, you establish certain criteria (for example, if the subject contains certain words) and then decide what Mail should do when messages meet criteria (such as move the e-mail to a specific folder or highlight it in a particular color). Using Rules is like having a really great personal assistant go through your inbox before you start looking at the messages. Here are just a few uses of Rules:

✔ Color-code e-mail based upon what e-mail address it's coming from

✔ Have a particular sound play when you get an e-mail from a specific person

✔ Automatically mark some e-mail as read

✔ Color-code e-mail based upon its subject

✔ Move specific messages into a folder

 Don't be confused: Rules are not specifically tied to handling or filtering spam. You can, and most likely will, use Rules to manage legitimate e-mail. We're discussing Rules here because the feature is very similar to the Junk Mail filter (which is actually a complex type of Rule).

Another example is to create a Rule to handle particular types of spam. For example, when the latest Windows virus hits, Larry might get a couple hundred of e-mails (because his address is on computers around the world). When he sees a wave of messages entitled `Wicked Screensaver` or `Your Application`, within a matter of minutes, he can set Mail to start trashing these. Here's how:

1. **Bring up the Mail preferences panel.**

2. **Click the Rules icon (see Figure 34-4).**

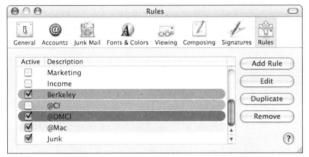

• **Figure 34-4:** Use the Rules panel to create and manage Rules.

3. **In the Rules dialog that appears, click the Add Rule button.**

4. **In the dialog that appears, type the Rule's name in the Description text box.**

Give your Rule a descriptive name, indicating what it does or what it applies to (an e-mail address, a particular virus, a certain subject).

5. **For the first criterion, select Any from the first drop-down list box, Subject from the second, and Contains from the third. Type** that movie **in the text box, as shown in Figure 34-5.**

Rules are case-insensitive by default.

6. **Click the plus sign after the first criterion to add another criterion.**

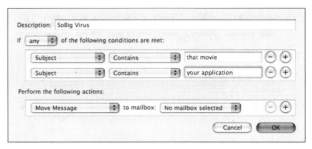

• **Figure 34-5:** Add as many criteria as you want to a Rule.

7. **For the second criterion, set the parameters to check whether the subject contains** Your Application.

The SoBig virus sent out e-mails titled `That Movie`, `Your Application`, `Thank You`, and so forth. For this Rule, Larry set up multiple criteria so that if the subject of an e-mail contains any of these phrases, it's picked up by his Rule.

8. **Add more criteria, if desired.**

9. **Under Perform the Following Actions, select Move Message from the first drop-down list and Trash from the second to move the message to the Trash (see Figure 34-6).**

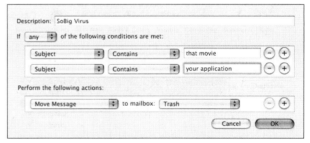

• **Figure 34-6:** The last step when creating a Rule is to indicate what to do when the criteria are met.

10. **Click OK to create the Rule.**

Stopping Spam before It Gets to You

The bulk of this Technique revolves around dealing with spam after it hits your mailbox (acknowledging that "spam happens"). But a more critical — and difficult — task is cutting down on the amount of spam that you receive. The quickest way to stop spam is to not have an e-mail address, but that's a drastic step that most people aren't willing to take these days. Here is some more practical advice:

- **Don't use an AOL, Yahoo!, MSN, or Hotmail e-mail account.** The big providers of e-mail service (commercial or free) are major targets for spammers. These users are frequently hit not because their address got put on a list but simply because spammers use every combination of names and popular domains — for example, @aol.com — that their spam software can come up with.

- **Watch what you sign up for online.** Most registration forms require your e-mail address and then assume you want to receive e-mail from that business. Although this isn't spam, technically, it's often e-mail that you don't want. Look for opt-out boxes during registrations.

- **Never respond to the spam that you receive.** This just lets spammers know that they've hit on an active e-mail address.

 Absolutely, positively do not follow the Click Here to Unsubscribe or Reply to Unsubscribe suggestions included in spam. These steps only confirm for the spammer that they had a valid e-mail address. The likely result? You'll get even more spam!

- **Try to keep your e-mail address off the Internet.** A large majority of spammed addresses come from spiders that scour the Internet looking for *someone@address.com* text. These are normally found on contact pages of Web sites or in public message boards.

- **Use separate e-mail addresses.** A smart move is to have one e-mail address for your friends and family, which is used (hmmm) only for your friends and family. Create a second e-mail address for work or school. Then, create a separate e-mail address that is only used for riskier behavior (like posting messages online). When this address becomes overrun with spam, delete it and create a new one.

 One of Mail's best features is its ability to easily manage multiple e-mail accounts. Using temporary e-mail accounts in the war against spam is far less of an inconvenience than you might think it is.

- **Pay attention to the law.** The United States government and many states are working hard to cut down on spam. The FTC also tracks spam, and some states are starting to sue spammers. Pay attention to what laws have been passed and what recommendations these government agencies have.

Bouncing spam

Recent studies have suggested that far and away the most effective method of stopping spam is to indicate that e-mail address wasn't valid. You can do this by bouncing the e-mail back to the sender. When you bounce a message, it indicates to the sender (or the sender's computer) that the e-mail address doesn't exist. With any luck, this might get you off the offender's list. Here's how Larry handles this:

1. **Click the Junk mailbox to view its contents.**

Over the course of the day, Larry's Junk mailbox gets filled up with the messages that either Mail thought was junk or that he manually marked as junk.

2. **Press ⌘+A to select every message.**

3. **Looking at the Subject names and From addresses, ⌘+click any messages that might not be spam (see Figure 34-7) to deselect them.**

• **Figure 34-7:** Select all the Junk messages and then deselect those that might not be spam.

You or the Junk filter might have erred in marking a message. In those cases, you don't want to bounce the message.

4. **Double-check to make sure that all the highlighted messages are spam.**

5. **Click the Bounce icon on the toolbar or press ⌘+Shift+B.**

6. **Click OK at the prompt (see Figure 34-8).**

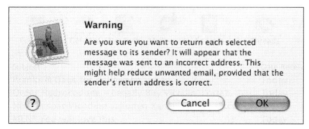

• **Figure 34-8:** Mail confirms that you want to bounce these messages.

After you bounce an e-mail, it's moved from the Junk mailbox into the Trash. When you empty the Trash, bounced e-mails are also be deleted.

7. **Review the remaining messages (which you marked as *not junk* in Step 3) and click the Not Junk button (see Figure 34-9) to tell Mail that a message wasn't spam.**

• **Figure 34-9:** If Mail wrongly marks a messsage as junk, you'll see a Not Junk button to undo that flag.

  The Not Junk button is just as important as the Junk button in teaching Mail how to identify bad e-mail.

There's a good chance that a percentage of the bounced messages will be returned to you with a Mail Undeliverable (or similar) message. This just indicates that the original sender's e-mail address was bogus, and you can delete the undelivered message. Or, you can make a Rule to automatically send undelivered mail to the Trash.

Other spam tools

You can use many other applications to combat spam. Here are five popular choices:

✔ **SpamSieve** (www.c-command.com/spamsieve/index.shtml, $20) is a very solid piece of software that adds junk mail filtering capability to other e-mail applications (like Mail, Eudora, Mailsmith, and Entourage).

✔ **Spamfire Pro** (www.matterform.com, $40) filters all your mail before it gets to your e-mail application.

✔ **SpamCop** (www.spamcop.net) provides you with spam-filtered e-mail for $30 per year and has tools to set up spam filtering software for entire companies.

✔ **Mailblocks** (www.mailblocks.com, $10) routes all of your existing e-mail addresses through a new Mailblocks address, filtering out the spam in the process. It works with most major e-mail applications, including Mail, and is ridiculously cheap.

✔ **SpamSlam** (www.ilesa.com, $25) is slightly different from other applications in that it uses two of the best spam-stopping techniques: namely, filtering spam based upon content (which is what Mail does) and requesting confirmation of e-mails from senders not in your Address Book.

35

Innovative iChat

Technique

Save Time By

- Memorizing the keyboard and mouse shortcuts that you need to know
- Customizing iChat
- Picking up some tips and tricks
- Seeing what alternatives to iChat are available

Chat is Apple's answer to America Online's Instant Messenger (AIM) application. The application works by using your .Mac account or an AIM account, if you have one. You can use it to communicate with other iChat users or AIM denizens.

In this Technique, we assume that you understand the fundamentals of using iChat, so we focus instead on some of the little extras that make using the application more productive. We begin with the keyboard and mouse shortcuts that you should be using, and then we go through some of the customizing techniques that you might not be aware of. Finally, we go through a few specific tips for common tasks and then mention some of the iChat alternatives.

Keyboard and Mouse Shortcuts

To be honest, there aren't a lot of shortcuts to be used within iChat. The principle is very basic: Type some text, and press Return. But still, you ought to be aware of the following shortcuts:

- **Option+Return:** Creates a carriage return

 By default, pressing the Return key sends the typed text within an Instant Message (IM) window. Therefore, to insert a return into a message (so that text goes onto the next line), use Option+Return.

- **⌘+L:** Logs you out
- **⌘+N:** Creates a new, private chat room
- **⌘+K:** Creates a hyperlink
- **⌘+1:** Brings up your Buddy List window (see Figure 35-1)
- **⌘+2:** Brings up the Rendezvous window

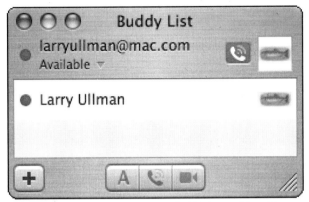

• **Figure 35-1:** Larry's Buddy List (while logged into his .Mac account) shows that his buddy Larry (using an AIM account) is logged in.

Rendezvous is Apple's technology that instantly recognizes other computers, hardware, and users on your network. iChat's Rendezvous window shows other AIM and .Mac users who are currently online and on the same network as you.

✔ **⌘+Shift+G:** Shows and hides the groups bar

✔ **⌘+Option+E:** Sends an e-mail to the selected user

✔ **⌘+Option+F:** Opens the prompt for sending a file

✔ **⌘+I:** Gets the info of a user selected in the Buddy List

The Get Info panel for a particular user serves two purposes. First, it displays some of that person's Address Book information (see Figure 35-2). Second, you can use it to associate specific actions with this user (see Figure 35-3). For example, you can configure a user's Info setting so that a specific sound is played when that person comes online or sends you a message.

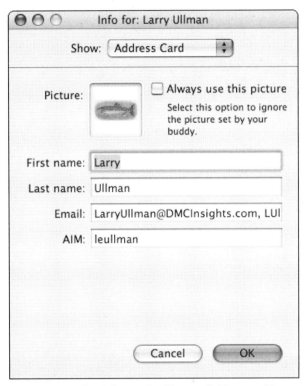

• **Figure 35-2:** Get Info on a buddy to edit his record in iChat.

✔ **⌘+Shift+I:** Gets the information for a user in an Instant Message

✔ **⌘+Shift+A:** Adds a buddy

✔ **⌘+S:** Saves the chat transcript

With the mouse — iChat is admittedly not a mouse-driven application — the most important pointers are these three:

✔ Click a person's name in your Buddy List to select her.

✔ Double-click a person's name in the Buddy List to send him an instant message (IM).

✔ Click the red button in the upper-left corner of the IM window to close the message.

• **Figure 35-3:** Set iChat to do certain things when
particular users log on or send you
messages.

Customizing iChat

Rather than go through all the preferences settings —
which you can do very well on your own — we're
going to concentrate on some of the most important
and interesting customizing options. All these fall
under the *useful* or *cool* categories with respect to
iChat.

✔ Use Rendezvous to help iChat automatically recognize people on your local network (see
detailed instructions in Technique 38).

✔ Enable the Show Status in Menu Bar option
(choose iChat➪Preferences➪General) to control
iChat without opening the application (see
Figure 35-4).

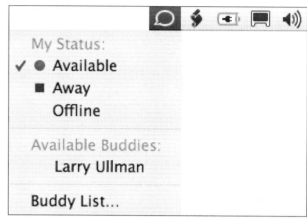

• **Figure 35-4:** iChat's menu bar icon lets you control the
application without making it active.

 iChat's Menu Bar tool (enabled in iChat's
General preferences) lets you set your status
and see who's online without opening iChat.
You can instant-message a buddy by selecting
his name from the menu bar list, at which
point iChat will open for you. iChat will also
launch itself if someone sends you an IM.

✔ Add a new icon to represent you during chat sessions by dragging it onto your icon in the Buddy
List window.

✔ Click your icon in the Buddy List window to be
given a choice of different icons that you've used
(as shown in Figure 35-5).

✔ Add a background to your IM by dragging an
image onto it.

✔ Have iChat use sounds to let you know when certain people come online or send you messages.

✔ Have iChat check your spelling while you type
(**hint:** to make you look smarter than you are!).

✔ Customize your status to make it more specific
and useful.

• **Figure 35-5:** Choose your icon from the list of icons you've used in the past.

iChat comes with the default status options of *Available* and *Away,* but you shouldn't have to restrict yourself to those. Follow these steps to create a custom status:

1. **Click the status text below your name.**

2. **In the pop-up menu that appears (see Figure 35-6), select Custom from either the Available or Away sections.**

3. **In the resulting text box, enter your new status label.**

4. **Press Return to make this status active (see Figure 35-7).**

Larry has created a Taking a Nap status for this example.

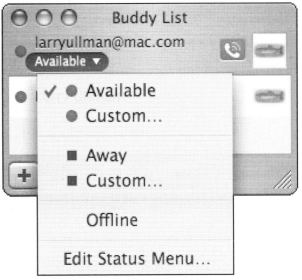

• **Figure 35-6:** Use the status pull-down menu to indicate your availability.

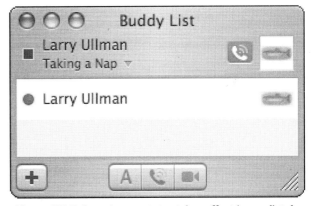

• **Figure 35-7:** Larry's new status takes effect immediately.

 Alternatively, you can use the Edit Status Menu option (refer to Figure 35-6) to create and manage multiple status options at once (see Figure 35-8). Select a message and click the minus sign below it to delete it. Click the appropriate plus sign to add a message. Double-click a message to edit it. Press Return (or click OK) when you are finished.

• **Figure 35-8: The Edit Status menu is a fast way to add or remove multiple statuses.**

Logging iChat Sessions

If you want to remember an idea that someone gave you, a URL that someone mentioned, or are just looking for proof of something someone once said, you can save your Instant Message session. To do so, while in an IM session, choose Save from the File menu or press ⌘+S. You'll be given a prompt so that you can save the file on your computer. (By default, the filename will be `Instant Message with Username`.)

Because of the unique format of an iChat sesssion, you can't just open it in any old text editor. To view the iChat logs, you need to open them in iChat. (This will happen automatically if you double-click the saved file.) Or, you can use Logorrhea (`http://spiny.com/logorrhea`, free), an application that can parse iChat logs and that provides some other nice tools for searching through them.

Transferring Files with iChat

Did you know that you can use iChat as a quick and easy way to transfer files? You can, and it's remarkably simple:

1. **Begin an Instant Message with a user.**

2. **Switch to the Finder.**

    Press ⌘+Tab, click the Finder Dock icon, or click the Desktop itself to switch from iChat to the Finder.

3. **Browse for the file that you want to attach.**

4. **Drag the file from the Finder onto the IM window in iChat.**

    Drag the image into the text box area (where you type) — not the main window itself.

 If the file is already open (like a Word document in Microsoft Word), you can attach the file by dragging its *proxy icon* (the icon of the file which appears in the title bar next to the file's name) onto the IM window. You can also use the Exposé or the ⌘+Tab drag-and-drop techniques, discussed in Techniques 13 and 8, respectively.

5. **Add some text (if desired) and press Return to send the file.**

    Depending upon what client the other user has, you will normally have to wait a bit while iChat requests approval from the receiver. Then the file appears in the main window of the Instant Message, along with its name (see Figure 35-9 for the sender's IM window).

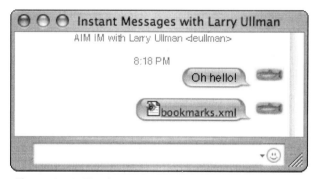

• **Figure 35-9: The file appears with its icon in your iChat.**

Here's some other stuff that you should know about sending files in iChat:

- ✔ You can send files to people running iChat or AIM.

- ✔ The File feature, in conjunction with Rendezvous, makes for a great way to send files to other people on your network (for example, co-workers).

✔ If you send images in iChat, they'll appear in the IM window, as shown in Figure 35-10. If you resize the IM window, the image will also be resized.

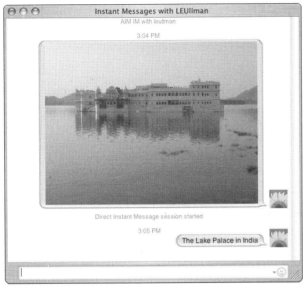

• **Figure 35-10: Images can be included inline (in the message) during an Instant Message.**

Using the Videoconference

The latest version of iChat is technically called *iChat AV* because of its audio/visual capabilities. With it, you can videoconference or audioconference with other iChat users. (It's like Buck Rodgers come to life!) Besides being really, really cool, this means that you can have free, long distance phone calls — while playing solitaire — or, if you're writing a book, videoconference with your coauthor in Switzerland, hypothetically.

To use iChat AV's videoconferencing feature, you'll need

✔ A FireWire video camera (like Apple's iSight)

✔ At least a 600 MHz G3 processor or better

✔ A high-speed Internet connection

 If you don't meet the above requirements and really want to give videoconferencing a whirl, check out iChatUSBCam (www.ecamm.com/mac/ichatusbcam, $10). It makes iChat work with many USB cameras (which are much cheaper than FireWire ones) and lowers the processor requirements.

If you only want to use the audio aspect, the requirements are more lax:

✔ A USB or built-in microphone

✔ A 56 Kbps dialup connection or better

iChat AV makes it very easy to set up an audioconference or videoconference. To use it, do the following:

1. **Connect a supported camera, if you have one.**

Apple created the iSight ($149) specifically for this task, but any FireWire camera should work.

2. **Open iChat.**

3. **Under iChat's Audio menu, make sure that Camera Enabled and Microphone Enabled are marked (see Figure 35-11).**

• **Figure 35-11: Turn on AV features at the bottom of the Audio menu.**

4. **Select someone to conference with from your Buddy or Rendezvous List.**

Other iChat users have one of two icons (which appears next to their iChat icon in the Buddy or Rendezvous List) indicating their capability for audio or video chatting:

► A **green telephone** indicates that they're ready for audio.

► A **green camera** indicates that they're ready for video.

 iChat indicates audio and video capability in the Buddy List via camera and telephone icons. A grayed-out camera icon indicates the user is currently videoconferencing with someone else.

5. **Begin an audio- or videoconference by clicking the green symbol next to the person's name.**

The user gets an invitation to join you for a conference, which he can either accept or decline. While the call is being set up, you will see your own image so that you can adjust the camera framing.

 If you have a camera and/or microphone but your partner does not, you can still start a one-way video- or audioconference. The person on the other end of the conference will see and/or hear you, and you will both be able to use the regular text Chat feature. To use this, select the other person in the Buddy List, and choose Invite to One-Way Video/Audio Chat, either from the contextual menu of the Buddy List entry or from the Buddies menu.

Here are some things to keep in mind when using the AV features:

✔ In the Video preferences panel (see Figure 35-12), lower the Bandwidth Limit for video to 500 Kbps to improve the audio quality.

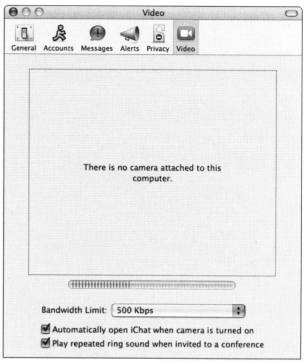

There is no camera attached to this computer.

Bandwidth Limit: 500 Kbps

☑ Automatically open iChat when camera is turned on
☑ Play repeated ring sound when invited to a conference

• **Figure 35-12: Use the Video panel to test and tweak your settings.**

✔ Press ⌘+Option+S to take a snapshot from the video feed.

✔ You can resize the video image or make it full-screen, but this slows down the performance of your computer.

 If you connect a video camera to your computer for videoconferencing, it can also be used to take a snapshot of you. This snapshot can be used as your representative icon in the operating system and certain applications. See Technique 16 to read how this is done in the Address Book.

Creating URLs

As you probably know, iChat automatically turns any typed or pasted URL into an active Web link. When it does so, it displays the URL text as the link name by default (see Figure 35-13). But you can create URLs with a specific name if you want.

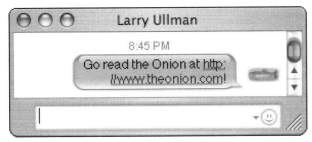

• **Figure 35-13:** URLs are automatically linked in Instant Messages.

 In order for iChat to automatically process URLs, they must include the initial `http://`, `https://`, `ftp://`, and so forth. Just using `www.sitename.com` will not work.

1. In the iChat Instant Message window, type some text that you want to be the name of the link.

2. Select the text.

3. Press ⌘+K.

4. In the resulting prompt, type the URL for the link (see Figure 35-14).

5. Press Return or click OK.

 Dragging a site's proxy icon (the icon which appears next to the URL in the location bar) from the Safari browser into iChat creates a link for that Web site using its name.

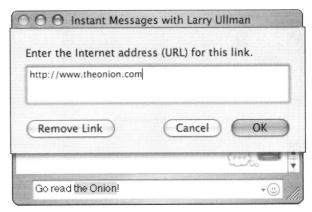

• **Figure 35-14:** Use the ⌘+K shortcut to make a named link.

Chatting with Multiple People at Once

As the final step in trying to convince you that iChat is a solid business application (as well as a way to catch up with your Aunt Karen), we show you how to chat with a whole group of people at once. Think of it as a meeting for telecommuters.

1. Select the first chat participant from your Buddy List.

2. Choose Invite to Chat from the Buddies menu.

The first person will be given the option of joining the chat; if he or she agrees, a chat window appears.

3. Drag other members of your Buddy List into the Participants drawer.

Drag and drop other buddies into the chat window's Participants section in order to add them to the chat.

Now everybody can chat at once, each seeing what the other is saying!

You can also begin a chat or Instant Message from other Apple applications, specifically Mail and Address Book. Each of these can be set to indicate when a person is available in iChat. If they are available, each application has an option for instant-messaging them or inviting them to chat.

Other Instant Messenger Tools

Just because iChat is free and ties in nicely to the rest of the operating system doesn't mean you have to use it. Or, for that matter, that doesn't mean it has to be your only IM client. The main reasons to use a different IM application are to have one with fewer features (if iChat is too much for you) or to use one that manages multiple IM accounts at once. Here are a few other options, each free and with its own benefits:

- ✔ **America Online's Instant Messenger** (www.aim.com) has been fully replaced by iChat but is still available. It only works with AIM accounts but has lots of bells and whistles like stock and news tickers.

- ✔ **Adium** (www.adiumx.com) is a bare-bones alternative to AOL's Instant Messenger. It only supports AIM but does so without banner ads and the other shiny baubles in the AIM application.

- ✔ **Fire** (http://fire.sourceforge.net) is our personal favorite and a great second IM client to use. It supports AIM (but not .Mac), ICQ, MSN, Yahoo! Messenger, and even IRC (Internet Relay Chat).

- ✔ **Proteus** (www.indigofield.com, donation requested) is like Fire in that it supports AIM, ICQ, MSN, Yahoo! Messenger, and IRC. Proteus is very customizable, works well with the Address Book, and has a lovely interface.

- ✔ **Yahoo! Messenger** (http://messenger.yahoo.com) only supports the Yahoo! format but allows videoconferencing with other Yahoo! Messenger users. You can even videoconference across platforms (Mac to Windows).

Part VI

Optimizing Your Network

The 5th Wave   By Rich Tennant

"I guess you could say this is the hub of our network."

36 Technique

Getting Your Mac Online

Save Time By

- ✔ Creating a location
- ✔ Using your modem to connect to the Internet
- ✔ Discovering other online timesaving techniques

Pretty much every computer is connected to a network of some kind or another, whether this network is a home setup, at the office, or just logging onto the Internet with your modem.

In this Technique, we discuss some of the tricks to get your Mac online. We cover everything that you need to know to quickly create new locations, and then we go through modem settings. Finally, we cover some tips and tricks for people who frequently switch locations (in other words, move their Mac).

Defining a Location

To connect your Mac to any network, including the Internet, you need to define a location. *Locations* allow you to define your network settings based upon where your computer is physically located and then save all those settings. If you have only one computer that never travels (a desktop machine), you need to define and use only one location. If you have a laptop that travels at all, you want to create multiple locations. You might have locations for

- ✔ Your home cable or DSL modem
- ✔ A dialup connection at home
- ✔ The network at your office
- ✔ When you visit your aunt and uncle in another state
- ✔ Traveling out of town for work

 When you move your computer — and therefore change networks — add a new network instead of altering your existing network settings. (That is, unless you've moved permanently or no longer need the original settings for some reason.)

If you opted for any Internet service at all when you first used Panther (or if you upgraded to Panther), you'll already have a location named *Automatic.* If you'll be using your computer in a new location (for example, if you take your laptop into work), you have to add another. To add a location, follow these steps:

 Every user of a networked Mac can use every location created by any user.

1. **Open System Preferences and click the Network icon.**

The Network icon is displayed both under Internet & Network and at the top of the window (see Figure 36-1).

• **Figure 36-1: Click Network to manage your locations.**

2. **Make sure that the Network panel is unlocked.**

If the padlock icon in the lower-left corner of the Network panel appears locked, you'll need to unlock it. Just click it, enter your administrative password at the prompt, and then press Return.

After you do this, you can make changes to the Network settings.

3. **Select New Location from the Location pull-down menu (see Figure 36-2).**

• **Figure 36-2: Adding a new location.**

 You can duplicate, rename, or delete networks by selecting Edit Locations from the Locations menu. This will bring up a prompt for managing your locations.

4. **Enter a descriptive name for this location in the prompt that appears (as shown in Figure 36-3) and then click OK.**

This is Larry's location for when he visits Bethany Beach, Delaware. Because this is the only Bethany he knows, it's a descriptive enough name. You might also use *At the Office* or *Home Broadband.*

5. **Select Network Port Configurations from the Show drop-down box.**

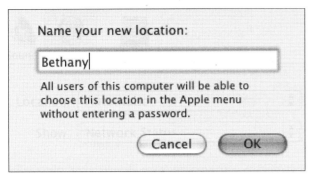

• **Figure 36-3: Give this location a name that lets you know where and when to use it.**

6. **Deselect any ports that this connection will not need (see Figure 36-4).**

• **Figure 36-4: Configure the network ports after adding a new location.**

Networks can be created by using many different ways of connecting to your computer, including

▶ Your modem

▶ A built-in Ethernet connection

▶ An AirPort or AirPort Extreme card

▶ A Personal Computer Memory Card International Association (PCMCIA) card (wireless or not)

▶ An Infrared Data Association (IrDA; infrared) connection

▶ A FireWire port

▶ A USB port

The Network panel automatically enables every port for a new location, but you have no need to keep them all on because most locations won't use multiple ports. Disable each port that won't be used, following these steps:

1. Select the port in the window.

2. Clear the check box to disable the port without deleting it.

3. Alternatively, click the Delete button and then click Delete at the prompt.

 Disabling a port and deleting it has the same effect. However, some ports cannot be deleted — like your internal modem and built-in Ethernet — but others can (like a second modem or a FireWire port).

7. **Select Network Status from the Show menu.**

Before you go any further, you should check whether your network is already fully functioning. If it is, go to Step 9. What you'll see (after selecting Network Status) is the name of the port being used (like *Built-in Ethernet*) and a red, yellow, or green bubble, along with some text. If you see a green bubble and the message that you are already connected to the Internet, you're good to go. If you see a yellow or red bubble, this means that the port is active but that an Internet connection hasn't been made. You'll then need to configure the port (see Step 8) or dial up to the Internet via your modem (again, go to Step 8).

8. **If your network isn't immediately recognized, select the appropriate port from the Show menu.**

If your active port didn't immediately get you an Internet connection, you'll need to configure it (or configure a modem connection and then make the phone call). Configure your port by using the appropriate following steps.

▶ See "Using a Modem" later in this section for a description of configuring a modem.

▶ See Technique 37 for a description of configuring AirPort or another wireless connection.

▶ If you have an Ethernet connection, use the information provided by your ISP or recommended by your router's manual (if you're using a router) to configure your Ethernet port.

9. Click the Apply Now button to use this network immediately.

10. Click the padlock icon to ensure that the network settings aren't changed.

 If you ever have trouble with the Network panel, click the Assist Me button at the bottom of the window or click the question mark icon (bottom right) to bring up Mac help.

Using a Modem

If you're still dialing up to get your Internet access, configuring your modem properly helps to improve the experience. To configure the modem, select Internal Modem from the Show menu in the Network panel. Obviously, if you don't have an internal modem, you need to select the appropriate choice from the Show menu. The most important considerations are the following:

1. Choose System Preferences⇨Network.

2. Select your location from the Location pull-down menu and your modem (probably Internal Modem) from the Show menu.

3. In the PPP tab (see Figure 36-5), enter the dialup settings that your ISP provided you. Enter your password so that every user can use this connection.

• **Figure 36-5:** The PPP tab is where you enter your ISP information.

4. Click the PPP Options button to configure your dialup settings and then click OK to return to the Network preferences dialog.

In the resulting prompt (see Figure 36-6), keep yourself online by setting it to prompt every so many minutes (30 at the most) to maintain the connection and deselect the Disconnect If Idle For *xx* Minutes option. If you frequently have trouble dialing in, you'll want to set Redial to 4 or 5, with a 5- or 10-second interval between redials.

 The first four options in the PPP Options panel have a big effect on when you go online and whether you stay online. Dialup connections are notoriously bad about kicking off users. Fine-tune these settings to minimize those occurrences. For example, if you get disconnected after 15 minutes or so, set the prompt to every 10 minutes to maintain the connection.

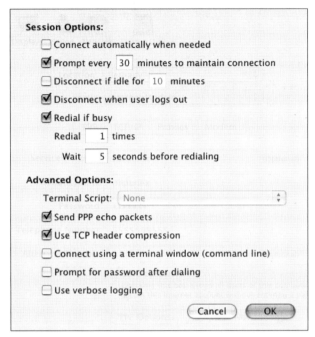

• Figure 36-7: Adjust the modem's behavior in the Modem tab.

• Figure 36-6: Set the PPP options to keep yourself online.

5. Don't worry about the TCP/IP and the Proxies tabs — you probably don't want to mess with them.

6. Use the Modem tab to make your life easier (see Figure 36-7):

▶ Turn off the sound if you get tired of hearing the end-of-the-world-like dialing-up noise.

▶ Under Connection, decide whether you want to be interrupted by incoming calls.

▶ Show the modem status in the menu bar (see Figure 36-8) to control your connection without using the Network panel.

7. Click the Apply Now button to activate your changes.

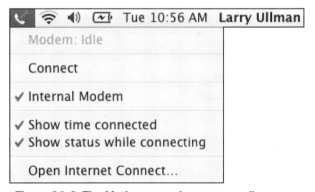

• Figure 36-8: The Modem menu lets you go online with ease.

You can also set multiple dialup settings (different phone numbers and passwords) in the Internet Connect application, which you can also access from the Modem menu bar tool.

What's a Protocol Anyway?

Networks make use of *protocols*. In layman's terms, these are guidelines for computers to speak to each other. Panther supports just about every protocol you can name, including

- ✔ **AppleTalk:** AppleTalk has been around for years and used to be how a Mac talked to other Macs and peripherals. People well versed in the protocol still use it although its popularity is dwindling.

- ✔ **TCP/IP (Transmission Control Protocol/Internet Protocol):** TCP/IP is the primary protocol for computers connecting to the Internet.

- ✔ **PPP (Point-to-Point Protocol):** PPP is used by modems to connect to the Internet.

- ✔ **PPPoE (Point-to-Point Protocol over Ethernet):** This protocol uses an Ethernet connection but simulates a dialup PPP session.

- ✔ **HTTP (HyperText Transfer Protocol):** HTTP is the default protocol for Web pages, which makes sense because you access sites by using http://. There's also HTTPS, which is a secure Web connection.

- ✔ **FTP (File Transfer Protocol):** FTP is a very common way to transfer files over the Internet (for example, to upload pages to a Web site). FTP is normally accessed by using an FTP application like Fetch or Transmit. There's also a secure version of this, called SFTP, which is replacing FTP for many users.

- ✔ **SMB (Server Message Block):** SMB is the most common way to share files with Windows users.

There's also Rendezvous, which is a special technology created by Apple to let computers automatically identify other computers and peripherals. It isn't a protocol in itself, although it uses these other protocols to function. This is discussed in Technique 39.

Networking Tips and Tricks

Setting up a network connection isn't the hardest thing in the world. After you create one, a lot of networking tips and tricks are at your disposal. We highlight the best of them here.

Switching locations on the fly

If you have multiple locations set up, you can easily switch from one to the other without going through the Network panel. The key is to use the Location menu (see Figure 36-9), found under the Apple menu. To switch locations, just select from the list of options there.

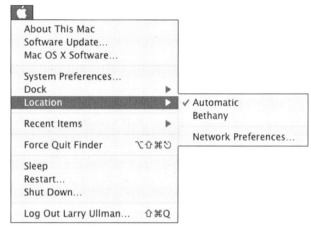

• **Figure 36-9: Quickly switch networks from the Apple menu.**

 The Location menu is also a quick shortcut to get to your Network preferences panel.

Another alternative is to use Location X (http://homepage.mac.com/locationmanager, $20). This utility adds a menu to the menu bar at the top of your screen. Furthermore, Location X lets you

- ✔ Order your list of locations so that they appear according to your demand for them.

- ✔ Set individual passwords for each location.

- ✔ Change e-mail settings, default Web page, time zone, and printer configuration.

- ✔ Use AppleScripts and shell scripts.

- ✔ Add to its feature set by using plug-ins.

Ordering connections

If you have several connections active in a single location — for example, an AirPort and an Ethernet connection — they both can be active at the same time. The important thing is that you can order these to give preference to the most reliable connection. If you have multiple ways of connecting to the Internet, you can order the connections so that the strongest option is used first, if it's available.

1. **Open the Network panel in System Preferences.**

2. **Select Network Port Configurations from the Show menu.**

3. **Click and drag any port to reorder them.**

 If you have several networks active and accessible to your computer, order your ports to use the best network.

Dialing with a calling card

If you're in a hotel or somewhere else where you might incur huge charges by dialing into an ISP, have hope. You can use your calling card to dial up. Most calling cards have a sequence of steps wherein you

1. **Dial the calling card number (1-800-888-8888).**

2. **Wait for the prompt and enter your member number (2222222).**

3. **Wait for the prompt and enter the phone number to call (555-555-5555).**

If you place all these numbers together, your modem will dial them all at once, missing the prompts. What you want to do instead is use commas to indicate two-second pauses. For example, you might change the modem telephone number to be 18008888888,,,2222222,,,5555555555. Use this as the Telephone Number value in the PPP tab (when you

show the modem configuration in the Network panel). You'll probably want to use this in a new location, for when you travel.

Using FireWire over IP

Finally, did you know that you can network a computer with a FireWire cable? We thought not. We're not talking about sharing an external hard drive but rather getting actual network access through the FireWire port. This feature is quite useful for transferring data between two Macs, if you

✔ Don't have an Ethernet cable

✔ Do have a FireWire cable

✔ Don't want to reboot one of the machines to use FireWire target mode (see Technique 51)

To use this:

1. **Plug a FireWire cable into both computers.**

2. **Open the Network panel.**

3. **Select Network Port Configurations from the Show menu.**

4. **Click the New button.**

5. **Give the connection a descriptive name.**

6. **Select Built-in FireWire from the pull-down menu.**

7. **Click OK.**

8. **Click Apply Now.**

9. **Follow the steps in Technique 39 for sharing an Internet connection or files.**

After you network two Macs with a FireWire cable, you can follow the steps in Technique 39 to share a Mac's Internet connection. Then the second computer can either access the Internet through the first computer or access files stored on the first computer.

37 Technique

The Wonderful World of Wireless Networking

Save Time By

- ✔ Buying the right equipment for your wireless network
- ✔ Creating your AirPort wireless network
- ✔ Using encryption for a more secure connection
- ✔ Finding the strongest network available

Wireless networks have increased in popularity in recent years partly because the technology has improved and the prices have come down. Simultaneously, the sales of Apple's laptops have increased, and many users use laptops as their primary computer instead of a conventional, wired desktop machine. The joys of a wireless connection can be seen in homes, college campuses, airports, and coffee shops. The wireless world is no longer restricted to only those with money to burn or a degree in Information Technology.

If you have the right hardware, creating and using a wireless network is amazingly simple. But you can still gain more knowledge to facilitate your wireless networking habits. In this Technique, we first discuss what you want in a base station and network card. Then we go over the basic steps of creating an AirPort network. After that, we go over encryption, which is an essential security concept. Finally, we show you some tips for speeding up your wireless network.

What to Look for in a Wireless Network

Wireless networking depends upon two things. First, you have an access point (a base station or router) that connects to the Internet (via a modem or over broadband) and passes along this connection to the computers. Second, each computer then needs a wireless network card to receive the information transmitted by the base station. In simplified terms, the access point (AP) is like a radio station sending out signals, and the network card is like an antenna, catching those signals out of the air.

In this section, we use the terms *router* and *base station* synonymously. Technically, a *router* is used to connect networks, like connecting a number of computers in a home or office to the Internet. A *base station* is a transmitter/receiver, used to handle wireless signals. Each of these often serves other purposes, like assigning IP addresses to computers, creating a firewall (see Technique 40), and connecting peripherals like printers. Manufacturers blur the lines in these definitions as well. For example, Larry's AP is called a router by D-Link (who makes it), but Marc's AP is an Apples AirPort Base Station. Both provide wired and wireless connectivity to both Macs and PCs alike.

You don't have to use Apple's AirPort Base Station or AirPort Card in order to have a wireless network. In fact, you can pretty much get most base stations to work with most network cards. When choosing a base station, look for the following features:

Your computer needs both a network card (like AirPort or AirPort Extreme) and the software for that card to work on your operating system in order to function. The AirPort software comes with Panther. The hardware is built-in for some higher-end models, and optional for others (labeled *AirPort ready* by Apple, meaning that the AirPort card must be purchased separately). If you want to use a non-Apple network card, make sure that the manufacturer also provides Panther-compatible software.

✔ **Built-in firewall:** Most routers have some sort of firewall or a Network Address Translation (NAT) system to protect your computer. See Technique 40 for more information.

✔ **Ability to also use a modem instead of an Ethernet Internet connection:** Most access points connect to the Internet via a broadband connection. More expensive routers also provide modems to use a dialup connection as a backup system. Alternatively, you can use a modem as a primary Internet connection, if one is built into your access point.

✔ **Support for a printer:** The latest AirPort Base Station includes a USB port to plug in a printer, letting you network this device. (More expensive printers come with Ethernet connections so that they may be plugged into any router.) Sure, your base station is wired to the printer, but your desktop model or laptop is freed.

If you can plug a printer into your access point, you can make your Mac even more wireless. And Rendezvous makes it easy for your Mac to find and use networked hardware (see Technique 38).

✔ **Ethernet ports to support wired computers:** Most access points are capable of networking computers wirelessly or by using a standard Ethernet cable. Having a couple of Ethernet ports is useful if you have computers without wireless cards or if a visitor wants to hop on your network via a computer that doesn't have a wireless card.

✔ **A long range:** There's a big difference between a base station's advertised range and its true range. This number is also affected by the materials used in the building where the network is (concrete and steel are killer), the distance the network covers, and how many/what kind of dense objects the connection must go through. You'll want a true range that's the size of your building but not so large that it'll be easily picked up by neighbors. Most base stations can broadcast up to around 100 feet, which is fine for apartments and smaller houses. People in bigger or multi-storied buildings might require multiple base stations to cover the entire area.

✔ **Support for encryption:** Encryption is critical to maintaining a secure wireless network. See "Understanding Encryption" later in this Technique for more.

We recommend buying a network card and base station from the same manufacturer to ensure that you'll be able to use encryption on your network. Encryption schemes are often incompatible between different manufacturers' hardware.

✔ **Ability to extend the antenna:** Some base stations can have their range expanded by adding to or otherwise extending the antenna.

✔ **Support for the 802.11g wireless protocol:** The current wireless protocol is 802.11b (Wi-Fi), but 802.11g is fast on its heels. This newer protocol supports faster transfer speeds (54 Mbps) but has the annoyance factor of disruption from cordless phones and microwave ovens. On the bright side, most 802.11g-capable equipment retroactively supports 802.11b as well. Apple's new AirPort Extreme uses 802.11g and 802.11b, whereas basic AirPort is 802.11b.

The big deal with the 802.11g protocol is the faster transfer speed. Before you spend the extra money on this better technology, you should realize that these improvements only affect transfers among computers within your network. The 802.11b standard already provides faster speeds than your Internet connection, so upgrading will not increase how fast you can download files or surf the Web.

✔ **Made by Apple:** Although you can use many different kinds of hardware with your Mac, you'll have the least amount of work to do and the highest degree of compatibility if you purchase Apple AirPort products. Further, most Macs are made to take an AirPort or AirPort Extreme Card without using up a PC Card slot (a common expansion area on desktop computers) or USB port.

Wireless Network Alternatives

Sadly, not that many manufacturers have created Mac OS X-compatible network cards. (In other words, they haven't developed the software or *drivers* for your Mac.) But if you would like to save yourself some money and give yourself more flexibility as to what network card you use, here are two manufacturers that put out drivers for OS X:

✔ **WirelessDriver** (http://wirelessdriver. sourceforge.net, free): WirelessDriver works on a couple of dozen cards (see the list at the Web site), but you won't get much in the way of support and it's not the most feature-rich driver to be found. Still, it is free.

✔ **IOXperts** (www.ioexperts.com, $20): For a reasonable cost, IOXperts offers its own 802.11b driver. It also works with a number of different cards from various manufacturers but has better support and development behind it. Visit this site for documentation, support, and a trial version of the driver.

Creating an AirPort Network

Because Apple believes that you don't need to be a rocket scientist to use its computers or equipment,

setting up an AirPort network isn't a Herculean task. In fact, even accessing a non-Apple base station with an Apple AirPort Card is pretty easy, thanks to the AirPort Setup Assistant. Here, then, is how you create your wireless network using this utility:

 To create an entirely non-AirPort network (where Apple makes neither the base station nor the wireless card), you'll need to go through similar steps but use the software provided by your hardware's manufacturer instead. You should have good instructions in the manuals that come with the base station and network card.

1. **Install the AirPort card on your Mac.**

 If you're installing the AirPort card yourself, follow the manual's instructions exactly. Be absolutely certain that the computer is off and cooled — and that you discharge any static electricity before touching your computer's innards.

2. **Turn on your Macintosh (if it isn't already) and make sure that you already have a working Internet connection.**

The base station will eventually use the same Internet connection information as your Mac (because it will replace your Mac in terms of connecting to the Internet). Before proceeding, make sure that your Mac can already access the Internet. If you've never connected to the Internet with your computer, your ISP will provide this information for you.

3. **Install and turn on your base station.**

Follow the manual's instructions that come with your base station. This might involve installing the antenna and then plugging in the power cord. (Yes, it will most likely be that simple.) If you use a modem to connect to the Internet, you'll need to connect the base station's modem port to a phone jack. If you use a broadband connection, you'll need to run an Ethernet cable from the base station to the cable or DSL modem.

Place your base station in a central location (as much as possible) to provide the maximum range throughout your home, office, or apartment. Try to keep it clear of walls (and out of closets) and away from electronic equipment that puts out or interferes with radio-like waves. This includes stereo speakers, microwaves, and cordless phones.

4. **Run the AirPort Setup Assistant on your Mac by double-clicking its icon in the Utilities folder.**

5. **On the introduction page (see Figure 37-1), select what you want to do and then click Continue.**

The AirPort Setup Assistant will let you join an existing network (AirPort or otherwise, despite what it might suggest) or set up a new one. If you're adding a new AirPort-enabled Mac to a wireless network, go for door number 1. To establish a new AirPort network, take option B.

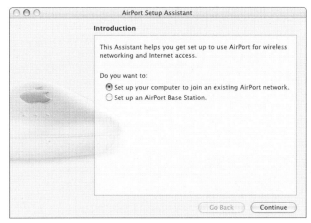

• **Figure 37-1: Use the AirPort Setup Assistant to connect to an existing network or set up a new one.**

6. **If you opted to set up an AirPort network in Step 5, follow through the remaining prompts, letting the AirPort assistant do the work.**

There will be a number of steps here, depending upon what decisions you make. The assistant will give you detailed instructions along the way. If you are ever unsure about an option, use the default choice recommended (or selected) by the assistant.

7. **If you opt to join an existing network in Step 5, the AirPort Setup Assistant will find it for you.**

If a password is required to join the network, enter the Wired Equivalent Protocol (WEP) key (see "Understanding Encryption").

If you have trouble connecting to an existing network after running through the AirPort Setup Assistant, select Other from the AirPort menu bar tool to be prompted (see Figure 37-2) for the network's name, password, and password type (like WEP 40/128-bit hex).

• **Figure 37-2: Use this prompt to manually add a wireless network.**

8. **Enjoy your wire-free world!**

Understanding Encryption

One of the problems with the growth of wireless networks is the increased security risk that they pose. You have to remember that when you use a wireless connection, all the data being transmitted is floating around the airwaves, ready to be intercepted. With that in mind, we present our list of things that you should know about security on wireless networks:

✔ **Use WEP.** Although most wireless networks use Wired Equivalent Protocol) to encrypt and decrypt transmitted data, WEP is not perfectly secure.

Hackers have cracked through WEP-protected networks. This means that someone can potentially listen in on the data transmission occurring between your computer and the base station. The end result is that someone can steal your passwords, bank account information (if you do online banking), and more! This security concern is the main disadvantage of using wireless networks over wired ones. Granted, for most home networks, it would take a long time for a hacker to crack your WEP (because of the smaller amount of traffic), but just don't fool yourself into thinking that WEP encryption is 100 percent safe.

✔ **Use at least 128-bit encryption.** WEP supports many levels of encryption, including 64-bit, 128-bit, and 256-bit. The more bits, the harder the encryption is to crack. Apple's AirPort Extreme supports up to 128-bit encryption.

✔ **Use a really, really good WEP key.** Your WEP key is like a password to the network. It can be either hexadecimal (restricted to the numbers 0–9 and the letters A–F) or ASCII (plain text). Come up with the most random key you possibly can.

✔ **Use encrypted network protocols whenever possible.** Secure Sockets Layer (SSL) connections to Web sites, MD5 authentication to e-mail servers, and Secure FTP (SFTP) connections for transferring files are far more secure options than the unencrypted alternatives.

The Virtues of VPNs

For the highest level of security on a wireless network, use an IPSec-based virtual private network (VPN). Setting that up usually requires knowledgeable network engineers, but Panther does have support for the concept now. If you need a little assistance creating an IPSec-based VPN, use a tool like VPN Tracker from equinux (www.equinux.com).

Finding Networks

Away from home or the office, you're not going to have much of a wireless experience if you can't find a network. The availability of wireless networks

creates *hotspots* — public areas where users can hop onto live connections. Some hotspots are intentionally freely available and legal to use; others require an hourly usage charge; and still others can be also used for free (thanks to someone's lax in security), but doing so is technically illegal.

 Another good reason to use and require WEP encryption on your wireless networks is that it prevents neighbors from piggybacking your connection. Without the proper key, other computers cannot use your access point.

The easiest way to find available networks is to adjust your Network settings accordingly:

1. **Open System Preferences.**

2. **Click Network, under Internet & Network.**

3. **Select your network card from the Show menu.**

4. **Click the TCP/IP tab.**

5. **In the resulting window (see Figure 37-3), select Using DHCP from the Configure IPv4 drop-down list.**

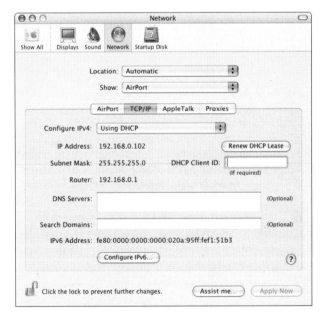

• **Figure 37-3: Use DHCP to let your computer find network connections.**

Dynamic Host Configuration Protocol (DHCP), a very common protocol, is the preferred method for most routers, wireless networks, and broadband connections. It allows your Mac to receive its connection information from the connection provider rather than establishing set parameters.

6. **Click the AirPort tab (if you're using an AirPort Card).**

7. **In the resulting window (see Figure 37-4), select Automatic from the By Default, Join drop-down list.**

Using this option will let your computer automatically log onto the strongest network.

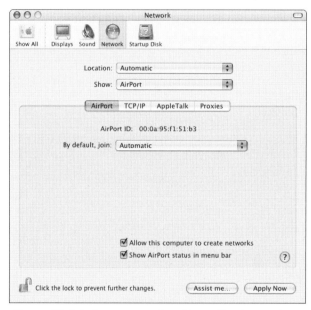

• **Figure 37-4: Let your computer choose the strongest network by not specifying one to join automatically.**

8. **If you want, select the Show AirPort Status in Menu Bar check box.**

This option makes seeing and switching among the available networks easier by using a menu bar tool (as shown in Figure 37-5).

9. **Click the Apply Now button to enact the new settings.**

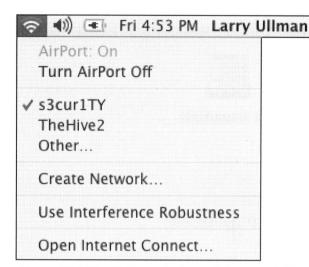

• **Figure 37-5: The AirPort menu bar tool shows available networks and lets you quickly switch among them.**

You can use many other tools to facilitate the process of finding networks. For starters

- ✔ **MacStumbler** (www.macstumbler.com, free): MacStumbler is a free (woo-hoo!) utility that finds wireless access points. Unfortunately, it only works with Apple's AirPort Card.

- ✔ **WiFi Finder** (www.kensington.com, $30): The WiFi Finder is a little device that finds wireless networks. It requires no other software and works independently of your Macintosh.

- ✔ **WiFinder** (www.wifinder.com): WiFinder is an online resource for finding publicly available wireless networks based upon geographic location. You can perform searches there, and it even lists both free and pay access points.

Good places to find wireless networks include

- ✔ Coffee shops
- ✔ Bookstores and libraries
- ✔ Airport concourses
- ✔ Hotel lobbies

In many urban environments, people will mark with chalk those areas where you can pick up wireless networks. This is *warchalking*. *Wardriving* is the process of driving around looking for open networks. Just remember that an *available* network is not the same as a network that you can *legally use*. And, note that if you can access a network, other computers on a network — and a network administrator — can see, and potentially access, your computer, too.

Technique 38

Sharing the Wealth with Rendezvous

Save Time By

- Being convinced to use Rendezvous
- Enabling and customizing Rendezvous
- Using Rendezvous with iChat and iTunes
- Using Rendezvous with hardware

Rendezvous is Apple's protocol for instantly recognizing other computers and devices on the same network. If you've never had to try your hand at networking, you won't be able to appreciate how wonderfully useful this technology is. In this Technique, we give you the skinny on what Rendezvous is, what you can do to configure it on your Mac, and how it works with some popular software and hardware.

Why You Should Use Rendezvous

Rendezvous, simply put, is the most valuable timesaving tool that you can use if you need to network computers and devices. Furthermore, Rendezvous brings some nice added features to many of the applications that you use on a daily basis. If you have a single computer that's not connected to any network all, you're not going to benefit from using Rendezvous. But for the rest of you, here's what Rendezvous lets you do:

- Find computers by name — not Internet Protocol (IP) address
- Locate people in iChat
- Listen to other music collections in iTunes
- Use a printer not connected to your computer

 In the non-Apple world, the Rendezvous concept is referred to as *Zeroconf,* for *zero configuration.* For more information on the technology as a whole, see www.zeroconf.org.

Setting Up Rendezvous

You don't *have* to do anything to begin working with Rendezvous, but you might want to make your computer more identifiable to others on the network by giving it a Rendezvous name. Here's how:

1. **Open System Preferences and click the Sharing icon (under Internet & Network).**

In the Sharing panel that appears (as shown in Figure 38-1), your computer name appears in the Computer Name text box. Your Rendezvous name will be your computer name plus the suffix `.local`.

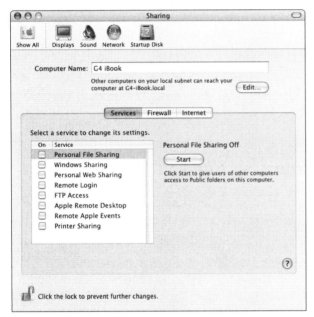

• **Figure 38-1: The Sharing panel controls how your computer is identified.**

 If your computer name contains characters that are invalid in Rendezvous (such as a space), Panther converts them to valid characters. For example, *G4 iBook* becomes *G4-iBook.local* in Rendezvous. Likewise, *It's a name!* becomes *its-a-name.local*.

2. **To change your Rendezvous name, click the Edit button.**

3. **At the prompt (see Figure 38-2), enter a new Rendezvous name in the Local Hostname box.**

 Certain characters aren't allowed in a Rendezvous name, including spaces and all punctuation. In other words, you have to stick to the alphabet, numerals, and the hyphen. Fortunately, this prompt doesn't let you enter characters that it doesn't like.

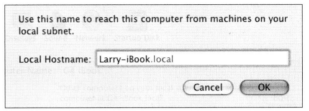

• **Figure 38-2: Use the prompt to create a new Rendezvous name.**

 Try to name your computer something meaningful to other computer users. They're the ones who'll see it in their Rendezvous-enabled applications, after all.

4. **Click OK.**

5. **Close System Preferences.**

 If Rendezvous doesn't recognize a computer, it names that computer *Macintosh.local*.

Using Rendezvous with Software

Rendezvous works with many applications, adding cool new features to already fantastic tools. Most of these applications come from Apple, naturally, but an increasing amount of third-party software supports Rendezvous. Here's a highlight of what each application brings to the table:

✔ **Safari:** Safari can find local Web addresses by using Rendezvous. To enable this, mark one of the three Include Rendezvous options of the

Bookmarks preferences panel (as shown in Figure 38-3). Then you'll see bookmarks for sites that Rendezvous finds added to your Bookmarks Bar, Bookmarks menu, or collections (in the Bookmarks window). (See Technique 28 for more on Safari.)

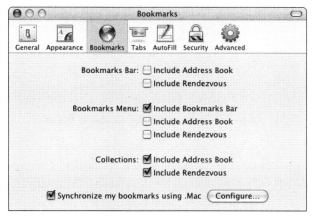

• **Figure 38-3: Larry has added Rendezvous bookmarks to his collections so they'll appear in the Bookmarks window.**

✔ **iChat:** iChat finds people on your network who are available for instant messaging, chatting, and video- or audioconferencing. Rendezvous automatically adds available people and removes them when they go offline. For more on how to do this, see the upcoming section, "Using Rendezvous with iChat."

If you use wireless networking in a public area, are in a large network, or dial up to a network by using a modem, you could easily become overwhelmed with the number of people that Rendezvous finds. In such a case, use iChat's Accounts preferences panel to disable Rendezvous.

✔ **SubEthaEdit** (`www.codingmonkeys.com/subethaedit`, free): SubEthaEdit (apparently it's former name, Hydra, was just too easy to spell) is a free text editor that allows multiple people to work together on the same document at the same time without worrying about messing up each other's work. It can be used over the Internet or on a network, using Rendezvous. It's a very innovative — and award-winning — application that's well worth considering.

✔ **Transmit** (`www.panic.com/transmit`, $25): This popular File Transfer Protocol (FTP) client lists local FTP servers using Rendezvous. Because it also supports Secure File Transfer Protocol (SFTP), Transmit is a good way to transfer files to networked users who've enabled Remote Login.

✔ **BBEdit** (`www.barebones.com/products/bbedit/index.shtml`, $179): The best of all possible text editors now supports Rendezvous for finding FTP and SFTP servers on your network. In this regard, it's much like Transmit except that it's a text editor, too.

✔ **Games:** Many games coming out now use Rendezvous to find other players. Aspyr (`www.aspyr.com`) was one of the first developers to start using this feature.

✔ **World Book 2003:** This encyclopedia application — which ships for free with Panther on new computer purchases — lets students share their work.

✔ **iTunes:** iTunes might just take the cake for cool Rendezvous features. It just has one Rendezvous feature, but it's a good one: Rendezvous on iTunes lets you listen to other people's music. For more on how to do this, see the upcoming section, "Using Rendezvous with iTunes."

Using Rendezvous with iChat

To automatically add available people and remove them from iChat when they go offline, follow these steps:

1. **Select the Use Rendezvous Messaging radio button when you start iChat AV for the first time (see Figure 38-4).**

• **Figure 38-4:** When you first use iChat, you are given the option to enable Rendezvous.

Alternatively, select the Enable Local Rendezvous Messaging check box in the Accounts preferences panel (see Figure 38-5).

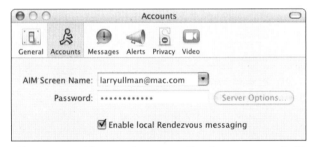

• **Figure 38-5:** You can always turn Rendezvous on and off in iChat through the preferences panel.

2. Open the Rendezvous window by using the Window menu or the ⌘+2 keyboard shortcut.

When you launch iChat or turn on Rendezvous in iChat, Rendezvous automatically finds other users on your network who are online. These people are displayed in the Rendezvous window (see Figure 38-6), which behaves almost exactly like your Buddy List.

• **Figure 38-6:** Rendezvous in iChat managed to find Larry's other self!

3. Chat, instant-message, or send a file to a found Rendezvous person as you normally would.

When you use Rendezvous, you now have two lists (windows) of people you can chat and IM with: your Buddy List and the Rendezvous window. You can work with both windows — and the people listed in them — exactly the same. Double-click a person's name to send him an Instant Message, Control+click a name to see a contextual menu, and so forth.

 Marc has found that using Rendezvous with iChat during business meetings is surprisingly useful and productive. After you have everyone recognized in your iChat, you can easily transfer files back and forth through the Instant Message window.

Using Rendezvous with iTunes

To set up Rendezvous and iTunes so that you can listen to other people's music, follow these steps:

1. On the computer that's sharing the music, open iTunes.

2. Open the iTunes Preferences panel and click the Sharing icon.

3. In the resulting Sharing panel (see Figure 38-7), enable the Look for Shared Music check box.

This setting actually lets you see other people's music — and while you're sharing yours, you might as well look for theirs, too.

• **Figure 38-7:** Enable sharing in iTunes to let others see (and hear) your good taste in tunes.

4. Enable the Share My Music check box.

5. Decide whether you want to share your entire library or just selected playlists.

6. In the Shared Name box, give your music a meaningful name.

 The shared name is for the benefit of other people on your network — not yours. You can leave them guessing with *Hip DJ 72* or be plain and descriptive with *Larry's Music*.

7. Decide whether you want to require a password.

By setting a password, you can let your friends listen in but keep your mean co-workers or annoying sibling out. The choice is up to you.

If you set a password, users see your collection listed but cannot see any specifics until they enter the correct password (see Figure 38-8).

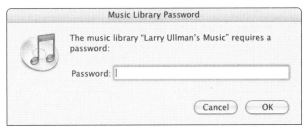

• **Figure 38-8:** You can password-protect your playlists if you want to share your music selectively.

8. Click OK to save the sharing settings.

You'll see a nice message reminding you that sharing music is for personal use only. In other words, this feature is not meant to be used as a radio station or as a way to steal music.

9. Now other users who've enabled Look for Shared Music will see your music collection and playlists in their collections window (see Figure 38-9).

Click the down-arrow next to the collection name to view the playlists.

• **Figure 38-9:** Other people's music collections appear in blue.

Look at the Status heading in the iTunes Sharing preferences panel to see how many users are currently connected to your iTunes (see Figure 38-10). You must keep your iTunes up and your computer awake for people to be able to continue listening in.

• **Figure 38-10:** Only one person is currently accessing Larry's music.

Using Rendezvous with Hardware

Rendezvous can be used with hardware as well as software. In these cases, instead of finding people in iChat or music in iTunes, Rendezvous helps you access networked devices. For example, with Rendezvous, you can easily use a printer not even connected to your Mac or find shared volumes on other computers. As of the time of this writing, Rendezvous can locate

✔ Other Macs (running OS 10.2 or later)

✔ Printers

 You can use Rendezvous to find a printer on your network or to find a printer connected to another computer on your network. Brother, Canon, Epson, Hewlett-Packard, Lexmark, and Xerox all create printers that support Rendezvous.

✔ Storage devices (like Redundant Array of Inexpensive Disks, or RAID)

✔ TiVo units

✔ Digital cameras

✔ Scanners

For specific information on using Rendezvous to find other computers and printers, see Technique 40.

Technique

39

Share the Love: Sharing Files, Printers, and More

Save Time By

✔ Comprehending the security risk when you share

✔ Sharing your Web sites

✔ Trading files with others

✔ Sharing your printer

✔ Sharing your Internet connection

Your Mac can interact with other computers on your network in many ways. For the beginner, this normally means accessing some other computer to view a Web page or retrieve files. But by making judicious use of Panther's Sharing features, you can easily and securely share your wealth with others as well.

The focus of this Technique is the many types of sharing that your Mac can do. We begin by addressing the security risks involved with these features. Then we move on to Web sharing: hosting Web sites on your Mac. Then we go into file sharing — a great way to move documents around. After that, you'll see how easily you can share your printer or Internet access with other users.

 If you find yourself frequently turning the different sharing tools on and off, consider SharingMenu, (`www.mani.de/en/`, free). This shareware (in every sense of the word) creates a menu bar item that gives you quick access to the various shares.

Safe Sharing

You should understand that sharing your computer brings some security risks. By letting others access your computer, you run the risk of them doing bad things to said computer. This could range from stealing information to crashing the system. This isn't to say that this *will* happen . . . only that it could. Here is a nonscientific hierarchy of the most-secure to least-secure sharing options; enable these (except Internet access) on the Services tab of the Sharing dialog of System Preferences:

✔ No sharing at all

✔ Personal Web Sharing

✔ Printer Sharing

✔ Internet access

You can feel pretty safe enabling Web, printer, or Internet access sharing. None of these require usernames or passwords nor allow access to your Mac's operating system or the file structure at large.

- Personal File Sharing
- Remote Login
- Windows Sharing
- FTP Access
- Remote Apple Events
- Apple Remote Desktop

 The most prudent decision that you can make is to turn on only those sharing services that you need — and when you need them. Turn off services when they're no longer necessary. Most importantly, never give out the username and password of a Mac's administrator. If others must be able to log on to your computer, set up a dummy, nonadministrative user for this purpose (use the Accounts panel under System Preferences for this purpose).

Sharing a Web Page

Web sharing is Apple's fancy description of hosting Web sites. Little did you know that your Mac has a very sophisticated Web-hosting tool built into it. With this feature, you can develop Web sites on your Mac — or, if your ISP allows it, host sites that are available to anyone in the world.

 Personal Web Sharing lets you access Web pages running on your own computer and also lets other computers on your network or the Internet access them. If you develop Web sites, you can now fully build them on your computer and then upload them to a live server after they're finished.

Personal Web Sharing lets you run static HyperText Markup Language (HTML) pages out of your Sites directory, but it doesn't have to stop there. With this tool — after the proper configuration — you can also run the following Web development tools:

- PHP scripts
- JavaServer Pages
- Common Gateway Interface (CGI) scripts
- WebObjects pages
- WebDAV

 For more information on any of these Web development tools, search Google or check out O'Reilly's MacDevCenter (`www.macdevcenter.com`). Marc has created an installer for adding PHP to your Mac (check out the Mac OS X software section of `www.entropy.ch`), and Larry has written many books about PHP (using a Mac as his test computer).

To turn on and use Web sharing, follow these steps:

1. **Open System Preferences.**

2. **Click the Sharing icon under Internet & Network.**

3. **Enable the Personal Web Sharing check box (see Figure 39-1).**

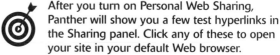 After you turn on Personal Web Sharing, Panther will show you a few test hyperlinks in the Sharing panel. Click any of these to open your site in your default Web browser.

4. **Place the files for your site within your Sites folder (in your Home directory).**

5. **Open Safari on your computer.**

6. **Go to** `http://localhost/~username` **(see Figure 39-2).**

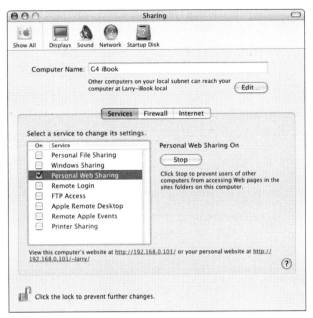

• **Figure 39-1: Web sharing is now running.**

• **Figure 39-2: This is the default Web page placed in a user's Sites directory.**

 If you attempt to go to `http://localhost` in your Web browser and it reports that the address cannot be found, Personal Web Sharing is not turned on.

What's in a Name (Or URL)?

After you enable Web sharing, you have many ways to access your Web site. From your own computer, you can point your browser to one of these two locations:

- `http://localhost/~username`

- `http://127.0.0.1/~username`

 The word `localhost` and the IP address `127.0.0.1` are two different ways to refer to your own machine (and they always refer to just your own computer). If your computer is on a network (online, that is), it will have a second IP address that is unique to your computer — `127.0.0.1` is how every computer refers to itself. This second address can also be used to find your machine in the Web browser.

- `http://your.ip.address/~username` (for example, `http://192.168.0.100/~username`)

From another computer, your Web site can be accessed through

`http://your.ip.address/~username`

Advanced Apache Management

Personal Web Sharing is really just the Apache Web server — the most popular (and arguably the best) Web server application available. From the Terminal application, you can control Apache with

- `sudo apachectl start` to turn on Personal Web Sharing

- `sudo apachectl stop` to turn off Personal Web Sharing

- `sudo apachectl graceful` to restart Personal Web Sharing

(continued)

Your Personal Web Sharing (Apache) relies upon the /etc/ httpd/httpd.conf file to control its behavior. You can modify this file if you know what you're doing. (You should probably back it up first, just in case.) For example, if only one user on your machine will use Personal Web Sharing and you'd rather use http://localhost or http://127.0.0.1 instead of http://localhost/~username or http://127.0.0.1/~username to access those pages, you can change these settings. You can also edit the httpd.conf file to turn on and off features you might want, like support for PHP or WebDAV.

Fun with File Sharing

If you want to share your stuff with other computer users or make it easier for them to share their stuff with you, you'll want to use file sharing. The two main tools for file sharing are

- ✔ **Personal File Sharing:** Personal File Sharing is an easy way to let other Mac users access the Public user folders on your Mac.

- ✔ **Windows Sharing:** You'll need to use Windows Sharing to let a Windows user access your files or use a Mac printer. From Windows, the user can go to //your.ip.address/username and then log in with your username and password. For this reason, you might want to create a new account without administrative privileges. (Choose System Preferences⇨Accounts to create the new user, making sure that the Allow user to administer this computer option is not enabled.)

Read on to discover how to easily use Personal File Sharing to transfer files between two Macs.

Personal File Sharing

To turn on and use Personal File Sharing:

1. **Open System Preferences.**

2. **Click the Sharing icon under Internet & Network.**

3. **Mark the Personal File Sharing check box (as shown in Figure 39-3).**

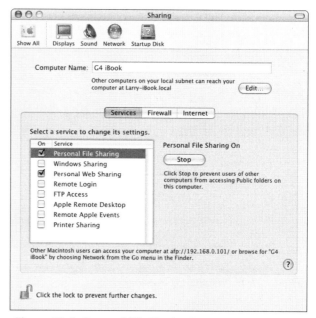

• **Figure 39-3: Personal File Sharing is now running.**

 After you turn on Personal File Sharing, text appears at the bottom of the Sharing window (above the padlock icon) that tells you how to access your computer.

4. **Place files to be shared within your Public folder (in your Home directory).**

5. **On another Mac, choose Network from the Finder's Go menu or press ⌘+Shift+K.**

6. **In the resulting window (see Figure 39-4), double-click the icon for the computer you want to access.**

• **Figure 39-4: In the Network window, open the computer you want to access.**

7. In the resulting prompt (as shown in Figure 39-5), click the Guest button.

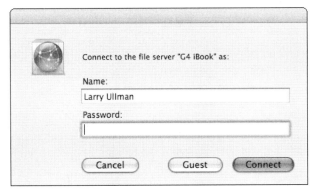

• **Figure 39-5:** Click the Guest button to access just the Public folders.

You don't need to enter a username or password.

8. In the resulting Finder window (see Figure 39-6), double-click the user's folder that you want to access.

• **Figure 39-6:** Each user's Public folder is now accessible.

9. In the resulting Finder window (see Figure 39-7)

• **Figure 39-7:** The contents of a Public folder.

▶ Transfer files to that computer by dropping them in the Drop Box folder.

▶ Transfer files from that computer if they are available in this window (like the Ch_40_figures folder in Figure 39-7).

10. As a security measure, go back to the Sharing panel and turn off Personal File Sharing when you're finished.

 When you disable Personal File Sharing, you're given an option of how quickly to disconnect it and what message to send to connected users. These messages appear in the Finders of connected Mac users.

Print Sharing

Between Rendezvous (Technique 38) and Printer Sharing, sharing one printer on a network is surprisingly easy. Here's how:

1. Make sure that the printer is turned on and connected to the primary computer.

2. On the primary computer, open the Sharing panel and select the check box next to Printer Sharing.

3. On the secondary computer, open the Printer Setup Utility (in the Utilities folder).

4. Click the down arrow next to Shared Printers (see Figure 39-8).

• **Figure 39-8:** Shared printers should automatically appear in the Printer Setup Utility.

5. Select the shared printer and click the Make Default icon.

6. Print to the shared printer as you would to a connected printer.

The next time you go to print a document, the networked printer will appear as the default printer (as long as it's turned on and connected and the primary computer is on). You can send your document to this networked printer as if it were connected to your Mac.

Sharing Your Internet Connection

A pretty cool feature built into Panther is the ability to share an Internet connection. This means that one Mac can be online (through a dialup modem, cable modem, DSL, or other type of Internet connection), and another computer can access the Internet through the first computer's connection.

 If you have multiple computers but use a modem dialup connection or don't have a router to allow multiple computers on a broadband network, use Internet Sharing.

Here's how to set up and enable Internet Sharing:

1. **Open System Preferences and click the Network icon.**

2. **Select Network Port Configurations from the Show menu (see Figure 39-9).**

3. **Make sure that at least two ports are active.**

   You'll need one port to provide this computer with Internet access and another port through which to connect to the second computer.

4. **Click the Apply Now button to activate the settings.**

5. **Select Sharing from the View menu.**

6. **Click the Internet tab.**

• **Figure 39-9: Check your active network ports before sharing a connection.**

7. **In the Share Your Connection From drop-down list, select the port where you get your Internet connection.**

   For example, this might be your AirPort or other wireless card, your modem, or your built-in Ethernet port.

8. **In the To Computers Using list, mark the check box next to the port through which the second computer will connect (see Figure 39-10).**

   For example, this might be your built-in Ethernet port.

9. **Click Start.**

10. **In the warning prompt that appears, click Start (see Figure 39-11).**

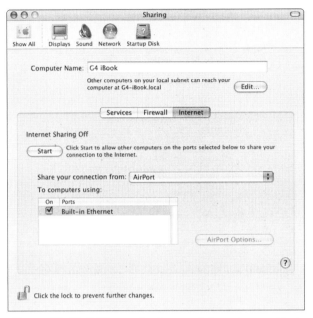

• **Figure 39-10:** Setting up to share an Internet connection.

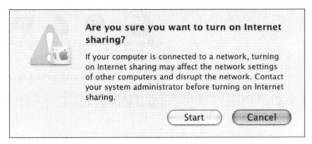

• **Figure 39-11:** Panther gives you one last word of advice before turning on Internet sharing.

11. Go to the Energy panel and set your computer so that it doesn't sleep.

Technique 40

Network Security

If your Mac is on a network, you need to be mindful of security. Whether your computer is on a company's intranet or just uses a modem to dial up to the Internet, if your computer ever talks to another computer, you have to be a little careful. Mac OS X is fairly secure in its default state (much more so than, say, um, Windows), but that doesn't mean you can't still learn a trick or two.

In this Technique, we suggest three steps to take. First, we show you what to do to secure your Mac. Second, we recommend that you run a firewall. Finally, we recommend some tools you can use to check for potential security violations. By following a few simple rules, you can use your computer without worrying about unwanted intruders.

Keeping Your Mac Secure

Network security is first and foremost a matter of turning off those features you aren't using. The Sharing System Preferences panel (see Figure 40-1) enables you to turn different features on and off by selecting or deselecting the check boxes on the Services tab. Each of these features adds functionality — but at the cost of decreased security. The most secure rules for sharing your computer are

• **Figure 40-1:** Turn off all Sharing options when they're not being used.

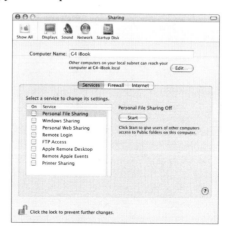

✔ **Leave all Sharing options turned off at all times, if you can.**

✔ **If you must use a type of sharing, enable it only as long as it's necessary.**

✔ **Try to use the most secure type of sharing for what you need to accomplish.**

Note the hierarchy in terms of security. For example, using the FTP Access options is less secure than Remote Login, but both can be used for the same purposes. (In Technique 39, we discuss Sharing in more detail.)

✔ **Use a firewall to protect your computer (see the following section).**

Using a Firewall

A *firewall* is a special type of security device that creates a barrier between your computer and others. It's normally created by using a combination of hardware and software. A firewall allows your computer to do everything it needs to do but prevents other computers, *Trojan horses* (software that lurks in the shadows and does malicious things without your knowledge), and the like from getting into your computer or your data.

Software firewalls

Earlier versions of Mac OS X had a built-in firewall but didn't provide a good graphical user interface to it. Most users resorted to using third-party applications such as BrickHouse (www.securemac.com) to easily manage their firewall. Fortunately for all of us, Panther includes a firewall configuration tool, also found in the Sharing panel.

 To protect your computer from outside intrusions, turn on the built-in firewall. The firewall is *exclusionary*, meaning that it will deny access through every port. (A *port* is a gateway into a computer.) If you need to turn on some Sharing features, you can then explicitly open those ports.

To enable a firewall, follow these steps:

1. **Open System Preferences.**

2. **Click Sharing, under Internet & Network.**

3. **In the Sharing panel, click the Firewall tab.**

 If you want something a little more user-friendly than the built-in firewall, check out **Firewalk X 2** (http://pliris-soft.com, $35) or **ContentBarrier** (www.intego.com, $60). Both are easy-to-use products, but they essentially provide the same functionality as the built-in firewall at a higher price.

4. **On the Firewall tab, click the Start button (see Figure 40-2).**

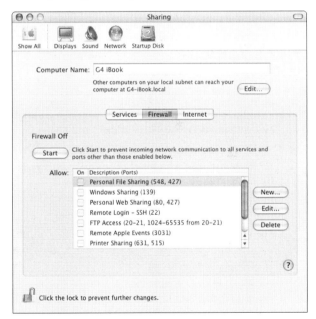

• **Figure 40-2: Use the Firewall tab of the Sharing panel to enable and control your firewall.**

 A firewall does not affect any outgoing traffic (things you do) except for your FTP application. If you have your firewall enabled, you might have difficulty accessing remote servers via FTP unless you select the Use Passive FTP Mode (PASV) check box on the Proxies tab of the Network dialog (see Figure 40-3).

• **Figure 40-3:** Enable PASV to use FTP when your Mac is behind a firewall.

5. **If you use any of the Sharing services, make sure the appropriate check box for that service is selected in the Firewall tab of the Sharing panel.**

6. **If you want others to be able to recognize you by using Rendezvous with iChat, select the iChat Rendezvous check box (see Figure 40-4).**

   For Rendezvous to work, it needs the freedom to scan certain ports. If you have a firewall enabled, other iChat users won't be able to see you unless you grant that access.

7. **If you want others to be able to listen to your iTunes collection, select the iTunes Music Sharing check box.**

   Again, iTunes Music Sharing won't work for other users unless the proper port is open.

 If you need a little assistance understanding how any item works, move your mouse over the item's description. A yellow box appears, displaying more information (see Figure 40-5).

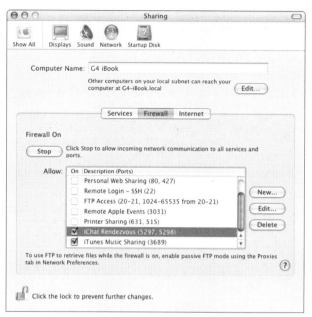

• **Figure 40-4:** At the bottom of the window are the options to let iChat and iTunes find your computer.

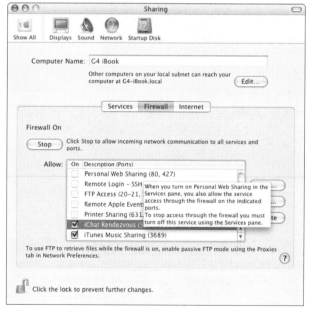

• **Figure 40-5:** Hover your mouse over a listing to receive helpful advice.

Hardware firewalls

Another common way to put your computer behind a firewall is to use some sort of router on your network. AirPort Base Stations and non-Apple routers create Network Address Translation (NAT) firewalls for your network. Essentially, the router itself is recognized as the machine being online: It's part of the wide area network (WAN). All the computers connected to the router are hidden from the WAN and are part of the local area network (LAN). If you have more than one computer at home, school, or the office, spending $100 on the right router might be your easiest option.

 Some routers will let you bypass the firewall for a particular computer through specific ports (see Figure 40-6). This is useful if you play games online, do video conferencing, and the like.

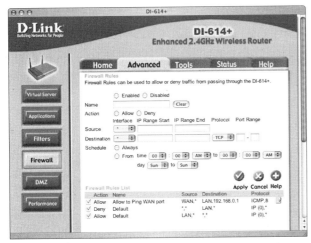

• **Figure 40-6: The D-Link router has a control panel for tweaking the firewall.**

Blocking Access to Specific Web Sites

If you'd like to keep people on your computer from accessing specific Web sites, you can do so by modifying the /etc/hosts file. Here's how:

1. **Open the Terminal.**

2. **Type** sudo pico /etc/hosts.

   This step opens the hosts file in the pico editor. Adding information to this file adjusts how your computer accesses Web sites.

3. **Enter the administrator's password.**

4. **At the end of the file in your text editor, add** 127.0.0.1 *url.com*.

   Replace *url.com* with the actual URL you want to ban. You can add as many items as you want here by using this syntax, with each going on its own line.

5. **Press Control+X to exit.**

6. **Press Y at the prompt to save the changes.**

7. **Press Return at the final prompt.**

8. **Restart your Mac.**

The next time any user attempts to go to the named URL in any browser, he will be redirected back to his own computer. This will result in either a default, meaningless Web page being displayed or a Server Not Found error message. This is a great way for parents to keep kids out of particular sites, for corporations to do the same, or to play practical jokes.

Checking for Security Problems

For the really paranoid (er, security conscious), you can use a number of applications to monitor network activity on your Macintosh. The intention of such software is to notify you of behind-the-scenes activity, thereby alerting you if something unexplained is going on. These tools won't catch people trying to break into your computer but will see whether something on your computer is trying to access the Internet without your knowledge. This could happen with Trojan horses and some applications (see the sidebar, "Applications and Your Network").

Applications and Your Network

Some applications will make use of a network connection without your knowing it. For example, an application might harmlessly check for software updates or check other computers on your network to ensure that multiple copies of the same software (that is, the same single-use serial number) are not being used repeatedly. It's up to you to interpret or abide by your licenses, but if you want to stop this behavior, run these commands in the Terminal:

```
sudo ipfw add 0 deny tcp from any to any
  3464
sudo ipfw add 0 deny tcp from any to any
  2222
```

You'll need to enter the administrator's password once, but both ports will be blocked.

Here are some popular tools for the job:

✔ **MacScan** (http://macscan.securemac.com, currently free in beta form)

MacScan looks for the various types of malicious software that lingers on your computer and tries to make connections to the outside world. If it finds any, you'll be notified and given the option to remove the offending application.

✔ **Little Snitch** (www.obdev.at/products/ littlesnitch, $25)

Little Snitch alerts you when any application attempts to use a network connection. You can then allow the connection to occur, deny it, or tell Little Snitch what to do when this happens.

✔ **Nmap** (www.insecure.org/nmap, free)

Nmap scans your computer for potential security holes, including open ports (gateways into your computer). It can work on an entire network or just a single computer.

Technique

Your Guide to .Mac: $100 Well Spent

Save Time By

- Finding out why to get a .Mac membership
- Working with iDisk
- Putting yourself online with HomePage
- Synchronizing your Address Book, calendars, and more with iSync

If you want an argument in favor of getting a .Mac account — or already have one and would like to learn a few new tricks — this is the Technique for you. A .Mac membership isn't cheap (currently $99 per year), but we have begrudgingly come to the conclusion that it's worth it. (And no, we're not getting paid by Apple to say that.) If you're not so sure, sign up for the free (free!) 60-day trial membership and see for yourself.

If you need a little arm-twisting, read the first section of this Technique, in which we discuss the best reasons to pony up the money for a membership. Next, you discover a few things about iDisk and how easy it is to use. After that, you see how to make Web pages on your .Mac site. Finally, we show you how to synchronize your Address Book contacts, iCal calendars, and Safari bookmarks with .Mac so that they're always available online . . . and backed up, to boot!

Top Ten Reasons to Use .Mac

If you require a little convincing (and that's okay: $100 bucks isn't chump change), here are our top ten best reasons to spend the money. A .Mac account will

10. Let you use iChat without creating an AOL account name.

9. Bring added functionality to many of Apple's applications.

8. Store your Address Book contacts and Safari bookmarks so that they're available and backed up online.

7. Offer you a Web presence (everyone needs a Web page).

6. Give you a pretty good virus-scanning utility.

5. Show you special tips and tricks for using your Mac.

4. Give you a pretty good backup utility.

3. Give you a remote 100MB disk space.

2. **Provide you with e-mail (and a Simple Mail Transfer Protocol [SMTP] server) while traveling.**

Your .Mac e-mail can be read via your mail client (Mail, Eudora, whatever) or online through the .Mac Web site. The online Webmail is really, really nice and easy to use, even providing you with access to your contacts if you synchronize your Address Book online. For more information, head to www.mac.com, log in, and then click Mail. If you're confused by anything, click the Help link for a useful pop-up window of assistance.

And from the home office in Topeka, Kansas, the number one reason to invest in a .Mac account is

1. **It offers up a very healthy amount of freebies, discounts, and other extras.**

Perhaps in response to some of the criticism that Apple has received over .Mac's initial release, Apple has been very, very good about offering up other goodies as they become available. These include

✔ Many free games

✔ Free versions of commercial applications

✔ Discounted software (including games)

✔ Discounted hardware

✔ VersionTracker.com memberships (both free and discounted)

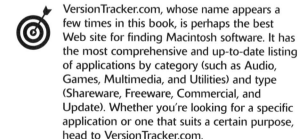

VersionTracker.com, whose name appears a few times in this book, is perhaps the best Web site for finding Macintosh software. It has the most comprehensive and up-to-date listing of applications by category (such as Audio, Games, Multimedia, and Utilities) and type (Shareware, Freeware, Commercial, and Update). Whether you're looking for a specific application or one that suits a certain purpose, head to VersionTracker.com.

✔ Free online training videos

We were both skeptical when we first signed up, but we have both gladly (and independently) rejoined for another year because it was well worth it. (Plus you get an @mac.com e-mail address, and how cool is that?)

You can set up an existing .Mac account or sign up for a free trial from the .Mac System Preferences panel (as shown in Figure 41-1).

• **Figure 41-1: Use the .Mac panel to sign up for, set up, or manage a .Mac account.**

I Like My iDisk: Storing Stuff Online

Your .Mac membership comes with *iDisk*, which offers 100MB of remote storage. Your iDisk can be used to

The 15MB of allowed e-mail space does not count against your 100MB of iDisk space. You can, of course, purchase more iDisk space if you need it.

✔ Host Web pages

✔ Back up important files

✔ Share files with other users

✔ Give yourself remote access to some of your stuff

✔ Download software from Apple and other developers

 An iDisk is a pretty handy thing if you have a fast Internet connection. If you don't, you might not find the iDisk to be that grand, particularly if you need to dial up every time you need to access the thing.

To use your iDisk, you're going to need to mount it on your computer first. As always, you have many ways of doing this:

✔ Press ⌘+Shift+I in the Finder.

✔ Choose Go⇨iDisk⇨My iDisk in the Finder (see Figure 41-2).

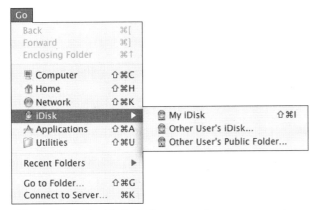

• **Figure 41-2: The Finder's Go menu gives you access to your iDisk as well as other people's.**

✔ Use Finder's preferences to add iDisk to the list of items that appear in the Finder windows (see Figure 41-3).

 If you list the iDisk in the Sidebar of the Finder windows, you can also directly save files there within applications from the Save dialog. Naturally, you can also then open files from your iDisk within an application by using the Open dialog. See Technique 10 for customizing the Finder window Sidebar.

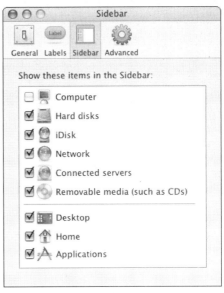

• **Figure 41-3: Make your iDisk a constant presence by adding it to the Finder window Sidebar.**

Your iDisk mounts as an icon on your Desktop. After you open this icon, you can work with the iDisk like any other folder in the Finder (as shown in Figure 41-4). You'll find that your iDisk is organized like your Home directory, with a couple of exceptions:

• **Figure 41-4: The root level of Larry's iDisk.**

✔ **Your Documents, Music, Pictures, Movies, and Library folders are all private and are not directly available to other users.**

 If you store items in the Documents directory, only users who have username and password access to your iDisk can see them. This is a good place to store files that you might need to retrieve while traveling.

✔ **Your Sites folder is where your Web pages go.**

 The URL http://homepage.mac.com/ *your_username* points directly to your Sites folder. This URL is case-insensitive, so http:// homepage.mac.com/YOUR_USERNAME and http://homepage.mac.com/*Your_Username* also work.

✔ **The Public folder is for sharing files with others.**

(See the section titled "Making your iDisk secure," later in this chapter.)

✔ **The Backup folder is where the Backup application stores files.**

You can download files from the Backup folder by using the mounted iDisk, but only the Backup application can modify this folder's contents (by adding or deleting items).

✔ **The Software folder is where Apple places Mac software that you might like.**

Updates to Apple applications appear in the Apple subfolder, whereas the Members Only subfolder contains bonus applications given out to .Mac members. You can find out about newly available software by visiting (in Safari) www.apple.com/software/ and www.mac.com (the .Mac home page).

Making your iDisk secure

The Public folder of your iDisk is automatically accessible to the world at large, so you want to be careful with it. Follow these steps to secure the folder:

1. **Open System Preferences.**

2. **Click the .Mac icon (under the Internet & Network heading).**

3. **In the .Mac dialog that appears, click the iDisk tab (see Figure 41-5).**

The iDisk preferences panel is used to tweak your iDisk settings. It takes a few seconds to load each time you click it while it attempts to synchronize with your iDisk.

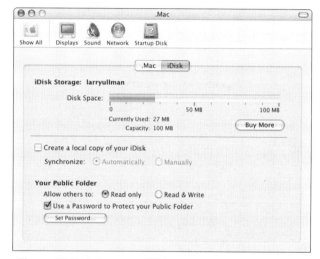

• **Figure 41-5: Adjust your iDisk settings in the .Mac panel.**

4. **Make sure that the Read Only radio button is selected under Your Public Folder.**

You can give people the option of both downloading (the Read Only radio button) and uploading (the Read & Write radio button) files to your Public folder. There's really no need to let users write to your iDisk unless you have to do some serious file sharing and don't want to use one of the many other file sharing tools available (see Technique 39).

5. **Select the Use a Password to Protect Your Public Folder check box.**

By marking this check box, you require users to enter a password to access this folder. You'll be given a prompt (as shown in Figure 41-6) to enter the password.

Enter a password to protect your Public folder:

Password: ••••••••

Confirm: ••••••••

Retype your password

Cancel   OK

• **Figure 41-6: Enter a password here twice to set it for your Public folder.**

 You can easily change your iDisk Public folder password by clicking the Set Password button in the iDisk panel.

6. **Close System Preferences.**

 You cannot turn off the sharing capability of the Public iDisk folder. The best you can do is password-protect it and remember not to place sensitive information there!

Using a Local Copy of Your iDisk

While you're in the iDisk panel, you can decide whether you want Panther to maintain a local copy of your iDisk. This means that your computer will keep a backup of your iDisk on your Mac. Larry personally finds this to be a little annoying and completely unnecessary for these reasons:

✔ In all likelihood, your iDisk is a backup of stuff already on your computer.

✔ If you have this set to automatically update, a good amount of time will be spent by your Mac syncing your iDisk with the local copy. This is really annoying.

✔ If you have to manually update the copy, you need to remember to do this.

Feel free to use this feature if you must, but Larry turned it off almost immediately and hasn't missed it since. That being said, if you're on a slow Internet connection and use the iDisk for storage, you can drop things in your local copy of the iDisk and then update the online version the next time you connect.

Using another .Mac member's iDisk

Just like you can let other people access your iDisk, you can easily access theirs with Panther. The iDisk submenu (under the Finder's Go menu, refer to Figure 41-2) gives you these options:

✔ **Other User's Public Folder:** To mount another user's Public folder, you need only his .Mac username. Mind you, you can download files from a person's Public folder, but you cannot add files to it, delete files from it, or otherwise change the Public folder's contents. If the folder is password protected, you'll be prompted to enter that password before you can read (download) any files.

 You can also mount a user's Public folder by using the Finder's Connect to Server tool (under the Go menu or press ⌘+K). Use `http://idisk.mac.com/username` as the address. If you use this method, you can bookmark an iDisk by adding it to your list of favorite servers (see Figure 41-7). To do so, just enter the connection address in the box and click the plus sign. Access a Favorite Server by selecting it from the list and clicking Connect. To quickly go back to any recently accessed server, click the clock icon (beside the plus) to view a pull-down menu of your server history.

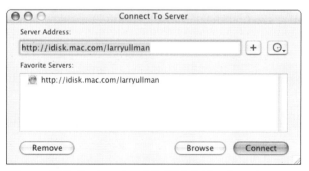

• **Figure 41-7: Bookmark Public iDisk folders by using Connect to Server.**

✔ **Other User's iDisk:** To mount someone else's iDisk, you'll need his .Mac username and password. If you have this, you can control that disk as if it were your own.

Working with Your .Mac Web Page

Along with the .Mac account comes your very own `http://homepage.mac.com/`*your_username_here* Web page. These days, anyone who's anyone has a Web page (as does everyone else), so it's about time you make your online presence felt. Just log on to the .Mac site (`www.mac.com`) and use the HomePage tools to create your pages. *HomePage* lets you pick a theme from one of many prefab templates and then add your own text, pictures, movies, or whatever to create your own page. If you know a little Web design, however, you can skip the HomePage hassle and manipulate your site with ease.

 Your .Mac member name will be part of your Web site address, so watch what you choose. That is, unless you're okay with telling your boss to check out `http://homepage.mac.com/JobHater53`.

1. Create the Web page on your computer.

 If you create a Web page within your Sites folder, you can see how it looks in your browser by going to `http://localhost/~your_username`.

2. Mount your iDisk by pressing ⌘+Shift+I in the Finder.

3. Open the Sites folder on the iDisk.

4. Copy all your site files to the iDisk.

5. Use your Web browser to visit `http://homepage.mac.com/`*your_username*.

 Images stored in your Pictures directory can be used in a Web page by setting the image source to `http://homepage.mac.com/`*your_username*`/.Pictures/`*imagename*.

Protecting Your Web Site

If you want to put your site online but want to restrict access to it, you can password-protect it. To do so, follow these steps:

1. Go to `www.Mac.com` **in your Web browser.**

2. **Log in with your username and password.**

3. **Click HomePage.**

4. **Do one of the following:**

▶ If you have multiple sites, select the site to protect from the list and then click Edit.

▶ If you only have the one site, click Protect (on the right side of the page).

5. **In the resulting page, select the On check box.**

6. **Enter a password.**

7. **Click Apply Changes.**

The next time that users visit your site, they'll be presented with a prompt to enter this password.

Using iSync with .Mac

The iSync application (which is available for free from `www.apple.com/isync`) was created by Apple to simplify the synchronization of certain types of data between two sources. For example, you can use it to update contacts between your Mac and a cellular phone. Or, you can synchronize your Safari Bookmarks, Address Book data, and iCal data (Calendars and To Do lists) with your .Mac account.

Synchronization provides three really keen benefits:

✔ A backup of your valuable data

✔ The ability to use these items on multiple computers

✔ Online access to your contacts (in Webmail) and bookmarks

After you synchronize your data from one Mac (computer A) to your .Mac account, you can then update the data on a second Mac (computer B) by using the same .Mac account. This is great if you've just acquired a new computer or you regularly use two different Macs. Furthermore, by synchronizing through .Mac, changes made to your data on one computer (say, a person's e-mail address in Address Book) can be updated on the second computer without the risk of losing other important information (like all the other Address Book data). For this to work, you only need to log in to the same .Mac account on both computers (using the .Mac section of System Preferences).

 Using iSync and .Mac together means that you can guarantee that you always have the most up-to-date version of your Address Book, Safari bookmarks, and iCal data on the computer that you're using.

To use iSync across two computers, follow these steps:

1. Use the .Mac System Preferences panel to set your .Mac username and password, if you haven't already.

2. Open the iSync application, found in the Applications folder (download it from Apple if you don't already have a copy).

3. Click the .Mac symbol (see Figure 41-8).

• **Figure 41-8:** iSync lists the available destinations at the top of its window.

4. In the dialog that appears, select the Turn on .Mac Synchronization check box.

5. Enable all the check boxes under This Computer.

   Here is where you select what information you want to be synchronized, choosing from Safari Bookmarks, Address Book Contacts, and iCal Calendars and To Do items. If you don't use any of these, you don't need to synchronize it.

6. Click the Sync Now icon.

   The first time you run the application, it will take a little time.

7. Access the second Mac (computer B).

   It doesn't matter whether the second Mac is on the same network as the first Mac. It doesn't even matter what username you use to log on to the second Mac. (The synchronized data is associated with a specific .Mac account, not the computer's username.)

8. Open iSync on the second computer.

9. Click the .Mac symbol.

10. From the For First Sync menu, choose Merge Data on Computer and .Mac.

 You're pretty safe using iSync unless you choose either of the Erase Data On options. These could have dire, unintended consequences. The Merge Data on Computer and .Mac option combines all existing data and is therefore the safest. If it runs across a conflict (two different records for an individual in the Address Book, for example), it asks you what to do.

11. Enable all the check boxes under This Computer (see Figure 41-9).

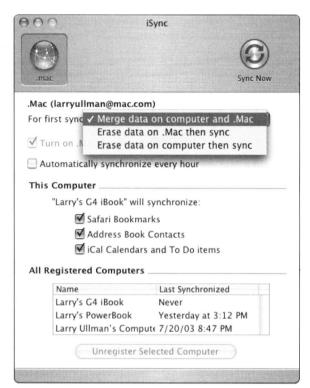

• **Figure 41-9:** Setting up iSync for the first time on a second computer.

12. **Click the Sync Now icon.**

The application first previews how much data needs to be reconciled. If it's more than five percent of the total data for any one application, you'll be prompted (check it out in Figure 41-10).

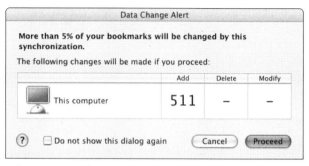

• **Figure 41-10:** iSync warns you before any major changes occur.

13. **After the application has finished, close iSync.**

14. **Restart iCal, Safari, or your Address Book to use the synchronized data.**

iSync is kind enough to remind you in a window at the bottom which computers have synchronized their data and when. You can also "forget" a computer (like one you got rid of) by selecting it from the All Registered Computers box and then clicking the Unregister Selected Computer button. (Refer to Figure 41-9.)

Part VII

Fast and Furious Multimedia

The 5th Wave   By Rich Tennant

THE NEW HOLLYWOOD   @RICHTENNANT

CUT! PASTE!

iTunes: Rockin' in the (Partially) Free World

Of the many free applications that Apple has included with its operating system, iTunes could just be the shining star. The first of the iLife products, iTunes has become so popular that even Windows users now have it. (Who would've thunk it?) All iTunes does is manage and play music, but that's a pretty useful thing. If you've never used iTunes before, this Technique will show you the fastest ways to use the application. If you're a seasoned iTunes veteran, you're still bound to discover many new, efficient techniques.

This Technique begins with the coverage of iTunes set-up routine — for first-time users. Then we discuss the most critical preferences settings and how to adjust the iTunes window itself. Afterwards, you'll see how to manage your music collection. Finally, we cover how to spend every last dime at the iTunes Music Store.

 Also see Technique 46, which specifically discusses burning CDs from iTunes, as well as Technique 38, which covers using iTunes with Rendezvous.

Setting Up iTunes

The first time you use iTunes, you'll be taken through the Setup Assistant. Here's what you'll see the first time you use iTunes:

1. Feast your eyes upon the iTunes Software License Agreement.

You're pretty much going to have to agree to this if you want to use the software. You can click the Decline button, but then the application will just quit . . . which kinda defeats your purpose.

 You'll see the iTunes agreement the first time you use iTunes and again after certain updates. You have the option of agreeing to it and using iTunes or declining it and not using the software. All in all, it doesn't really matter what the agreement says then, does it? Let's hope there's nothing important in there. . . .

2. **Welcome to iTunes (see Figure 42-1)!**

This is just a welcome page. You can cancel this process and go directly into the application, but then you'll need to manually tweak every setting using iTunes preferences. Take the smart road and click Next to advance.

• **Figure 42-1:** The iTunes welcome page begins the Setup Assistant.

3. **Select your Internet Audio settings (see the choices in Figure 42-2) and then click Next:**

▶ *Do you want to use iTunes to handle Internet audio?* Don't have iTunes modify your Internet settings if your Web browser already handles audio content as you'd like it to.

▶ *Should iTunes connect to the Internet automatically when it needs to (for example, to retrieve the track listings for a CD)?* If you have an always-on connection (like cable modem, DSL, and such), select the Yes radio button. If you have a dialup connection, select the No radio button.

A cool feature of iTunes is the ability to look up CD and song names online. However, you don't necessarily need to be connected to the Internet to use this. If you import a CD, you can look up the songs later. The next time you're online, select the entire imported CD and then choose Get CD Track Names from the Advanced menu.

• **Figure 42-2:** Set your Internet audio settings now and forget about them.

4. **Decide whether you want iTunes to search for MP3 and AAC music files that you already have (see Figure 42-3).**

If you have music files on your computer, go ahead and select the Yes radio button. If you know that you don't, select the No radio button.

If you don't have any audio files on your computer when you first run iTunes, don't bother having iTunes search for them. It'll only be a waste of time.

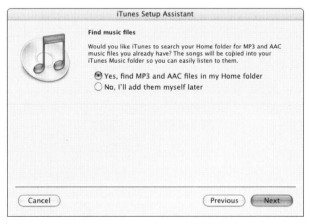

• **Figure 42-3:** Send iTunes off on a useful search or a wild goose chase.

5. **Decide whether to go to the iTunes Music Store (see Figure 42-4).**

• **Figure 42-4: The final step in the Setup Assistant.**

Finally, iTunes will obligingly take you right to the iTunes Music Store to start filling up that hard drive (and emptying your wallet at the same time). We leave this choice up to you. If you do go visit, don't forget to read "Blowing Your Paycheck at the iTunes Music Store," later in this chapter.

Tweaking Your Preferences

After you get iTunes up and running, you should immediately customize your preferences to make it work exactly as you'd like it to. If you used the Setup Assistant, many settings will already be determined. Our best advice for tweaking iTunes follows. We'll take you step by step through the preferences panels, omitting only the cosmetic issues:

1. **Open the iTunes preferences by pressing ⌘+, (comma) or choosing Preferences from the iTunes menu.**

2. **In the On CD Insert drop-down list box of the General panel (as shown in Figure 42-5), choose from four options of what iTunes should do when inserting a CD:**

   ▶ Show the songs on the CD

   ▶ Begin playing the CD

   ▶ Import the songs from the CD (copy them to your music collection)

   ▶ Import the songs from the CD and then eject the disc

   In all likelihood, you'll most often want to leave this on the Show Songs setting. That being said, if you're about to rip your entire music collection onto your computer, set iTunes to import the songs and eject the CD to facilitate the process.

 You can also set the Finder to automatically open audio CDs in iTunes.

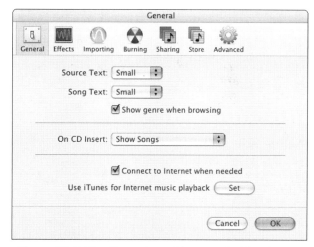

• **Figure 42-5: The General panel lets you decide what to do when CDs are inserted and how to work with the Internet.**

3. Click the Effects icon and select the Sound Check check box (see Figure 42-6).

This setting ensures that iTunes automatically adjusts the song volume so that it maintains a consistent level. Opting for this saves you the hassle of constantly adjusting the volume.

• Figure 42-6: Use the Effects panel to provide a consistent listening experience.

4. Click the Importing icon (see Figure 42-7) and set your import configurations.

These values are critical if you import a lot of music from CDs. The Import Using drop-down list affects how large the files will be and where you can play them. The Setting drop-down list also affects how large the files will be and how good they'll sound. For more on these settings, see the sidebar "A Word on Music Formats," elsewhere in this chapter. Finally, the Create File Names with Track Number check box dictates whether CD track numbers are used in filenames.

 We discuss the iTunes Burning panel in Technique 46, where we cover burning CDs in general.

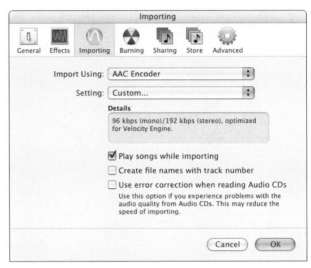

• Figure 42-7: The Importing panel is very important if you import a lot of music.

5. Click the Sharing icon (see Figure 42-8) and decide whether you're a borrower, a lender, or both.

• Figure 42-8: Share your music with others on your network.

The Sharing panel has two main settings:

▶ **Look for Shared Music** controls whether iTunes should look for other music collections on your network. If your iTunes finds other people's music collections, they appear as a blue-colored playlist in the left-hand column. You can then access any of those songs — and potentially the playlists — that user created.

 You cannot change the information of a song on another user's computer, alter a rating, increase the play count, or copy songs to your computer. If a particular song was purchased through the iTunes Music Store, you need that user's access information to play it.

▶ **Share My Music** determines whether you let others listen to your iTunes. If you decide to share your music — and you really ought to, to be nice — you can decide whether to share every song (the entire library) or specific playlists (and therefore, specific songs). While you're at it, give your share a descriptive name and password-protect it if you want to make sure that only friends tune in. After you turn on this feature and click OK, you'll be given the Sharing Music Is for Personal Use Only prompt (as shown in Figure 42-9) where you should select the Do Not Show This Message Again check box.

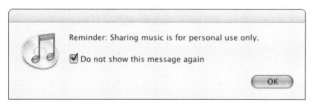

• **Figure 42-9: Yes, yes. Stealing music is bad. We get it!**

 As long as other people have sharing turned on and their iTunes up, you can listen to their songs. Similarly, sharing your songs will have little, if any, performance effect on your computer and will not interfere with your listening to iTunes as you want to.

 Technique 38 shows you — using detailed instructions — how to share your music with other users on your network.

6. **Skip the Store panel for now.**

This pertains to the iTunes Music Store, which we discuss later in the chapter.

7. **Click the Advanced icon (see Figure 42-10). Here, you can**

• **Figure 42-10: Use the Advanced panel to dictate whether iTunes manages your music files.**

▶ Use the Change button to tinker with the Music folder location.

 If you move your music files from one drive to another or want to use iTunes on a different music collection, change the Music folder location in the Advanced preferences panel.

▶ Set the Streaming Buffer Size to Large. (You really should.)

▶ Select the Keep iTunes Music Folder Organized check box. (Trust the app.)

There are two schools of thought when it comes to letting iTunes manage your music files. If you don't want to think about this process at all, let iTunes do the work and don't go meddling in the Music folder yourself. On the other hand, if you like a more hands-on approach, turn off the Keep iTunes Music Folder Organized option and you'll never have your files rearranged just because you made some edits to a file in the iTunes application (like changing a song or album name).

▶ Select the Copy Files to iTunes Music Folder When Adding to Library check box. (Again, let iTunes do the work.)

You can override the iTunes setting that copies music to your folder when added to your library by holding down the Option button when you drag a song into iTunes. That way, you can listen to a track with iTunes without making it part of your permanent collection.

8. After you tweak all your settings, click OK.

9. Enjoy iTunes!

A Word on Music Formats

When you import music into iTunes and onto your computer, you have to make a few decisions first. These decisions affect the size that each file takes up on your computer and the sound quality that it provides. It's important to realize that there's an inverse relationship between the two: the higher the quality, the larger the file size. All the important sound settings can be made using the two pull-down menus found in the Importing preferences panel.

iTunes supports four audio formats:

✔ **AAC:** AAC is the default setting for iTunes. It provides a better quality than MP3 at a smaller file size. The only drawback to AAC is that not all computers or players can recognize the format. If you play your music as MP3s in a CD player or don't use an iPod as your portable device, avoid this format until it's better supported.

✔ **AIFF:** AIFF is an uncompressed standard format for sound files on the Macintosh. It provides great quality but at a high price in terms of disk space. A CD is in AIFF format normally, taking up around 700MB (as opposed to 70MB in MP3 format).

✔ **MP3:** MP3 is the format that started the whole digital music boom. It turned music into files one-tenth of their normal size without significantly sacrificing sound quality.

✔ **WAV:** WAV is the Microsoft version of AIFF. Yuck!

Besides the format used, iTunes lets you adjust some of the specific settings, by choosing Custom from the Setting pull-down menu. After you do this, you'll find three pull-down menus for configuration. First, the Stereo Bit Rate affects both your file size and the sound quality. The higher the bit rate, the higher the quality and the bigger the file. The 128 Kbps is the default setting, but you might want to up this some, particularly if you're likely to burn audio CDs from your iTunes collection, in which case there will be potentially noticeable quality loss. Larry normally opts for a setting of 192 Kbps, which is a nice compromise between quality and file size.

Next, you'll want to leave both the Sample Rate and Channels settings on Auto. There's no need to mess with these.

Making the iTunes Window Look the Way You Want

Before doing your thing with iTunes, you ought to customize the iTunes window. Start with which version of the window you'd like to see:

✔ **The full-screen version** (as shown in Figure 42-11)

✔ **The optimal version:** To view the full iTunes screen optimally (so that it takes up as much space as needed or as it can), Option+click the green button in the upper-left corner of the window.

✔ **The minimized version** (see Figure 42-12): Switch to this format by clicking the green button. Click on the green button again to go back to the full-screen version.

• **Figure 42-11:** Both the full-screen and optimal versions of iTunes looks more or less like this.

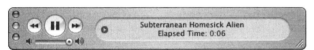

• **Figure 42-12:** Use the minimized version of iTunes to display the bare necessities.

Within the minimized version, you can still see the song name and time. Click the song name to rotate among song, artist, and album. Click the time to rotate among song length, how much of the song has been played, and how much is remaining. Click the small circle on the left to switch between the display and the equalizer. If multiple tasks are going on (like importing a CD or copying music to an iPod), clicking this circle cycles through that information as well.

✔ **The really small version** (see Figure 42-13): If you're in the minimized version, you can make it smaller by resizing the window, using the lower right-hand corner.

• **Figure 42-13:** If you want to control iTunes and nothing more, use this window version.

Within the full-screen version, you can do a lot to customize the window.

1. **Bring up the View Options menu (as shown in Figure 42-14) by choosing ⌘+J or choosing View Options from the Edit menu.**

• **Figure 42-14:** Customize the iTunes window like you would any window in the Finder.

2. **Select check boxes for every column you want to view.**

3. **Clear those check boxes for every column that you don't need (or don't need regularly).**

Yes, we're talking about Beats Per Minute.

The only column that you cannot remove or even move is the Song Name. Notice that it's not listed in the View Options menu (refer to Figure 42-14).

4. **Click OK.**

5. **In the iTunes window, click and drag the column names to rearrange them.**

6. **Control+click any column heading to bring up its contextual menu (see Figure 42-15).**

• **Figure 42-15:** Use contextual menus in iTunes to work with the window settings.

7. **Choose Auto Size All Columns to adjust the column widths automatically.**

 Notice that you can also add and remove columns via the contextual menu (if you don't feel like using the View Options prompt).

Managing Your Music

After you import or purchase a slew of music, you'll need to be able to manage and navigate through it with ease. In this section, we cover the best techniques, without any of the beginner step-by-step stuff you've probably already figured out.

Editing song information

You can edit information for individual songs in many ways:

✔ **Select a song and press ⌘+I to bring up the Get Info panel.**

✔ **Click within any one field to change just that field.**

✔ **Select multiple songs and press ⌘+I to edit information for several songs at once.**

With this method, you'll only want to tweak broad factors, like the artist name, the year of release, the album name, and the genre.

 If you keep your music organized, you'll find that editing songs becomes really quick thanks to iTunes' AutoFill feature. From your existing library of artists, albums, and genres, iTunes will guess what you're typing in these fields and fill it in for you.

Searching for tracks

iTunes supports two methods for finding specific songs: browsing and searching. Our three best tips for finding a song or artist are

✔ **Click the Browse button (it looks like an eye, in the upper-right corner) or press ⌘+B to open and close the browsing panels (see Figure 42-16).**

• **Figure 42-16:** The Browse button appears at the top of the iTunes window.

 Use the Browse tool to browse by genre, artist, or album.

✔ **Choose a category from the Search pull-down menu to narrow your search before you enter your keywords (see Figure 42-17).**

The Search box in iTunes immediately begins searching as soon as you begin typing. This is both handy and a pain. If you know you're searching specifically for an artist or a song, select this option first, and then enter your keywords.

Managing Your Music

✔ **Select a playlist in the left-hand column to browse or search within it.**

By default, the Search and Browse tools look through an entire collection, but you can limit both of these by selecting a playlist and then searching or browsing (see Figure 42-18).

• **Figure 42-17:** Fine-tune a search by clicking the magnifying glass icon.

• **Figure 42-18:** Browse through parts of your library by first selecting a playlist.

Creating playlists

You can save yourself a lot of time, or just kill some time, by playing around with playlists. Here are some of the cool things that we've come to appreciate:

✔ **Press ⌘+Delete to remove a song or playlist without getting the confirmation dialog. (Deleting a song from a playlist does not remove it from your collection; to do that, remove a song from the Library list.)**

✔ **Create a new playlist by**

  ▶ Selecting a bunch of songs and then Shift+clicking the Add button.

  ▶ Selecting a bunch of songs and dragging them into a blank area in the Source column.

  ▶ Selecting a bunch of songs and pressing Shift+⌘+N.

✔ **Option+click the Add button to create a Smart Playlist.**

Smart Playlists are relative newcomers to the world of iTunes. Standard playlists have set songs in them (selected by dragging the song from the Library into the playlist). Smart Playlists let you set parameters (such as artist name, year the song was released, your ranking of the song, genre, and more). iTunes will then create a playlist that matches your criteria. You can further limit your Smart Playlist to a certain length, like eight hours of total music (say, if you're taking an eight-hour car trip).

Adding album covers

If you like eye candy with your iTunes (and we're not talking about the Visualizer toy here), you'll love the artwork feature added in iTunes 4. It brings you one step closer to having the CD but without the fragile jewel case (or the liner notes). The songs that you purchase at the iTunes Music Store come with the artwork already. For the other 2,000 songs you have in your collection, you'll need to manually add album covers. Or, if you actually have, you know, better things to do, try these:

✔ **Fetch Art for iTunes** (`http://staff.washington.edu/yoel/fetchart`, **free**).

This script automatically scans through Amazon.com for the songs you select and retrieves the appropriate artwork. You can then review and approve the downloaded images.

✔ **Find Album Artwork with Google** (http://www.dogheadbone.com/projects.php, **free**).

If Fetch Art for iTunes doesn't come through, download and use this AppleScript to search Google's images pages for the album cover. From there, you can download and install it.

Blowing Your Paycheck at the iTunes Music Store

The iTunes Music Store looks like it just might be the most popular (legal) music downloading software around. It was an immediate hit with Mac users, and now our lesser Windows brethren can finally understand exactly the kind of things that we've been crowing about for years: 50 percent innovation, 50 percent really, really cool.

To use the iTunes Music Store (let's just call it the *iTMS* for short), you need either an Apple ID or a .Mac account. First, click the Music Store option in the Source column. Then click the Sign In button next to Account (on the far right of the screen) and you'll be taken through these steps that follow. If you have a .Mac account, Apple most likely already has your credit card, saving you a step (for better or for worse).

Within the preferences panel, click the Store icon to adjust a few of its preferences (see Figure 42-19). This is what you need to know:

✔ **If you don't want to be tempted, clear the Show iTunes Music Store check box.**

✔ **If you're of the instant gratification type, opt for one-click shopping.**

✔ **If you prefer larger debits on your credit card, go with the Shopping Cart.**

 If you use the iTMS shopping cart, the Music Store playlist becomes an expandable folder that shows both your purchased music and your shopping cart. You can add items to the shopping cart over multiple sessions and buy them all when that paycheck comes in.

✔ **If you're on a slow network connection (read: modem), select the Load Complete Preview Before Playing check box to improve your preview quality.**

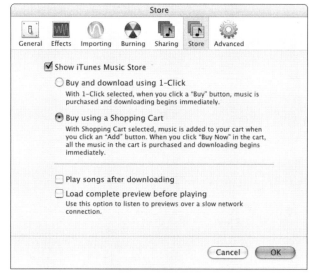

• **Figure 42-19:** Adjust the iTunes Music Store settings in the preferences panel.

Within the iTMS itself (see Figure 42-20), here are a few shortcuts with which you should familiarize yourself (so that you can spend more time buying). These are

✔ **⌘+[(opening bracket):** Takes you back a page

✔ **⌘+] (closing bracket):** Takes you forward a page

 The ⌘+[and ⌘+] shortcuts also work to move forward and back among the panels of the Preferences and Get Info panels.

• **Figure 42-20:** The iTunes Music Store, with its main buttons and tools along the top of the window.

✔ Click the house icon to go to the iTMS main (home) page.

✔ Click the Browse button (the eye) to browse the entire iTMS by genre, artist, or album.

✔ The Search box has a pull-down menu that lets you limit the scope of your search.

Use the Search pull-down menu to make your searches faster and more accurate. Better yet, use the Power Search for extended searching.

Technique 43

Working with iPhoto

Save Time By

- ✔ Discovering some of the best practices for working with iPhoto
- ✔ Managing your growing digital library
- ✔ Presenting your photographs online

If you have a digital camera and you're not using iPhoto already, you're really missing out. iPhoto is a simple, yet effective, application for managing your digital photographs. In this Technique, we shy away from the basics (such as importing and viewing images), instead focusing on the best and quickest ways to do specific things within the application. Then we address your digital library: what to do with all those images you've imported over the years. Finally, we demonstrate a couple of techniques for posting your images as an online, viewable catalog.

 iPhoto is a great application and seems to be more than sufficient for nearly every user. If it's not to your liking, many people use iView Media ($30) or iView MediaPro ($160). They're both available from www.iview-multimedia.com, where you can also download the free iView Catalog Reader for managing your library.

Best iPhoto Practices

The basics of using iPhoto are easy to master, but you can do a number of little things to use the application more productively. We go through these in somewhat random order.

Preferences

Some of the settings in the iPhoto's preferences panel will affect your productivity, such as

- ✔ What to do with a double-click:
    - ▶ Open in Edit view
    - ▶ Open in a new window
    - ▶ Open in another application (see Figure 43-1)

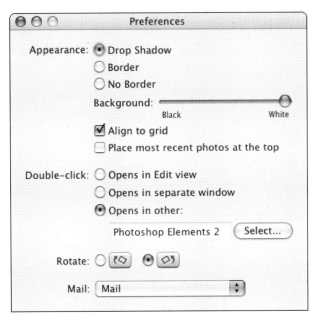

• **Figure 43-1:** iPhoto's Preferences panel.

 Whatever you decide to do with the double-click setting, click the Select button to choose your external editor, such as Photoshop Elements. Just Control+click an image to bring up a contextual menu that offers you the option of editing the image in your external editor (see Figure 43-2).

✔ **Rotate:** Different cameras display rotated images in different directions (clockwise versus counter-clockwise). Change your rotate button to match your camera so you can easily adjust how the image is displayed.

 If your Rotate setting works correctly for you most of the time but you need to rotate an image the other way on occasion, hold down the Option button while clicking Rotate within the main iPhoto window.

✔ **Mail:** One of the nice features in iPhoto is the ease in which you can e-mail a picture to some-one. In order for this feature to work, however, iPhoto must know what mail application you use. Establish that here, select an image in the main

iPhoto window, and then click Email to be prompted (see Figure 43-3) for how the photo should be formatted when you send it.

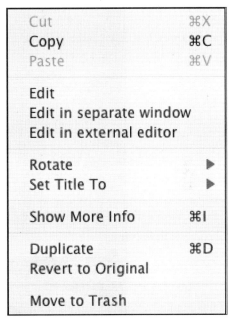

• **Figure 43-2:** iPhoto's contextual menu offers quick access to frequently used features.

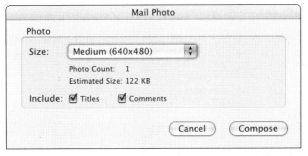

• **Figure 43-3:** When e-mailing a picture, you can adjust the image's size and information in iPhoto first.

Creating a new Photo Album quickly

The iPhoto application uses Photo Albums to help you organize your digital images. Even though all your images are primarily stored in the Photo Library — the first item listed in the left-hand column — subsets can be grouped into albums, organized based upon theme, location, and so forth. (Think of Photo Albums as the equivalent of the iTunes playlist.) You can create a new Photo Album by choosing New Album from the File menu and then dragging all your images into this new folder, but this method is faster:

1. **Open iPhoto.**

2. **Select Photo Library in the left column to view all your images.**

3. **⌘+click images to select the images for the Photo Album.**

4. **Drag these images into the blank area in the left-hand column, below the Trash.**

   You'll see a green plus circle appear, along with the number of images being moved in a red circle.

5. **The new album (Album-1) will appear with the photos in it (see Figure 43-4).**

• **Figure 43-4:** The new Photo Album is automatically created by iPhoto.

6. **Double-click the new album's name to change it.**

7. **Delete the default name, type a new one, and you're done!**

 You can also create a new album by dragging a folder of images from the Finder into the iPhoto Library list column. The album is created with the same name as the folder, and all the images are imported automatically.

Editing images with ease

After you import your images, you might want to tweak them some. This can be accomplished by using iPhoto's basic tools or with an external application such as Adobe Photoshop, Adobe Elements, or the open source The GIMP. We don't have space in this book to discuss basic editing techniques, but here are our best editing-related tips:

✔ **Set your preferences for a default action when you double-click (refer to Figure 43-1); otherwise, use the contextual menu (refer to Figure 43-2).**

   If you want to use iPhoto for your editing, make this explicit in your preferences (by selecting Opens in Edit View under Double-Click). If you'd rather use another application, set the double-click to launch that (by using the Select button after selecting Opens in Other). In either case, when you want to edit an image using other than the default tool, Control+click to see your options.

✔ **If you use a separate iPhoto window for editing, customize its toolbar.**

   The separate iPhoto windows have a toolbar at the top, like most other Panther windows. The window can be customized by using the Customize Toolbar option under the Window menu. This brings up a palette of tools (see Figure 43-5) that you can add to the window's toolbar. Drag items from the palette to the toolbar to create a custom toolbar.

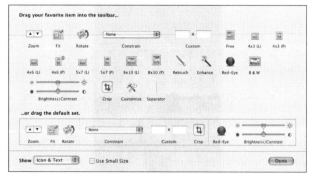

• **Figure 43-5:** Customize the window toolbar to display the tools you use most.

✔ **After you edit a photo, you can undo the effects by selecting Revert to Original from the contextual menu that appears when you Control+click an image.**

This feature works even after you've quit and returned to iPhoto because iPhoto doesn't let you make alterations to the original photo. Instead, it creates a copy of the image and makes changes to it.

Working with Your Digital Library

If you take a lot of digital photographs, your hard drive will quickly fill up with images. This isn't ideal for your computer and, more annoyingly, will bog down iPhoto every time you use it. From the experience of importing and managing several thousand photos (no, we are not making that up), here is our best timesaving advice for importing, managing, and storing your digital photographs.

Importing images

One of the ways in which iPhoto has grown is its streamlined importing capability. You can now hook up your camera to your Mac (depending upon the camera and the Mac) and import your images directly into iPhoto.

✔ **Let iPhoto erase the camera contents after each transfer.**

As Marc has painfully discovered, if you use your camera's media card for photos and movies (which many cameras are now capable of), you can easily forget the movies and accidentally delete them by manually reformatting the media. By letting iPhoto take care of deletions, your photos will be deleted, but everything else will remain untouched. Just mark the Erase Camera Contents after Transfer check box before clicking the Import button (under the Import tab).

✔ **Use a media reader adapter instead of a direct connection to your camera.**

For very little money — $10–$20 — you can purchase a media adapter so that you can access your virtual "rolls of film" without using your camera. In all likelihood, such a connection would be much, much faster than the likely USB cable that your camera uses, particularly if you pick up a FireWire model. After you mount a media card, you can import the images by dragging them from the Finder into iPhoto.

✔ **If you want to import movies recorded on your camera, use Apple's Image Capture application.**

Image Capture is a multifunction tool that doesn't get much press. It can be used to do everything from sharing cameras and scanners to importing contents from a media card.

✔ **Have iPhoto store your photographs in your Pictures directory.**

That's what it's there for, after all. Plus, your images will be backed up with the rest of your Home directory.

 You can import an image from a disk (instead of a camera) by dragging the folder containing the images into the photo viewing area of iPhoto. The application will use the folder's name as the film roll name. If your folder is nested with subfolders, each subfolder becomes its own film roll.

Managing your images more efficiently

After downloading a batch of images, you usually want to rotate the ones in portrait orientation first. We recommend this timesaving procedure:

1. **Make sure that you can view most of the images and you can see the orientation clearly.**

Use the Zoom slider to present the images at an appropriate size.

2. **Select all the images that need to be rotated clockwise.**

You can select multiple images by ⌘+clicking.

3. **Click the Rotate button.**

Remember to use the iPhoto Preferences to set the default rotation direction.

4. **Select all the images that need to be rotated counterclockwise.**

5. **Hold down Option while clicking Rotate.**

After an image is in iPhoto, you can

✔ Drag it into Photoshop or another application for editing.

✔ Click the Desktop button (under the Organize tab) to set the selected image as your Desktop (see Figure 43-6).

• **Figure 43-6:** Use the Organize tools to quickly do common things with an image.

✔ Send it to a buddy by dragging it into an iChat Instant Message window.

 Deleting an image in iPhoto doesn't actually delete the image from your hard drive. You must empty iPhoto's Trash to formally remove the photograph (which also deletes the image from your computer).

How Many Megapixels Are Enough?

Today's digital cameras take images starting at 2 megapixels and easily going up to 5 or 6 megapixels, even for consumer-level cameras. But how many megapixels do you really need to use? All digital cameras let you adjust the size (in number of pixels) and quality (based upon format and compression) of the pictures that they take. Choosing a lower image size has many benefits:

✔ You can fit more images on whatever media your camera uses.

✔ You use far less disk space.

✔ You won't slow down iPhoto like choosing larger images does.

✔ You get smaller file sizes, which makes placing images on the Web or e-mailing them easier.

The only reason why you won't want to use less than the maximum number of pixels is if you plan on printing the images in sizes larger than 5 x 7 inches. Images with small file sizes result in poor image quality in a print that size.

Our advice is to use an image size around 2–3 megapixels but at the highest image quality. This gives you a high-enough resolution for editing and lets you use an image as your Desktop without stretching — but still gives you a very printable picture.

Storing your images to save space and time

You don't want to keep all your photographs in iPhoto at all times for three reasons:

✔ Digital images take up an incredible amount of disk space.

✔ iPhoto's performance suffers.

✔ Finding images is much harder.

If your Photo Library is nearing 650MB, burn your archived images to a CD to save space:

1. **Select the Photo Library in the left-hand column.**

2. **Click the Information button (which bears an *i*) at the bottom of the column.**

If you select the entire Photo Library, the information panel will show you how large it is on your hard drive.

3. **Click Burn (under the Organize tab) to archive the library to a disc.**

4. **Insert a blank CD-R (you'll be prompted for one).**

5. **Click the now-flashing Burn button.**

6. Click Burn in the Burn Disc prompt.

7. After the CD has been made, close iPhoto.

8. Switch to the Finder.

9. Find the Photo Library folder.

Presumably this is in your ~/Pictures directory.

10. Delete the entire Photo Library folder.

11. Insert the CD at any point in time to review the stored images.

If you need help managing your libraries, check out

✔ **iPhoto Buddy** (http://nofences.net/iphotoBuddy, free): iPhoto Buddy makes managing multiple iPhoto libraries easier. You can work with subsections of your digital collection, even if they're located on different media (your hard drive, CDs, and so forth).

✔ **iPhoto Library Manager** (http://homepage.mac.com/bwebster/iphotolibrarymanager.html, free): This application works much the same as iPhoto Buddy but is AppleScript-able.

Creating an Online Photo Album

Putting your photos online is really easy if you have the right software. If you have a .Mac account, you can put your photos online by following these steps:

1. Select a Photo Album in the left-hand window.

2. Click HomePage.

3. Edit the page title, picture frame style, and so forth from the Publish HomePage dialog (see Figure 43-7).

4. Click the Publish button.

You can only publish up to 48 images at once by using these steps. If you have more images than that in a Photo Album, break them up into multiple albums.

iPhoto uploads all the images.

The beauty of this system is that iPhoto automatically resizes the images to be more Web-friendly and creates a page of thumbnails.

5. When iPhoto is finished, it gives you the URL for your new site (see Figure 43-8).

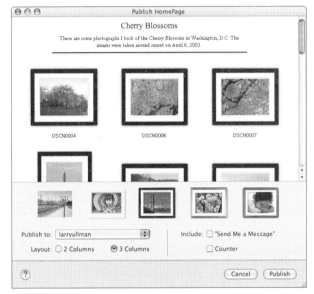

• **Figure 43-7:** Quickly customize how you want your Web site to look.

• **Figure 43-8:** You are prompted after iPhoto finishes uploading your new site.

You can also use the .Mac Slides Publisher tool to turn your online pictures into a screen saver for other Mac OS X users.

If you don't have a .Mac account, you still have options. Both of these tools will generate the Web pages for you, but you need to have your own Web site in order to make them public (or be able to host Web sites on your computer, see Technique 39). After one of these applications creates the pages, just upload them to their final destination. (Your ISP — which will most likely provide a limited amount of free Web space — or Web hosting company will provide you with the requisite details.)

✔ **Use Image Capture.** The Image Capture application can also build Web pages for you. After you connect a camera, open Image Capture. Then choose Build Web Page from the pop-up menu. The Web pages themselves will be created and stored in your ~/Pictures folder.

✔ **Use a commercial tool like Image Rodeo** (www. imagerodeo.com, $30). Image Rodeo, although not free, ties in nicely with iPhoto and provides some more sophisticated features than the other tools listed. Specifically, it has many available templates and lets you define your own.

Staying on Schedule with iCal

Technique 44

Save Time By

✔ Making your own Calendar

✔ Memorizing the important keyboard shortcuts

✔ Subscribing to and publishing Calendars

✔ Discovering the best tips and tricks for using iCal

✔ Exploring alternatives to iCal

iCal is Apple's nice little scheduling application that, along with the Address Book, pretty much means that you never need to buy any Personal Information Management (PIM) software again. Not only does iCal have all the features that you would ever use, but it also uses a standard format that makes it compatible with alternative software. This is a great asset if you share calendars with other users who might (or might not) also be using a Mac.

In this Technique, you find out the fundamental keyboard shortcuts and some best-usage techniques. Then you see how to easily subscribe to someone else's calendar and publish your own calendars online. After that, pick up some cool tips and tricks for using iCal. Finally, you see some of the alternatives that you can use if iCal doesn't suit you. But first, make sure that you know how to create and use a basic Calendar.

Creating Calendars and Events

Everything in iCal relies upon one basic thing: a Calendar, which is more than just a collection of hours, days, weeks, and months. A Calendar is a collection of data — including all those elements, plus events (scheduled occurrences) and To-Do list items — grouped into subjects.

iCal comes with two Calendars from the start: Home and Work, meant to record your personal and work happenings, respectively. You can subscribe to other calendars (see "Subscribing and Publishing"), like U.S. holidays, the schedule of Chicago Bulls games, listings of movie releases, and more. Or, you can add your own Calendars.

Here are the benefits of this multi-calendar structure:

✔ Search and browse Calendars by subject (work versus home versus school).

✔ Share specific Calendars with others. (Share a work Calendar but not your personal one.)

✔ Color-code your life to make managing your schedule easier.

To create a Calendar, just do this:

1. **Choose New Calendar from the File menu.**

A new Calendar will appear in the Calendars list in the upper-left column of the iCal window (see Figure 44-1).

• **Figure 44-1: Create a new Calendar here.**

2. **Type the new Calendar's name.**

After you create a new Calendar, it's named Untitled by default but is already highlighted. Just begin typing to rename the Calendar.

3. **Press Return to finish the renaming.**

4. **To hide any Calendar, clear the check box next to its name.**

 The check box next to a Calendar's name indicates whether that Calendar (and its events and To-Do items) is visible. By toggling these check boxes, you can more easily see only the information you want.

5. **To change a Calendar's properties, click the *i* in the lower-right corner of the iCal window to bring up the Info panel (see Figure 44-2).**

Within the Info panel, you can

▶ Rename a Calendar (click its name).

▶ Change its color (click the arrows next to the color).

▶ Add a description.

• **Figure 44-2: The Info panel, showing the details for a calendar.**

More important than knowing how to create a Calendar is how to add an event. Follow these steps:

1. **Select a Calendar by clicking its name in the Calendars window.**

 Choose which Calendar the event goes in before it can be added. If an appropriate Calendar doesn't yet exist, use preceding steps to add one.

2. **Double-click under the event's date (or start date) to add the event.**

The easiest way to add an event is to double-click the day of the event. Be sure to click underneath the day's number rather than the number itself (which will display that day's events, rather than add a new event).

3. **Click the *i* in the lower-right corner of the iCal window to bring up the Info panel (if it isn't already visible).**

4. **Enter the event's information by clicking the fields in the Info panel and typing the proper values (see Figure 44-3).**

• **Figure 44-3:** The Info panel, showing the details for a specific event.

Adding and editing events from the Info panel is very easy. Just click a field (like the event name or date), type in the new values, and press Return. Click the All-Day box to schedule the event for the entire day or for several days.

iCal's Main Keyboard Shortcuts

iCal, like most applications, has oodles of keyboard shortcuts available. Rather than provide an un-learnable list of them all, here are the most useful for performing common tasks:

✔ **⌘+N:** Creates a new event (Calendar entry)

✔ **⌘+K:** Creates a new To-Do item

✔ **⌘+R:** Refreshes the selected Calendar

✔ **⌘+Shift+R:** Refreshes every Calendar

✔ **⌘+T:** Moves to today

✔ **⌘+Shift+T:** Gives you the Go to Date prompt (as shown in Figure 44-4)

✔ **⌘+1:** Switches to the Day view

✔ **⌘+2:** Switches to the Week view

✔ **⌘+3:** Switches to the Month view

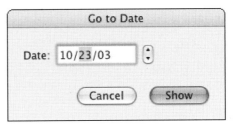

• **Figure 44-4:** Use this prompt to jump to another date.

✔ **⌘+→:** Moves you to the next unit (day, week, or month)

✔ **⌘+←:** Moves you back a unit (day, week, or month)

✔ **⌘+I:** Hides and shows the Information panel (see Figure 44-5)

✔ **⌘+Option+T:** Hides and shows your To-Do list

✔ **Tab:** Cycles you through the events

• **Figure 44-5:** The Info panel shows an event in detail.

Best iCal Practices

Using iCal is easy, but using it well is a whole different matter. Here are some of our best suggestions for getting the most out of this application.

✓ **Keep many different organized calendars.**

iCal comes with two Calendars for starters: Work and Home. Get in the habit of creating new Calendars for special projects, particular events, or when the Calendar will be shared with others.

 It's so easy to color-code your calendars and turn them on and off that there's no reason not to use several different ones.

✓ **Use iSync and a .Mac account to back up and synchronize your Calendars across multiple computers (see Technique 41).**

✓ **Use iSync to synchronize your Calendars with an iPod or a PDA.**

✓ **Discover what contextual menus will do for you (see Figure 44-6 and Figure 44-7).**

As with any application, most of the common tools are easily accessible by using a contextual menu. Just Control+click an item — like a To-Do list task in Figure 44-6 or a Calendar in the Calendars window in Figure 44-7 — to see what shortcuts are available.

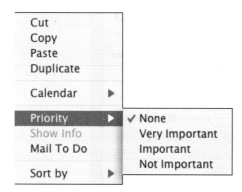

• **Figure 44-6: A contextual menu for a To-Do item.**

• **Figure 44-7: A contextual menu for a Calendar.**

 You have a Search box at the bottom of the iCal window!

✓ **Select a Calendar and then enter part of an event's name to quickly find that event.**

✓ **Double-click your way to a shortcut.**

Double-clicking creates a new Calendar, a new event, or a new To-Do item, depending upon what blank area you double-click. For example, double-clicking in the Calendars window creates a new Calendar; double-clicking a date creates a new event; double-clicking in the To-Do list creates a new task.

Subscribing and Publishing

The primary role of iCal is to handle your own scheduling, but you can also subscribe to other people's calendars and publish your own so that others can see it.

Where to find subscriptions

You can subscribe to different calendars for all kinds of reasons. Maybe you want a calendar that lists all the San Antonio Spurs games or all the major Hollywood movie premieres. You can find such calendars and many others like them through these sources:

- ✔ **Apple:** `www.apple.com/ical/library`

- ✔ **dotmac.info:** `www.dotmac.info/index.html/category/6/`

When you find a calendar that you want to subscribe to, just click the <u>Subscribe</u> link provided on the Web site. This brings up iCal, and you'll be prompted to subscribe to that calendar (see Figure 44-8).

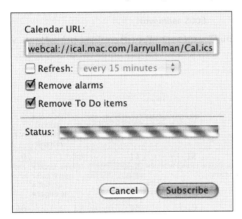

• **Figure 44-8: Subscribe to online calendars.**

The calendars to which you subscribe don't have to be corporate and impersonal. For example, you can subscribe to a friend's calendar to see where and when her band will be playing. After someone publishes a calendar to .Mac or another service, he can provide you with a URL. To subscribe to it, choose Calendar⇨Subscribe and enter that URL in the prompt that appears (refer to Figure 44-8).

The subscription prompt has three options:

- ✔ Refresh

- ✔ Remove Alarms

- ✔ Remove To-Do Items

The last two are normally recommended because they get rid of Calendar items that won't mean much to you. The refresh tells iCal to automatically compare your subscribed version of the calendar every so often (15 minutes, every hour, every day, or every week), updating your copy as necessary. You can also manually update a subscribed calendar by choosing Refresh from the Calendar menu.

Publishing your Calendar with .Mac

In order to share one of your Calendars (so that others might subscribe to it), you must first publish it online. For example, you could create a Calendar of your travel schedule or your children's band practices and then share this with family members via the Internet. Whenever you make changes to your Calendar, those who have subscribed to it can also retrieve these changes.

To publish a Calendar by using your .Mac account, follow these simple steps:

1. **In the left-hand column, select the Calendar that you want to share.**

2. **Choose Publish from the Calendar menu.**

3. **In the Publish Name box of the dialog that appears (as shown in Figure 44-9), give the calendar a title.**

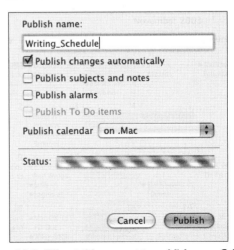

• **Figure 44-9: Fill out this prompt to publish your Calendar.**

Your Calendar's title must abide by standard URL rules. This means that non-alphanumeric characters such as punctuation and spaces are replaced by representations. For example, the title *Writing Schedule* becomes *Writing325Schedule,* which is not the desired result. Instead, use *Writing_Schedule,* which is acceptable.

4. **Decide whether to update the Calendar automatically.**

This option is important for keeping subscribers abreast of your most current Calendar.

5. **Decide what extra parts of the Calendar you want to share:**

► Subjects and notes

► Alarms

► To-Do items

6. **Make sure that On .Mac is selected in the Publish Calendar pull-down menu.**

7. **Click the Publish button.**

When iCal is done, you'll see a message indicating two URLs for the Calendar (see Figure 44-10). The first is for those who use iCal; those who don't can use the second URL to view your Calendar with a browser.

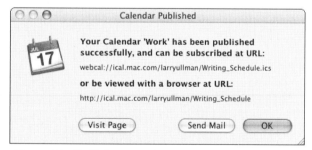

• **Figure 44-10:** Make note of the URLs for your Calendar.

8. **Give the URLs to family, friends, and co-workers.**

You can also click the Send Mail button to start spreading the news.

Publish your Calendar without .Mac

If you don't have a .Mac account, you can publish your Calendar with these other tools:

✔ **iCal Exchange:** www.icalx.com

✔ **iCalShare:** www.icalshare.com

✔ **Your Mac:** If you have a permanent Internet connection (broadband, not dialup), you can use the WebDAV features of your Mac to publish iCals. A good tutorial on doing so is at www.gregwestin.com/webdav_for_ical.php.

iCal Tips and Tricks

iCal can do many things, but here are two features and add-ons that are to our liking.

iCal and Mail

iCal works with your Address Book and the Mail application in an unbelievably easy way. From the Contracts stored in your Address Book, you can add potential attendees to events and then have iCal and Mail send them e-mails and handle their replies with respect to attending. What a brilliantly simple way to schedule meetings or family gatherings.

1. **Create an event in iCal.**

2. **Make sure that the Information panel is visible.**

3. **Press ⌘+Option+A to open the People window (see Figure 44-11).**

4. **Drag names from the People window onto the event in the Information panel.**

The event displays the list of attendees as you add them.

5. **Click Attendees and then choose Send Invitations from the pop-up menu that appears (see Figure 44-12).**

iCal opens your Mail application and sends the message.

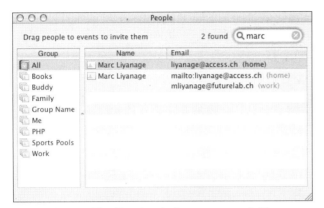

• **Figure 44-11: The People window uses your Address Book data.**

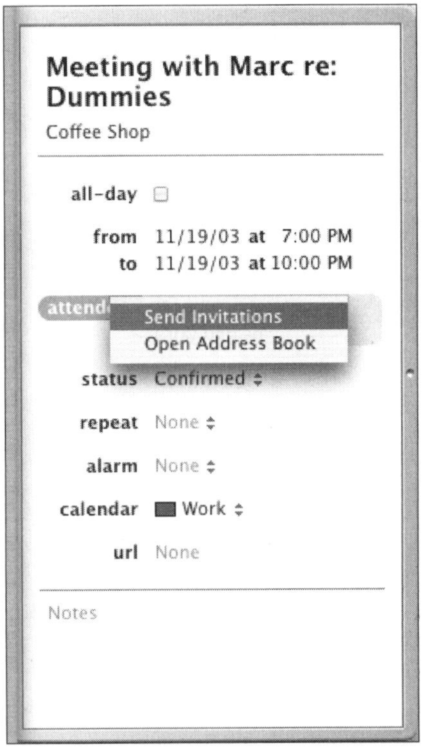

of accepting the event and the option of e-mailing you her response.

• **Figure 44-13: iCal sends an e-mail inviting people to an event.**

AppleScript

iCal is, naturally, AppleScript-able. If you're savvy with the tool, you can write your own. If you'd rather ride on the coattails of others (which is fine), check out some of the AppleScript resources listed in Technique 60.

Among the 250 AppleScripts that Doug Adams provides at his Web site (www.malcolmadams.com/itunes/index.shtml, then look for iCal in the left column), you'll find a couple of particular note to iCal users. For example:

✔ **iCal Calling iChat:** This script automatically changes your iChat status message (normally Away or Available) so that it reflects your Calendar's schedule. For example, if you have a meeting with Marc from 1 until 3, this script changes your iChat status during that time to read *Meeting with Marc.* You'll find both a free version available and a $5 version that has more features.

✔ **iCal Calling iTunes:** This script uses iCal to schedule iTunes playlists. You can have iCal start and stop playing different lists that you create in

• **Figure 44-12: Send attendees an invitation to the event.**

All the participants then receive an e-mail inviting them to the event (see Figure 44-13). When a recipient clicks the embedded link, she is given the option iTunes. For example, you can have iCal automatically start a playlist or radio station when you log on in the morning and then stop iTunes when you go to lunch. This script also comes in both a free and a $10, more feature-rich, version.

Exploring Alternatives to iCal

If iCal isn't to your liking (and we really couldn't image why that'd be the case), look into these alternatives that provide some of the iCal functionality.

✔ **Mozilla** (www.mozilla.org/projects/calendar, free): Mozilla, the makers of the excellent Mozilla, Camino, and Firebird Web browsers, also makes a calendar tool that works in the Mozilla Web browser. It uses the same format for its calendars as iCal, which means that you can use Calendars you create in it with iCal or subscribe to Apple-provided calendars with Mozilla.

 If your office needs a good (and free) scheduling system, you can use iCal on the Macs, and Mozilla's calendar on Windows and Linux.

✔ **PHP iCalendar** (http://phpicalendar.sourceforge.net/nuke, free): PHP iCalendar is a PHP-based calendar application. It also uses the iCal format but only allows you to view calendars . . . not edit them.

✔ **PandoCalendar** (www.pandacorner.com/PandaSystems/PandoCalendar.html, free): If you want a bare-bones calendar, try PandoCalendar. It has a basic interface, lets you schedule things, and doesn't overwhelm you with features.

Snapping Screenshots Fast

Whether you want to show some cool onscreen thing to a friend, need to do some debugging work with tech support, or are writing a book, being able to quickly and easily take shots of your screen is a valuable trick to know. You can always whip out your camera, take a picture of the screen, have the film developed, and scan in the photograph, but we think that you'll like the techniques outlined here better.

We start by going over the built-in system tools that Panther has to offer: Screen Capture and Grab. After that, special attention is given to Snapz Pro X, the granddaddy of screenshot applications. Finally, you see a couple of other options, should these not be to your liking.

Taking Screenshots with Screen Capture

Screen Capture is part of the operating system, which means that it is available with every application that works with OS X. Screen Capture is triggered by several keyboard shortcuts:

 Don't be confused by the Image Capture program found in the Applications directory. Despite its name, this application does not capture screenshot images. Its actual role is to import images from a digital camera. It can also be used to network and share a digital camera or scanner.

↙ **To capture the entire screen, press ⌘+Shift+3.**

↙ **To capture part of a screen, press ⌘+Shift+4.**

The cursor will then turn into a cross-hairs icon. Click and drag over an area (see Figure 45-1) to select it. When you release the mouse button, the image is taken, and you'll hear a snapshot sound.

• **Figure 45-1: The Screen Capture tool highlights in gray the area to be captured.**

The keyboard shortcuts for image capturing are listed under Keyboard Shortcuts of the Keyboard & Mouse System Preferences panel.

You can capture a window or object by using this last method; or, follow these steps to get a more precise screenshot:

1. **Press ⌘+Shift+4.**

Again, the cursor turns into the cross-hairs icon.

2. **Press the spacebar.**

The cursor turns into a camera icon.

3. **Move the camera cursor over the window or object that you want to capture.**

When you move the cursor over an object, it becomes highlighted.

4. **After you highlight the window that you want, click the mouse anywhere on the window or object to take the screenshot.**

 You can take screenshots of items in the background as long as you can see a piece of them. For example, if you're in Microsoft Word and can see a corner of a Finder window, you can get a screenshot of the whole Finder window by highlighting and taking a shot of just the visible portion.

Here are a couple of things that you should know when using this method:

✔ **Screen Capture saves the screenshots as PDFs.** No other format options are available. That being said, you can use the Preview application's Export feature (under File) to covert a PDF to a JPG, TIFF, PNG, and more.

✔ **The screenshots are automatically saved to your Desktop with such useful names as Picture 1, Picture 2, and so forth.**

✔ **You cannot capture the cursor.**

✔ **Unlike digital cameras, which normally allow you to adjust the size of the picture taken in pixels, you cannot change the resolution of shots in Screen Capture.** You can adjust the size of your screenshots only by adjusting the resolution of your monitor.

✔ **With the ⌘+Shift+4 shortcut, you can toggle back and forth between a section of the screen and a window by continuing to press the spacebar.**

✔ **With the ⌘+Shift+4 shortcut, press Escape to cancel the operation.**

✔ **If you hold down the Control key while triggering the screenshot utility (using either ⌘+Shift+3 or ⌘+Shift+4), the image is sent to the Clipboard and is not saved as a file.**

 Hold down the Control key to send the captured image to the Clipboard. Then you can paste this image into an e-mail, a document, or an iChat session.

If you'd rather place an image within the document you're working on instead of creating an image as a file on your computer, here's how:

1. **In your document, place the cursor where you want the image to go.**

2. **Toggle over to the application where you'll want to take the screenshot.**

3. **Capture the image while holding down the Control key.**

Holding down the Control key copies the image to the Clipboard. You can use ⌘+Control+Shift+3 to capture the entire screen or ⌘+Control+Shift+4 to capture a section of the screen or an entire window.

4. **Toggle back to your document.**

5. Press ⌘+V to paste the captured image from the Clipboard into your document.

Taking Screenshots with Grab

The other option for taking screen shots is Grab. Grab is located, appropriately enough, in the Utilities folder. It has certain benefits over the built-in Screen Capture tool. With it, you can

✔ **Capture the cursor.**

✔ **Decide what cursor to view.**

 If you want a cursor in your screen shots, select the cursor type from Grab's Preferences panel (see Figure 45-2).

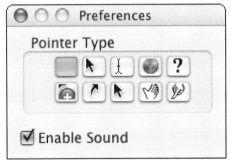

• **Figure 45-2: Use the Preferences panel to tell Grab what cursor to capture, if any.**

✔ **Capture images in TIFF format.**

Whereas Screen Capture takes only PDFs, Grab takes only TIFFs.

✔ **Use a more intuitive menu system rather than keyboard shortcuts.**

Grab comes with its own keyboard shortcuts, which are also duplicated in the Capture menu (see Figure 45-3). These are

✔ **⌘+Shift+A:** Captures a selection of the screen

✔ **⌘+Shift+W:** Captures a window

✔ **⌘+Z:** Captures the whole screen

✔ **⌘+Shift+Z:** Brings up Timed Screen (see Figure 45-4)

• **Figure 45-3: Use the Capture menu in lieu of or to remind you of the keyboard shortcuts.**

Timed Screen captures let you take images while you're in the process of doing something. This is the easiest way to capture complex actions, like dragging a document onto an application's icon.

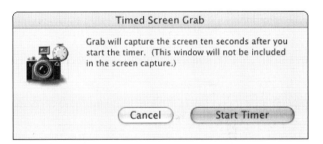

• **Figure 45-4: Grab can take delayed snapshots.**

After Grab has done its magic, it loads the image as a new document. This can then be saved as a file anywhere on your computer by pressing ⌘+S or selecting Save from Grab's File menu.

In the earlier "Taking Screenshots with Screen Capture" section of this chapter, we discuss how to capture images and paste them into a document. If you're using an application that supports Services (like TextEdit), you can accomplish the same thing by using the Grab tool as a Service.

1. **In your document, place the cursor where you want the image to go.**

2. **Decide what Service you'll need to use.**

   ▶ If you want to capture the whole screen (not necessarily the current one), you need to use the Screen Service.

➤ If you want to capture a part of any screen (not necessarily the current one), use Selection.

➤ If you want to capture the entire screen but need a few seconds to get yourself organized, use Timed Screen.

3. **From the application menu, choose the appropriate service from Services⇨Grab (see Figure 45-5).**

The Screen Grab prompt appears.

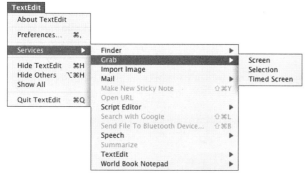

• **Figure 45-5: You can use Grab as a Service in applications that support it.**

4. **To capture the entire screen, toggle to whichever view you want to capture and then click anywhere outside the prompt (see Figure 45-6).**

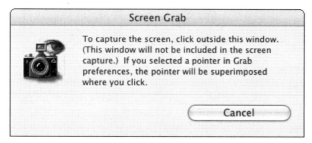

• **Figure 45-6: Follow the instructions to capture the entire display.**

To capture a part of the screen, toggle to whichever screen you want to use and then click and drag over the area that you want captured (see Figure 45-7).

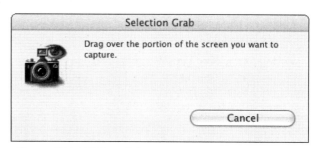

• **Figure 45-7: Click and drag to grab a section of the screen.**

 You can also click a window once to have it automatically captured.

If you chose Timed Screen, you have ten seconds to set up the screen as you want it.

5. **Toggle back to your document.**

You'll see the image already inserted into it.

Using Snapz Pro X

Snapz Pro X from Ambrosia Software (www.ambrosiasw. com, $29) has long been the preferred screenshot utility for Mac writers and developers. In part, this is because there were no good alternatives (like Grab) prior to OS X. If you need to do any serious amount of image capturing, Snapz Pro X is definitely the way to go. Here's what it can do for you:

➤ Take images in many formats (JPG, GIF, PNG, TIFF, BMP, PICT, PDF, and Photoshop)

➤ Resize images

➤ Perform color conversions (say from color to black and white)

➤ Create borders for your images

➤ Capture or create video

If you haven't used Snapz Pro X before, here is all you need to do to take a quick screen capture:

1. **Open the application by double-clicking its icon (assuming you've installed it).**

Snapz Pro X will load and then run in the background, hidden from you until you press the proper keyboard shortcut.

2. **Press ⌘+Shift+3 to bring up the Snapz Pro X interface.**

3. **Click one of the buttons across the top to choose your capture type.**

Your options are

- ▶ Screen (the whole screen)

- ▶ Objects (documents, windows, and such)

- ▶ Selection (a selected area of the screen)

- ▶ Movie (video)

4. **If you select Objects in Step 3, click the object that you want to capture.**

5. **If you select Selection in Step 3, click and drag to select an area to capture.**

6. **If you have Snapz Pro X set to let you choose a filename (under Capture Options in the main panel), you'll be prompted for the file's name.**

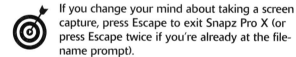 If you change your mind about taking a screen capture, press Escape to exit Snapz Pro X (or press Escape twice if you're already at the filename prompt).

If you're already using Snapz Pro X, there are plenty of timesaving techniques that you can use:

- ✔ In the Snapz Pro X Extras folder, you'll find three AppleScripts for automating the utility.

- ✔ You can automatically resize your images as you take them, using the scale menu (see Figure 45-8).

- ✔ Set the default filename for the image from the Preferences tab and disable Choose File Name in the main tab.

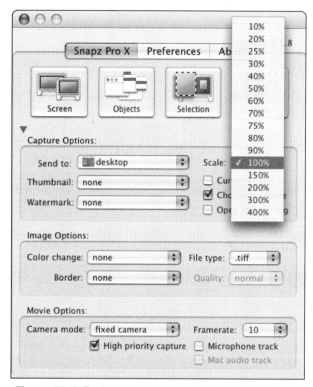

• **Figure 45-8: Resize your images with Snapz Pro X.**

 If you need to make a series of numbered images like Steps 001.tiff, Steps 002.tiff, and so on, let Snapz Pro X do the work for you. Set the Prefix for the filenames under the File Naming Settings section of the Preferences tab (for example, Steps). Each screen capture will be named starting with that prefix and numbered sequentially.

- ✔ Use the File Creator drop-down menu to associate the taken image with a particular application (see Figure 45-9).

- ✔ Have Snapz Pro X automatically change the coloring of the image (see Figure 45-10).

- ✔ Hold down the Control key to zoom in where the cursor is currently pointing (when using the Objects or Selection options).

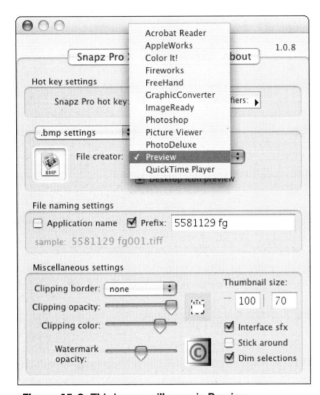

• **Figure 45-9:** This image will open in Preview.

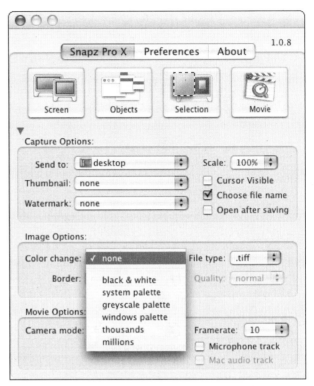

• **Figure 45-10:** Use the Color Change menu to take, for example, black and white images instead.

✔ Change the modifier keys to have Snapz Pro X launch by using a different key combination than the default.

✔ When capturing objects, use the Shift key to add or subtract objects to the selection.

 Snapz Pro X was in version 1 when this book was written, although the beta of Snapz Pro X 2 was in development. Version 2 seems to offer improved performance and more advanced video and audio capturing.

More Screenshot Utilities

Although you're pretty well covered in the screenshot area between Panther and Snapz Pro X, you can explore some alternatives. The main reason to use any of these is that they're both cheaper than Snapz Pro X and more feature-rich than Panther's tools:

✔ **ScreenShot Plus** (www.pidog.com/screenshotplus, $5 recommended) uses Apple's screenshot tools but lets you resize the images and use different formats like JPG, TIFF, and Photoshop.

✔ **Constrictor** (www.sticksoftware.com/software/constrictor.html, $10) is small and very customizable. It has a timer, lets you choose a backdrop for your images, offers a range of image types, and, like Snapz Pro X, lets you dictate what application the screenshot should open in by default.

✔ **FreeSnap** (www.efritz.net/software.html, free) supports different image formats, can resize your snapshots, is AppleScript-compatible, and is free, free, free!

Technique 46

Working with CDs and DVDs

Save Time By

✔ Telling your system how to handle different discs

✔ Burning CDs

✔ Making CD labels and inserts the easy way

✔ Using shareware to catalog your discs

In this Technique, we discuss every possible timesaving technique there is related to CDs and DVDs. If you have a CD-write (CD-R), CD-rewrite (CD-RW), DVD-write (DVD-R), or DVD-rewrite (DVD-RW) drive in or attached to your Mac, you'll be able to find some good tips here for burning CDs, making labels, and getting organized. If you don't (and there are a few of you out there still), you should at least go through the first section to tell Panther how to handle your discs.

Setting Your System Preferences

Setting System Preferences to automatically handle discs is an important configuration step to take. Adjusting these settings once saves you a lifetime of making decisions later.

1. **In the Finder, open the Finder Preferences panel.**

2. **Click the Sidebar icon (see Figure 46-1).**

• Figure 46-1: Use the Sidebar panel to tweak the Finder window Sidebar settings.

3. Select the Removable Media check box.

This setting makes your discs appear in the Sidebar of Finder windows when they're mounted (as shown in Figure 46-2). It applies to disk images as well as CDs and DVDs.

• **Figure 46-2:** You can easily access inserted discs via the Finder window Sidebar.

4. Click the General icon.

5. Select the CDs, DVDs and iPods check box (see Figure 46-3).

• **Figure 46-3:** Show discs on the Desktop to make them readily available.

This setting guarantees that mounted discs also appear on the Desktop.

6. Open System Preferences and click CDs & DVDs (under Hardware).

7. Use the pull-down menus to tell Panther what to do when different types of discs are inserted (see the choices in Figure 46-4).

For most users, the default settings will work just fine. How and what you change depends upon how you use your computer. If you always burn CDs from iTunes and never from another application (like the Finder, Backup, or Disk Utility), you can set blank CDs to trigger iTunes. The same applies to blank DVDs: Open iDVD when they're inserted. If you don't use the default Apple application for a particular disc type (for example, you don't use iPhoto or DVD Player), choose your preferred application in the CDs & DVDs System Preferences panel.

• **Figure 46-4:** Save yourself a step by customizing these settings.

 Use the CDs & DVDs System Preferences panel to indicate the default action for different media. You can then overrule this action as needed (like make a CD using the Finder and not iTunes, or open a picture CD in iView Media instead of iPhoto). When those times come, let Panther open the default application and then switch over to (or open) the application you'd rather use.

Scripting CDs

If you want to get really fancy, you can set Panther to run specific AppleScripts when different types of discs are inserted. All you need to do is choose Run Script from the appropriate pull-down menu in the CDs & DVDs preferences panel (see the accompanying figure) and then select the script on your hard drive, using the prompt that appears.

Sample ideas might include opening Backup when a blank CD is inserted and automatically running a particular type of backup. Alternatively, an AppleScript could run a command line utility and write the event log to your CD instead of the hard drive.

You can create the scripts yourself or download them from any of the common AppleScript resources online. The best AppleScript sites include

✔ Mac Scripter: www.macscripter.net

✔ Apple: www.apple.com/applescript

✔ Script Web: www.scriptweb.com

See Technique 60 for more.

Burning CDs

If you have a CD-R drive built into your Mac or attached externally, you can easily rip audio, video, or data CDs at your leisure. Considering the cheap cost of blank CD media, this has become a nearly ideal medium for today's computer users. Making CDs in Panther isn't rocket science, but we'll go

through a few tips and tricks that you can use in the different applications. Specifically, we target the Finder, iTunes, iPhoto, and Disk Utility.

 Panther's built-in disc-burning applications are sufficient for most users. If you want something a little nicer and more customizable, Toast from Roxio (www.roxio.com, $100) is the reigning king.

Making CDs in the Finder

Unless you've told Panther to do otherwise (by your setting in the CDs & DVDs panel), the Finder will ask you what to do when a blank disc is inserted (see Figure 46-5). At this point, you can choose a specific application to open and give the disc a name. After you do this, the disc will be mounted on the Desktop. A faster way to create discs in the Finder is to do this:

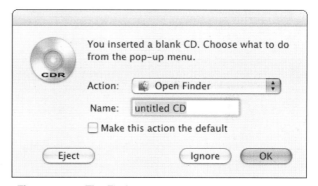

• **Figure 46-5:** The Finder prompt when blank media is inserted.

1. Set the preferences to show discs in the Finder window Sidebar (see earlier in this chapter; refer to Figure 46-1).

2. Insert a blank disc.

3. Give the disc a name at the prompt.

4. Open a Finder window.

   The blank disc should appear in the Sidebar of the Finder window (see Figure 46-6).

Figure 46-6: Blank CD-Rs appear in the Sidebar (called Backup Images here).

5. Use the content area of the window to find the files that you want to write to the disc.

6. Drag your files onto the blank disc icon in the Sidebar.

7. Click the Burn icon (looks like a fallout shelter sign) in the Sidebar window to create the disc.

 Mount disc images in the Finder Sidebar to create discs using only a single window.

Making an audio CD in iTunes

The crucial considerations for making CDs in iTunes are tweaked in the iTunes Burning preferences panel (as shown in Figure 46-7). Use the radio buttons to dictate what format your CD will be:

✔ **Audio:** For an audio CD, select the Use Sound Check check box to give the CD a more consistent volume level. Set the Gap Between Songs to 2 Seconds. Under Effects, set Crossfade Playback to 2 Seconds for a more professional feel.

✔ **MP3:** The MP3 format retains information about a file. For example, it associates the artist name, song, album, and so forth with the file. This information is lost when you make a standard audio CD. MP3 CDs also hold about ten times as many songs as standard audio CDs.

 In order to make an MP3 CD, which many new compact disc players can play, the songs must be in MP3 format. If you use the AAC encoder when you import music, these might not be playable on many other devices.

✔ **Data:** A data disc is just that . . . and probably something you don't want to be doing with iTunes. If you want to create data discs, just use the Finder like you would with any other CD.

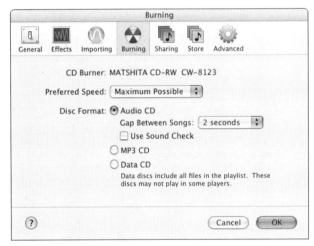

• **Figure 46-7: Tell iTunes what kind of CD to make.**

Making picture CDs in iPhoto

To burn a CD in iPhoto, all you need to do is select a photo album in the left-hand column and then click the Burn icon. It's just that simple. Making CDs in iPhoto retains all your album information along with the images. If you'll be using these CDs on your Mac or sharing them with other Mac users, this is perfect. If what you want instead is just a disc of images, use the Finder, Toast, or Disk Utility to burn a data disc instead.

iPhoto cannot copy photo libraries and albums across multiple discs. You'll have to either subdivide your collection and burn it separately or use the Finder and lose all the photo data.

When an iPhoto CD is loaded onto another Mac, it can be displayed in iPhoto, retaining all the information from the original user. The new user can do anything with the images he wants except for editing them (unless the images are imported first). You can eject a CD in iPhoto by dragging the disc icon onto the iPhoto Trash icon, just as you would in the Finder (see Figure 46-8).

• **Figure 46-8:** Drag a CD to the iPhoto Trash to eject it.

 Also see Technique 43 on using iPhoto to manage your digital library.

Making data CDs in Disk Utility

If you want something a little fancier than the Finder for your data CD burning, fire up the Disk Utility application (found in your Utilities folder). One of its coolest features is the ability to make and then burn a disk image based upon a folder.

1. **Open Disk Utility by double-clicking its icon in the Applications⇨Utilities folder.**

2. **Choose Image from Folder from the Images⇨New menu.**

3. **Select the folder to use.**

4. **In the Convert Image dialog that appears (see Figure 46-9), enter a name for this image and save it on your Desktop.**

Notice that you can adjust the properties of this image by using the Image Format and Encryption menus.

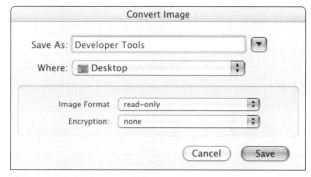

• **Figure 46-9:** The new disk image prompt.

5. **After the image has been created, select it in the left-hand column.**

6. **Click Burn to make a CD.**

Some of the sample uses of this feature are

✔ Make an exact copy of your Home directory (assuming it's less than 650MB).

✔ Make multiple copies of the same directory.

✔ Redistribute software, organized as you see fit.

Making Labels and Covers

After you've made your CD, you can get really fancy and make a nice label and cover for it. These applications simplify the process.

✔ **disclabel** (www.smileonmymac.com/disclabel, $30): This application works tightly with iTunes, iPhoto, and iDVD so that you can import track listings and images directly from them. The application is AppleScript-able and can be used to make disc labels, jewel case inserts, and DVD covers.

✔ **CoverStar** (www.autostylus.com, $20): If you find yourself constantly cranking out CD and/or DVD backups, audio CDs, photo CDs, and whatnot, chances are you've got stacks of identical-looking CD and DVD jewel cases — probably because you haven't had the time to create individual covers for each disc. If that's the case, this app can help. CoverStar automatically generates artwork from images, filters, data info, and graphics to create jewel case booklets, tray cards, and disc labels in six different styles so you don't have to sweat it out on your own. The app can pull images from iPhoto and Safari, import playlists from iTunes, screen out fonts that you don't want to use, calibrate your printer for optimum results, and more. This shareware demo won't allow you to print or save files until you register.

✔ **Discus** (www.magicmouse.com/_discus.html, $39): Discus creates labels and inserts and comes with 1,000 different background images and bits of clip art. It runs on both the Mac and Windows and uses over 15 different languages.

✔ **UnCoverIt** (www.iwascoding.com/uc/, $15): UnCoverIt doesn't create labels, but it does make covers for CDs, Zip disks, and other common media. It works nicely with iTunes and iPhoto to create content listings.

Alternatively, a quick search on Google will turn up CD label templates that work with common applications (such as Photoshop and Word) if you don't mind doing a little work yourself.

Finally, here's a nice trick for creating a track list from a playlist in iTunes:

1. **In the left-hand column of iTunes, select the playlist you just burned.**

2. **Use the contextual menu or the Show View Options tool to edit what columns are shown.**

   Obviously, you'll want to include the title and artist name at the very least. Depending upon how detailed you want the track listing to be, you can also include the album name and track length.

You'll most likely want to track your rating, the last time the song was played, and the genre.

3. **Rearrange the columns as needed.**

4. **Choose Export Song List from the File menu.**

   This creates a tab-delimited text file containing the information from iTunes. This, then, can be imported into any other application to make your disc label or jewel case insert.

5. **Open the created text file in TextEdit, BBEdit, or Word.**

6. **Edit the text as you want and then print it for your CD insert.**

Managing a Disc Collection

If you make a lot of discs, you'll find a third-party application to help you manage your collection useful. By using one of these, you can locate a file, photograph, or song without inserting and browsing dozens of discs. Here are three of the available applications:

✔ **DiskCatalogMaker** (http://hp.vector.co.jp/authors/VA008942/library/diskcatalogmaker, $18): DiskCatalogMaker uses a simple interface to catalog discs. After you register discs with the application, you use its search engine to quickly find the file you're looking for.

✔ **DiskTracker** (www.disktracker.com/index.shtml, $30): DiskTracker lets you browse or search cataloged discs. It also has a built-in (but basic) label-printing tool.

✔ **CDFinder** (www.cdfinder.de, $25): Use this to build a detailed (and customizable) catalog of the files that you've burned to CD, stored in Zip disks, or have on your iPod. This catalog can be used to make labels or can be exported into other applications.

If none of these is to your liking, check out VersionTracker (www.versiontracker.com), searching for *catalog,* or more generically, *disks.*

Getting More Than Music out of Your iPod

Save Time By

- ✔ Using your iPod as an external hard drive
- ✔ Storing data securely on an iPod
- ✔ Making backups to an iPod
- ✔ Synchronizing your Contacts and schedules to the iPod with iSync
- ✔ Keeping Notes on your iPod

If you already own an iPod, we don't have to tell you how great it is for listening to music while you're on the road. What you might not know is that your iPod can do a lot more than play music. In this Technique, we tell you about some of those other useful and timesaving capabilities.

First, we look at some of the things that you can do with the tools included in Panther. Next, we show you useful tricks with third-party programs and shareware tools. Many of these use the features of the iPod in new and creative ways.

All of these uses will, of course, require free space on your iPod (anywhere from a few kilobytes to a gigabyte or more, depending upon what you're trying to do), so if you have it filled to capacity with music already, you'll have to make some room first. If you run into this problem, read the final section to see how to clean out some space.

Using the iPod for Data Storage and Transfer

The iPod is a very good place to store important files. By doing so, you create backups and can take your stuff with you when you travel. Because the iPod connects to the Mac via a FireWire connection, you can transfer even very large files efficiently.

Here are some things you can do with the iPod:

- ✔ Transfer media files between computers (like large video files from a DV camera).

- ✔ Retain disk image (.dmg) files of big software installers for installation of the same software on several identical machines (useful if you work in a computer lab).

- ✔ Keep sensitive information on the iPod instead of the computer's hard drive so you can always take it with you (see "Secure, Encrypted Storage on the iPod").

> ✔ Store backups of the most important data. (See "Backing Up Your Data to an iPod," later in this Technique.)

> ✔ If you're a system administrator responsible for many Macs, store a bootable OS on the iPod to diagnose and repair broken OS X installations.

The organization of your data on the iPod is really simple:

> ✔ Use iTunes to manage your music on the iPod.

> ✔ Use the Finder to store nonmusic files and folders that you want to carry around or just store there. (The iPod, when mounted, appears like any other volume on the Desktop or Finder window, with an iPod icon.)

 The place on the iPod where the music is stored is hidden from the Finder. Similarly, your nonmusic files are not visible in iTunes. Therefore, the iPod provides a perfect and clean separation between the two kinds of data.

 Because the music directories are hidden in the Finder, you usually cannot mess up anything. However, if you're using the Terminal or disk- or file-management utilities, you can see these hidden music directories. You should never erase or otherwise modify your music files outside of iTunes.

Secure, Encrypted Storage on the iPod

If you have sensitive data that you want to keep in a really safe place, this is for you! Create an encrypted virtual volume in the form of a disk image on the iPod. This is secure for two reasons:

> ✔ **The data doesn't stay on your computer's hard drive.** When you're done working with your data,

you simply disconnect the iPod, and nobody can get physical access to your sensitive information.

> ✔ **The data is encrypted and password-protected by using the state-of-the-art, 128-bit Advanced Encryption Standard (AES) encryption built into Apple's disk images.**

Mac OS X already includes everything that you need to create a disk image:

1. **Make sure that your iPod is connected to your Mac.**

2. **Open Disk Utility.**

Disk Utility is stored in the Utilities folder, naturally.

3. **In the Disk Utility main window, choose New Image from the toolbar.**

4. **In the resulting prompt, enter a name for your encrypted disk image in the Save As box, as shown in Figure 47-1.**

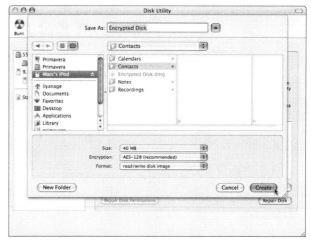

• **Figure 47-1:** Settings for the new, encrypted disk image.

5. **Still in the Save As dialog, choose your iPod from the Where pull-down menu or from the list of volumes in the left column (if the more expanded prompt is shown).**

6. Pick a reasonable size for your disk image from the Size pull-down menu — the smaller the better — and enable AES encryption by choosing it from the Encryption pull-down menu.

7. Make sure that the Format drop-down list box is set to Read/Write Disk Image.

8. Click Create.

9. At the prompt that appears, enter a new password.

Pick a password that's hard to guess.

 If you lose this password, you'll lose all your data on the encrypted volume. You can't recover a lost password! Because your encrypted data is most likely very important to you, you absolutely must not lose this password. Also, remember to make regular backups of this disk image.

 As always, storing the password in the key-chain is a big timesaver, so you should enable it. However, if you are really paranoid about the data on this disk image, clear the Keychain option in this case and just type in the password every time. See Technique 52 for information on passwords and the Keychain Access application.

10. Disk Utility automatically mounts the new volume, and you can immediately begin storing files there.

11. When you're finished transferring files, eject the virtual volume by dragging it to the Trash on the Dock.

From now on, you have to double-click the disk image file on the iPod volume every time you want to work with the data. The disk will mount, and you can use it like any other removable medium to store files and folders there (see Figure 47-2).

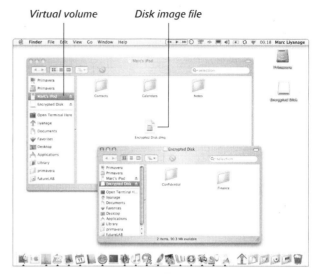

• **Figure 47-2:** The disk image file on the iPod and the virtual volume where the confidential data is stored.

Backing Up Your Data to an iPod

You can back up your data to an iPod in several ways, including simply dragging files and folders to the iPod in the Finder. We also show you two backup programs in this section.

Regardless of the method that you use, keep in mind that the iPod differs from the typical backup medium in a few ways:

✔ **Its hard drive is geared toward light use during music playback.** Don't perform full backups to it every day. Writing and reading massive amounts of data very often could shorten the iPod's life span.

✔ **The iPod's capacity is probably a lot smaller than your computer's hard drive.** Be selective and back up only important files, like your documents. Leave out things like applications or drivers, which you can always reinstall from installation CDs.

Using .Mac and Backup

If you're a .Mac member (currently $99 per year, see Technique 41 for more information), you can use Apple's Backup utility. Starting with version 2.0, it can back up to an external FireWire drive, which is exactly what an iPod is.

If you haven't already installed Backup on your computer, you should do so now. You can download the software after you log in to the .Mac member Web site at www.mac.com.

 For more detailed instructions on using Backup (without an iPod), see Technique 48.

To set up Backup for the first time, do the following:

1. Launch Backup by double-clicking the Backup icon in the Finder (presumably in the Applications or Utilities folder), which looks like a small umbrella.

2. Choose Back Up to Drive from the pop-up menu in the upper-left corner of the Backup window.

3. Decide what to back up by selecting the check box for each item that you want to back up.

Backup shows you a list of items in your Home directory (see Figure 47-3). For a full backup, choose everything. However, we suggest leaving out as much as you can. For example, you don't need to back up the iTunes collection because it takes a lot of space (and thus backup time) and because you can always reimport the music from CDs. Further, there's a good chance you already have a backup of your music collection on the iPod, anyway!

4. Use the + button to add other items to the list, especially items that aren't stored in your Home directory.

5. Click the Set button to choose the backup location.

6. Click the Create button in the dialog that pops up.

7. In the Save dialog that appears, select your iPod in the list of available volumes on the left.

• **Figure 47-3:** The list of items to back up in the application's main window.

8. In the Save As text box, enter a descriptive name for this backup.

Marc used *Laptop-backup* in the example (see Figure 47-4).

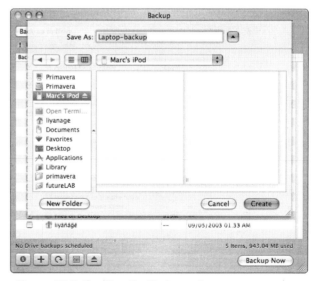

• **Figure 47-4:** Creating the Backup set.

9. Click Create to make the new backup location and return to the main Backup window.

10. Perform the backup by clicking the Backup Now button.

 You can set up automated, scheduled backups by using the Schedule button at the bottom of the window (the one that looks like a calendar). You have to make sure that your Mac is turned on, your iPod is connected to your Mac, and you are logged in at the scheduled time. You could, for example, leave your machine running through the night and have it start the backup at a fixed time. This way, your computer does the hard work while you're sleeping.

Using Carbon Copy Cloner

Apple's Backup utility is tied to a .Mac membership, even if you only back up to local drives and not to the .Mac servers. However, if you don't have a .Mac account, you can choose from plenty of other tools to perform backups. An inexpensive and reliable one that we like is Carbon Copy Cloner by Bombich Software (www.bombich.com/software/ccc.html; free but donation requested).

Do this to back up your computer:

1. Launch Carbon Copy Cloner (see Figure 47-5).

2. In the main window, pick a source disk from the drop-down list.

3. Remove any unwanted items from the Items to Be Copied list.

To remove an item, select it from the Items to Be Copied list and click the Delete button (the red circle with the slash through it).

4. From the Target Disk drop-down list, select your iPod.

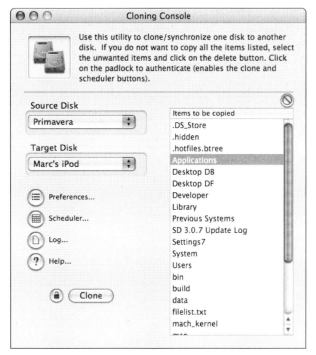

• **Figure 47-5: The main window of Carbon Copy Cloner.**

5. Click the Preferences button to edit your preferences.

Carbon Copy Cloner can create two kinds of backups: identical, bootable copies; and disk images. In the preferences dialog that appears (see Figure 47-6), select the Create a Disk Image on Target check box unless you really plan to boot from the iPod later on. Booting from the iPod can be handy in case of a problem with your computer's main startup disk. Click Save to close the preferences dialog.

6. Click the little lock symbol and enter your password in the dialog that appears.

7. Finally, click the Clone button to start the backup process.

The backup usually takes a while, so plan on getting a bite to eat or taking a nap while it does its thing.

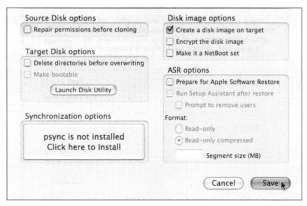

• **Figure 47-6:** Carbon Copy Cloner's preferences window.

Emergency Rescue iPod

If your computer's startup hard disk gets corrupted, you need to boot from a secondary device in order to repair and/or rescue the main disk. The iPod is an ideal device for this purpose.

You can install a stripped-down Mac OS X package onto the iPod, which includes Apple's Disk Utility for hard drive first aid. Optionally, you can add third-party hard disk repair products such as Norton Utilities (www.syamantec.com), DiskWarrior (www.alsoft.com), or Data Rescue X (www.prosofteng.net).

To create a bootable emergency Mac OS X installation on your iPod, follow these steps:

1. **Insert the first Mac OS X installation CD.**

2. **Launch the installer and follow the onscreen instructions.**

A reboot might be required (see Technique 1 for more information).

3. **In the Destination screen, select your iPod volume and click Continue.**

By default, the reformat option is disabled, which is probably what you want (so you don't erase any existing data or songs on your iPod).

4. **Click the Customize button as soon as it appears.**

5. **Make sure to remove as many of the optional Mac OS X components as possible.**

This includes printer drivers, language versions, and so on. You really want a bare-bones system to save space on the iPod.

6. **After the installation is complete, unplug the iPod to make sure that your computer boots from the main disk and then reboot your Mac.**

7. **Open the Finder, connect the iPod, and install any other disk repair utilities that you have.**

To boot from the iPod when an emergency actually happens, plug in your iPod and hold down the Option key during a reboot. You should see a list of connected, bootable devices. Click on the iPod icon and click the right arrow to continue the boot process.

Synchronizing with iSync

Apple adds more PDA-like features to the iPod's software all the time. Currently, this means read-only access to your iCal and Address Book data. (You can't edit this data through your iPod.) Somehow these Contacts and Calendars need to be synchronized from your computer to your iPod, and that's what the iSync program does.

To set up synchronization, do the following:

1. **Launch iSync.**

2. **Choose Add Device from the Devices menu and double-click your iPod's icon in the Add Device dialog that appears (see Figure 47-7).**

3. **In the iSync dialog, click the Sync Now button to perform the first synchronization.**

 For maximum efficiency, allow iSync to launch and synchronize whenever you connect your iPod by marking the Automatically Synchronize When iPod Is Connected check box. This way, the data on the iPod is always up-to-date without you having to think about synchronizing (see Figure 47-8). Click the iPod icon in iSync's main window to see these settings.

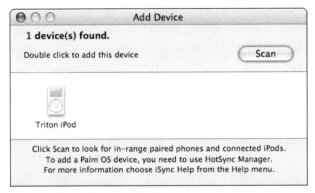

• **Figure 47-7: Add your iPod to iSync's list of devices.**

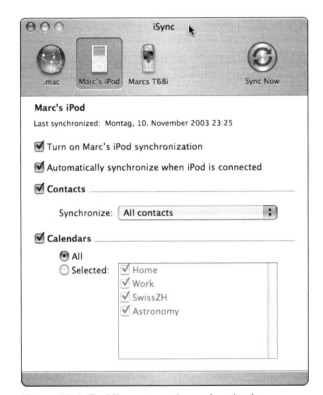

• **Figure 47-8: Enabling automatic synchronization.**

 You can view your Contacts and Calendars under Extras on your iPod.

Keeping Notes on Your iPod

The new iPods (with a dock connector) can store text Notes in addition to Contacts and Calendars. To store Notes, simply drag short text files such as grocery shopping lists, To-Do items, and so forth to the Notes folder on the iPod in the Finder (see Figure 47-9).

• **Figure 47-9: Storing small text Notes on the iPod.**

Some specialized freeware and shareware tools are available to make working with iPod Notes even quicker. We picked out a few of them, as described here.

Using Notes on older iPods

If you own an older iPod that doesn't directly support Notes, various utilities are available to pack up Notes as Contacts and store them in the Contacts list. This trick works fine for most short Notes.

A good utility that does this is the free Text2iPod X. Simply drop your Note text file onto the application's icon, and it will store it on the iPod, if it's connected. The program is available at `http://homepage.mac.com/applelover/text2ipodx`.

OmniOutliner

If you use the (highly recommended) OmniOutliner program to organize information, you'll appreciate a little script addition to the program called OmniOutliner iPod Export. It exports an outline directly to the iPod. It even supports older iPods by storing the Note disguised as a Contact (see Figure 47-10).

• **Figure 47-10:** Export an OmniOutliner outline file directly to an iPod.

You can download the script for free at www.omnigroup.com/applications/omnioutliner/extras/.

Driving directions

PodQuest is an application that allows you to download driving directions from the MapQuest service to your iPod. It installs an icon in your menu bar. From there, you can look up directions (see Figure 47-11) and download them directly to your iPod.

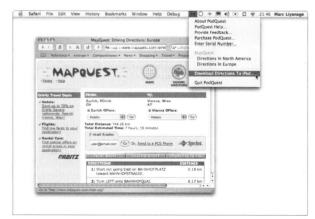

• **Figure 47-11:** Download driving directions from MapQuest to the iPod.

To download PodQuest, go to www.mibasoft.dk/podquest.html ($9.95).

Housekeeping on the iPod

After you use your iPod for a while for music playback and data storage, it might fill up. For many reasons, including being able to do some of the other things that we mention in this chapter, you might want to clean out the data on it quickly. You have three choices to free up space on the device:

- ✔ Erase music via iTunes.
- ✔ Erase data on the iPod volume from the Finder.
- ✔ Reformat the drive with the Disk Utility program, which erases everything (both music and data).

The nice thing about the way the data is stored on the iPod is that your music and your other data are kept completely separate. If you erase files on the iPod in the Finder, you won't lose any of your music; if you clean up music in iTunes, you won't lose any of your data.

If you want a completely fresh start, reformat the iPod by using Disk Utility. Be sure to select the indented iPod volume in the list at the left. Open the Erase tab in the right half of the window and then click the Erase button (see Figure 47-12).

The next time that you launch iTunes, it responds as if a new iPod has been connected and asks you what to do.

 Do not reformat your iPod unless you're prepared to completely wipe out everything on it!

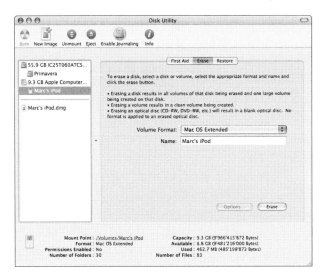

• Figure 47-12: Reformatting the iPod.

Useful Hardware You Might Consider

We cover a lot of software-related tips in this chapter, but we also have a few extra tips about useful hardware additions for your iPod.

The first is a recommendation for special sealing earphones by Etymotic Research (www.etymotic.com). They are more expensive than regular earphones (ranging from $130–$330), but they sound so incredibly good that we would spend the money again anytime. The improvement over the regular earphones that come with the iPod is truly remarkable. These earphones are inserted into the ear canal, and they seal tightly. This means that ambient sounds are filtered out almost completely, and you can listen at lower sound levels. The blocking of ambient sound is especially useful for listening to music during long flights. These things really demonstrate how good the iPod sounds!

The second useful addition for older iPods is a special FireWire cable made by SiK, called HotWire (www.sik.com). It's a special, power-only cable that you can use to charge your iPod's battery by connecting it to your Mac's FireWire port. Unlike with a regular cable, the iPod won't mount as a disk on the computer, so you can continue to use it as a music player while still charging it. On the newer iPods, you can use a regular cable and immediately eject the iPod's disk right after it is mounted automatically. This will have the same effect.

Part VIII

Security and Maintenance

"Hey you bunch of loser jocks! This happens to be an AirPort, and I got it to go with my iBook, and you wouldn't even know what to do with it!"

Better Backups with rsync and .Mac

Save Time By

✔ Reviewing smart backup policies

✔ Performing backups with rsync

✔ Using Apple's Backup application

✔ Exploring alternative backup applications

If you care about any of the data on your computer, you better back it up. It's that simple. Although today's computers are more reliable than their predecessors, you absolutely *must* back up your stuff. Accidents still happen, hard drives crash, laptops get dropped, and computers are stolen. Without a backup, you're in trouble if any of these things happen to you.

We begin this Technique by going over the best backup policies to abide by. Then we take you through an easy and free backup utility, rsync, which works with your Mac's command line. After that, we demonstrate Apple's Backup software, which is available to .Mac members only. Finally, we mention several other third-party tools that might be to your liking if rsync or Backup don't fit your needs.

Maybe you've never lost data. Maybe you don't even know anyone who has. Still, you should back up your computer (either the entire hard drive or just the most important files). It costs very little, doesn't take much time, and makes you look like a savvy, pre-emptive computer user.

Smart Backups

Before we get into how to back up your computer, a brief discussion of the best policies is warranted. When planning a backup strategy, be sure to

✔ **Back up your data frequently.** Ideally, you should back up your Home directory daily and your entire computer weekly or monthly.

When it comes to making backups, the question to ask yourself is, "How much data can I afford to lose? One day's worth? A week's worth?"

✔ **Make multiple backups.** You don't want to discover after your computer crashes that your backup is also corrupted. Use multiple backups and rotate them — use one backup set for a month, use a second for a month, then go back to the first for a month, and so forth.

✔ **Back up to different media.** You should also rotate your backups among external hard drives, CDs and DVDs, and so forth.

✔ **Make sure that one backup is in a different geographical location than your computer.** If you have a backup of your computer in your home office and the house burns down, you've lost everything.

 Leave one of your multiple backups in a fireproof safe, at school, at the office . . . somewhere other than where your computer is.

✔ **Test your backup.** If you have a spare computer or drive, restore your backup. Otherwise, restore part of your backup. Doing this before you have to confirms that the backup worked and that you'll know what to do when the time comes.

rsync: Using the Command Line to Back Up

If you don't mind a little command line work, you can use the rsync utility to perform your backups. The benefits of using rsync include

✔ It's free!

✔ It's very, very fast.

✔ rsync copies only the changed files, thus saving time and disk space.

 Most backup utilities perform *incremental* backups: That is, they copy only altered and new files, and unchanged files aren't copied after the initial backup. rsync takes this one step further by copying only the altered *parts* of a file. For example, if you edit a text file, the new changes are copied . . . not the entire file.

✔ It doesn't need to be run as an administrator.

✔ It maintains file ownership and permissions.

✔ Did we happen to mention that it's free?

The only drawbacks to this application are

✔ You must use the Terminal.

✔ You can't back up to a CD or DVD.

✔ It has no pretty graphical user interface to admire.

✔ It has problems backing up resource forks. (See the sidebar, "rsync, Resource Forks, and Why You Should Care about Them," for what this means and why it might be important.)

✔ You can't deduct the purchase price from your taxes.

You can use rsync in many ways. The three most important and common are

✔ Backing up files *locally* (from one drive to another on your computer)

✔ Backing up files *remotely* (from your computer to a remote computer)

✔ Backing up files locally from a remote computer

 One of the benefits of using rsync — in fact, this is pretty much why it was created — is that you can use it to back up files either to or from a remote server (assuming that it's also running rsync). If you're a Web developer, this can be a very handy tool!

To use rsync, pull up the command line tool (the Terminal application) and enter a command with this basic syntax:

```
rsync -options sourcedirectory
    targetdirectory
```

For example, a simple way to use the tool would be to run this command:

```
rsync -a ~/Documents/WorkFiles/
    /Users/Shared/MyWorkFiles
```

This would copy the entire contents (the a means that an exact copy should be made) of the WorkFiles directory (located within the Documents folder of the current user's Home directory) to a folder called MyWorkFiles, located in the Shared users folder. By copying these files over to the Shared users folder, other Mac users can access them. Repeated uses of this command will insure that the most recent versions of the files in Larry's WorkFiles folder are copied over to the public directory.

rsync syntax options

The most important options are (these can, and often are, combined)

- ✔ a: Creates an exact archive.

- ✔ n: Runs a test backup to show you what rsync will do without actually doing it.

 If you're a little nervous about using rsync, run it with the -n option to see what files it will copy without actually copying the files (see Figure 48-1). The -a indicates that an exact archive should be created, the -z says to use compression, but the -n dictates that a trial run should be taken first.

```
Larry-iBook:~ larry$ rsync -azn ~/Documents /
Volumes/40\ GB\ Firewire/G4\ iBook\ Backup/
building file list ... done
Documents/.DS_Store
Documents/.localized
wrote 133 bytes  read 28 bytes  322.00 bytes/
sec
total size is 6148  speedup is 38.19
Larry-iBook:~ larry$
```

• **Figure 48-1: Run a test backup to see what will happen.**

- ✔ v: Gives you a verbose response.

- ✔ z: Uses compression to save space.

- ✔ --exclude: If you would prefer not to back up certain files, use the --exclude option. For example, to exclude the contents of the Preferences directory, use

```
rync -az --exclude=Preferences/
    /Users/larry /Volumes/Backup
```

- ✔ --progress: If you want to see a progress report, use, --progress.

- ✔ --quiet: If you don't want a lot of feedback, use --quiet. (This is essentially the opposite of the verbose option.)

- ✔ --stats: To see some statistics on the backed-up data, use --stats (see Figure 48-2).

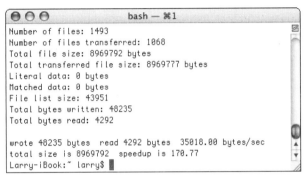

```
Number of files: 1493
Number of files transferred: 1068
Total file size: 8969792 bytes
Total transferred file size: 8969777 bytes
Literal data: 0 bytes
Matched data: 0 bytes
File list size: 43951
Total bytes written: 48235
Total bytes read: 4292

wrote 48235 bytes  read 4292 bytes  35018.00 bytes/sec
total size is 8969792  speedup is 170.77
Larry-iBook:~ larry$
```

• **Figure 48-2: Get more detailed reporting with** --stats.

 If you use a trailing slash with your source directory name, you'll back up that directory's contents but not the directory itself. In other words, rsync -az ~/Documents/ /target copies everything in Documents to the target without making a Documents folder.

Backing up Home to an external hard drive

A good way to use rsync is to back up your Home directory to an external hard drive. Follow these steps to do just that:

1. **Mount an external drive.**

You can use an external FireWire or USB drive, or even a Zip disk if it's large enough.

2. **Open the Terminal by double-clicking its icon in the Utilities folder.**

3. **At the prompt, type** ls /Volumes/ **to list the drives (see Figure 48-3).**

Before using `rsync`, make sure that your drive is available. This command lists the currently connected drives, along with their names.

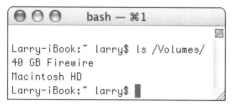

```
Larry-iBook:~ larry$ ls /Volumes/
40 GB Firewire
Macintosh HD
Larry-iBook:~ larry$ ▊
```

• **Figure 48-3:** Larry's computer has a main drive (Macintosh HD) and an external drive (40 GB Firewire) mounted.

4. Type rsync -azn ~/ /Volumes/<*drive*>/*path/to/ destination* (see Figure 48-4).

```
Larry-iBook:~ larry$ rsync -azn ~/ /Volumes/40\ GB\ Firewire/
G4\ iBook\ Backup/
building file list ... done
Desktop/558129 fg5603.tiff
Desktop/558129 fg5604.tiff
Library/Preferences/.DS_Store
Library/Preferences/com.apple.finder.plist
wrote 50348 bytes  read 36 bytes  33589.33 bytes/sec
total size is 137105992  speedup is 2721.22
Larry-iBook:~ larry$
```

• **Figure 48-4:** Test the backup.

You'll want to use the a and z flags to archive and compress the files. Also use n to preview the operation. The directory being backed up is Larry's Home directory (~/), and it's also being backed up to (in this case) /Volumes/40\ GB\ Firewire/G4\ iBook\ Backup. Because the Terminal has problems with spaces in filenames, spaces must be *escaped* (preceded with a backslash) in all path names. (In the Finder, the drive is called 40 GB Firewire, which is then shown as 40\ GB Firewire in the Terminal.) See Technique 55 for more on escaping and using tab completion or the Finder to easily enter path names.

5. If everything's okay, run rsync by using rsync -az —progress —stats ~/ /Volumes/<*drive*>/ *path/to/folder* (see Figure 48-5).

```
Larry-iBook:~ larry$ rsync -az --progress --stats ~/
/Volumes/40\ GB\ Firewire/G4\ iBook\ Backup/
     9205 100%   0.00kB/s    0:00:00
    23582 100%   0.00kB/s    0:00:00
       35 100%   0.00kB/s    0:00:00
    12365 100%   0.00kB/s    0:00:00

Number of files: 1820
Number of files transferred: 4
Total file size: 137090277 bytes
Total transferred file size: 45187 bytes
Literal data: 45187 bytes
Matched data: 0 bytes
File list size: 50320
Total bytes written: 64625
Total bytes read: 84

wrote 64625 bytes  read 84 bytes  129418.00 bytes/sec
total size is 137090277  speedup is 2118.57
Larry-iBook:~ larry$ ▊
```

• **Figure 48-5:** Running the actual backup.

In all likelihood, running this command won't reveal or cause any problems (it's just a backup, after all), but if you see a Permission Denied message, or it seems like an extraordinary amount of information is about to be copied, you might want to rethink your `rsync` command.

To actually run the backup, drop the n option. Your resulting command will now be in this form:

```
rsync -az --progress --stats ~/
    /Volumes/<drive>/path/to/folder.
```

6. Check the destination drive in the Finder to make sure that the files were backed up.

Another cool thing about `rsync` is that you can use a `cron` (a UNIX task-scheduling program) to automatically call `rsync` at set times. This way, you can back up your computer at regular intervals (say, every night) without any extra effort. See Technique 53 for more.

rsync, Resource Forks, and Why You Should Care about Them

One of the problems with using rsync is that it doesn't recognize old-style resource forks, which might be lingering on your computer. Resource forks are still used by a number of UNIX applications that have been brought into the Mac OS X platform. This means that some of the backed up files stored via rsync might not be usable when restored to your Mac. For this reason, you should rely upon rsync for your personal files and not the applications or the operating system as a whole. You should also test rsync by restoring some files to make sure it works.

As an alternative, you could look into the ditto command, which does support resource forks. See the manual for ditto (type **man ditto** in the Terminal) for more information. Another command line option is asr (Apple Software Restore). Its specific purpose is to copy disk images to make clones of drives.

Backup for .Mac Users

If you have a .Mac account, you have a pretty good backup tool already — appropriately called *Backup* — which is free for all .Mac users. (Remember that a .Mac membership costs $99 per year, but you get some pretty nice other features as well.) In the latest version of Backup, you can copy files to

- ✔ Hard drives
- ✔ Removable drives
- ✔ CD-Rs and CD-RWs
- ✔ DVD-Rs and DVD-RWs
- ✔ iDisks
- ✔ iPods

In fact, Backup can now perform backups over multiple volumes or types of volumes. For instance, you can back up your entire hard drive to a combination of DVDs and CDs.

For more information on backing up files to your iPod, see Technique 47.

 If you have a .Mac account, you can also use iSync to back up (or synchronize) your Address Book data, iCal Calendars, and Safari bookmarks online.

The best way to demonstrate all the timesaving techniques involved with Backup is to run through a quick example, highlighting the key points along the way.

Getting started with Backup

1. **Open Backup.**

Backup takes a second to open while it checks the status of your iDisk. Your current iDisk usage is shown at the top of the Backup window (see Figure 48-6).

• **Figure 48-6: Start here to use Apple's Backup application.**

2. **Select one of the three backup options from the pull-down menu (as shown in Figure 48-7).**

▶ **iDisk:** If you select your iDisk, you don't need to do anything more except connect to the Internet — go to the section, "Deciding what to back up," later in this Technique.

Trial .Mac members can only back up stuff to their iDisk. These files are lost if you drop your membership. Use Backup only if you plan on keeping your account.

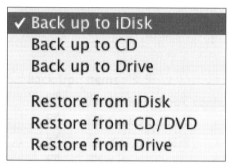

• **Figure 48-7: Back up to your iDisk, an optical disc (CD or DVD), or a drive.**

▶ **CD:** If you choose CD, Backup displays how many CDs are required at the bottom of the window.

▶ **Drive:** If you choose Drive, follow these steps:

1. Click the Set button, next to the pull-down menu.

2. Click the Create button at the prompt (see Figure 48-8) to make a new backup location. If you've already created a backup location, click Open instead.

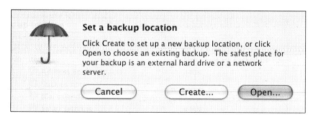

• **Figure 48-8: This prompt appears if you choose to back up to a drive.**

3. Navigate to where you want to create the backup or navigate to the existing backup location and then press Return.

Deciding what to back up

After you've decided where to back up your data, the next important decision — in fact, the most important decision — is what to back up. The Backup utility uses *QuickPicks,* which automatically identifies common files and file types (see Figure 48-9). These include

- ✔ Safari bookmarks
- ✔ Keychains
- ✔ Address Book contacts
- ✔ Stickies files
- ✔ iCal Calendars
- ✔ AppleWorks stuff
- ✔ iPhoto and iTunes libraries
- ✔ Microsoft Office documents
- ✔ Mail

• **Figure 48-9: Use QuickPicks to decide what to back up.**

To back up any of these items, mark the check box next to its name in the Back Up column. To see more details, select the item and click the Info button (which bears a lowercase *i*) or press ⌘+I to bring up the Info panel (as shown in Figure 48-10).

• **Figure 48-10:** Use the Info panel to preview a group of files or fine-tune your selections.

To add items to be backed up, you can click the plus button and navigate to the item, or drag the item from the Finder and drop it into Backup.

 The easiest and most thorough way to use Backup is to drag your Home folder into the application.

If you don't like the list of options made available to you, use the Edit menu (see Figure 48-11) to quickly make changes to the list.

Finalizing the backup

The last step is to click the Backup Now button. You'll be prompted for a backup name if burning to a CD/DVD (you might as well use the default). Then you'll see a progress bar while Backup continues.

After the backup has finished, click the calendar icon at the bottom of the screen. A dialog in which you can schedule regular backups appears (see Figure 48-12). You can perform regular backups to drives or your iDisk but not to a CD or DVD.

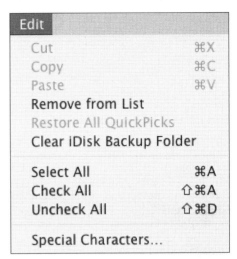

• **Figure 48-11:** Use the Edit menu to remove items or select and clear all the items at once.

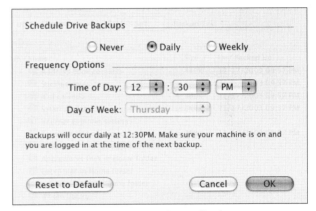

• **Figure 48-12:** After you use the application once, you can schedule incremental backups.

 The downside to using Backup is that if you stop paying for .Mac, you can no longer use this application. Therefore, any backed-up files must be backed up by using a different system before you cut your service, or else!

Other Backup Options

If none of the above options are to your liking (perhaps they're too expensive or too geeky), here are some other backup utilities that you might appreciate.

- ✔ **Dantz Retrospect** (www.dantz.com, $129): Retrospect is a long-standing backup application for Mac users. It's pricey but has a lot of useful features, including scheduled backups, the ability to search through catalogs of backed-up files, and backing up computers over a network.

- ✔ **Déjà Vu** (http://propagandaprod.com, $15): Déjà Vu is a very simple backup utility with a nice interface and the ability to run backups unattended (read: you can back up your computer while you're sleeping). It runs as a System Preferences panel and will even let you back up to networked servers via common protocols.

- ✔ **ChronoSync** (www.econtechnologies.com, $20): ChronoSync is actually designed to be a synchronization utility between two computers, like a laptop and a desktop. But because of this functionality, it can also be used for backups. If you have multiple computers and no synchronization capability, this is the tool for you.

- ✔ **SilverKeeper** (www.silverkeeper.com, free): SilverKeeper is a free product put out by LaCie, a maker of hard drives, optical drives, and other products. It's a simple application, but the price is right and it can back up to pretty much any type of drive (CDs, DVDs, external hard drives, and so forth).

- ✔ **Carbon Copy Cloner** (www.bombich.com/software/ccc.html, donation): We mention Carbon Copy Cloner many times in this book and for good reason. It makes a complete backup of your hard drive as a bootable drive. In other words, you can back up your disk to a FireWire drive or an iPod and then run a computer from that device.

On a different note, both CMS (www.cmsproducts.com) and Maxtor (www.maxtor.com) make FireWire hard drives — ranging in price from $300 to $500 — that back up your Mac at the touch of a single button. Rather than having to invest in both an external hard drive and backup software, you can meet both needs with one of these products.

Technique 49

Battling Viruses

Save Time By

✔ Knowing about viruses

✔ Avoiding viruses in the first place

✔ Using Virex to quash infections

✔ Checking out third-party software to fight viruses

Mac users have always been somewhat fortunate because relatively few viruses target the Mac operating system. Some people have complained that there isn't much software written for the Mac, but the upside is that not many viruses are written for the Mac, either. Still, one has to be careful.

In this Technique, we tell you what you need to know about viruses, how you can avoid getting them, and what to do if your Mac becomes infected. We focus on using McAfee's Virex for this purpose, but we list other options at the end of this Technique, too.

What You Should Know about Viruses

A *virus* is a special type of application that is able to make copies of itself. Viruses can be either mere nuisances that do nothing but spread themselves around or malicious evildoers that try to destroy your data or create security holes. Roughly speaking, the three kinds of viruses are

✔ **Worms:** Worms are the A-list celebrities of viruses — they get all the attention. Worms spread via e-mail applications (Outlook Express on Windows is a particular favorite), removable media (such as CDs or Zip disks), or network *holes* (open gateways into your machine; again, Windows provides for plenty of these). Every time a new worm comes out, you hear about it in the news as it spreads around the globe, shutting down servers and causing billions of dollars in damage.

✔ **Trojan horses:** A *Trojan horse* pretends to provide a service (like remembering your Web passwords) but really does something else in the background (like e-mailing your Web passwords to somebody else). Trojan horses spread by people downloading and installing software that they assume to be safe.

✔ **Macros:** *Macro viruses* use advanced features of scriptable applications as their medium for trouble. They are attached to documents and are activated when that document is opened. The most common problem involves Microsoft Word. Simple macro viruses wreak havoc with the application in question; more troublesome macros use your e-mail client to propagate themselves.

 Because of the problems with macro viruses, many applications (like Microsoft Word, see Figure 49-1) prompt you before enabling the macros.

• **Figure 49-1:** Microsoft Word asks whether you want to use the macros in the document being opened.

Again, other operating systems have much more trouble with viruses than Mac OS X does, but you should still be careful. Continue reading to see what you can do to limit your risk of infection and what you can do should the worst happen.

Things You Can Do to Limit Viruses

What's more important than knowing what to do should your computer become infected is knowing how not to get infected in the first place. These are our best practices for protecting your Mac:

✔ **Use a firewall on your network.** Many worms spread through network holes. *Firewalls* — special software that establishes a barrier between a network and the Internet — prevent traffic from going through these holes. Whether you're using a single computer on a dialup connection or you're one of a dozen computers on a network, you can use a firewall. See Technique 40 for more information, including how to enable firewalls on your Mac (see Figure 49-2).

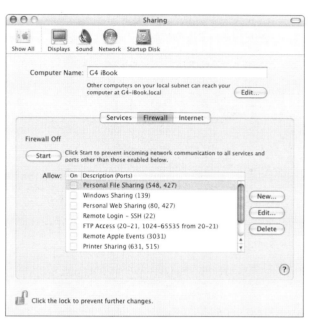

• **Figure 49-2:** Panther's built-in firewall configuration panel.

✔ **Be careful whom you give your e-mail address to.** If few people have your e-mail address, you have less of a chance that folks will send viruses to you. It's that simple.

 Limiting the visibility of your e-mail address minimizes the number of viruses and spam that you are subject to. Try to keep your e-mail address off public message boards and Web pages. You can also follow the anti-spam suggestions from Technique 34.

✔ **Don't open attachments to e-mails.** Receiving a virus as an attachment to an e-mail is not a security risk. It's when you open this attachment — that's when the trouble starts. If you really want to be safe, don't open *any* attachments. If you find this rule to be unreasonable and excessive (and it is), scan attachments with antivirus software and abide by the next rule.

✔ **Don't open executable attachments in e-mails.** Many Trojan horse viruses work by posing as one thing while being another. For example, several popular viruses were spread as a file with the extensions .txt.vbs or .jpg.exe. People recognized .txt and .jpg as benign, but the .vbs (Visual Basic Script) and .exe (executable) extensions were actually the ones that counted. These are both specifically Windows examples, but you get the point.

 To be safe with e-mail attachments, always try to open them with a specific application rather than double-clicking them. See Technique 23 for particular methods for opening files.

✔ **Keep your antivirus software up-to-date.** Something like 500 new viruses are discovered each month. If your antivirus software is out-of-date, you might as well not even have it.

We discuss one popular antivirus application, McAfee's Virex, in the section "Using Virex," later in this Technique.

 Many virus applications, like Virex, provide for automatic updates each time they run. This is a very good thing (but does require an Internet connection).

✔ **Perform daily virus scans.** If you have a virus application, run it every time you log in as an extra precaution. Most antivirus applications give this as an option in their preferences.

✔ **Don't network with Windows computers.** A Windows virus can't infect your computer, but that doesn't keep it from trying and trying and trying, which can be an annoyance. If you can, avoid networking with Windows computers. If you must, make sure that the Windows users do everything they must do to protect their machine.

✔ **Be careful if you use Virtual PC.** You can be affected by Windows viruses if you run a version of Windows on your Mac that uses Virtual PC. If you do, be supremely careful with what you do in the virtual environment.

✔ **Use Rules in Mail.** When the next wave of Windows worms hits, we're usually pelted with hundreds of messages. You can't do anything

to stop it, but you can establish a Rule in your Mail application to automatically delete these annoyances (see Figure 49-3). Technique 34 shows you how to set up a Rule in detail.

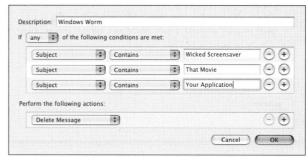

• **Figure 49-3: Define Rules to handle annoying Windows worms.**

✔ **Turn off all Sharing tools.** This goes along with using a firewall to shut down network holes. Your Mac comes with every Service turned off as the default; none are turned on unless you specifically do so. If you turned something on at one time and don't need it anymore, be certain to turn it off. Services are controlled through the Sharing System Preferences tab, which we discuss in Techniques 39 and 40.

✔ **Don't assume that you can trust something just because it comes from someone you know.** The most successful worms worked because they used a person's Address Book to send themselves out to the world. John Smith receives an e-mail from his friend, Jane Doe, so he opens the attachment, launches the virus, and inadvertently sends it to everyone in his e-mail client's Address Book. Even if someone sends you a file purposefully, he might not know whether it has a macro virus attached to it.

✔ **Scan every file you download, borrow, take from CD, copy from a disk, and so forth, with a virus tool.** If you have a virus application — and you should have one — use it to scan files that are new to your computer. Even if they come from a reputable source, like from a CD-ROM, it can't hurt.

✔ **Let people know if they sent you a virus.** Help yourself by helping others. If someone sent you a virus, she might not even know it.

✔ **Eat healthy, get regular exercise, and take your vitamins.** So this last step keeps *you* from getting a virus, not your computer. It's still sound advice.

 Although it won't prevent getting viruses, keeping regular backups of your data makes it easier to recover after a virus strikes.

Tips for Those Who Also Use Windows

Okay, this is a book on the Macintosh, but some of you might also use Windows on a regular basis. We all have our crosses to bear. If you have to use Windows, here are a few quick tips on minimizing viruses on that operating system:

✔ Don't use Outlook Express.

✔ Don't use Internet Explorer.

✔ Turn off every feature that you don't use.

✔ Have Windows display file extensions.

✔ Use an antivirus application and keep it up-to-date.

One reason why Windows is less secure is that many applications — like Outlook Express and Internet Explorer — are tied into the operating system as a whole. Vulnerabilities in those applications can be used to manipulate vulnerabilities in Windows.

Using Virex

McAfee's Virex (www.mcafee.com) is a popular antivirus application, partially because it comes free with your .Mac account (although that does cost $99 per year). Using it is simple, but using it efficiently and effectively requires a little more thought. Here are some suggestions if you already have the application:

1. **Open Virex by double-clicking the Virex icon found in either the Applications or Utilities folders.**

2. **Open the Preferences panel (see Figure 49-4).**

3. **Within the Preferences panel, select the following check boxes:**

  ▶ **Automatically Scan at Login**

    You want Virex to scan automatically so you don't need to think about it.

  ▶ **Perform an Advanced Scan of Applications and Macros for Previously Unknown Viruses**

    Although this option takes longer, it's much more thorough.

  ▶ **Check for New Virus Definitions at Launch**

    What's the point of using Virex if it isn't up-to-date? If you have a permanent Internet connection, take advantage of this feature.

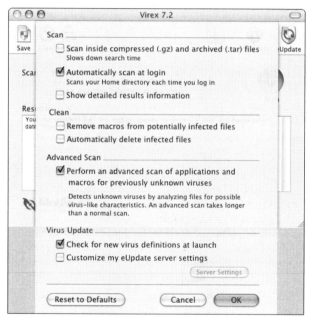

• **Figure 49-4: The Virex Preferences panel.**

4. **Click OK to exit the Preferences panel.**

5. **In the main screen (see Figure 49-5), select Home from the Scan drop-down list.**

6. **Select the Clean Any Files Infected with a Virus check box.**

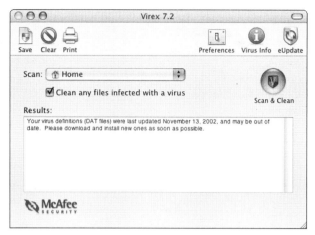

• **Figure 49-5:** The Virex main window.

7. Exit the application.

8. Once a week or so, launch Virex, select All Local Volumes from the Scan drop-down list, and then click the Scan & Clean button to inspect your entire computer (see Figure 49-6).

If you use StuffIt Expander (www.aladdinsys. com) to decompress files, you can set it to automatically scan files when decompressing them through the Expanding tab of the Virex Preferences panel (see Figure 49-7).

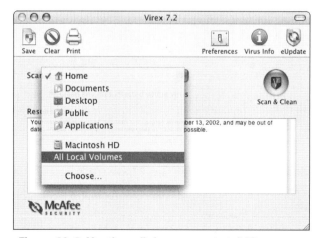

• **Figure 49-6:** Use the pull-down menu to tell Virex where to scan.

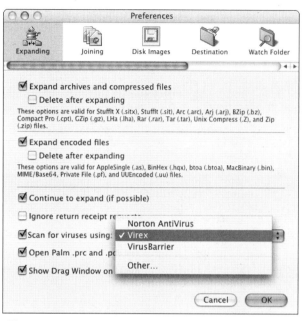

• **Figure 49-7:** Have StuffIt Expander scan files that you download or get from other sources.

Other Antivirus Software

We highlight using Virex as a protection tool because it's the current application of choice for your beloved authors. But there are other options, as always:

✔ **Norton AntiVirus** (www.symantec.com/nav/ nav_mac/, $70): Norton's AntiVirus is a solid application and has been around for a long time. In fact, Norton's other applications have been integral to maintaining Macs for years. Norton AntiVirus (NAV for short) performs live updates of its virus definitions to stay current and will certainly do the trick.

✔ **Intego VirusBarrier X** (www.intego.com/ virusbarrier/home.html, $60): VirusBarrier performs automatic updates and can run at all times to keep an eye out for potential problems. VirusBarrier also works well with Intego's other security products like NetBarrier. You can also buy packages containing multiple products.

Technique 50

Keeping Your Software Up-to-Date

Save Time By

- ✔ Keeping your operating system up-to-date
- ✔ Knowing the best way to update other applications
- ✔ Staying on top of software updates

Keeping your operating system and applications up-to-date is an important aspect of maintaining your computer. In terms of performance, security, and features, the time that you spend updating software should be considered time well spent.

We begin this Technique discussing how you can update your operating system (it's pretty simple, if you didn't know). Then we discuss some best practices when it comes to updating other applications found on your computer. Finally, we go through a few references that you can use to stay informed when updates become available.

Using Software Update

Keeping your operating system up-to-date is an absolute must for these two reasons:

- ✔ **It's the only way for Apple to plug security holes.** One of the downsides of Panther's UNIX underpinnings is that your Mac is now vulnerable to UNIX security issues as well. Although this is unfortunate, it means that a whole world of knowledgeable programmers out there are catching these problems when they occur. Having security holes in your computer is a bad thing. Continuing to have security holes after they've been made public is even worse.

- ✔ **It's the only way for Apple to fix bugs.** Nobody's perfect, and Apple's no exception. The more complex a piece of software is, the more likely it is to have bugs. Apple's pretty good about fixing bugs, but you'll need to update your software in order for those fixes to take effect.

The Software Update utility (see Figure 50-1) is the tool to use to perform all operating system updates. Just check the boxes next to the items you want to install and then press Return to begin the process. (You'll then be prompted for the administrator's password.) Software Update has the added benefit of updating other Apple applications as warranted, like iTunes and QuickTime. Although you can access this tool through

System Preferences, choosing Software Update from the Apple menu (see Figure 50-2) is much faster if you want to quickly update your computer (you can run an update at your prompting or schedule updates to occur periodically). In fact, the Software Update panel in System Preferences (see Figure 50-3) is actually the preferences page for the Software Update utility.

• **Figure 50-1: Apple's Software Update application makes it easy to maintain Panther.**

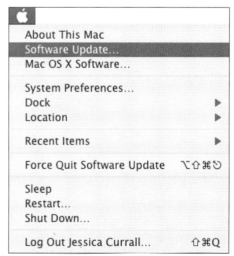

• **Figure 50-2: Use the Apple menu to quickly access Software Update.**

• **Figure 50-3: Use System Preferences to adjust Software Update settings.**

Updating your software using these tools is fairly straightforward, but here are some best practices of which you ought to be aware:

✔ **Set Software Update to run weekly.** You can no longer specify a day and time for it to run, so you're best off choosing Weekly from the Check for Updates pull-down menu. This menu is located on the Update Software tab of the Software Update preferences panel (refer to Figure 50-3). At some random time — probably while you're doing something critically important — Software Update will pop up and do its thing.

 Because you have to enter your password to run any updates, you can't update your OS at night or when you are away from your computer.

✔ **If you don't have a high-speed Internet connection, select the Download Important Updates in the Background check box.** With this option, also in the Software Updates preferences panel (refer to Figure 50-3), you can continue using your computer while the files are downloading. Then you'll be notified that the installation is ready to take place.

✔ **Have Software Update ignore the updates that you don't need.** As an example, if you don't have an iPod, you won't need to update your iPod software. The same applies to applications you don't use. You can effectively delete anything by following these steps:

1. Run Software Update and select the item to be ignored in the list of updates that appears.

2. ⌘+click to select multiple items (as shown in Figure 50-4).

3. Choose Ignore Update from the Update menu or press ⌘+Delete.

   You'll be prompted to confirm this action (see Figure 50-5). Rest assured that you can also reaccess deleted updates later (like after you've purchased that iPod).

• **Figure 50-4:** ⌘+click to select and ignore multiple installers.

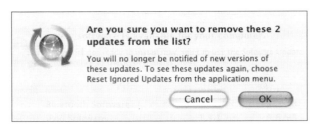

• **Figure 50-5:** Like emptying the Trash, ignoring updates gives you a confirmation prompt.

4. To reactivate an update that you've previously deleted, choose Reset Ignored Updates from the Software Update menu.

 If you have multiple Macs to update, opt for the Install and Keep Package or Download Only options. Using these methods, you can download the new installations once and then run them on multiple computers.

 If you use the Install and Keep Package update method, you'll find the installed package in the /Library/Packages folder after the installation is complete. Panther will open this directory in a new window for you.

Updating Other Applications

Application updaters work in two different ways: Some modify the existing software, and others replace the existing software. Using either of these is straightforward enough (and they should come with instructions), but make and keep a backup copy of the software before performing the update just in case problems occur.

Although we've never personally experienced a problem, proactive users should back up their files before updating any software. This is especially true when it comes to installing major updates to the operating system. Although unlikely, an update gone awry can potentially wreck your system.

Updates versus Upgrades

There are technically two kinds of software changes for applications: updates and upgrades. *Updates* are normally minor version changes (like from 7.0 to 7.0.1) that fix bugs and security holes. These are the most important (for obvious reasons) and should be provided for free from the application's manufacturer. *Upgrades* are normally major version changes (like from 6.0 to 7.0) that add features. These will normally cost you money and are a much larger download (or will come with their own CDs). In this Technique, we primarily focus on updates.

Although calling something an *update* as opposed to an *upgrade* is largely a syntactical difference, some people have taken issue with Apple for releasing what seems to be an update (going from Mac OS X 10v.2 to 10v.3) and charging $129 for it. Considering the number of features added to each new release, Apple could just as easily silence the critics by calling the versions Mac OS XI, XII, and so forth. Or by not charging quite so much. . . .

Some applications come with their own updaters built into the software. Again, you'll see two general types of built-in updaters:

✔ **Automatic updaters:** For example, QuickTime has its own updater, called QuickTime Updater. Cocktail (www.macosxcocktail.com; see Figure 50-6), a utility that performs various system maintenance routines, checks for newer versions as well.

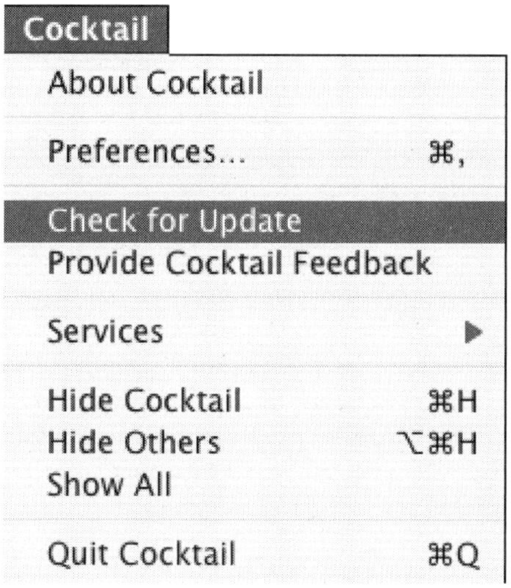

Cocktail	
About Cocktail	
Preferences...	⌘,
Check for Update	
Provide Cocktail Feedback	
Services	▶
Hide Cocktail	⌘H
Hide Others	⌥⌘H
Show All	
Quit Cocktail	⌘Q

• **Figure 50-6: One of the features of good applications, like Cocktail, is the ability to check for updates.**

Some advanced applications automatically check for updates at set periods of time (every two weeks, for example) or every time the application starts.

✔ **Links to a supporting Web page:** Other applications let you check for updates by taking you to their Web sites. Although this isn't as useful, it's still an easy way for you to keep your software up-to-date.

To see if an application has some sort of updating system built-in, check the application's manual or help files. Or, look in logical places: the Preferences panel, under the application menu, or under the Help menu. Finally, you can always check the manufacturer's Web site to see if they have any updates listed.

Staying Informed about Updates

Before you can update any software, you need to be aware that an update is available. Although Apple's Software Update utility checks this for you (with respect to Apple software), you need an easy way to keep informed for everything else. Here are some recommended resources to keep informed about what updates are available:

✔ **VersionTracker** (www.versiontracker.com): There is a whole cult around VersionTracker, which is one of the premier application information sites around. Some fanatics check it daily to see what updates are available for their favorite applications. It's also a great way to see what's new for Mac OS X and to find alternatives to tools you're already using.

.Mac users have been thanked by Apple with a free one-year subscription to VersionTracker. Anyone can use VersionTracker for free, but those with a membership can take advantage of more useful tools (membership starts at $25 per year).

✔ **MacUpdate** (www.macupdate.com)**:** MacUpdate
is similar to VersionTracker but is free. The site
e-mails you when particular applications are
updated and lets you create custom watch lists
to track your favorite software.

✔ **Apple mailing lists** (http://lists.apple.com)**:**
Apple maintains a number of mailing lists for various subjects. Almost all of them have a moder-
ate amount of traffic, so signing up shouldn't
overwhelm your inbox. Most important with
respect to updates is the "security-announce"
list, which notifies you of security-related updates
available for the operating system. Sign up for
this, and you'll be one of the first to know when
a new patch comes up.

✔ **Apple Developer Connection e-mails** (http://
developer.apple.com)**:** You don't have to be a
software engineer to be a member of the ADC.
This free membership provides you with a ton
of information. You can also sign up for the
ADC update e-mail, which lets you know when
new software or upgrades to existing applications come out. It's not as exhaustive as
VersionTracker, but it is another useful resource.

✔ **Application e-mails:** Many manufacturers have
mailing lists that you can sign up for that are not
(thankfully) spam. If you want to know when a
new version of StuffIt or BBEdit is available, sign
up at the appropriate Web site or when you register the application.

Securing Files

Technique 51

Save Time By

- ✔ Working with FileVault, Panther's tool for file encryption
- ✔ Working with other encryption software
- ✔ Really, really deleting a file

Security comes in many forms: for example, the security issues involved with Internet transactions, or the physical security of making sure that someone can't steal or physically tamper with your computer. There's also the issue of protecting your passwords (see Technique 52). This Technique is all about securing individual files and folders on your computer. If your computer never leaves the house, this might not be a concern, but if you work in an office or travel with your Mac, protecting sensitive documents is critical.

The primary tool for accomplishing this is FileVault. In this Technique, we show you how to use that most efficiently. Then we show you some other popular shareware options, just in case FileVault isn't sufficient for your needs. Finally, we let you in on the Secure Empty Trash feature added to Panther, which lets you safely (and permanently) delete files.

Making the Most of FileVault

FileVault is a new technology to Panther. FileVault makes use of a 128-bit version of the Advanced Encryption Standard (AES) to encrypt your stuff. (*Encryption* is the process of translating data into an unreadable form, requiring a password or similar key to make it legible again.) After you enable FileVault, it encrypts and decrypts the contents of your Home directory while you work, meaning that you'll automatically have this security without needing to constantly manage the process.

 If you use FileVault, make sure that you store everything within your Home directory. Anything kept outside of the ~/ structure will not be protected!

 FileVault is new to Panther, which means that it might not be 100 percent reliable. Keeping unencrypted copies of your stuff and storing it in a secure location is prudent. For example, you could routinely back up your Home directory to CDs or an external hard drive and place those in a home safe or underneath your mattress. (Well, we're just kidding about the mattress, but you get the idea.)

To enable and use FileVault

1. **Open the System Preferences panel.**

2. **Click Security, under Personal.**

3. **Click Set Master Password.**

   The Master Password is used to control access to every encrypted Home directory on the computer. The files themselves are encrypted using both it and the user's login password.

4. **In the dialog that appears (see Figure 51-1), enter the password twice and a hint whose answer is hard-to-guess, if you want.**

• **Figure 51-1: Set a master password before enabling FileVault.**

 If you lose or forget your master password and your login password, you are up a creek without a paddle, to put it politely. Whatever you do, make sure this never happens, or you might as well say goodbye to all your stuff. That being said, don't make your password obvious — and don't write it on a note taped to your computer.

5. **Click OK.**

6. **Click the Turn on FileVault button (see Figure 51-2).**

 FileVault cannot be turned on while other users are logged into your computer. Make sure that you're the user only logged in before proceeding.

• **Figure 51-2: Enable FileVault here.**

7. **Enter your master password at the prompt (see Figure 51-3). (It doesn't bode well for you if you've already forgotten it.)**

   A dialog appears that warns you of the consequences of forgetting your master password.

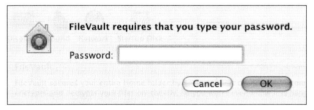

• **Figure 51-3: Enter your password.**

8. **Click the Turn on FileVault button (which appears in a prompt) after you've read the warning (see Figure 51-4).**

You are now ready to turn on FileVault protection.

WARNING: Your files will be encrypted using your login password. If you forget your login password and the master password is not available, your data will be lost forever.

Once you turn on FileVault, you will be logged out and FileVault will encrypt your entire Home directory. Depending on how much data you have, this could take a while. You will not be able to log in or use this computer until the initial setup is completed.

Cancel Turn On FileVault

• **Figure 51-4: The very stern warning reminds you to remember your password.**

9. **Log back in after FileVault is finished doing its thing.**

FileVault will log you out and then spend a few minutes encrypting your Home directory. How long this takes depends on the size of your Home directory.

While you're in the FileVault control panel (refer to Figure 51-2), you might consider selecting the check boxes for these other security features, too:

✔ Require Password to Wake This Computer from Sleep or Screen Saver

✔ Disable Automatic Login

✔ Require Password to Unlock Each Secure System Preference

✔ Log Out After *x* Minutes of Inactivity

Each of these features makes your computer more secure but also slightly more tedious to work with. If you're the only one who uses your computer and it's in a safe place, leave these cleared. If you have sensitive data on your computer, keep your Mac in an environment where others can access it — or just generally want the peace of mind — enable these options.

Other Encryption Tools

If FileVault doesn't exactly float your boat, you can use a number of other applications to encrypt and decrypt files. We cover some of the most popular in this section.

> One of the downsides of FileVault is that it will slow down your computer when you're working with files in your Home directory. If you'd rather not risk that or if you require only certain things to be protected, use one of the other pieces of software discussed in this section of the chapter.

Disk Utility

Apple's Disk Utility allows you to create encrypted disk images, using the same encryption protocol as FileVault. One benefit is that you can mount the disk image only when you need it. Second, you can encrypt only those files that need it: for example, leaving the 8GB of music on your hard drive untouched.

To use Disk Utility

1. **Open Disk Utility by double-clicking its icon in the Utilities folder.**

2. **Choose New⇨Blank Image from the Images menu.**

3. **In the resulting dialog (see Figure 51-5), make the following selections:**

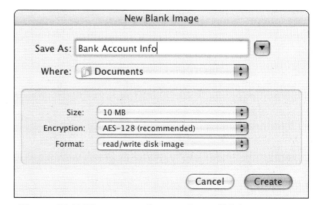

New Blank Image

Save As: Bank Account Info

Where: Documents

Size: 10 MB

Encryption: AES-128 (recommended)

Format: read/write disk image

Cancel Create

• **Figure 51-5: The prompt for creating a disk image.**

▶ Give the image a name in the Save As box.

 For added security, give your disk image a creative name that doesn't indicate its purpose (in other words, don't use a give-away like *Bank Account Info*). This will keep people from wanting to investigate the disk image. On the other hand, if you're likely to forget that the disk image named *Brautigan Thesis* is actually your bank information, use a more meaningful name and trust that the encryption will safely protect your data.

▶ Decide where to save the image, using the Where drop-down list.

▶ Select an appropriate size from the Size drop-down list.

The size of your disk image is a cap on how much information it can store. It's also how much room the file will take on your hard drive, so choose this value wisely.

▶ Select AES-128 in the Encryption drop-down list.

This is the key step in making a secure disk image.

▶ Leave Read/Write Disk Image selected in the Format drop-down list.

4. **Click the Create button.**

5. **At the prompt (see Figure 51-6), enter a password twice and then click OK.**

• **Figure 51-6: This password allows access to the disk image and its files.**

 If you store the disk image password in your keychain, you can open it without entering the password. This means that anyone else with access to your computer can as well. Make a decision between security and convenience here.

6. **Copy files to the mounted disk image.**

The disk image will automatically be mounted by the operating system. You can now use it like any other disk.

7. **Eject the disk when you're finished with it.**

8. **To reaccess the files, remount the disk image.**

StuffIt

If you pay for the full version of Aladdin System's StuffIt (www.stuffit.com, $80), you can create encrypted StuffIt and Zip archives. A password is required to access those contents.

Mac GNU Privacy Guard

Mac GNU Privacy Guard (http://macgpg.sourceforge.net, free) is a free implementation of the popular Pretty Good Privacy (PGP) software. It provides a framework for using PGP within other applications, like Mail, Entourage, or Eudora. It requires a little bit of configuration and work on your part, but the price is right.

PGP

This is the commercial version of PGP software (www.pgp.com, $50), which you can use to encrypt your e-mail and create secure disk images. Although it's not free, it is easier to get started with than the Mac GNU Privacy Guard.

SubRosaSoft and CodeTek Studios

Both SubRosaSoft (www.subrosasoft.com) and CodeTek Studios (www.codetek.com) develop numerous security-related products including larger scale packages. For example, CodeTek's SafeData Technology Suite ($50) cleans out your Internet history, encrypts and decrypts files, and securely trashes files.

Sending Secure E-mail

If you need to send encrypted mail, Panther now includes support for the professional Secure Multipurpose Internet Mail Extensions (S/MIME) e-mail encryption standard. This tool requires that both the sender and receiver get a personal S/MIME certificate, which can be had for free at www.thawte.com.

Setting up this feature requires a few steps, but after it's set up, it works pretty well. If both users have a certificate, the certificate will be transmitted along with the message. This certificate can then be added to the Address Book (technically, the certificate will be added to your keychain, assuming that the user is in your Address Book) so that it's associated with the sender. Thereafter, when you send that person an e-mail, you will see an additional option in the mail composition window to send the e-mail securely (you'll see a small button with a lock icon, next to the Signature pull-down menu).

• **Figure 51-7: Secure Empty Trash provides a level of security that the Department of Defense would endorse (literally).**

Using the Finder's Secure Empty Trash

Also new to Panther is the Secure Empty Trash option, found under the Finder menu (see Figure 51-7). Whereas the normal Empty Trash option simply deletes the files in the trash bin, Secure Empty Trash deletes those files by writing over them, renaming them, and so forth, before actually throwing them away. Think of it like crumpling a piece of paper, putting it inside a bag, and then throwing the bag away.

 Unlike with the normal Empty Trash command, you cannot recover a file from Secure Empty Trash. For this reason, we advocate double-checking the contents of the Trash before proceeding. (You can see what's in the Trash by clicking its icon in the Dock.)

A Terminal Solution

The Secure Empty Trash Finder feature, like many utilities, is duplicated as a command-line utility. From the Terminal, you can securely delete files by using the `srm` command.

```
srm filename
srm foldername
```

The `srm` command takes several options, including

- ✔ I: Prompts you for each item being deleted
- ✔ r: Empties directories
- ✔ s: Does a simple, secure deletion
- ✔ m: Does a medium-level deletion
- ✔ z: Zeroes the blocks on the hard drive (that means it uses blank data to cover the hard drive where the deleted file was)
- ✔ v: Gives you a verbose response

So, a nice and secure command-line deletion can be accomplished by using

```
srm -mz filename
```

This feature is pretty easy to use. Just follow these steps:

1. **Trash a file by moving it to the Trash or by pressing ⌘+Delete after selecting it.**

2. **Choose Secure Empty Trash from the Finder menu.**

3. **Click OK at the prompt.**

 If you'd rather not see the "Are you sure?" warning, clear the Show Warning Before Emptying the Trash option under the Finder's Advanced preferences panel (see Figure 51-8) or hold down the Option key while selecting Secure Empty Trash (or Empty Trash) from the Finder menu.

• **Figure 51-8: Clear the empty Trash warning if you trust you know what you're doing.**

4. **Watch the Trash progress bar in action.**

You'll probably notice that Secure Empty Trash takes much longer than the standard method. This should make sense, considering the many extra steps taking place behind the scenes.

 Although this new feature is nice, keep in mind that most potential snoops don't know how to recover data that has been deleted through ordinary means, either. The Secure Empty Trash option is great if you have truly sensitive data to delete or if you fear that someone who really knows what they are doing might get hold of your computer. But unless either of those applies to you, save yourself some time by sticking to the standard Empty Trash.

Technique 52

Proper Password Policy

Save Time By

- ✔ Coming up with a secure password
- ✔ Getting the most out of Apple's password management utility
- ✔ Knowing how to change your login password

The security of your computer partially depends upon the passwords you use to log in, access Web sites, and encrypt files. The first step is to choose a good, secure password. The second step that you should take is to use Apple's keychain technology to manage your passwords for you. Finally, we discuss the important information that you should know about changing and using your login password.

To improve both the convenience and security of using your computer, the Mac OS X operating system uses *keychains:* virtual places to store and retrieve sensitive information. The first time you use any "key" (a password required by a file or encrypted disk image, your .Mac account information, login values used by Web sites), you are given the option — through a prompt or check box — of storing that information in the keychain. The passwords and such are kept in a secure format so that they are not easily viewable. Your keychain (the collection of all of your keys) is unlocked when you log into your Mac, and the different keys are then automatically used as needed. (For example, when you go to a Web site or attempt to open a password-protected file, the proper values will be entered for you.) Although Panther handles all of this seamlessly, it also comes with the Keychain Access utility, which gives you more specific control over your keys and keychains.

Creating a Good Password

Good security begins with selecting good, secure passwords. You should abide by certain rules when coming up with your passwords. Here is the party line on passwords:

Do use

- ✔ A combination of letters and numbers
- ✔ A combination of upper- and lowercase letters
- ✔ At least eight characters
- ✔ A combination of symbols and punctuation, if allowed

Don't use

- ✔ Words that are in a dictionary
- ✔ Names, words, or numbers that are meaningful to you
- ✔ Too-obvious passwords, such as names of your pets, children, or spouse; or digits from your phone number, address, birthday, or Social Security number
- ✔ The same password for multiple things

 The most important consideration is that your login password is unique. Moreover, keep your login password distinct from the root user's password, if one has been set.

The problem with these rules is that they can make remembering your passwords impossible. So what are you to really do?

- ✔ **Use the Keychain Access to remember your passwords. See "Working with Apple's Keychain Access" later in this Technique for more.**

- ✔ **Use the first letters of the words in a phrase to come up with a password.**

  Just like you used the mnemonic Roy G. Biv to memorize the colors of the rainbow, you can take a phrase and create an abbreviation to create a memorable password. For example, the abbreviation for the phrase *Larry Ullman and Marc Liyanage wrote a book together* creates the password *LUaMLwabt*. This makes for a pretty decent password, and it's not impossible to recall.

- ✔ **Take existing words and add numbers and punctuation.**

  For example, you can take the word *original* and turn it into *Or!gina_L*. This password uses upper- and lowercase letters, numbers, and punctuation.

- ✔ **Go ahead and write down important passwords but store them securely.**

  One of the golden rules is not writing down your passwords. This sounds like a great idea but is

impractical, particularly when you consider the fact that if you forget your login password, you'll be in trouble. If you must, make a note of your password, but don't

- ▶ Post it on your monitor.
- ▶ Leave it in a desk drawer.
- ▶ Indicate what the password is for.
- ▶ Keep it in your wallet.

Working with Apple's Keychain Access

Mac OS X's main tool for managing passwords is Keychain Access (see Figure 52-1). This application stores and retrieves your passwords, including those used by

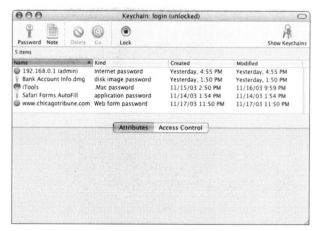

• **Figure 52-1: The Keychain Access tool makes password management easy.**

- ✔ Web sites
- ✔ E-mail accounts
- ✔ FileVault
- ✔ iChat
- ✔ .Mac accounts

✔ Encrypted disk images

✔ Wireless networks

✔ Servers

 Check out Technique 51 for how you can use the Security panel to require passwords to access your computer after it's been sleeping, idle, and so forth.

Panther will use the keychain automatically, so there's little you need to do to enable it. However, note these best policies here:

✔ **Use the keychain as much as possible.** This is a good, secure application, designed to make your life easier. Take advantage of this!

✔ **Make a very secure login password.** The keychain uses your login password as its master password. If someone can get into your computer and guess your master password, he can then get access to all your other passwords.

✔ **Regularly back up the keychain database.** The keychains are stored in your ~/Library/Keychains directory. They are automatically backed up if you back up your entire Home directory, or you can manually move the files from there to a CD or a USB thumbnail drive (a small, portable hard drive).

 The Backup application will automatically present your keychain database as an option to back up.

✔ **Use the keychain menu bar tool.** If you do a lot with keychains, choose Show Status in Menu Bar from the View menu. This creates a menu bar shortcut to keychain-related tasks (see Figure 52-2).

✔ **Change the keychain settings for improved security.** Your keychain automatically unlocks when you login and then remains unlocked. This can be a security risk, particularly if others have access to your computer when you step away. To change this behavior, select Change Settings for

Keychain *Keychain Name* from the Edit menu. Use the resulting prompt (see Figure 52-3) to secure your keychain.

• **Figure 52-2: Make the most of Keychain Access by using the menu bar tool.**

• **Figure 52-3: Change a keychain's settings for heightened security.**

✔ **When prompted, grant applications permission to always allow access to the keychain.** When an application needs to access the keychain, you see a prompt that lets you choose to deny this, allow this once, or always allow this action. You might as well always allow this so that you won't have to worry about it in the future.

You can also use your keychain to store sensitive data, like your ATM PIN or credit card information, by creating a Note. This is a more secure option than placing such information in a plain text file or a Sticky note. You might want to use this for recording social security numbers, listing the serial numbers of your computers and other valuable equipment, or for securing sensitive work-related secrets. In short, with the Keychain Access utility, you can encrypt and protect any little tidbit you want.

Here's how to create a secure Note:

1. **Open Keychain Access by double-clicking on its icon in the Applications⇨Utilities folder.**

2. **If no keychain is visible, click Show Keychains to display the keychain drawer and select your keychain.**

3. **Click Unlock and enter your password if the keychain is locked.**

4. **Click Note.**

5. **In the resulting prompt (see Figure 52-4), type your note's name in the Name box.**

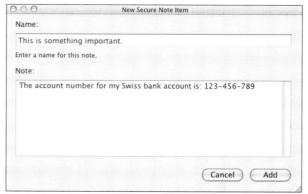

• **Figure 52-4: Use Keychain Access for important information other than passwords.**

6. **Type the text of your Note in the Note box.**

7. **Click Add to add the Note.**

You'll be returned back to the Keychain Access application itself. To later view the contents of any note, just follow these steps:

1. **Open the Keychain Access application.**

2. **Click on the note's name in the list of keychain items.**

When you select an item in the main listing, you'll see its information in the bottom half of the window. This will include the item's name, creation date, and modification date. You will not, at this point, see any of the secure values themselves (like a note's contents or a password).

3. **Check the Show note box that appears under the item's name (in the bottom half of the window).**

4. **Enter your login password at the prompt.**

To view a note, you'll need to enter the Keychain Access password at the prompt. This is the same value as your login password, unless you've changed the Keychain Access password separately.

5. **You'll now see the note's contents in the bottom half of the window.**

Using Open Firmware Password

To really protect your computer, make use of the Open Firmware Password utility. If you enable this feature, people cannot access your computer by booting from another volume. This also means that you'll need to enter this password to boot from a CD-ROM or even zap your PRAM (the process of resetting your computer's special parameter memory, which is sometimes required to fix erratic behavior). The basic steps, which are detailed at `http://docs.info.apple.com/article.html?artnum=106482`, are

1. **Make sure that your computer supports Open Firmware Password (see the Web page).**

2. **Download the installer.**

3. **Install the Open Firmware Password application.**

4. **Open the application.**

5. **Enable the Require Password to Change Open Firmware Settings option.**

6. **Enter the password twice.**

7. **Click OK.**

8. **Quit the application.**

Changing Login Passwords

Routinely changing your login passwords is a smart security policy. Some operating systems prompt you to do this every so many months, although Mac OS X does not. (It's a nice security check, but it's kind of an inconvenience, too.)

To change your login password

1. **Open System Preferences.**

2. **Click Accounts, under System.**

3. **Select your account from the list in the left column (see Figure 52-5).**

• **Figure 52-5:** Change your login password in the Accounts System Preferences panel.

4. **Highlight the dots that currently appear in the Password box and then press Delete.**

5. **Enter your current password at the prompt (see Figure 52-6).**

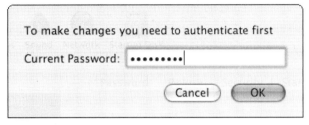

• **Figure 52-6:** Before making any changes, you need to authenticate yourself.

6. **Enter your new password in the Password box.**

7. **Enter the password again in the Verify box.**

8. **Click the lock to save the settings.**

 When you change your login password, Panther will also change your Keychain Access password. If these are not the same, your keychain will not be unlocked when you log in.

Resetting the Administrator's Password

If you forget the administrator's password, you still have some hope: The Mac OS X Installation discs will let you reset this value. Boot your computer from the first installation CD. When the installer begins, choose Reset Administrative Password from the Installer menu and follow the prompts.

Technique 53

Useful Utilities

Save Time By

- Using TinkerTool, a wonderful and free utility
- Understanding and using cron, a scheduling application
- Seeing a couple of other good utilities

A big part of using your Mac effectively is choosing and using the right tool for the job. In this book, we discuss a variety of software options, but we don't have room to mention all of our most recommended applications. In this Technique, we will go over the benefits — both timesaving and cosmetic — of using a couple of more utilities.

Special attention is first given to *TinkerTool,* one of the best free applications around. Then we mention *CronniX,* a graphical user interface to the cron scheduling utility. Finally, we give brief notice to a smattering of other software worthy of your consideration.

Working with TinkerTool

TinkerTool, which we mention in other Techniques of this book because it's so helpful, is available from www.bresink.de/osx/TinkerTool.html for free. Some of the best features of TinkerTool are the abilities to

- Show hidden files in the Finder
- Disable animation effects
- Dim hidden applications in the Dock (see Figure 53-1)

• **Figure 53-1: With TinkerTool, hidden applications have their Dock icons dimmed (like Preview on the right).**

✔ Align the Dock on the top, bottom, left, or right (rather than the center) of the screen

✔ Add a pair of arrows to both ends of a scroll bar

✔ Set system fonts (see Figure 53-2)

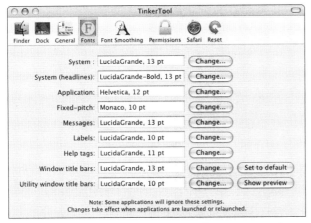

• **Figure 53-2: Use TinkerTool to set different system fonts.**

✔ Add features to Safari (see Figure 53-3)

As you can see from this list, some of these features are merely cosmetic, whereas others are very practical. TinkerTool has been consistently developed over the years, and many of its most popular features have been incorporated into the operating system already. Especially considering its cost — free! — you have no reason not to make use of TinkerTool.

The popularity of TinkerTool has spurred its creator to break it into two separate products: TinkerTool and TinkerTool System. The former (free) is expressly for personalizing a user's setting, whereas the latter (approximately $10) can make system-wide alterations.

• **Figure 53-3: TinkerTool can enable Safari's debug menu, which is very useful for Web developers.**

Automating Tasks with cron

One of the cool technologies built into Unix is `cron`, a command-line utility for scheduling actions. Seasoned UNIX users will define a `crontab`: a list of what actions your operating system should take when. The `cron` *daemon* (a perpetually running process) calls the commands set in the `crontab` when the time is right. You can control all of this from the Terminal (see the "Using cron in the Terminal" sidebar), but the easiest way to control `cron` is to use CronniX (`www.koch-schmidt.de/cronnix/`, free).

Some example uses of a `cron` are to

✔ Schedule backups

✔ Access Web pages

✔ Perform maintenance

✔ Retrieve stock quotes

✔ Schedule interactions with databases

The CronniX utility also lets you view the system `crontab` file (see Figure 53-4) and provides an interface for scheduling your own actions. If you have a need for `crons`, you'd be crazy not to use CronniX.

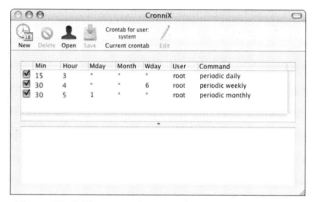

• **Figure 53-4: The operating system runs these commands between 3 and 5 a.m.**

As an example, your Mac relies upon privileges in order to properly deny or allow access to files. These privileges can become muddled, having undesirable results. Fortunately, the permissions can be easily fixed by running the Disk Utility's Repair Disk Permissions tool (under the First Aid tab). But how are you to remember to do this? By letting CronniX do it for you, of course! Follow these steps:

1. **Open CronniX by double-clicking its icon after you've installed the application.**

2. **Choose File⇨Open System Crontab.**

You can establish `crons` for any user, but this one should run on an administrative level, so you'll need to open up the System Crontab.

3. **Click New.**

4. **In the resulting prompt (see Figure 53-5), enter 0 as the minute and 12 as the hour.**

This task will run at noon every day.

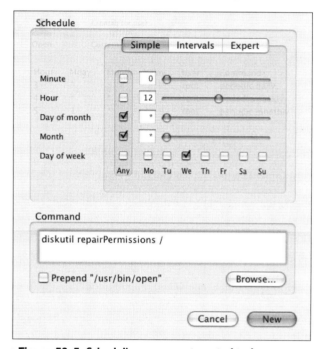

• **Figure 53-5: Scheduling a new automated task.**

5. **Still in the same prompt, click the Any box for the day of the month and the month.**

This task will run one day each week (Wednesday) but should not be limited to a specific date (1 through 31) or month.

6. **Set the day of the week to We.**

7. **For the command, enter** diskutil repairPermissions /.

To run the Disk Utility's Repair Disk Permissions command on the whole hard drive, enter this code (the slash indicates that the repair should be applied to the entire drive).

8. Click New.

You'll now see the command added to the list of scheduled tasks.

9. Save the added task by pressing ⌘+S.

10. Enter the administrator's password at the prompt.

Because the added task runs as the administrator, you'll need to authenticate yourself.

11. Quit CronniX by pressing ⌘+Q.

Using cron in the Terminal

The `cron` utility uses the information stored in the `crontab` file to know what commands to run when. You can edit the `crontab` file in your default text editor by typing **crontab -e** in the Terminal. The syntax for a `crontab` entry is confusing and critical. What you'll see is

```
* * * * * command
```

The five asterisks represent, in order from left to right, minutes, hours, days, months, and days of the week (from 0 to 6, with 0 being Sunday). Using an asterisk for one of those parameters means that value is not limited. You can also set ranges with hyphens or list discrete elements separated by commas. Here are some examples of `cron` entries that you can add to your crontab file:

```
0 16 * * * calendar
```

This displays a calendar every day at 4 p.m.

```
0,15,30,45 8-17 * * 1-5 open
'http://finance.yahoo.com'
```

This opens Yahoo!'s finance page in your default Web browser every 15 minutes between 8 a.m. and 5 p.m., Monday through Friday.

Other Useful Utilities

The following utilities are not meant for everyone, but you ought to be aware of their existence. There's not much to say about how to use any of these, but understand that the applications themselves are good timesaving tools.

✔ **Pacifist** (www.charlessoft.com, $20): Pacifist lets you access specific files and folders from package installers. This is very useful if you know you need a particular item but don't want to reinstall all the software again. If you'd like to get one file from one of Apple's huge installers, Pacifist can really simplify and hasten that process.

 CharlesSoft also makes a free product called DockDisks, which adds mounted disks (CD-ROMs, DVDs, disk images, and so on) to your Dock. With this tool, you can access mounted disks without going to the Desktop.

✔ **Cocoa Gestures** (www.bitart.com, free): Cocoa Gestures is a clever little tool that lets you associate actions with mouse movements. For example, you could set it so that when you Option+click a file and move up your mouse, the Get Info panel appears. Marc uses Cocoa Gestures to associate mouse movements with the Back and Forward Safari buttons. The Cocoa Gestures functionality is far more useful than you might imagine, and its free price makes it worth trying. If you like Cocoa Gestures, bit*art* Consulting also offers the $30 CocoaSuite, with many, many added features, including

▶ Turn your laptop's trackpad into a virtual scroll wheel.

▶ Change existing menu shortcuts in applications.

▶ Quickly run AppleScripts.

✔ **Konfabulator** (www.konfabulator.com, $25): Konfabulator is an application that runs widgets (little segments of code designed to perform specific tasks) written in JavaScript. Even if you don't know how to write JavaScript code, this is far more useful than you might imagine because you can download hundreds of widgets at the Web site. Sample widgets can

▶ Download stock quotes

▶ Get weather reports

▶ Act as clocks or alarm clocks

▶ Play games

▶ Manage to-do lists

Konfabulator is definitely one of those must-see-to-believe applications. The price might seem a little high, but the widgets are free, meaning that $25 buys many, many tools at once.

✔ **AutoPairs** (www.jwwalker.com, free)**:** AutoPairs is a System Preferences addition that constantly runs in the background. It's useful for programmers in particular by making a matching quotation mark, parenthesis, bracket, or curly brace whenever the initial one is typed. For example, if you type a left bracket ([), AutoPairs adds the right bracket (]) and places the cursor between the two so that you can begin typing. Besides saving you an extra keystroke here and there, it helps you avoid errors caused by forgetting a closing mark.

Part IX

The Scary Or Fun Stuff

The 5th Wave   By Rich Tennant

DAD ADDS MULTIMEDIA SOUND AND GRAPHICS TO THE TRADITIONAL CAMPFIRE GHOST STORY.

Technique 54

Controlling Cellphones with Bluetooth

Save Time By

✔ Setting up your Bluetooth connection quickly

✔ Hooking up your cellphone with the OS X Address Book

✔ Dialing your cellphone from within any application

✔ Synchronizing Contacts and Calendars with your cellphone

✔ Remotely controlling your Macintosh

Mac OS X includes extensive support for *Bluetooth,* which is a wireless networking standard. Many new Macintosh computers now have Bluetooth hardware built in. It is an exciting and versatile technology, and in this Technique, we show several examples of how Bluetooth can help you save time.

Many new cellphones are Bluetooth-enabled. With only a bit of configuration, you can have your computer and your cellphone talk to each other and exchange data. This one-time setup procedure is what we look at first. We also take you on a tour of the things that you can do with Apple's own applications, and then we highlight some useful third-party applications.

What Is Bluetooth?

Bluetooth (www.bluetooth.com) is a wireless communications protocol used to connect up to seven compatible devices to each other within a limited range, usually less than 30 feet. Designed to be small and inexpensive, integration into today's digital entertainment and communications gadgets is technically and economically feasible. The list of Bluetooth-enabled devices now includes mobile phones, portable music players, digital cameras, printers, laptops, PDAs, and even computer mice and keyboards.

Bluetooth can carry data and voice. Some wireless phone headsets use Bluetooth instead of a cable to connect the headset (usually a tiny, battery-powered ear clip and microphone) to the mobile phone.

Because it doesn't require a clear line of sight between the communicating devices, Bluetooth is also more convenient than infrared connections. You can leave your mobile phone in your pocket and still use it to connect to the Internet with a PDA or receive a phone call on your headset.

Compared with other technologies, Bluetooth is designed for lower cost, shorter range, and slower speed than the AirPort/802.11x family of wireless networking protocols. (You know, WiFi and its cousins?) It is also more versatile. Whereas you use AirPort to connect your computer with medium to high speed to other computers on a network, you use Bluetooth to connect your computer to small communications and entertainment devices.

Bluetooth was initiated by computer and telecommunications heavyweights such as IBM, Intel, Ericsson, Nokia, and Toshiba. Bluetooth has been around for about six years, but only recently did all the puzzle pieces like Bluetooth-enabled cellphones, computers with Bluetooth hardware and software, and applications that actually provide some useful service become widely available. Now Macintosh users can finally benefit from the technology.

If you want to find out more about it, start by visiting Apple's Bluetooth Web site at `www.apple.com/bluetooth`.

Getting Started with Bluetooth

In order to follow the steps in this Technique, both your computer and cellphone need to be Bluetooth-enabled. On the computer side, if you own a new Macintosh, especially an aluminum series PowerBook, it already includes everything you need for Bluetooth communications. For Macs without built-in hardware, you have to use a USB Bluetooth *adapter.* This is a tiny device that plugs into the USB port. (Apple sells one for about $50 in the Apple Store, Figure 54-1.)

In any case, you can determine whether your computer's Bluetooth system is working by checking the Bluetooth system control panel, in the Hardware section of System Preferences. If there is a problem, the Bluetooth Device Name is displayed as Not Available.

Figure 54-1: A USB Bluetooth adapter, manufactured by D-Link.

If the device isn't available and you use a USB adaptor, you need to check it by following these steps:

- Unplug and replug it.

- Make sure that it's seated firmly in the USB port.

- Try another USB port, preferably one directly on the computer.

On the cellphone, you have to make sure that

- **Bluetooth is enabled.**

  It is usually disabled when not used to save battery time.

- **The cellphone is in Discoverable mode, either permanently or just for the next few minutes.**

Both of these settings vary with each cellphone manufacturer, so just browse the phone's menu options or check the documentation for your phone.

Setting Up Your Connection

The Bluetooth control panel is also where you set up the connection between the computer and phone. This process — *pairing* two devices — is a security feature to assure that nobody can interact with your Bluetooth equipment without you knowing it.

To set up the connection between computer and phone:

1. Open the Bluetooth control panel and click the Devices tab (see Figure 54-2).

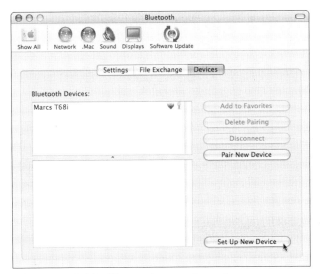

• **Figure 54-2:** The Bluetooth control panel.

2. Click the Set Up New Device button.

The Bluetooth Setup Assistant launches. Click the Continue button to start.

3. Select the Mobile Phone radio button on the Select Device Type screen (see Figure 54-3) and then click Continue.

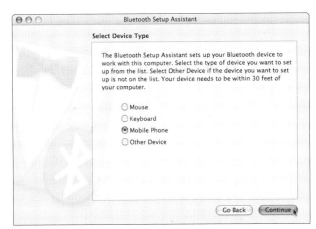

• **Figure 54-3:** Select your Bluetooth device type.

4. On the Bluetooth Mobile Phone Set Up screen, select your phone from the list and then click Continue (see Figure 54-4).

If your device doesn't appear in the list, make sure that it's still in Discoverable mode and that it's within a short distance of your computer.

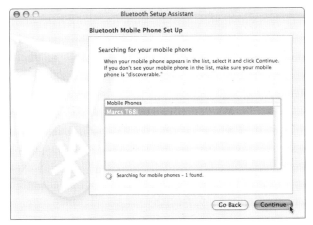

• **Figure 54-4:** Searching for devices in range.

5. Still on the Bluetooth Mobile Phone Set Up screen, enter a numeric passkey and then click Continue (see Figure 54-5).

You can enter whatever numeric combination you want as your passkey.

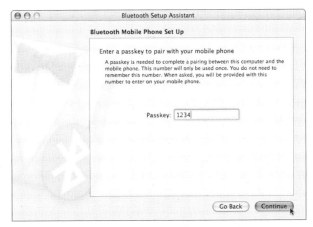

• **Figure 54-5:** Enter your passkey here.

6. On your cellphone, choose the Add to Paired option when the phone asks you how to pair the two devices (see Figure 54-6).

The specifics for your device might be slightly different, but basically you need to tell the device to accept the request coming from your Mac.

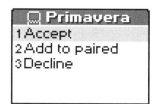

• **Figure 54-6:** The phone asks how to proceed with the pairing request from the computer.

7. When your cellphone asks you to do so, enter the same passkey set on your Mac (see Figure 54-7).

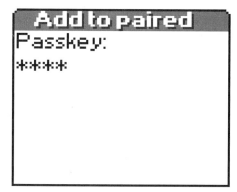

• **Figure 54-7:** Enter the passkey on the phone.

8. Click Continue on your Mac after you set up the phone.

Now you have to choose what services to enable with your device.

9. Select all the offered services (see Figure 54-8) and then click Continue.

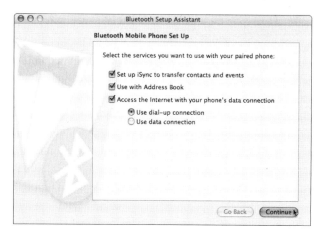

• **Figure 54-8:** Choose Bluetooth services here.

10. (Optional) Enter the Internet connection settings that you wish to use while you're on the road (see Figure 54-9).

Ask your mobile carrier or ISP for this information if you don't know it. This step is optional, and you can leave the fields empty if you don't plan to use the Internet connectivity. But don't deselect the Internet connectivity in the previous screen in this case — just leave the fields blank. Some of the tricks that we show you won't work unless the phone is configured for Internet access. Then click Continue.

You're finished setting up the connection (see Figure 54-10).

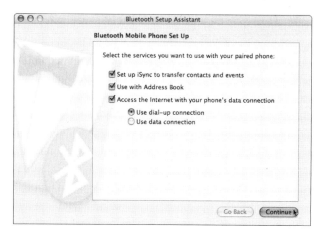

• **Figure 54-9:** Internet connection settings.

• **Figure 54-10:** See your list of known devices after successful pairing.

11. **Click the Quit button to leave the Bluetooth Setup Assistant.**

The phone is added to the list of paired devices.

You're now ready to explore the various Bluetooth features.

Working with Your Address Book

The most elegant and useful features of Bluetooth are in Apple's Address Book application. To use these features most effectively, make sure that you always keep all Address Book entries up-to-date, especially the mobile phone numbers.

First, you need to tell Address Book to watch your mobile phone. To do that, click the little Bluetooth button near the upper-left corner of the window (see Figure 54-11; look for the angular capital B). The button should turn blue — now you're ready to use your cellphone from within Address Book.

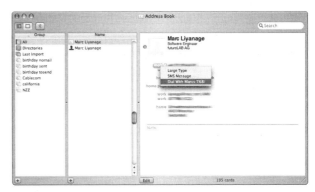

• **Figure 54-11:** Click the Bluetooth button to use it with the application.

Dialing from within Address Book

To call somebody directly from within the person's Address Book entry, click the category word to the left of the phone number (such as *mobile* or *work*) that you wish to dial (see Figure 54-11). A pop-up menu appears. Choose the Dial With option. Your cellphone should now be dialing the number.

 Using the Address Book to call people is much faster than dialing the cellphone itself.

Display incoming call alerts

If you keep the Address Book open and connected to your phone in the background, it will pop up a small dialog if somebody calls you (see Figure 54-12). Usually you will just pick up the phone and accept the call like you usually do (or click the Answer button). If you are unable to take the call however, you can use one of the other options offered by the dialog:

✔ Voice Mail forwards the call to your voice mailbox so the caller can leave a message there.

✔ SMS Reply rejects the call and allows you to send a short text message to the caller's cellphone (like "I'm in a meeting right now, will call back").

✔ Log Call will add a short entry to the Notes section of the person's card in the Address Book.

✔ If the incoming cellphone number is not yet known in the Address Book, an Add Card button lets you add a new card in the Address Book for the calling person.

Figure 54-12: An incoming call alert.

Sending and receiving SMS messages

SMS stands for Short Message Service, a feature available on some, slightly more advanced, cellular networks. Using SMS, a short alphanumeric message of up to 160 characters can be sent to a cellphone. The receiving device will display the message and allow you to respond. Replacing the functionality people used to get from pagers, SMS messaging is much like Instant Messaging using a phone.

If you use your cellphone to send text messages, you know how awkward and annoying typing them on a tiny phone keypad can be. When using Address Book, you can send and reply to text messages with the comfort of your computer keyboard.

Here's how to receive and reply to an incoming message:

1. **If somebody sends you a message and Address Book is hooked up to the phone, your computer displays the text in a pop-up window (see Figure 54-13).**

2. **Click the Reply button if you want to write back.**

An empty text field appears.

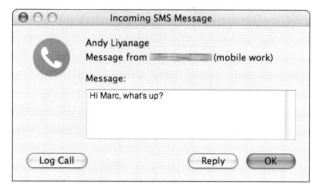

• Figure 54-13: An incoming SMS.

3. **Type in your message and then click Send (see Figure 54-14).**

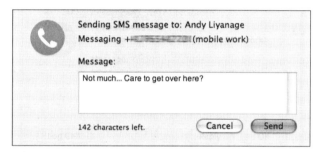

• Figure 54-14: Writing the SMS reply.

To send a new message:

1. **Open the Address Book.**

2. **Find the person's card to whom you want to send the message.**

3. **Click the Mobile category label to the left of the mobile phone number.**

4. **Choose SMS Message from the pop-up menu that appears (see Figure 54-15).**

5. **Type your text into the field that appears and then click Send.**

 Your Mac has a much better keyboard than the phone's 10-digit keypad! Use your Mac when you can.

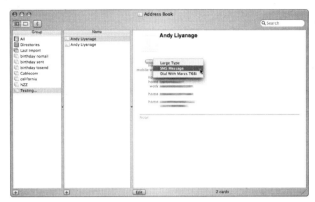

• **Figure 54-15:** Use the pop-up menu to send an SMS.

Dialing Your Phone from a Text Selection

You can download a great little (and free!) application called T68iDialer that dials phone numbers that you select in any piece of text. For example, if you find a phone number on the contact page of a company's Web site, T68iDialer lets you select that phone number with the mouse and then dial it immediately on your cellphone. How cool is that?

This program currently works with the T39m, T68m, or T68i Ericsson cellphones. It might work with others, and because it's free, you can just try it with no commitment. As of this writing, we don't know of a similar utility for other cellphones, but they're bound to come along sooner or later.

T68iDialer publishes a service to accomplish its function. (See Technique 27 on Services for more information about how Services work.)

Do this to try out the T68iDialer:

1. **Download the latest version from** www.macupdate.com/info.php/id/8913.

2. **Move the application into the Applications folder.**

3. **Log out of your Mac and log back in.**

4. **Launch any program that supports Services.**

Mail would be a good choice because many e-mail messages end with a signature that includes phone numbers.

5. **Select a phone number and choose Mail⇨Services⇨Dial Number (see Figure 54-16).**

• **Figure 54-16:** Select a phone number in any application and choose the Dial Number Service.

6. **If it's not already running, T68iDialer launches and inserts the phone number into the corresponding field in its main window.**

7. **Click Dial to dial the number (see Figure 54-17).**

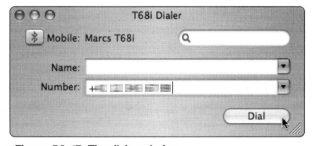

• **Figure 54-17:** The dialer window.

 Enable the Service Dial Immediately option in the program's preferences. That way, you won't have to click the Dial button anymore. Instead, T68iDialer dials the selected number as soon as you choose the Service menu command.

Synchronizing with iSync

Bluetooth-equipped cellphones usually also have an Address Book and a Calendar. Some, but not all, of these phones can be synchronized with the Address Book and iCal data on your computer with Apple's iSync application.

Synchronization means that

✔ All data is available in both places.

✔ Any additions or changes made on either the computer or the mobile phone will be effective on the other device, too.

For example, if you add to your cellphone's address book the contact information for a person you meet, this information will automatically be transferred into a new card in your Address Book application on the Mac the next time you synchronize the computer with the cellphone. On the other hand, if you add a new card for a person while working at your computer, you will not have to remember to also store the person's mobile phone number into your phone manually because synchronization will do this for you automatically.

To find out whether your particular phone (or a phone that you're thinking about buying) can be used with iSync, go to Apple's device compatibility list at www.apple.com/isync/devices.html. The best way to be sure is to check that list . . . or to try it out before buying, if possible.

Setting up iSync

To start synchronizing with your phone, you need to add it to iSync's list of devices.

1. **Launch iSync.**

2. **Choose Add Device from the Devices menu.**

Your phone should appear in the list of recognized devices (see Figure 54-18). If it doesn't, put your device into Discoverable mode and try again.

• **Figure 54-18: Adding a new device to iSync.**

3. **Double-click the phone to add it to iSync's list.**

4. **In the For First Sync drop-down box, choose the option that you prefer.**

You usually want the Merge Data on Computer and Device option unless you really want to erase all existing Contact and Calendar information on the phone (see Figure 54-19).

5. **Use the check boxes and pull-down menus to indicate what to synchronize (contacts and calendars).**

6. **Click Sync Now.**

After you set up iSync to work with your cellphone, you only have to click Sync Now to start the synchronization. It usually takes a while, especially for the first synchronization. You should sync regularly because this feature is most useful when all data is up-to-date all the time.

 You should enable the iSync menu bar icon in the application's preferences, which you can find in the iSync menu. This allows you to start a synchronization very quickly without having to first launch iSync.

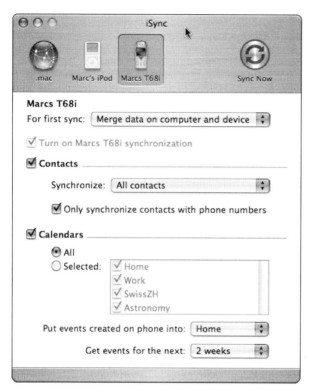

• **Figure 54-19:** iSync synchronization options.

Your Cellphone as a Remote Control

If you use a Sony Ericsson cellphone (or a Palm PDA), you can use one of the hottest Bluetooth-related utilities, Salling Clicker (http://homepage.mac.com/jonassalling/Shareware/Clicker/SEMC, $10). It installs a menu on your phone that allows you to control your computer from the phone or to view information about the computer on the phone's display. Examples of some things you can do include

✔ Starting, stopping, or skipping music in iTunes

✔ Displaying information about the current iTunes song

✔ Controlling DVD playback

✔ Adjusting or muting the sound volume

✔ Controlling slides in a presentation program, including the ability to display slide notes on the phone's display

What's more, Salling Clicker has a proximity sensor. You can use this to trigger certain actions when you (or more accurately, your cellphone) enter or leave the proximity of your computer. Examples include

✔ Stopping iTunes or muting the volume when you leave

✔ Restarting iTunes when you return to the machine

✔ Changing your iChat availability when you leave or return.

Here's how to quickly get started with Salling Clicker:

1. **Download and install the software.**

2. **Open the Salling Clicker panel in System Preferences.**

3. **Click Select Phone and choose the cellphone on which you'd like the menu installed.**

   Again, if it doesn't appear in the list, make sure that the phone is in Discoverable mode.

4. **Back in the main Salling Clicker window, click the Publish Menu button to install the menu on your phone (see Figure 54-20).**

5. **If it worked, you can now control your Mac from your phone.**

   The location of the menu in the phone's screens varies depending on the model that you have. On Marc's T68i, it's under Connect⬦Accessories. Have fun!

• **Figure 54-20:** Publish the menu to the cellphone.

Storing Notes and Pictures on a Cellphone

Modern Bluetooth phones can accept text and picture files. The text feature is especially handy for storing items like shopping lists, travel itineraries, travel directions, and so forth.

Panther includes the Bluetooth File Exchange application to send files to and from a mobile phone. Make sure to select the Show Bluetooth Status in the Menu Bar check box of the Settings tab of the Bluetooth control panel (see Figure 54-21). That way, you always have instant access to the File Exchange application by choosing the Send File command from the menu (see Figure 54-22).

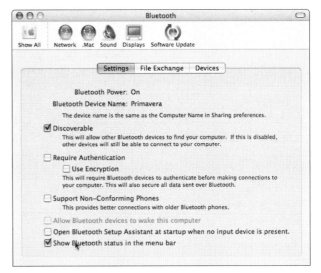

• **Figure 54-21: Enabling the Bluetooth menu.**

• **Figure 54-22: Sending files directly from menu bar.**

An even quicker way to send short snippets of text to your cellphone is to use a Services menu command:

1. **Download the free Services menu extension called BlueService, available from** www.devon-technologies.com/freeware.php.

2. **Copy the BlueService file into the** Library/Services **folder in your Home directory.**

3. Log out of your Mac and log back in (to enable the newly-added Service).

4. In an application that supports Services, select a piece of text and then choose the Send to Bluetooth Device Service.

In order for this to work, the application needs to actively support Services, and not all do yet. Try it out in a Cocoa application like Safari or Mail first.

5. Your note should be transmitted to the cellphone.

The phone will ask you whether you want to accept the file. Choose Accept to do so and store the file in the phone's memory. (The details vary with each cellphone manufacturer, so check the documentation for your particular model if it's not clear how to accept a file.)

55 Technique

The Terminal, the Finder, and You

Save Time By

- Getting around within the Terminal
- Making the Terminal and the Finder work together
- Editing in the Terminal

The *Terminal* is Panther's bridge between the beautiful Mac interface and the awesome UNIX infrastructure. Still, you don't have to be a UNIX geek to use and appreciate this application. After you understand the basics of getting around and have picked up a few key commands, you'll see how useful the Terminal can be.

In this Technique, we begin with the quickest and easiest ways to move around within the Terminal. Then we demonstrate some cool and handy tricks to use, including how you can use the Terminal and the Finder together. Finally, we cover some efficient ways to make edits in the Terminal.

 If you have some UNIX and command line experience, you'll be thrilled to see how most of those skills (plus a few more) apply to your Mac. If you've never tinkered in this area before, this and the subsequent Techniques will open a whole new — and quite cool — universe to you.

Navigating within the Terminal

When you start using the Terminal, you learn pretty quickly that the standard Finder navigation techniques don't work. In fact, without mastering some commands, you can't get anywhere in the Terminal. Luckily, figuring out these things is not all that hard.

The Terminal window greets you with a lot of information (see Figure 55-1). The most important of this is the command prompt line itself, which is where you'll find the cursor. This line is formatted as

```
Computer Name: Current Directory Current User
```

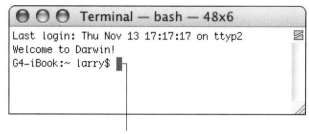

Command prompt line

• **Figure 55-1: The basic Terminal window.**

In Figure 55-1, you can tell that Larry is connected to his G4 iBook, that he is in his Home directory (indicated by the tilde; ~), and that he is logged in as the user named `larry`. The $ reflects what kind of user Larry is logged in as (a normal user, whereas a number sign indicates a root user).

If you ever forget where you're at, you can use the `pwd` (print working directory) command to have the Terminal tell you (see Figure 55-2).

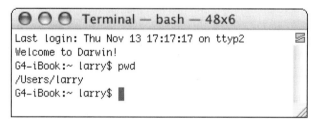

• **Figure 55-2: Use the** `pwd` **command to find yourself (but not in a New Age-y way).**

Getting around in the Terminal

Now that you know where you're at, it's time to get a move on. To move around within the Terminal, you use the `cd` (change directory) command, like this:

```
cd /path/to/directory
```

To go to the Applications directory, you would enter **cd /Applications** (as shown in Figure 55-3). This is the equivalent of double-clicking or otherwise opening a folder in the Finder.

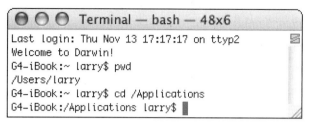

• **Figure 55-3: Larry is now in the** `/Applications` **directory, which is also indicated by** `/Applications` **after the colon.**

When it comes to moving around, here are certain facts that you should know:

✔ `/`: A forward slash is called the *root directory*.

 The root directory is the topmost folder on your computer and is the equivalent of opening your main hard drive in the Finder. If you have multiple hard drives or partitions, the one with the operating system will be at the root level, whereas the others will be found under `/Volumes`.

✔ `~`: The tilde refers to the Home directory of the currently logged-in user.

✔ `.`: A single period refers to the current directory.

✔ `..`: Two periods refer to the parent directory of the current directory.

Those are just the basics — here are some other things that you should know to use this tool effectively:

✔ Use `cd` to go to your Home directory.

✔ Use `cd ~` to go to your Home directory.

✔ Use `cd ..` to go up one directory.

 The current directory is referred to as `.` or m. The parent directory of the current one is `..` or `../`. A subdirectory is simply `directoryname` or `directoryname/`.

Tab completion

The best tool to use in the Terminal — which you absolutely must use — is tab completion. *Tab completion* automatically completes words for you, requiring less typing and cutting down on the number of errors that you might make. For example, to use tab completion to move into the Mac OS X TST FD folder within the Books folder within the Documents folder of your Home directory (as a completely hypothetical example), do this:

1. **Open the Terminal application, which can be found in the Utilities folder.**

2. **In the Terminal window, type** cd.

The command that you want to eventually type is

cd ~/Documents/Books/Mac\ OS\ X\ TST\ FD

For this example, manually type the first part (cd). Now we'll show you how to use tab completion as much as possible.

 Spaces in filenames are allowed in the Finder but not in the Terminal because a space delineates a command. To work around this potential problem, *escape* the space by using the backslash, as in Mac\ OS\ X\ TST\ FD, which looks like Mac OS X TST FD in the Finder. Escaping is the process of preceding problematic characters with a backslash, so that they don't cause problems. In this example, the backslash-space combination will be interpreted as a space character.

3. **Type** ~/Doc **(see Figure 55-4).**

In order to get to this destination, you must first go into the Documents directory. Because the Terminal automatically starts you in your Home directory, you can make a relative path to it (just start typing **Doc**) or you can be extra precise by starting with ~/. This is then followed by Doc, and remember: Capitalization matters!

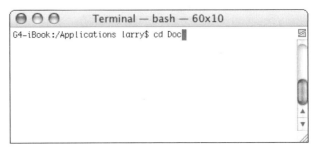

• **Figure 55-4: Tab completion lets you type a minimum of characters.**

 You can move around by using either absolute or relative paths. An *absolute path* is accurate no matter where you're currently located. A *relative path* is only accurate with respect to your current location. For example, /Users/ larry/Documents/Books/ is an absolute path (as is ~/Documents/Books/), but Documents/ Books/ is relative (and accurate as long as Larry is currently in his Home directory).

4. **Press the Tab key.**

The remaining folder name (Documents/) should be filled in automatically.

 If the Terminal cannot find a match for tab completion, it will do nothing. If it finds several matches, it will either do nothing or complete the text that all the matches have in common. For example, if a directory contains filename. txt and filename.pdf, and you type **fi** and try to do a tab completion, the Terminal returns filename. (with the period).

5. **Type Bo and press the Tab key.**

The folder name Books/ is filled in automatically.

6. **Type Mac and press the Tab key.**

The folder name Mac OS X TST FD is filled in automatically.

7. **Press the Return key to complete the command (see Figure 55-5).**

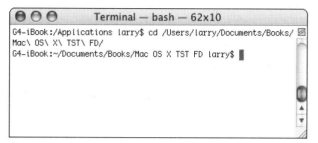

```
G4-iBook:/Applications larry$ cd /Users/larry/Documents/Books/
Mac\ OS\ X\ TST\ FD/
G4-iBook:~/Documents/Books/Mac OS X TST FD larry$ ▌
```

• **Figure 55-5:** Execute a long command with a minimum of typing.

You can use tab completion on files as well as directories. You can also use it with practically any command, not just `cd`.

Viewing directory contents

If you're in a directory and need to see what's there, use the `ls` (list) command. The `ls` command presents you with a list of a directory's contents, much like you would see in a Finder window . . . but without the icons.

✔ **Type ls to list the basic contents of the current directory.**

✔ **Type ls -G (uppercase G) to show the list in color (assuming that Disable ANSI color is not disabled in the Terminal⇨Window Settings⇨Color panel).**

✔ **Type ls -a to show every file, including hidden ones.**

The `-a` flag makes the `ls` command show many other items. These include *hidden* files (filenames begin with a period), a line for the current directory (marked by a single period), and a line for the parent directory, if applicable (marked with two periods).

✔ **Type ls -l to show more file information.**

✔ **If you like, you can combine parameters, like `ls -al` or `ls -aG`.**

✔ **Add a directory name to view a directory other than the one you're in. Here are three different ways to do it:**

```
ls /Applications/Utilities
```

See Figure 55-6.

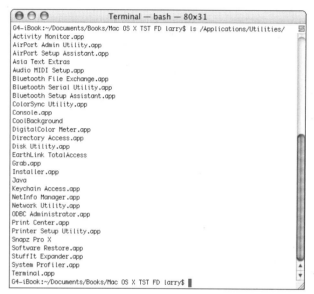

```
G4-iBook:~/Documents/Books/Mac OS X TST FD larry$ ls /Applications/Utilities/
Activity Monitor.app
AirPort Admin Utility.app
AirPort Setup Assistant.app
Asia Text Extras
Audio MIDI Setup.app
Bluetooth File Exchange.app
Bluetooth Serial Utility.app
Bluetooth Setup Assistant.app
ColorSync Utility.app
Console.app
CoolBackground
DigitalColor Meter.app
Directory Access.app
Disk Utility.app
EarthLink TotalAccess
Grab.app
Installer.app
Java
Keychain Access.app
NetInfo Manager.app
Network Utility.app
ODBC Administrator.app
Print Center.app
Printer Setup Utility.app
Snapz Pro X
Software Restore.app
StuffIt Expander.app
System Profiler.app
Terminal.app
G4-iBook:~/Documents/Books/Mac OS X TST FD larry$ ▌
```

• **Figure 55-6:** You can view a directory's contents without being in it.

```
ls -G ~/Documents
ls -al /usr/local/php
```

Navigating among open Terminal windows

The Terminal opens a new window for you when you load the application, but you don't need to restrict yourself to just a single session. You can open more windows by selecting New Shell from the File menu or using the ⌘+N keyboard shortcut.

Each Terminal window opens with the default user logged in and located in their Home directory. There is no relationship between the multiple Terminal windows, and no history is maintained from one to the other.

Working with multiple Terminal windows is great if you're trying to accomplish many things at once. Or, if you are doing some work in one directory, and other work in another, you can use two windows (one for each directory) so that you don't have to keep moving yourself around.

After you have multiple Terminal windows open, you can easily move from one to the other:

- ✔ **Use ⌘+← and ⌘+→ to move back and forth.**

- ✔ **Use ⌘+~ to rotate among them.**

- ✔ **Use ⌘+1 to access the first window, ⌘+2 to access the second, and so forth.**

Other commands

Here are a few other must-know commands that we should mention:

- ✔ `clear`: **Clears the Terminal screen**

- ✔ **Control+C: Stops the currently running command.**

- ✔ `exit`: **Logs out (see Figure 55-7)**

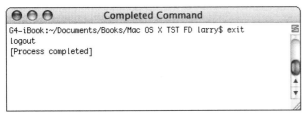

- • **Figure 55-7: When you're done using the Terminal, log out with** `exit`.

 You can set the Terminal to automatically close the window after you exit. Check out Technique 59 or the Shell panel of the Window Settings panel.

Terminal Tips and Tricks

In the next four techniques, we cover various tips and tricks involving broader subjects — finding files, handling output, viewing files, and customization. Here we include a few miscellaneous little tricks that you'll appreciate as well.

Getting help

The world of UNIX is a world of commands, but you'd have to be a genius to remember how to use them all. Fortunately, you don't have to. Most commands come with a help manual (called `man` files) you can read. For example, to find help for the `ls` (list) command, do the following:

1. **Open the Terminal.**

2. **Type** man ls.

This displays the manual for the `ls` command (see Figure 55-8).

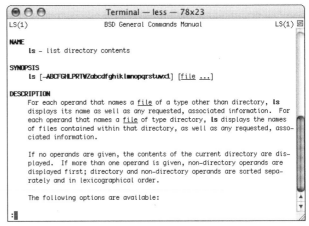

- • **Figure 55-8: The manual for the** `ls` **command.**

3. **Press the spacebar or the F key to go forward.**

4. Press the B key to go backward.

5. Press Q to quit (at any time).

 Many commands also have a help option, which is like a short version of the manual. If it's supported by a command, you would type **command --help** to see that command's help.

A command of history, or a history of commands

Along with tab completion, one of the best ways to save time is to make use of the Terminal's memory. We don't mean memory in a RAM sense, but rather that the Terminal remembers your history of commands. For example, you can use history to re-enter a previously used command:

1. Press the up arrow to display the previously entered command.

Continue to press the up arrow to find earlier commands.

2. Press the down arrow if you went too far.

3. Edit an existing command as needed.

4. Press Return to re-execute it.

A more elaborate but related tool is the history command.

1. After you've used the Terminal for a while, type history and press Return (see Figure 55-9).

The history command shows you what you've done (in order), numbering each.

2. Type !*n* to repeat a command listed by history, where *n* is the line number associated with the command (see Figure 55-10).

As you can see in Figure 55-9, each command is numbered. To rerun the pwd command, for example, type !4 and then press Return.

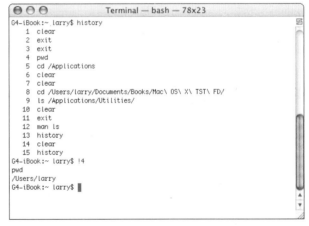

• **Figure 55-9:** The history **command reveals the commands you've recently entered.**

• **Figure 55-10:** Repeat commands with the !*n* **syntax.**

3. Type !*command* to repeat the last version of a specific command (see Figure 55-11).

This version of the history trick tells the Terminal to repeat the last version of whatever the command was. For example, !ls might actually call ls /Applications/Utilities, which you had previously entered.

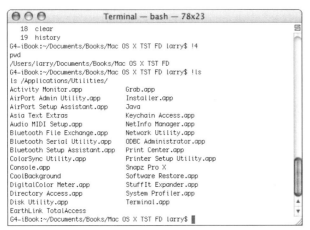

• **Figure 55-11:** The history tool also provides shortcuts by command name.

Do not use the `!command` trick with the `rm` (remove) command. Doing so will most likely permanently remove something that you might not have wanted to remove. Or, it might attempt to remove something that you've already deleted (because that command has already been run).

4. Use the `!command:p` or `!n:p` syntax to see what a command would be (see Figure 55-12).

The `:p` addition will remind you of what a particular command was, rather than execute it. You can use it with the numbering system (`!4:p`) or with the command syntax (`!ls:p`).

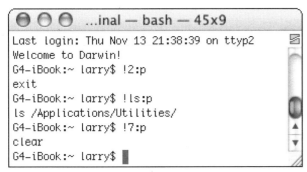

• **Figure 55-12:** The `:p` flag gives you a preview of what command a shortcut would be.

Role playing: Executing commands as another user

One final trick that you'll inevitably need to know is how to execute commands as other users. Most likely, you'll need to execute a command as a more powerful user (like root, see the sidebar). Or, you might want to access another user's files (on your Mac or another). The `sudo` command lets you run a command as another user.

In the following example, we'll show you one use of `sudo`: controlling the built-in Web serving application.

You need to use `sudo` when you get a permission-denied error message in the Terminal.

1. Open a Terminal window.

2. Try starting Apache by using `apachectl start` (see Figure 55-13).

The Apache Web server can be controlled through the Sharing System Preferences panel or via the command line by using `apachectl`. However, you will need to be an administrator to use the command line. Therefore, trying to control Apache as yourself will create errors.

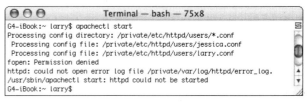

• **Figure 55-13:** Even administrators cannot start Apache when logged in as themselves.

3. Type `sudo apachectl start`.

To run any command as a more powerful user, preface it with `sudo`.

4. Enter your administrative password at the prompt (see Figure 55-14).

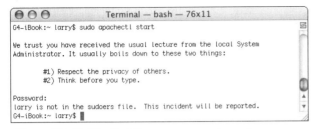

• **Figure 55-14:** The first time you use `sudo`, a strong warning is displayed.

The `sudo` command will recall your administrative password for five minutes after you last used it. If you don't use `sudo` for a few minutes, you'll be required to enter the password again.

Creating a Root User

Your Mac has many users on it, users that are entirely different than those you use to login and access the computer. Of these system users, the most critical is the *root* user. The root user has unlimited powers but is not enabled by default. This is a good thing as it protects your computer from highly detrimental mistakes (only the root user can do very serious damage).

On the other hand, power Mac users who know what they are doing appreciate being able to work as the root user sometimes. Switching over to the root account lets you do those things you need to do without preceding each command with `sudo`. To use the root user feature, you must enable it and create a password, by following these steps:

1. **Open the NetInfo Manager application, which is found in the Utilities folder.**

2. **Select Enable Root User from the Security menu.**

3. **Read the prompt (shown here) and click OK.**

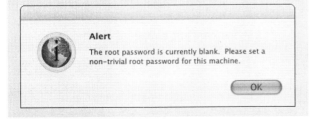

4. **Use the second prompt (see the accompanying figure) to enter the new password and then click OK.**

5. **Enter your administrative password at the prompt in the Authenticate dialog (as shown here) and then click OK.**

6. **Quit the NetInfo Manager.**

7. **In the Terminal, type** su root **and press Return.**

8. **Enter the new root user's password.**

9. **Be very, very, very careful!**

Even though you can create a root user password, you really, really should avoid doing so unless you really know what you're doing and absolutely need a root user.

Making the Terminal and the Finder Play Together Nicely

One of the nice things about the Terminal is how easily it interacts with the Finder. Here's you'll find a couple of tricks to make interactions between the two more seamless.

Using the open command

The open command is a pretty useful little tool. It will use the Finder to open a file, directory, or even a URL. Essentially, open works in the Terminal exactly like how opening a file, folder, URL, or application works in the Finder.

✔ open .: **Opens the current directory in a Finder window (see Figure 55-15)**

• **Figure 55-15:** The open **command makes quick transitions between the Terminal and the Finder.**

Marc has created an AppleScript that can be added to your Finder window toolbars (www.entropy.ch/software/applescript/welcome.html, free). When you click it, it opens the Finder directory in the Terminal.

✔ open *directoryname*: **Opens the directory in a Finder window**

✔ open /Applications/*application_name*: **Opens the application**

Applications in the Applications folder can also be opened by using the -a (open with application) flag. (For example: open -a Calculator.app.)

✔ open http://www.espn.com: **Opens the URL in your default Web browser**

✔ open -a ApplicationName *filename*: **Opens that file in the particular application**

✔ open -e *filename*: **Opens the file in TextEdit**

Drag and drop with the Finder

If the tab completion trick that we discuss earlier isn't good enough for you, here's another timesaver: You can drag and drop items from the Finder into the Terminal.

1. **Open a Terminal window.**

2. **Type cd, followed by a space.**

3. **Switch to the Finder.**

4. **Navigate to the directory that you want to use in a Finder window.**

5. **Click the directory's proxy icon in the window's title bar and drag the icon into the Terminal window.**

6. **Switch back to the Terminal (see Figure 55-16).**

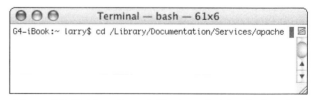

• **Figure 55-16:** Dragging a folder into the Terminal copies that folder's path there.

7. **Press Return to execute the command.**

You can drag and drop anything from the Finder into the Terminal, including folders, files, and applications.

Editing between the Terminal and the Finder

You can also make edits between the Terminal and the Finder. You'll use the Clipboard (of course) to temporary store and retrieve text, but you have two ways of using it:

- ✔ You can select text in the Terminal by using the mouse and then pressing ⌘+C to copy it.

- ✔ You can use the `pbpaste` and `pbcopy` commands.

These last two commands are very handy but not until you're familiar with *piping*. Head over to Technique 57 for information on piping and how to use it with `pbpaste` and `pbcopy`.

Technique 56

Managing and Finding Files Fast

Save Time By

✔ Manipulating your files from the command line

✔ Working with directories

✔ Using the `find` command to locate your stuff

✔ Using the `locate` command to find your stuff

There's no shortage of things that you can do with the Terminal and a command line interface. Many of them, including managing and finding your files, can actually be done faster in the Terminal than they can in the Finder. Plus, the command line options provide for flexibility and automation of tasks that cannot be replicated elsewhere.

In this Technique, you find out the easiest ways to copy, move, rename, and delete your files and directories by using the Terminal. Then you see two different ways to search your hard drive for files and directories.

Copying, Moving, Renaming, and Deleting Files

Managing your files in the Finder is easy to do and relatively quick. But you can also perform the same tasks in the Terminal with many benefits. For example, you can

- ✔ **Move or copy files** from one folder to another without having multiple windows open.

- ✔ **Delete files** without having to empty the Trash. (It's a one-step process.)

- ✔ **Manage files** by using just a few commands rather than a bunch of keyboard shortcuts.

- ✔ **Apply changes to files** that meet a certain naming scheme.

To copy a file, use the `cp` (copy) command:

```
cp source target
```

For example, to make a copy of the myfile.jpg called myfile2.jpg (both of which are in the current directory):

```
cp myfile.jpg myfile2.jpg
cp ~/Documents/Books/chapter.doc ~/Desktop/chapter.doc
```

To copy an entire directory, add the `-R` flag (you must use a capital R):

```
cp -R myfolder ~/Desktop/myfolder
```

 The `cp` command does not warn you if you are about to overwrite an existing file (as the Finder does). To prevent doing something you'll regret, use the `-i` flag: `cp -i source target`. Then `cp` will prompt you before overwriting an existing file (see Figure 56-1).

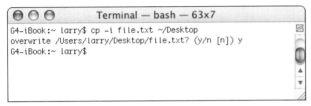

• **Figure 56-1: The `-i` flag tells the Terminal to prompt you before overwriting any files.**

What a Difference a Slash Makes

Note the obscure difference between `cp -R myfolder` and `cp -R myfolder/`. The former copies the directory and its contents to the destination. The latter, because of the trailing forward slash, copies the contents of the directory but not the folder itself. The result of this can be very messy. It can be very confusing to beginners, especially because the tab completion always appends the forward slash. This also applies to the `mv` command.

If you want to move a file, use the `mv` command:

```
mv source target
```

For example

```
mv myfile.txt ~/Desktop/myfile.txt
mv ~/Desktop/afolder /Volumes/Main/afolder
```

 Like the `cp` command, the `mv` command does not warn you if you are about to overwrite an existing file. Again, use the `-i` flag to be prompted when this might happen.

There is no actual rename command in the Terminal. Instead, use `mv` and provide a new name:

```
mv myfile.txt newname.txt
mv ~/Desktop/afolder ~/Desktop/bfolder
```

 The `mv` command cannot create a path, whereas `cp` can. In other words, if you try to copy filename.txt to `/Users/larry/Document/newfiles/filename.txt` and the newfiles directory doesn't exist, the `cp` command will create it for you.

To delete a file, use the `rm` (remove) command:

```
rm filename
rm mydocument.doc
```

 Be very, very careful with the `rm` command. Unlike deleting something in the Finder — which places the item in the Trash to be deleted (emptied) or recovered later — the `rm` command is an immediate deletion. The command does have a `-W` (capital W) flag that attempts to undelete a deleted file. It might let you undelete a file for a few minutes after deletion, but you can't count on that.

The `rm` command can also delete directories, using the `-R` flag:

```
rm -R mydirectory
```

 Command names (`rm`, `cp`, `mv`) are case-insensitive, so `RM`, `Cp`, and `mV` will work equally well. Flags (like the `-R` flag added to `rm`), filenames, and directory names are case-sensitive.

As with `cp` and `mv`, the `-i` flag asks for confirmation before completing the action.

 The absolute worst command that you can ever use is `rm -R /`, which attempts to delete everything on your computer. To avoid running this risk, do not use `rm` with `sudo` (see Technique 55), do not use `rm` when you're logged in as root, and always use the `-i` option to be prompted before disaster strikes.

Another common Finder trick that is replicated in the Terminal is the ability to make an alias. In UNIX terms, these are symbolic links and are created with the ln (make link) command.

```
ln -s file alias
ln -s directory alias
```

Creating and Listing Directories

If you're in the Finder, you always see a directory's contents whether you are in icon, list, or column view mode. In the Terminal — as you might have noticed — you won't see any directory contents unless you specifically ask for them by using the ls (list) command. (See Figure 56-2.)

```
ls
ls ~ (Figure 56-2)
```

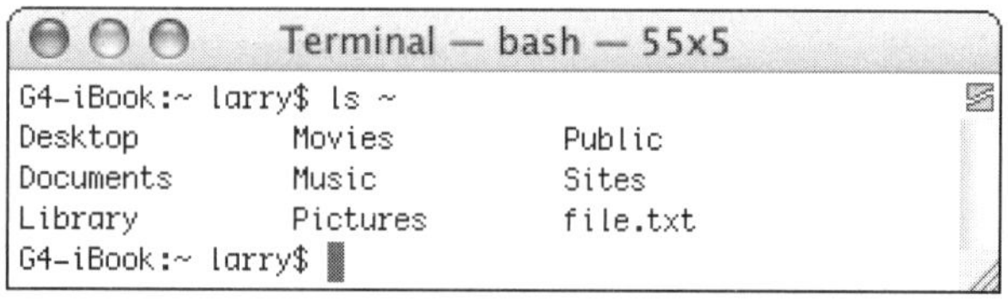

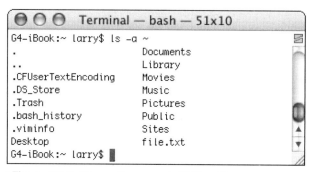

• **Figure 56-2: The listed contents of Larry's Home directory.**

The nice thing is that the ls command lets you view the contents of a directory you're not even in! For example, to see the contents of the Games folder, use

```
ls /Applications/Games
```

Like most commands, ls takes several arguments.

✔ -a: **Use** -a **to view every file, including hidden ones (see Figure 56-3).**

✔ -A: **Use** -A **to view every file, including hidden ones, but not list the current and parent directories (see Figure 56-4). The current and parent directories are represented by one and two periods, respectively.**

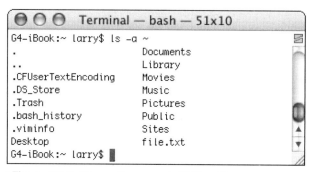

• **Figure 56-3: The** -a **flag reveals hidden files.**

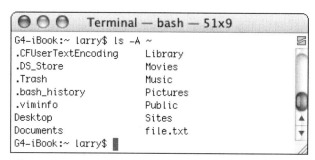

• **Figure 56-4: The** -A **flag is like** -a, **but it omits the current and parent directories.**

✔ -l: **Use** -l **to view more information about the directory contents (see Figure 56-5).**

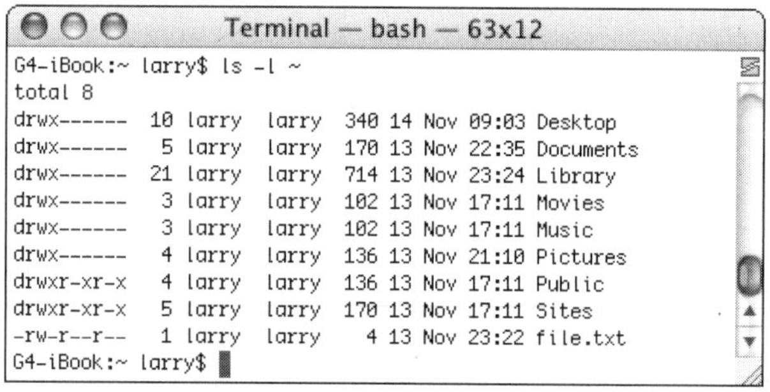

• **Figure 56-5: The** -l **flag shows permissions, ownership, modification date, and more.**

✔ -r: **Use** -r **to sort the directory contents in reverse order by name.**

✔ -S: **Use** -S **to sort the directory contents by size in descending order.**

✔ -t: **Use** -t **to sort the directory contents by time in descending order.**

In the Finder, you can create a new directory by making a new folder. In the Terminal, you use the mkdir (make directory) command:

```
mkdir directoryname
mkdir junk
```

Again, with this command, you can even make a directory without being in the parent directory:

```
mkdir ~/Documents/By\ Application/Excel
```

Conversely, the rmdir (remove directory) command deletes an empty directory:

```
rmdir directoryname
rmdir junk
rmdir ~/Documents/By\ Application/Excel
```

 To delete a full directory, you need to use rm -R directoryname. **To delete an empty directory, use** rmdir directoryname.

Using Wildcards

The true power of the basic Terminal commands comes with using certain wildcards to make less-specific statements.

✔ *: **The asterisk represents zero or more characters.**

✔ ?: **The question mark represents a single character.**

✔ [ ]: **You can place options within brackets.**

For example, if you have a folder full of images, you can move all the JPGs with

```
mv *.jpg /path/to/new/destination
```

Or, you can delete all the files that begin with the word chapter:

```
rm -i chapter*
```

The best way to learn how to use wildcards is to test your command first by preceding it with echo. The result of this is to display (in the Terminal screen) the affected files rather than actually affecting the files (see Figure 56-6).

```
● ● ●        ...inal — bash — 46x5
G4-iBook:~ larry$ echo rm D*
rm Desktop Documents
G4-iBook:~ larry$ ▊
```

• **Figure 56-6: Use** echo **to preview the results of a command.**

 Run your rm commands with echo first to see what the effect will be before you remove a bunch of files.

Using the find Command

The find command alone is a really good reason to use the Terminal. It provides a quick and flexible search capability. Although find has a number of options, the easiest way to use it is like so:

```
find -f directory --name 'filename'
```

For example:

```
find -f ~/Documents --name 'chapter.doc'
```

To search for a file in the current directory, use

```
find . --name 'filename'
```

Other options include the ability to search for files by type. A type of f restricts the find to files, and d limits it to directories.

```
find -f ~ --name 'book*' -type f
find -f ~ --name 'book*' -type d
```

You can add a number to the end to indicate a modification date within a certain number of days from now. The following applies only to files modified in the last 24 hours:

```
find -f ~ --name 'book*' -type f -1
```

The find tool can also be used without a filename, in which case it returns all the contents for the named directory and all its subdirectories, as shown in Figure 56-7:

```
find ~/Sites
```

```
● ● ●              ...minal — bash — 47x9
G4-iBook:~ larry$ find ~/Sites
/Users/larry/Sites
/Users/larry/Sites/.localized
/Users/larry/Sites/images
/Users/larry/Sites/images/apache_pb.gif
/Users/larry/Sites/images/macosxlogo.gif
/Users/larry/Sites/images/web_share.gif
/Users/larry/Sites/index.html
G4-iBook:~ larry$
```

• **Figure 56-7: All the directory contents and subdirectory contents are listed by using** find.

In this way, the find tool can be a much more potent version of the ls command. In fact, another easy to remember trick is to use the -ls flag with find, as shown in Figure 56-8:

```
find ~/Sites -ls
```

```
● ● ●                     Terminal — bash — 108x9
G4-iBook:~ larry$ find ~/Sites -ls
249349   0 drwxr-xr-x   5 larry   larry       170 Nov 13 17:11 /Users/larry/Sites
249350   0 -rw-r--r--   1 larry   larry         0 Nov 13 17:11 /Users/larry/Sites/.localized
249351   0 drwxr-xr-x   5 larry   larry       170 Nov 13 17:11 /Users/larry/Sites/images
249352   8 -rw-r--r--   1 larry   larry      2326 Nov 13 17:11 /Users/larry/Sites/images/apache_pb.gif
249353   8 -rw-r--r--   1 larry   larry      2829 Nov 13 17:11 /Users/larry/Sites/images/macosxlogo.gif
249354   8 -rw-r--r--   1 larry   larry      3698 Nov 13 17:11 /Users/larry/Sites/images/web_share.gif
249355  16 -rw-r--r--   1 larry   larry      5754 Nov 13 17:11 /Users/larry/Sites/index.html
G4-iBook:~ larry$
```

• **Figure 56-8: The same directory as in Figure 56-7, displaying more information.**

All in all, the find tool is one of the most useful command line utilities. As an example, if you're looking for a file called something like quotes.doc or quotations.doc, and it's somewhere in your Documents directory, do this:

1. **Open a Terminal window.**

2. **Type find -f ~/Documents --name quot*.doc -type f and press Return (see Figure 56-9).**

This command searches through the Documents directory (and its subfolders) looking for a file whose name begins with *quot* and ends with *.doc*.

```
● ● ●                Terminal — bash — 94x7
G4-iBook:~/Documents/Other Documents larry$ find -f ~/Documents --name quot*.doc -type f
/Users/larry/Documents/.DS_Store
/Users/larry/Documents/.localized
/Users/larry/Documents/Books/.DS_Store
/Users/larry/Documents/Other Documents/quotes.doc
quotes.doc
G4-iBook:~/Documents/Other Documents larry$
```

• **Figure 56-9: The directories searched and the files found are returned.**

3. **If you see your desired file, open it with** open /path/to/*filename*.

4. **If you don't see your desired file, rerun the** find **with a new command.**

You can also use grep to find files. grep is a regular expressions tool (*regular expressions* being a very useful, and not easy to learn, method of creating patterns to match). For more information, see a good UNIX (or regular expressions) book or search the Internet for tutorials.

Using the locate Command

Another option for finding files is to use the locate command. But before you can use this, you need to create the locate database and then update this database frequently. The updatedb command is used to create and update the locate database.

1. **Open a Terminal window.**

2. **Type** sudo /usr/libexec/locate.updatedb **to create the database.**

3. **Type** locate *filename* **to look for a particular file.**

As you can see, locate is faster than find but requires the initial creation of a database (which is really just an index) in order to function. Here are some tips for getting the most out of this simple command:

✔ Run the updatedb tool frequently (to update the database) in order for your searches to be up-to-date and accurate.

✔ Create a cron (see Technique 53) to automatically run the updatedb command.

✔ Use wildcards in your filename to create a more flexible search.

✔ For a good tutorial on locate, see www.kingcomputerservices.com/unix_101/using_find_to_locate_files.htm.

Technique 57

Piping and Redirecting Output with the Terminal

Most beginning command line users are able to execute simple commands in the Terminal to accomplish basic tasks. But the advanced user also understands the concepts of standard input and output: controlling *where* a command's results are directed. You can do this with piping and redirection output. This Technique focuses primarily on those two subjects, but we first discuss a few other useful commands that can be used in conjunction with piping.

Handy Commands to Use with Piping

This book's Techniques relating to the Terminal cover the most efficient ways to use the most common and useful commands, but we also want to mention a few other tools that you'll likely appreciate. These commands can be used independently, but you'll find them particularly useful in conjunction with piping and output redirection.

The wc (word count) command is used to count the number of lines, words, and characters in a file:

```
wc filename
wc chapter57.txt
```

The output of this command is very simple. It returns the number of lines, words, and characters (see Figure 57-1). In the figure, for example, you can see that the Installer Log File contains 0 lines, 3,803 words, and 47,647 characters. If you only want to see some of these values, use the different flags to control output:

- l: For lines
- w: For words
- c: For characters

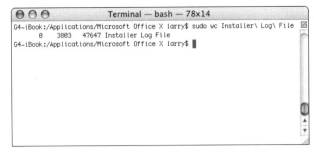

• **Figure 57-1:** Run `wc` to get statistics on a file.

You can also change the position of the flags to control the order in which results are returned. For example, `wc -wl filename` returns just the number of words and lines; `wc -cw filename` returns the number of characters and *then* the number of words.

 You can use the `wc` command with piping to return the number of items in a directory. For more information, see "Combining Commands with Pipes."

 As with everything in the Terminal, command names (`wc`, `sort`, `ps`) are case-insensitive, so `WC`, `Sort`, and `pS` will work equally well. Flags (like the `-w` flag added to `wc`), filenames, and directory names are case-sensitive.

The `sort` command sorts a file alphabetically and returns the sorted list:

```
sort filename
```

The `sort` command takes several arguments to adjust its parameters:

- b: Ignores any blank spaces at the beginning of a line
- d: Sorts in phone-directory order (ignoring everything but letters, numbers, and blank spaces)
- f: Performs a case-insensitive sort
- r: Sorts in reverse order

 You can actually use `sort` to see whether a file is already sorted: Use `sort -c filename`.

The `ps` command lists currently running processes (think *process status*). A *process* is UNIX-speak for a running application, service, or technology. This command is very easy to use:

```
ps flags
```

The relevant parameters (flags) for this command are

- a: Shows all processes, not just the ones you're running
- c: Shows a minimal version of the process name
- m: Sorts the list of running processes by memory usage
- r: Sorts the list of running processes by CPU usage
- U: Shows the process for a particular user

 The functionality of the `ps` command is duplicated in the Finder by the Process Viewer utility.

Finally, the `du` command displays disk usage statistics. It takes several flags:

- k: Returns the statistics in megabytes
- h: Makes the result more readable for humans
- s: Shows the results for every file
- c: Totals the statistics

Here are several practical examples of this command. To view

- Total disk usage of the current directory, type **du -sh** (see Figure 57-2).

...al — bash — 43x5
G4-iBook:~ larry$ du -sh
3.9M .
G4-iBook:~ larry$

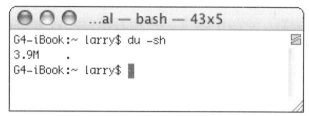

• **Figure 57-2: Larry's Home directory uses a whopping 3.9MB of space.**

- Disk usage of individual files in the current directory (and its subdirectories), type **du -h** (see Figure 57-3).

...al — bash — 45x24
0B ./Library/Internet Plug-Ins
0B ./Library/Keyboard Layouts
20K ./Library/Keychains
4.0K ./Library/Logs/CrashReporter
4.0K ./Library/Logs
12K ./Library/Preferences/ByHost
8.0K ./Library/Preferences/Explorer
120K ./Library/Preferences
0B ./Library/Printers
0B ./Library/Safari/Icons
72K ./Library/Safari
0B ./Library/Snapz Pro X/Watermarks
0B ./Library/Snapz Pro X
0B ./Library/Sounds
2.0M ./Library
0B ./Movies
0B ./Music
36K ./Pictures
0B ./Public/Drop Box
0B ./Public
12K ./Sites/images
20K ./Sites
3.9M .
G4-iBook:~ larry$

• **Figure 57-3: The** du **command can show the size of every file.**

- Disk usage of a specific directory, type **du -h ~/Desktop** (see Figure 57-4).

...al — bash — 44x6
G4-iBook:~ larry$ du -h ~/Desktop
1.0M /Users/larry/Desktop/Ch 64 figures
444K /Users/larry/Desktop/Ch 65 figures
0B /Users/larry/Desktop/Ch_66_figures
1.7M /Users/larry/Desktop
G4-iBook:~ larry$

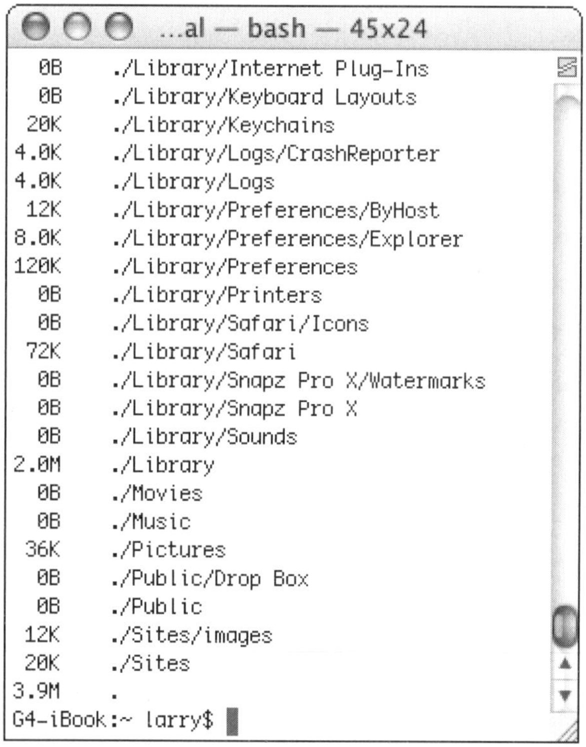

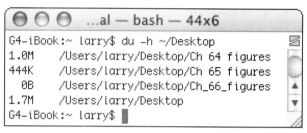

• **Figure 57-4: You can limit** du **to a specific directory.**

- Size of a specific file in kilobytes, type **du *filename*** (see Figure 57-5).

Terminal — bash — 55x7
G4-iBook:~ larry$ du ~/Desktop/558129\ fg6602.tiff
144 /Users/larry/Desktop/558129 fg6602.tiff
G4-iBook:~ larry$

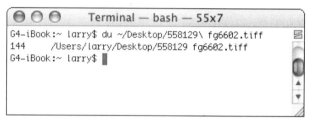

• **Figure 57-5: Show a file's size.**

Combining Commands with Pipes

Pipes are one of the most important timesaving command line tools. As you can see, commands normally send their *output* (the result of the command) to the *display* (the Terminal). By using pipes, you can send the output of one command to be used as the input for another. This is accomplished by the *pipe operator*, a vertical bar (found above the backslash key), to join multiple commands together:

```
output_command | input_command
```

For example, here's how you would find the number of processes that you have running:

1. **Open a Terminal window.**
2. **Type** ps -auxU *username* **to see all your processes.**

3. Type ps -auxU *username* | wc -l **to view the number of your processes (see Figure 57-6).**

```
G4-iBook:~ larry$ ps -auxU larry
USER    PID %CPU %MEM   VSZ    RSS TT STAT STARTED    TIME COMMAND
larry   660  2.0  0.4  67060   1652 ?? S   11:20AM  0:01.04 /Library
larry   647  0.0  0.9  89056   3380 ?? S   11:20AM  0:01.89 /System/
larry   651  0.0  0.4  44900   1724 ?? Ss  11:20AM  0:00.51 /System/
larry   654  0.0  0.6  95320   2544 ?? S   11:20AM  0:00.47 /System/
larry   656  0.0  2.9 120940  11232 ?? S   11:20AM  0:03.69 /System/
larry   659  0.0  3.7 132072  14468 ?? S   11:20AM  0:13.88 /Applica
larry   662  0.0  1.3 107880   5020 ?? S   11:20AM  0:01.14 /System/
larry   663  0.0  2.2 152024   8800 ?? S   11:20AM  1:24.72 /Applica
larry   646  0.0  1.2  82764   4784 ?? Ss  11:20AM  0:01.16 /System/
larry   665  0.0  0.2  18644    800 std S  11:20AM  0:00.29 -bash
G4-iBook:~ larry$ ps -auxU larry | wc -l
      12
G4-iBook:~ larry$ 
```

• **Figure 57-6: Use the pipe with multiple commands to fine-tune your results.**

Or, if you want to see how many items you have in a particular directory, do this:

1. **Open a Terminal window.**

2. Type ls *directoryname* **to list the files in the directory.**

3. Type ls *directoryname* | wc -l **to view the number of files in the directory.**

4. Type ls -A *directoryname* | wc -l **to view the number of files in the directory, including hidden files (see Figure 57-7).**

```
G4-iBook:~ larry$ ls ~
Desktop        Movies        Public
Documents      Music         Sites
Library        Pictures      file.txt
G4-iBook:~ larry$ ls ~ | wc -l
       9
G4-iBook:~ larry$ ls -A ~ | wc -l
      14
G4-iBook:~ larry$ 
G4-iBook:~ larry$ 
```

• **Figure 57-7: Use the pipe with multiple commands to fine-tune your results.**

Or, if you want to find every file with an extension of *TIFF* or *TIF* or *tiff* or *tif*, you can use the find command with grep:

```
find . | grep -i tif
```

We don't cover the grep command much in this book, but you'll get a sense of what it can do from this example. The find command returns all the files in the current directory and subdirectory. This list is then sent to the grep utility, which removes every file that doesn't include some version of *tif* (the i flag means that it should ignore case). The result of grep is then sent to the Terminal (see Figure 57-8).

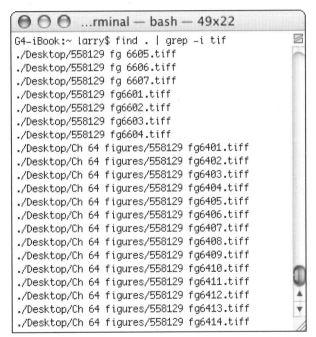

```
G4-iBook:~ larry$ find . | grep -i tif
./Desktop/558129 fg 6605.tiff
./Desktop/558129 fg 6606.tiff
./Desktop/558129 fg 6607.tiff
./Desktop/558129 fg6601.tiff
./Desktop/558129 fg6602.tiff
./Desktop/558129 fg6603.tiff
./Desktop/558129 fg6604.tiff
./Desktop/Ch 64 figures/558129 fg6401.tiff
./Desktop/Ch 64 figures/558129 fg6402.tiff
./Desktop/Ch 64 figures/558129 fg6403.tiff
./Desktop/Ch 64 figures/558129 fg6404.tiff
./Desktop/Ch 64 figures/558129 fg6405.tiff
./Desktop/Ch 64 figures/558129 fg6406.tiff
./Desktop/Ch 64 figures/558129 fg6407.tiff
./Desktop/Ch 64 figures/558129 fg6408.tiff
./Desktop/Ch 64 figures/558129 fg6409.tiff
./Desktop/Ch 64 figures/558129 fg6410.tiff
./Desktop/Ch 64 figures/558129 fg6411.tiff
./Desktop/Ch 64 figures/558129 fg6412.tiff
./Desktop/Ch 64 figures/558129 fg6413.tiff
./Desktop/Ch 64 figures/558129 fg6414.tiff
```

• **Figure 57-8: Use a pipe with grep to help narrow a search.**

Another good use of piping is to find the largest directories on your computer. You can do this by combining the du and sort commands (see Figure 57-9).

```
du -sk * | sort -nr
```

```
000          Terminal — bash — 65x11
G4-iBook:~ larry$ du -sk * | sort -nr
2088    Library
2068    Desktop
36      Pictures
24      Documents
20      Sites
4       file.txt
0       Public
0       Music
0       Movies
G4-iBook:~ larry$
```

• **Figure 57-9: Use piping to find the largest directories by size.**

The du -sk * syntax calculates the size of all the items (indicated by the asterisk) in the current directory. (Larry was in his Home directory when he ran it, so it will check his files.) This is then piped through the sort command, which places this list in numerically reverse order. You can be more exhaustive by using cd to go into a directory and then use the history command's !du to repeat this piping procedure:

```
cd Library

!du
```

As a final example of using pipes, you can use the pbpaste and pbcopy commands, which allow you to move data on and off the Clipboard while you're working with the command line. This means that these two commands are the ultimate glue for transferring text between regular Mac applications and UNIX tools:

✔ pbpaste **outputs the current contents of the Clipboard (presumably put there by a standard Mac OS X application) to the Terminal.** You then use output redirection or a pipe to feed this output to a file or to a second UNIX program that does something useful with the data.

✔ pbcopy **works the other way around, putting data onto the Clipboard.** The data is placed on the right side of a pipe, which means that the output of some other UNIX program is piped into pbcopy. The output of the first program is stored on the Clipboard, where it can be accessed from Mac applications by pressing ⌘+V.

As an example, here's how to use these commands to create a TextEdit file that lists the contents of the /etc directory:

1. **Open a Terminal window.**

2. **Type** ls -A /etc | pbcopy **and press Return (see Figure 57-10).**

The ls command is executed (the -A means it should list everything), but you won't see any results displayed in the Terminal. Instead, they're pasted onto the Clipboard.

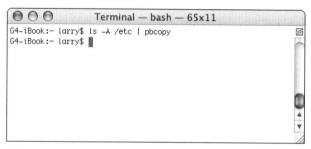

```
000          Terminal — bash — 65x11
G4-iBook:~ larry$ ls -A /etc | pbcopy
G4-iBook:~ larry$
```

• **Figure 57-10: Send the results of a command to the Clipboard.**

3. **Open TextEdit.**

4. **Create a new document.**

5. **Press ⌘+V to paste the Clipboard contents into the document (see Figure 57-11).**

Alternatively, you can use pbpaste to take the Clipboard contents and do something with them. For example, if you're writing an e-mail and want to know how long it is, do this:

1. **Open your e-mail message in Mail.**

2. **Select the entire message body by pressing ⌘+A.**

3. **Open a Terminal window.**

4. **Type** pbpaste | wc -w **and press Return (see Figure 57-12).**

• **Figure 57-11: The results of the** `ls` **command have been passed into the TextEdit document.**

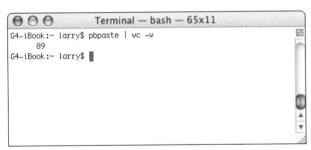

• **Figure 57-12: Piping the Clipboard contents through the word count command.**

5. If you wanted, you could store the number of words back in the Clipboard by using `pbpaste | wc -w | pbcopy`.

A more advanced level of piping uses the `tee` command. `tee` lets the output go to a command but also saves it to a file (think of it like a plumbing T, where the water splits in two opposite directions):

```
output_command | tee filename | input_
    othercommand

ls -A /path/to/directory | tee ~/
    contents.txt | wc -l
```

The above command lists (`ls`) all (`-A`) of the contents of a directory. Instead of displaying these contents, they are instead stored in a text file called `contents.txt` (located in the Home directory). The result of the `ls` command is also sent to the `wc` command, which returns the number of items (by counting the number of lines).

Redirecting Output

Your Terminal uses the notion of STDIN (standard input), STDOUT (standard output), and STDERR (standard error) to control the flow of information. These are each channels for information to travel through. For example, the `ls` command receives arguments through the Terminal (STDIN) and sends its results to the Terminal screen (STDOUT). But it doesn't have to work this way. As you can see with piping, you can send the standard output to another command rather than the Terminal. Likewise, a command can take its input from the output of another command. You can also add files to the mix by using output redirection.

To indicate that a command should take its input from a file, use `<`:

```
command < sourcefile
```

Use `<` in cases where the command normally takes its input from the keyboard. Many commands — including `more`, `head`, `tail`, `pine`, and `vi` — take filenames as arguments by default, so using `<` is unnecessary.

Comparatively, to redirect standard output to a file instead of displaying it in the Terminal screen, use `>`:

```
command > filename
```

For example, you can create a text file listing the contents of a directory by using

```
ls -la ~/Documents >
    ~/Desktop/documents_listing.txt
```

You should be aware that this technique overwrites any existing file contents and creates the file if it doesn't already exist. If you want to build upon an existing file or not risk overwriting a file, use >:

```
command >> filename
```

This syntax appends the output to the existing file, adding it at the end. For example:

```
ls -l ~/Documents >> ~/Desktop/listing.txt
ls -l ~/Music >> ~/Desktop/listing.txt
ls -l ~/Pictures >> ~/Desktop/listing.txt
```

Essentially, this how your system logs function: All messages created by the process being monitored are appended to the existing system log.

The > operator erases any existing contents in the named file. To be extra careful, use > instead!

Viewing and Editing Text Files

The last of the major Terminal techniques that we discuss deals with viewing and editing text files. Although you can easily do this in the Finder with TextEdit, BBEdit, and the like, here are some good reasons for working with text files in the Terminal:

- ✔ Accessing hidden files is easier in the Terminal.
- ✔ If you're already in the Terminal, you might not want to switch applications.
- ✔ You might already be working on a remote server.

In this Technique, you master two basic commands for viewing a text file. Then you see two other handy commands that will display only a portion of a text file — a real timesaver. Finally, you see how to perform basic edits of a text file in the Terminal by using the pico editor.

Viewing Files

Because UNIX comes with a gazillion little utilities, each of which does a specific thing, separate commands exist for viewing files as well for editing files. Obviously, you can use an editing tool to just view a file, but why would you want to? By using one of the two commands for viewing a file, you can simplify the experience.

cat

The cat command is actually short for *concatenation,* which is the process of appending one thing to another. The command's intention is to take several files as arguments and then display them all in order, as if their contents constituted one large file. You can use cat to do this, showing multiple files at once, or you can use it to display a single file (see Figure 58-1).

The syntax for this command is simply

    cat filename

For example, to view the Apache Web Server's configuration file, type

```
cat /etc/httpd/httpd.conf
```

```
●○○                  bash — ⌘1
G4-iBook:~ larry$ cat /etc/httpd/httpd.conf
##
## httpd.conf -- Apache HTTP server configuration file
##

#
# Based upon the NCSA server configuration files originally by Rob McCo
ol.
#
# This is the main Apache server configuration file.  It contains the
# configuration directives that give the server its instructions.
# See <URL:http://www.apache.org/docs/> for detailed information about
# the directives.
#
# Do NOT simply read the instructions in here without understanding
# what they do.  They're here only as hints or reminders.  If you are u
nsure
# consult the online docs. You have been warned.
```

• **Figure 58-1: Use** `cat` **to view Apache's configuration file.**

These two examples demonstrate how you can use `cat` to view multiple files at once (each appended to the next):

```
cat myfile.txt myfile2.txt
cat myfile.txt ~/Documents/myfile2.txt
   ~/ Desktop/myfile3.txt
```

You can make `cat` a little more useful by using either the `-n` flag to number the lines as they're displayed or by using `-b`, which numbers all but the blank lines. You can also use `cat` with the pipe or output redirection. (For more on output redirection and piping, see Technique 57.) For example:

```
cat myfile1.txt myfile2.txt > newfile.txt
```

creates a new file (named `newfile.txt` in this example) by putting the other two (`myfile1.txt` and `myfile2.txt`) together.

This command tells you how many lines the two files together contain (1,687 in the example shown in Figure 58-2):

```
cat myfile1.txt myfile2.txt | wc -l
```

• **Figure 58-2: Use** `cat` **to pipe two files through the** `wc` **command.**

Do not try to concatenate two files with the command `cat myfile1.txt myfile2.txt > myfile1.txt`. **This will not append the** `myfile2.txt` **contents to** `myfile1.txt`, **but rather destroy the original** `myfile1.txt` **contents and then add the** `myfile2.txt` **contents to it. If you want to concatenate** `myfile1.txt` **to** `myfile2.txt`, **do so in a new file.**

more or less

The `cat` utility is great for quickly looking at a file — even though that's not what it was originally intended for — but it lacks certain features. Namely, you can't move around too much within the `cat` command. As a step up from this, UNIX normally comes with a `more` command, which displays a file one page at a time. After the `more` command is displaying a file, you can then press the spacebar (or the F key) to paginate forward or Q to quit.

Sadly, your Mac doesn't have `more` on it. What it has instead is its successor, `less` (and no, we're not making this up). The `less` command is faster than `more` and lets you page backward, too. To use `less`, simply type

```
less filename
```

For example (the result of the second command is displayed in Figure 58-3):

```
less ~/Documents/myfile.txt
less /etc/httpd/httpd.conf
```

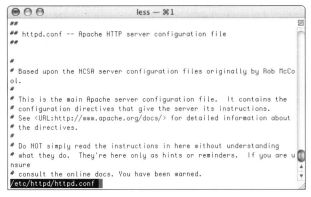

• **Figure 58-3: Use** `less` **to view a file one page at a time.**

Familiarize yourself with `less` because all `man` pages are displayed by using it. For more on the `man` (manual) command, see Technique 55.

Here are the basic commands for moving around after you're in `less`:

✔ Press H at any time to see all the commands (see Figure 58-4).

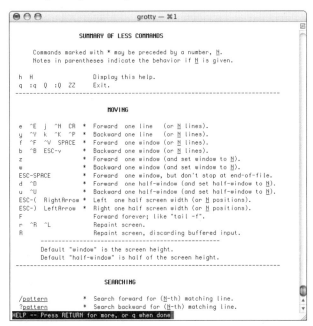

• **Figure 58-4: The help page for** `less`.

✔ Press F to scroll forward one page.

✔ Press B to scroll backward one page.

✔ Press Return to scroll forward one line.

✔ Press D to scroll forward one-half page.

✔ Press Y to scroll backward one-half page.

✔ Press Q to quit.

You can also precede the `d`, `b`, `f`, `Return`, and `y` commands with a number to move that many lines. For example, `10f` moves forward 10 lines, and `20b` moves backwards 20 lines. Similarly, `g` preceded by a number goes to a specific line. (`1g` goes to the first line, and `169g` moves to line 169.)

Type **man less** or **less --help** to see all the options, including how to perform searches.

Your Mac has a utility called `more` on it, but it's the same thing as `less` (it's not really `more`, it's just called `more`). In fact, if you check out the manual for `more` (`man more`), you'll see the manual for `less`. Marc's explanation for this phenomenon is that sometimes less is more. You can't argue with that.

Viewing Parts of Files

If you don't need to view an entire file, you have no reason to use `less`. Viewing just the part that you need saves time. Use the `head` command to view just the first few lines of a file or `tail` to view just the last few lines:

```
head myfile.txt
tail ~/Documents/file.txt
```

Both of these commands take an `n` flag to dictate how many lines to display (see Figure 58-5 and Figure 58-6):

```
head -n 5 /etc/httpd/httpd.conf
```

• **Figure 58-5:** When using head, **you can view just the first few lines of a file.**

```
tail -n 15 /etc/httpd/httpd.conf
```

• **Figure 58-6:** When using tail, **you can view just the last several lines of a file.**

The tail command has a couple of other useful flags. These are

✔ -r: **Shows the lines in reverse order**

✔ -f: **Keeps the** tail **utility running** (tail will continue to show the last lines of a file — even as lines are added to the file — until you press Control+C to stop it)

 You can view system logs with tail by using tail -f logname. **This will keep the** tail utility running, persistently updating you as the system log changes. In other words, the last ten lines (the default number of lines to display) are always displayed onscreen, even as lines are added to the log. This is essentially the functionality duplicated with the Console utility. This is extremely useful to Web developers and system administrators.

Editing Files

If you want to edit files in the Terminal, you have several options:

✔ pico: **A bare-bones application**

✔ vi: **A more advanced text editor**

✔ vim: **A modified version of** vi

✔ emacs: **Perhaps the most powerful text editor**

To keep this simple, we briefly discuss pico in this chapter. If you find yourself doing command line editing frequently, you ought to learn vim or emacs. (Panther doesn't actually have vi on it, just vim.) Here is the good, the bad, and the ugly about vi, vim, and emacs:

✔ **They're all very powerful after you master them.**

✔ **They're difficult to master and not even remotely intuitive to learn.**

✔ **Never, under any circumstances, suggest to someone that** vi **or** vim **or** emacs **is any better or worse than any other text editor.**

If you do, you'll never hear the end of that person's diatribe. (This is a point of serious contention among computer geeks.)

 In Technique 59, we demonstrate how to set your default text editor.

The pico editor is really easy to use. Here's all you need to know:

1. Type pico *filename* **to open a file.**

 Type **pico new***filename* to create a new file with that name.

2. Type the text you want (see Figure 58-7).

This might seem like an absurd statement. As a comparison, `vim` requires you to press I to begin inserting characters. You cannot just type away on other applications.

• **Figure 58-7:** Working in the `pico` **text editor.**

3. **Press Delete to remove characters.**

Again, as a comparison, to delete characters in `vim`, you press the X key.

4. **Press Control+O to save your work.**

After you press this command, you'll be prompted with what filename to use (see Figure 58-8). Press Return to use the default filename listed. To change the filename, press the Delete key to delete the default name and then type in the new name.

• **Figure 58-8:** Saving a file in `pico`.

5. **Press Control+X to exit** `pico`.

If you haven't saved your work, you'll be given the option to do so (`pico` calls the changes a *modified buffer*) before exiting.

6. **To copy or cut a section of code, do this (you cannot use the mouse to move around, you must use the arrow keys):**

a. Place your cursor where you want to begin.

b. Press Control+Shift+6 to mark the beginning of the area to be copied.

c. Move your cursor to the end. (The selected text will be highlighted.)

d. Press Control+K to cut the selected text.

e. Move the cursor to where you want to paste the text.

f. Press Control+U to paste the selected text.

 `pico` **doesn't actually have a** `copy` **command. To copy some text, cut it, paste it back in its original place, and then paste it again in the new location.**

Don't forget that you can also edit text files by using Finder tools — but launch those from the Terminal. For example:

✔ `open -e filename`: Opens a file in TextEdit

✔ `open -a applicationname filename`: Opens a file in the named application

✔ `bbedit filename`: Opens a file in BBEdit

 BBEdit also has an option to open hidden files directly in the application.

Technique 59

Customizing Your Terminal

Save Time By

✔ Using the Terminal Preferences panel to adjust its behavior

✔ Working with Terminal Preferences files

✔ Choosing a shell

✔ Creating special files to set shell settings

✔ Checking out freeware for working with the Terminal

Because the previous several Techniques — and much of what the more advanced Mac user does — depends upon the Terminal application, knowing how to adjust its behavior is well worth the time spent. In this Technique, we begin with the different preference settings the application itself has to offer and how they relate to using this tool most effectively. Then we show you the benefits of the different shells that you can use. (A *shell* is a tool that allows you to interact with the operating system.) Afterward, you figure out how to use special preferences files that affect your shell. Finally, we discuss a few cool related freeware and shareware applications.

Adjusting Terminal's Preferences

The Terminal actually has two different areas for setting its preferences:

✔ The Terminal Preferences panel (see Figure 59-1)

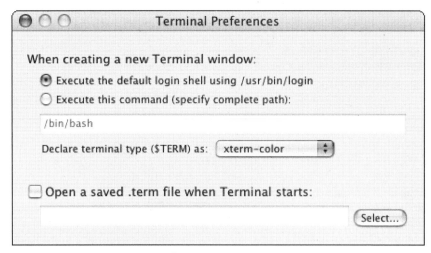

• **Figure 59-1: The Terminal Preferences panel has limited uses.**

✔ Window Settings, also called *Terminal Inspector* (see Figure 59-2)

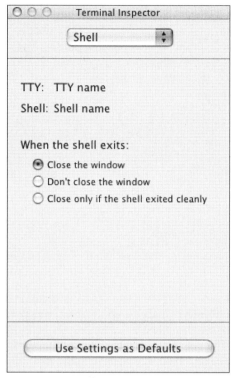

• **Figure 59-2: The Terminal's Window Settings controls much of the Terminal's behavior.**

Each of these is accessible under the Terminal menu. The Terminal Preferences panel is great if you know what you're doing, whereas the latter is for more general-purpose and cosmetic adjustments.

The Terminal Preferences panel has three settings:

✔ What to execute when a new Terminal window is created

✔ How to identify the type of Terminal

✔ What, if any, `.term` file to open when a new Terminal window is created

You probably don't want to mess with the first two, but the last can be handy, as you'll see in the section "Creating Terminal Preferences Files" later in this Technique.

The Window Settings dialog lets you adjust many different features. Each setting can be altered by selecting the general option (listed next) from the pull-down menu at the top of the window. Each subsequent panel uses some combination of radio buttons, check boxes, and/or pull-down menus.

✔ **Shell:** The only thing you can do here is dictate what the Terminal does when you exit a shell. Most likely, you'll want to close the window.

 To change what shell you use by default, use the Terminal Preferences panel. Read about the different shells in the upcoming section, "Choosing Your Shell."

✔ **Processes:** Don't touch the processes unless you really, really know what you're doing. For most, the best use of the Processes panel is to see what processes are running, particularly if you have some going in the background.

✔ **Emulation:** The Emulation panel lets you control how the Terminal behaves (in other words, what other tools it behaves like). You probably don't want to mess around here unless you decide to turn on the audio and visual bells.

✔ **Buffer:** The Buffer panel controls how much of the data the Terminal has received is retained in memory. You definitely want to enable this, and the 10,000-line default is sufficient for most users. You can also tweak the Scrollback settings here.

✔ **Display:** Use the Display panel to set how your Terminal looks (see Figure 59-3). You can choose a cursor, a font, and how characters look on the screen. Most importantly, select the Enable Drag Copy/Paste of Text check box so you can easily copy and paste between the Terminal and the Finder.

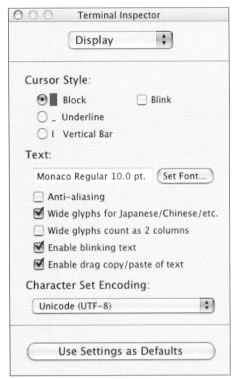

• **Figure 59-3:** Use the Display panel to make your Terminal more cosmetically pleasing.

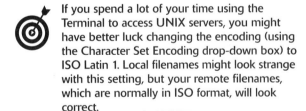

If you spend a lot of your time using the Terminal to access UNIX servers, you might have better luck changing the encoding (using the Character Set Encoding drop-down box) to ISO Latin 1. Local filenames might look strange with this setting, but your remote filenames, which are normally in ISO format, will look correct.

✔ **Color:** This panel is completely cosmetic, but what's wrong with that? Most likely you'll want to use black text on a white background for legibility, but if you don't worry about your eyesight, go wild. You can even use an image as the background, although you'll have to be careful with the text color or else you'll have a hard time using the Terminal (see Figure 59-4).

• **Figure 59-4:** For the truly stylish Terminal geek, use an image for the background.

✔ **Window:** This panel is also cosmetic but is worth tinkering with. You'll want to set the dimensions of the Terminal so that it fits nicely on your screen. The title section of this window lets you give your Terminal a useful or silly title. In Figure 59-5, for example, the Terminal title shows the current command being run (vim) and the keyboard shortcut to access this window (⌘+1).

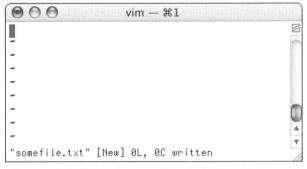

• **Figure 59-5:** Customize your Terminal title with the Window panel.

If you use the Terminal a lot, you can save a lot of time by giving your Terminal windows a useful title. By doing so, you'll be able to easily select the right Terminal window by seeing its name in Exposé or when it's minimized in the Dock. We recommend that your Terminal title comprise

▶ The active process name

▶ The .term filename (if a .term file — see "Creating Terminal Preferences Files" — is being used)

▶ The command key (⌘) shortcut

 You can also resize the Terminal window at any time by clicking and dragging the lower-right corner. This is likely to mess up the existing Terminal display, though.

✔ **Keyboard:** The Keyboard tool is just downright fantastic for people who use the Terminal regularly. It allows you to map commands or text to certain key combinations.

For example, with the Keyboard tool, you could make a shortcut to list the current directory's contents as you want them:

1. **Open the Keyboard panel of the Window Settings (see Figure 59-6).**

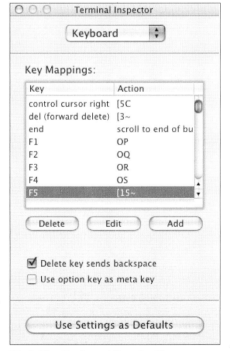

• **Figure 59-6: The Keyboard Terminal Inspector panel.**

2. **Select the F5 line in the list of keys.**

3. **Click the Edit button.**

4. **In the resulting dialog, select Shift from the Modifier drop-down list.**

5. **Leave the Action drop-down as is ("send string to shell").**

6. **In the text box, type** du -sk * | sort -nr **(see Figure 59-7).**

This is the basic command that you want to execute. It returns a list of files or folders and their disk usage, sorted from most to least.

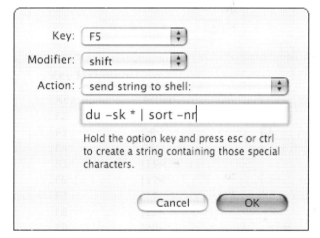

• **Figure 59-7: Use the prompt to add a keyboard shortcut.**

7. **Hold down the Option key and then press Return.**

The Option+Return combination adds a Return to the end of the command so that you don't have to press Return after using the keyboard shortcut.

8. **Click OK or press Return.**

9. **To use the shortcut, press Shift+F5 (or Shift+fn+F5 on a laptop).**

See the results in Figure 59-8.

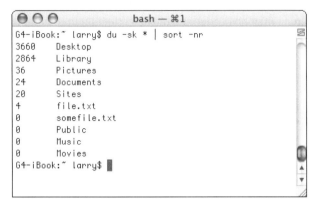

• **Figure 59-8:** Create keyboard shortcuts to run common commands quickly.

You can also add new keyboard shortcuts (instead of editing existing ones) by clicking the Add button in the Keyboard panel.

After you customize the Terminal, click the Use Settings as Defaults button. If you want to create a temporary set of preferences, use a `.term` file, which we discuss in the next section.

Creating Terminal Preferences Files

Because people who use the Terminal tend to use it a lot, changing your settings for each circumstance would be inconvenient. To work around this, you can create `.term` files, which are like saved Terminal settings.

1. **Create a Terminal folder within the** `~/Library/Application Support` **folder.**

2. **Open the Terminal.**

3. **Adjust the settings as necessary.**

See the previous section for which settings you want to work with.

4. **Choose Save from the File menu (or press ⌘+S).**

5. **In the resulting dialog (see Figure 59-9), type a name for your settings in the Save As text box and save the file in the** `~/Library/Application Support/Terminal` **folder.**

• **Figure 59-9:** The Terminal creates a `.term` file when you save a window.

To use the `.term` file, you can

✔ Choose it from the File⇨Library menu (see Figure 59-10).

✔ Drag the `.term` file from the Finder onto the Terminal icon.

✔ Double-click the `.term` file (if it's set to open in the Terminal by default).

After you create a `.term` file, you can edit it in any text editor.

You can edit a `.term` file with ease, although you'll find that trying to change colors in the file is ridiculously hard.

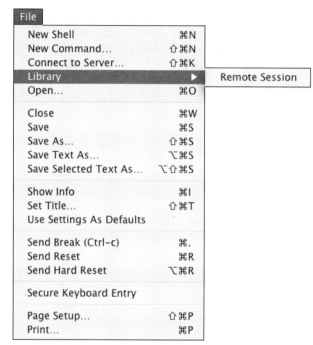

• **Figure 59-10: Your saved** `.term` **files appear as options in the File⇨Library menu.**

Even more handy than saving your preferences, your `.term` files can automatically run commands when they're opened.

1. Create a new `.term` file by using the preceding steps in this section.

2. Open the saved `.term` file in any text editor.

3. Look for the code that reads

`<key>ExecutionString</key>`

4. Between the `<string></string>` tags on the following line, type the command that you want to run.

To execute multiple commands, separate each with a semicolon.

5. Save the file.

The next time you open this `.term` in the Terminal, the commands are executed.

You can have the Terminal use this `.term` automatically by selecting it in the Terminal Preferences panel.

Choosing Your Shell

When you're running the Terminal, you're really using a shell. A *shell* is a tool that allows you to interact with the operating system. In other words, from the command line, you don't tell the OS anything directly. You tell the shell what you want to do, and the shell makes it happen. This is only really important in that you must understand what shell you are running to be able to configure it. Your Mac has all the popular shells:

- `sh`: The Bourne shell.
- `csh`: The C shell.
- `tcsh`: A enhanced version of the C shell (called the *T shell*).
- `bash`: The Bourne Again shell. (Yes, that is its name.)
- `zsh`: A geeky, lesser-used shell that's very powerful.

Panther's Terminal uses the `bash` shell by default, but Jaguar runs `tcsh`. If you'd rather go back to using `tcsh` or any other shell, follow these steps:

1. Open the Terminal Preferences panel.

2. Select the Execute This Command (Specify Complete Path) radio button.

3. Enter /bin/*shellname* **as the command.**

All the shells are located in the /bin directory. To use `tcsh` instead of `bash`, type **/bin/tcsh** in the text box (see Figure 59-11).

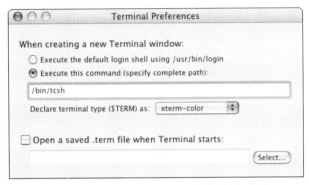

• **Figure 59-11:** You can tell the Terminal which shell to use.

4. **Close the Terminal Preferences panel to save your settings.**

 Features like tab completion, using the asterisk as a wild card, and many other tricks are parts of your shell, not the operating system or the Terminal. You can learn more about any shell by typing **man bash** or **man tcsh** (for the man files on each) in the Terminal.

Customizing Your Shell

Knowing what shell you're using is important because then you can create special files to customize its behavior. Each shell automatically loads a configuration file when a new shell is created (like when you open a new Terminal window). You can use these configuration files to

- ✔ Print a message.
- ✔ Create shortcuts for common commands.
- ✔ Adjust your environment settings.
- ✔ Automatically execute commands.

In these steps we demonstrate how to configure your shell, using some sample configuration ideas:

1. **In the Terminal, type** pico *filename,* **where *filename* is the appropriate file for your shell.**

If you're using bash, type **pico .bash_profile**. If you are using tcsh, type **pico .tcshrc**. You don't have to use pico to edit these, but because they are hidden files (note the initial period in the filename), you won't see them in the Finder.

 See Technique 58 for how to use the pico text editor.

2. **To have the Terminal print a message, type** echo "This is a message.".

The echo command prints out a string. You can use anything as your message.

3. **To have the Terminal execute a command, type it on its own line.**

For example, you could have the Terminal show you a calendar by entering **cal** on its own line.

4. **Set your default text editor by using** setenv EDITOR */path/to/editor.*

If you'd like your shell to use a particular editor by default (for example, vi or emacs), change this environmental setting. All the command line editors are in /usr/bin, so setenv EDITOR /usr/bin/vim makes vim your default editor.

5. **Create aliases.**

If you're using tcsh, type **alias aliasname 'command'** — for example, **alias mysite 'ssh -l user www.mysite.com'**. If you're using bash, use alias aliasname='command'.

Aliases let you use shortcuts for longer commands.

6. **Save the file and close** pico.

7. **Create a new shell/Terminal window (by pressing ⌘+N) to use the customization file (see Figure 59-12).**

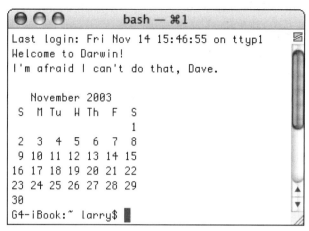

● ● ●   bash — ⌘1

```
Last login: Fri Nov 14 15:46:55 on ttyp1
Welcome to Darwin!
I'm afraid I can't do that, Dave.

     November 2003
 S  M Tu  W Th  F  S
                   1
 2  3  4  5  6  7  8
 9 10 11 12 13 14 15
16 17 18 19 20 21 22
23 24 25 26 27 28 29
30
G4-iBook:~ larry$ ▮
```

• **Figure 59-12:** Thanks to the customization file, a calendar and a message are displayed automatically.

 A great site for information about configuring shells is `www.dotfiles.com`.

Shareware Tools for Working with the Terminal

You can use dozens of different shareware and freeware applications in conjunction with the Terminal. Some of the best free tools are

✔ **Terminal Pal** (`http://freshlysqueezedsoftware.com/products/freeware.fss`) lets you launch .term files from the Dock, which saves you the step of loading the Terminal and then selecting the .term file from the File⊅Library folder.

✔ **Terminal Here plug-in** (`www.pyehouse.com/lynn/termopen.php`) creates a contextual menu item that allows you to instantly open the Terminal but in the current directory.

✔ Marc's very own **Open Terminal Here** script (`www.entropy.ch/software/applescript/`) resides in your Finder window toolbars and opens the current directory in the Terminal.

✔ **Terminal Services** (`http://homepage.mac.com/stas/terminalservices.html`) creates a service for running the selected text in the Terminal. Another service option that it provides is to fetch a URL in the Terminal by using the `curl` tool.

✔ **Connect 4** (`http://members.tripod.com/boneheadproductions/connect4/`) lets you play the popular game in the Terminal. (Well, Connect 4 was popular when you were eight, anyway.)

✔ **Fortune** (`www.vushta.com/fortune/`) brings the classic UNIX `fortune` utility to the Mac. What does it do? It provides you with a random fortune when you open a new Terminal window.

Technique 60

AppleScript and You

Save Time By

- ✔ Creating your own AppleScripts in no time
- ✔ Seeing examples of why you want to use AppleScripts
- ✔ Knowing what resources are available to you

The first thing that you should know about AppleScript (if you don't know already) is that it's a wonderfully powerful tool, giving you an easy way to automate repetitive tasks. AppleScript is a small, easy-to-learn programming language that can control one application or act as glue between many different apps. It's also one of those rare technologies that can be used by beginners and advanced programmers alike. If you don't have the time nor inclination to learn a new programming language, you can use other people's AppleScripts or quickly record your own. If you're the inquisitive type and have some spare time on your hands, the sky's the limit as to what you can accomplish.

Entire books are dedicated to AppleScript, so you won't master the technology in this chapter, but the novice can get a good taste, and the experienced AppleScript user can pick up a new timesaving trick or two. We start by showing how fast and easy it is to create your own scripts. Then we demonstrate some of the better uses of AppleScript. Finally, we point you in the direction of some AppleScript resources to further your knowledge.

The Easiest Way to Write Scripts

The default tool for creating AppleScripts is the Script Editor, found in the Applications⇨AppleScript folder. Use this simple application to write, record, test, and run your AppleScripts. As a quick example of how easy it is to record your own scripts, read on as we create an AppleScript that opens and tweaks two Finder windows. As you'll discover, many applications — including practically all from Apple — are *scriptable,* meaning that you can use AppleScript to control them (to varying degrees). Specific applications are also *recordable,* meaning that you can click the record button in the Script Editor, do what you want in another application, click stop in the Script Editor, and the Script Editor application will have translated all of your actions into the AppleScript language. Not all scriptable applications are recordable, sadly, but starting by recording an AppleScript is a great way to learn the language.

Choose File⇨Open Dictionary to find a list of scriptable applications and what properties those applications have. In this example, we use the Finder, which is both scriptable and recordable. After following through this example, you can open up the dictionary and use it to parse some of the information in the recorded AppleScript.

In this example, we'll show how you can record actions taken in the Finder to make a new (marginally useless) AppleScript:

1. **Open the Script Editor by double-clicking its icon in the Applications⇨AppleScript folder.**

2. **Click the Record button (see Figure 60-1).**

• **Figure 60-1: Use the buttons at the top of the Script Editor window to record and run your AppleScripts.**

3. **Go to the Finder.**

Navigate to the Finder however you want to, including clicking the Desktop or using the ⌘+Tab method.

4. **Create a new window by pressing ⌘+N.**

5. **Move to your Home directory by pressing ⌘+Shift+H.**

6. **Move the window to the upper-left corner of the screen.**

7. **Create another new window by pressing ⌘+N.**

8. **Move to the Applications directory by pressing ⌘+Shift+A.**

9. **Make sure the window is in list view mode by pressing ⌘+2.**

 For most of these steps, we use keyboard shortcuts (because we're keyboard shortcut kind of people), but the Script Editor will also follow most mouse actions as well. For example, you can select Applications from the Go menu instead of pressing ⌘+Shift+A.

10. **Move this window to the lower-right corner of the screen.**

11. **Return to the Script Editor.**

12. **Click the Stop button.**

You'll see the resulting AppleScript in the Script Editor (see Figure 60-2).

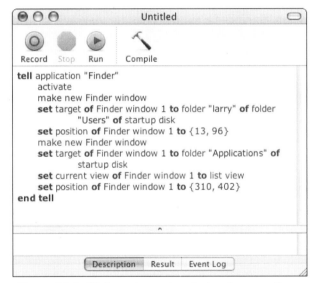

• **Figure 60-2: All the actions taken during the recording are translated by the Script Editor.**

13. **If you want, run the new script by clicking Run.**

You see two new windows created. This is a trivial (but still kind of cool) use of the technology. If you need to open and move two windows, there's really no faster way to do it!

14. **If you really like this script (and who wouldn't?), choose File⇨Save.**

In the resulting prompt (see Figure 60-3), you can choose a name and destination for the script. The pull-down menu lets you choose a format, the most useful of which are Script and Application. If you choose Application, the Save dialog lets you specify its properties (see Figure 60-4), such as Run Only, which means that the script runs but is not editable.

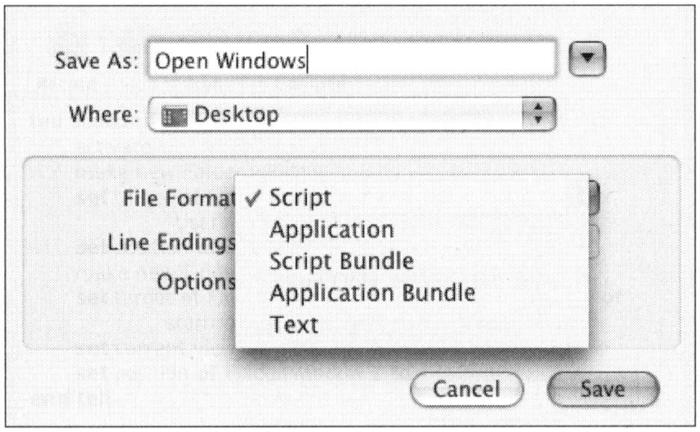

• **Figure 60-3: Save a script to use or review later.**

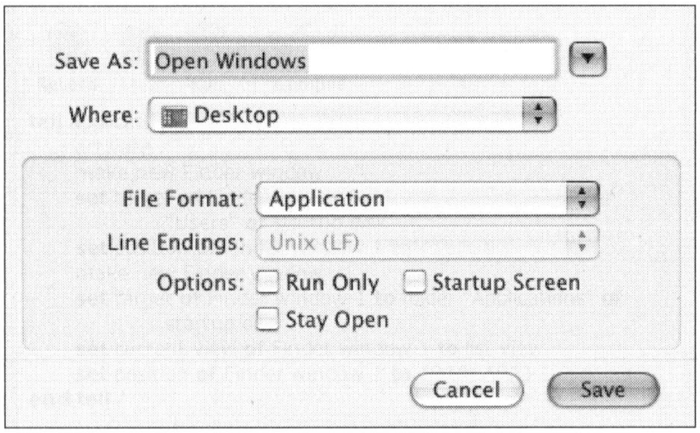

• **Figure 60-4: An AppleScript application can be run without going through the Script Editor.**

15. **Run the script.**

If you saved (in Step 14) the script as an application, you can run it by double-clicking the saved script in the Finder. If you saved the script as a

script, you can run it by double-clicking it, making it load in the Script Editor. Then click Run.

How you save your AppleScript is important. If you save it as a script, you'll need to go back through the Script Editor to run it every time, but it does allow you to re-edit the script. On the other hand, if you save a script as an application, you can more quickly run it, but you'll never be able to edit it in the Script Editor again (if you need to make changes later).

16. **If you want, edit the script to alter its behavior.**

Assuming that you did not save the script as an application, you can open it in Script Editor and make alterations by typing within the main window. Click on either Compile or Run to check the syntax of your work. (Run will both check the syntax and try to run the script.)

Add a description of your script — when you created it, what it's used for, why you did certain things, and so forth — by typing it in the Description box at the bottom of the Script Editor application. This will help jog your memory the next time you go to edit or even run a script.

Basic AppleScript Commands

As you'll quickly see from recording simple AppleScripts, the language uses just a few English-language-like commands. The most essential of these are

✔ `tell`: The `tell` statement normally gets the ball rolling and states what application should do what thing (command or sequence of steps), as in `tell application "Finder"`.... Each `tell` is concluded with an `end tell`.

✔ `activate`: The `activate` command makes an application (the one mentioned in the previous bullet for `tell`) active. Applications can be told to do things without being made active.

✔ `open`: The `open` command, as you might expect, tells an application to open a file or a URL, in the case of Safari.

✔ `set`: `set` is used to assign values to variables.

✔ `quit`: The `quit` command quits an open application. (AppleScript is literal that way.)

✔ comments: Adding comments to your scripts goes a long way toward helping you learn the language and remember what you're doing at this point of the script. To add a comment to your script, precede it with two hyphens, like this:

`--This is a comment.`

In the previous example, we recorded a script, but you can write them from scratch by firing up Script Editor and typing away (a new script window is created when you launch the application). You'll need to use the right commands, the proper syntax, and refer to the correct objects and attributes of the application being scripted (which you can find by using the Open Dictionary option in the Script Editor's File menu). Click on Compile to check your syntax and click on Run to test the AppleScript. You can view the Result and Event Log panels at the bottom of the Script Editor for more information on how your script performed.

Four Fabulous Reasons to Use AppleScripts

Perhaps the easiest way to learn AppleScript and appreciate its value is by seeing what can be done with it. You can download hundreds of excellent AppleScripts from the Web (many of which we mention elsewhere in this book) to examine and try or use the AppleScript features built in to the operating system. Here are just a few of the many practical uses of AppleScripts:

✔ **Script menu:** Your Mac comes with a slew of AppleScripts already, found in the `/Library/Scripts` directory. These scripts are not only nice suggestions for what you can do, but they also encourage you to use the Script menu. The Script menu resides in your menu bar and gives you quick access to your AppleScripts. Some of

these scripts retrieve stock quotes for you, get weather forecasts, or open Web pages. See Technique 9 for more information.

✔ **Folder Actions:** With Folder Actions, you can assign a script to be run when certain actions happen within a particular folder. An AppleScript might alert you when a file is added to a folder (like your Drop box for file sharing), convert an image dropped into a folder, or make an archive (compressed version) of the folder when it's changed. See Technique 12 for more information.

✔ **Create a startup routine (see Figure 60-5):** If you go through a set routine each day when you start your computer, you can have AppleScript perform this for you. Although you can start applications from Startup Items in the Accounts panel, an AppleScript can go one step further by also opening Finder windows, starting iTunes playing, and launching Web sites.

• **Figure 60-5:** This AppleScript executes when Larry starts his computer.

An AppleScript for your startup routine is a great, great time saver. It can be added to your Startup Items to automatically run when you log on or removed from your Startup Items with a single click if you're traveling.

✔ **iTunes:** If you use iTunes a lot — and we really, really do — you'll find that it's a great reason to use AppleScript. Doug Adams has over 200 iTunes-related AppleScripts available for download from his site (www.malcolmadams.com/itunes). AppleScripts can be used to tune into your favorite online radio station when you log in or play "Happy Birthday" when iCal sees it's your special day.

All the examples in this Technique demonstrate routines that can be automated with AppleScript. You can actually make entire applications with AppleScript after you really get the hang of the technology.

AppleScript Resources

Sure, you could search Google and browse through the returned results to find some of the best AppleScript resources available, but we'll save you the trouble. The granddaddy of them all (but of course) is the AppleScript page of Apple (www.apple.com/applescript), featuring dozens of premade scripts available for most Apple applications.

Each of the following sites has sample code available as well as information and tutorials:

✔ Macscripter: www.macscripter.net

✔ ScriptWeb: www.scriptweb.com

✔ AppleScript Sourcebook: www.applescriptsourcebook.com

If you're a power UNIX user or do a lot with the Terminal, look into osascript, a tool for performing interactions between command line tools and AppleScript.

In terms of software, these are some of the tools that work well with AppleScript:

✔ **AppleScript Studio** (www.apple.com/applescript/studio)**:** Part of the free Xcode studio, the AppleScript Studio is a nice tool for developing more intricate AppleScript applications. You'll find Xcode on one of the Panther installation discs (number 4 at the time of this writing), in an Installs directory within the Applications folder for brand new Macs, or you can download it from Apple's Web site.

✔ **Script Debugger** (www.latenightsw.com, $190)**:** Late Night Software puts out a wonderful AppleScript tool called Script Debugger. It's not cheap, but it's a very simple and powerful application for the serious AppleScript coder.

✔ **Smile** (www.satimage.fr/software/en/softx.html, free)**:** Smile falls somewhere between the Script Editor and the AppleScript Studio. It's a basic script editor but also has a lot of graphical user interface tools included to help you make more interactive applications.

61

Technique

Entertaining Yourself with Screen Savers

The Mac has always been a pretty operating system, complete with some pretty nice screen savers. Unlike all those boring ones that Windows users see — most of which just promote Microsoft and its products — your Mac can display flying toasters, an aquarium, or complex fractals. Even though screen savers no longer serve any practical purpose whatsoever (it's virtually impossible to burn an image onto your display), there's nothing wrong with some good old-fashioned eye candy.

This Technique is long on cool and short on boring. We begin with some information about Panther and screen savers. This section will be practical for most users, and you'll see some nice tips. Next, we tell you where you can get more screen savers (for those of you addicted to them) and how to install the suckers. Finally, we show you one way-cool trick, which is of absolutely no practical benefit to you at all! All in all, you're not going to find much in the way of increasing your productivity here (just the opposite, in fact), but all work and no play makes Jack a dull boy, right?

Configuring Screen Savers in Panther

If you don't like screen savers, you should at least read this section of the book to know how to turn the things off. If you do like screen savers, you should read this section to discover how to configure them. If you're indifferent towards screen savers, read this anyway. What do you care?

You can control your screen savers from the Screen Saver tab of the Desktop & Screen Saver panel of System Preferences (see Figure 61-1). The left column lets you choose what screen saver to run. The right column displays a preview of the selected screen saver. Under the preview is the Options button that lets you configure the selected screen saver (for those that are configurable; see Figure 61-2) and the Test button to preview it.

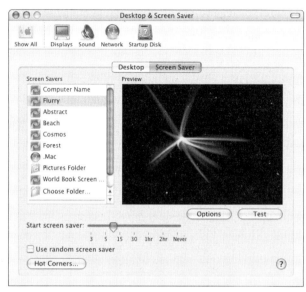

• Figure 61-1: Control your screen saver settings here.

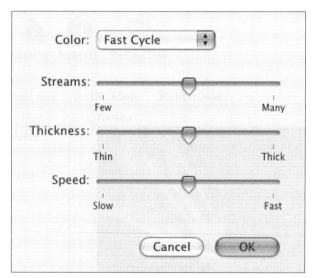

• Figure 61-2: If a screen saver can be configured, clicking the Options button brings up this panel.

Toward the bottom of the Screen Saver tab are two important controls:

✔ **A Start Screen Saver slider that lets you control when to start the screen saver:** You can set the screen saver to start after a certain amount of idle time or never at all. Keep in mind that if this value is longer than the sleep or display sleep settings in the Energy Saver panel (see Figure 61-3), you'll never, ever see the screen saver. Your machine will go to sleep before the screen saver ever kicks in.

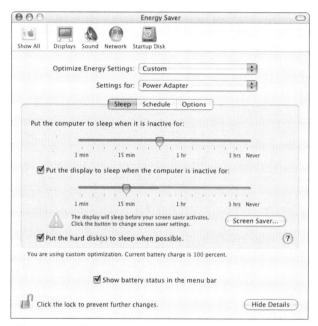

• Figure 61-3: Your computer's Energy Saver settings could affect whether you ever see the screen saver.

 To disable screen savers, set the Start Screen Saver slider (in the Screen Saver panel) to Never. It doesn't matter which screen saver is selected.

✔ **A Hot Corners button that lets you set hot corners:** Here's our advice: Don't use hot corners to activate your screen saver. Save them for Exposé, which is far more useful and important than a screen saver. Also, there's a decent chance that you'll set a hot corner to activate the screen saver and then inadvertently hit that corner when you're working (or playing a game) and momentarily throw your whole system out of whack. If you're doing a presentation, you might find the Disable Screen Saver hot corner useful (configurable by clicking on the Hot Corners button), but if you're doing a presentation, you ought to disable screen savers entirely anyway.

 The Desktop & Screen Saver and Exposé panels both let you set the hot corners for screen savers and Exposé functions.

The Desktop & Screen Saver panel isn't the only place that affects how screen savers run on your computer (the Energy Saver panel gets into the mix). Another, much more critical option can be found within the Security panel of System Preferences (see Figure 61-4). There you can set Panther to require a password when the computer is awoken from sleeping or just returns from displaying a screen saver. This will protect your computer while you're away, assuming that you're in a multi-user environment (like an office) or have some rambunctious pets that like to walk across your keyboard.

 The best, perhaps only, reason to set a hot corner to activate your screen saver is if you set up your computer to require a password to return from displaying a screen saver. If you're in a multi-user environment, select the Require Password to Wake This Computer from Sleep or Screen Saver check box in the Security panel (see Figure 61-4), and then move your cursor to the hot corner before you leave your desk. By using this method, you can quickly secure your computer before you walk away from it. (Any mischief-makers will have to enter your password before wreaking their havoc with your system.)

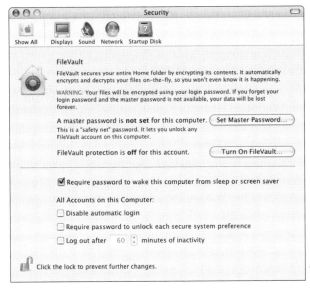

• **Figure 61-4: The Security panel option can force users to enter a password to reactivate the computer.**

Adding to Your Screen Saver Library

Your Mac comes with a half-dozen screen savers out of the box, but you don't have to be satisfied with those. You can download and use dozens of screen savers. Here are some Web sites where you'll find collections you can download:

✔ **LOOPS:** http://loops.pardeike.net

✔ **epicware:** www.epicware.com/macosxsavers.html

✔ **Apple:** www.apple.com/downloads/macosx/icons_screen savers/

✔ **VersionTracker:** www.versiontracker.com/macosx/screensavers

✔ **WhiteBox:** http://s.sudre.free.fr/Software/WBSoftware.html

These are some of our particular favorite individual screen savers:

✔ **After Dark X + Fish:** `http://en.infinisys.co.jp/product/adx/index.shtml`, $10

   After Dark was *the* screen saver for many years. Then people stopped using screen savers entirely (or so the story goes). Then came Marine Aquarium (see the next bullet), which opened up the world's eyes to how fun a screen saver can be. The latest version of After Dark, put out by Infinisys, has many different modules, from the toasters to the aquarium to a Mandelbrot set. Definitely worth the sawbuck!

✔ **Marine Aquarium 2:** `www.serenescreen.com/product/maquariumx/index.php`, $20

   Marine Aquarium 2 (from SereneScreen) creates a beautiful virtual fish tank, using dozens of different types of fish plus a healthy dose of coral. You can run this as a screen saver or all by itself. Another version of the Marine Aquarium is available that displays the current date and time on a crystal located in the tank.

To install a screen saver, follow these steps:

1. **Download the file from the Web site.**

2. **Decompress and/or mount the downloaded file.**

   The downloaded file is most likely in some sort of compressed format, like `.sit` or `.gz`. You'll need to use StuffIt Expander to decompress it. If the file then has a `.dmg` extension, double-click it to mount it as a disk image. After you have either a folder or a disk image left (see Figure 61-5), you can install the file.

3. **Move the screen saver file to** `~/Library/Screen Savers`, **where** ~ **refers to your Home directory (see Figure 61-6).**

   The screen saver itself has a `.saver` file extension. Move this into your Library/Screen Savers folder to add it to your available entertainment.

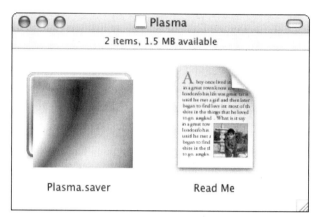

• **Figure 61-5:** The downloaded screen saver, as it appears as a mounted disk image.

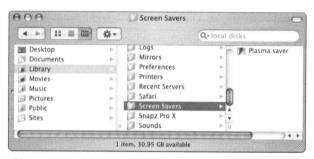

• **Figure 61-6:** Add the new screen saver to your Screen Savers folder.

 If your Library folder doesn't already have a Screen Savers directory, create one. You can also add screen savers to `/Library/Screen Savers`, which makes them available to all users. If you do this, though, they won't be backed up with the rest of your stuff and can easily be lost during operating system upgrades or transitions from one computer to another.

4. **Open System Preferences.**

 You cannot select and use your screen saver unless you open the Screen Saver panel *after* the screen saver has been added to your system. If the panel was open when you added the new file, quit and restart System Preferences.

5. **Click Desktop & Screen Saver.**

6. **Click the Screen Saver tab.**

7. **Select and configure the new screen saver (see Figure 61-7).**

   The screen savers that you've installed appear in the middle group of listings in the left-hand column.

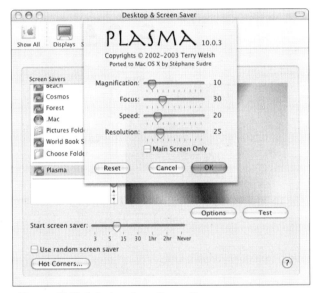

• **Figure 61-7:** Select and configure the new screen saver.

 Here's another really cool way to add screen savers: Use iPhoto. Your photo albums in iPhoto are automatically added as potential slideshows at the bottom of the list of screen savers. You can select a photo album to run as a slideshow and even configure it (see Figure 61-8).

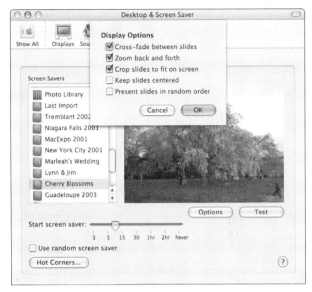

• **Figure 61-8:** Select and configure a new screen saver from iPhoto images.

Using the Desktop as a Screen Saver

In a Technique that discusses nothing but eye candy, this trick takes the cake. You can have a screen saver — any screen saver — run in place of the Desktop image. It'll slow down your computer like few other things can, but it looks *so* cool.

 Unless you have a Quartz Extreme-compatible computer with a really good processor (or a dual-processor, ideally), don't plan on doing anything else when running a screen saver on your Desktop. We found this to be really sluggish on a 550 MHz G4 PowerBook but not too bad on a 933 MHz G4 iBook.

One way to make this happen is to hack in manually:

1. **Open up your Terminal application.**

2. **Type** /System/Library/Frameworks/Screen saver. framework/Resources/Screen saverEngine.app/ Contents/MacOS/Screen saverEngine -background **and press Return.**

In a second or two, you'll see the current screen saver being used as your Desktop image (see Figure 61-9).

• **Figure 61-9:** Running the Flurry screen saver as the Desktop.

3. **Press Control+C to stop this effect.**

 If you have multiple monitors, one monitor runs the screen saver while the other has a solid black background.

If you'd rather not mess with the Terminal and want something a little easier to turn on and off, try either of these tools:

✔ **CoolBackground:** http://software. couthouis.com, free

CoolBackground has been tested under Panther and optimized for G5 processors. Its simple interface (see Figure 61-10) lets you select which

screen saver to use as the Desktop and has buttons to start and stop the process.

• **Figure 61-10:** CoolBackground is a good tool for turning your Desktop into a major distraction, er, screen saver.

✔ **Desktop Effects:** http://flyingmeat.com/ freestuff.html, free

Desktop Effects is a no-frills tool, essentially just giving you a Start/Stop button to control the screen saver. It will automatically use your current screen saver as the Desktop.

 You can create a similar but far less performance-taxing effect by setting your Desktop to use a Pictures folder and automatically change the picture every so many minutes. Although this doesn't have the flair or activity of some of the other options, it effectively creates a slideshow on your Desktop.

Index

Symbols & Numerals

A

F

Family Pack, advantages of, 10
Fast User Switching
  automatic login and, 22
  enabling, 40–41
  logging out, 36–38
  menu location, 75
  user accounts, 10
Favorites
  adding items, 125–126
  files, opening, 190
  Internet Explorer, 233–234
  launching applications with, 180
fax software, usefulness of, 9
features
  benefits of Panther, 9–10
  disabling for performance, 27–29
FetchArt for iTunes, 339
File Buddy
  file property manipulation, 148
  finding files with, 156
File Exchange application, Bluetooth, 426–427
file extensions
  changing, 144–145
  searching for, 155
file formats
  audio files, 336
  screenshots, 358
File menu, overview, 74
file sharing, types of, 312
file type, searching for files by, 155
File Vault, security, 10
filenames
  changing, 143–144
  file extensions, 144–145
files
  automatically opening, 24
  deleting manually, 161
  editing commands (Terminal), 454–455
  e-mail attachments, adding, 270
  iPod, security and encryption, 370–371

locked, deleting, 148
locking, 143
management tasks, 438–440
opening (Finder), 188–189
opening from within an application, 191–192
opening with specific applications, 189–190
overwriting, 198
permissions and, 146–147
properties, 141–142
saving, 195–198
search results, opening, 153
searching for by content, 154
searching for, Find dialog, 153–156
searching for, Search box, 151–153
setting default application for, 193–194
sharing with other operating systems, 149–150
tracking and identification, 144
transferring with iChat, 282–283
viewing commands (Terminal), 451–454
FileVault
  configuring, 400–401
  overview, 399
Find by Content searches
  optimizing, 157–158
  performing, 154
Find Clipboard, 206
find command (Terminal), 441–442, 447
Find dialog
  displaying, 64
  features, 153–156
  performance techniques, 157–159
Finder
  actions, 9
  applications, adding to Startup folder, 176
  applications, launching, 177–178

column view, usefulness of, 83–84
files, opening, 188–189
icon view, usefulness of, 80–81
iDisk, adding, 323
improvements to, 9
input devices and, 76
iPod files and, 370
items, defined, 55
list view, usefulness of, 81–83
navigation, column view, 57–58
navigation, icon view, 55–56
navigation, list view, 56–57
navigation, overview, 54
navigation, view modes, 54–55
preferences panel, Advanced tab, 72–73
preferences panel, displaying, 64
preferences panel, General tab, 70
preferences panel, Labels tab, 70–71
preferences panel, overview, 69–70
preferences panel, selecting default view, 57–58
preferences panel, Sidebar customization, 86
preferences panel, Sidebar tab, 71–72
preferences panel, window opening options, 56
scroll bars, 87
Search box, 151–153
Sidebar, usefulness of, 86–87
Terminal, working together, 435–437
themes, changing, 77
View Options panel, accessing, 73–74
Finder menu, overview, 74
FinkCommander, installing applications, 169
Fire chat program, 286